IN THE SHADOW OF THE UNITED STATES CAPITOL

IN THE SHADOW OF THE UNITED STATES CAPITOL

CONGRESSIONAL CEMETERY AND THE MEMORY OF THE NATION

Abby Arthur Johnson
and
Ronald Maberry Johnson

Washington, DC

Library of Congress Control Number: 2012947502
ISBN 978-0-9860216-0-2 paperback (alk. paper)
ISBN 978-0-9860216-2-6 hardcover (alk. paper)

New Academia Publishing
PO Box 27420, Washington, DC 20038-7420
info@newacademia.com - www.newacademia.com

We dedicate this book to the many volunteers who, over the past two centuries, contributed vision, time, and energy in maintaining and affirming the unique status of Congressional Cemetery as a place of national memory.

Contents

PREFACE

In the Shadow of the United States Capitol delineates the history of
Congressional Cemetery from its establishment in 1807 to its bicentennial anniversary in 2007. In this well documented study, Abby
and Ronald Johnson address the unique, national legacy of the
burial ground. Owned by Christ Church, located on Capitol Hill,
the cemetery functioned in part as the federal burial ground during
the antebellum period. Elaborate funeral processions to the burial
ground and the placement of cenotaphs over the federal graves underscored the status of Congressional Cemetery as the first national
burial ground. The era of federal involvement drew toward an end
during the Civil War, when the cemetery began a period of decline
that extended to the establishment of a preservation organization in
1976. The authors address both the period of decline and the subsequent restoration of the historic site.

The Johnsons have written the most complete and comprehensive study of Congressional Cemetery. The narrative draws upon a
rich trove of primary sources that reach back to the establishment
of Christ Church in 1794 and its subsequent correspondence with
the United States Congress regarding Congressional Cemetery.
These documents include records maintained by both the parish
and Congress, which participated in numerous federal burials at
the cemetery. The monograph builds in part upon the only previous studies of the site, both of which are unpublished: Cathleen
Breitkreutz's "Historic Landscape and Structures Report for Historic Congressional Cemetery" (2003), funded by the Architect of the

Capitol, and Julia A. Sienkewicz's "Historic American Landscapes Survey: Congressional Cemetery" (HALS No. DC-1, 2005). *In the Shadow of the United States Capitol* provides an important, memorable narrative focused on life and death in the federal city.

The authors' presentation of the founding and early history of the cemetery and its unique connection to the federal government, especially the United States Congress, is thorough, accurate, well-presented, and immensely valuable to have in print. They chronicle the ways in which this burial ground—like most cemeteries created prior to the 1830s and the rise of the rural cemetery movement—was owned and operated as a church cemetery. Nonetheless, it gained national significance due to its connection with the emerging federal government as the burial place for government leaders who died in Washington, D.C. As part of this narrative, the Johnsons demonstrate how the boundaries between public and private, sacred and secular, were blurred in the early republic.

Indeed, as a work of scholarship, *In the Shadow of the United States Capitol* will appeal to students of American political and cultural history and especially to those interested in the relationship between the public and private sectors. As the Johnsons persuasively demonstrate, Congressional Cemetery held a unique position until the Civil War as a private cemetery that fulfilled a public function as the national cemetery.

The authors' deft analysis of the decline of Congressional Cemetery and its eclipse by Arlington National Cemetery forms perhaps the most important contribution of this study. The subsequent revitalization of the site by the private Association for the Preservation of Historic Congressional Cemetery is similarly well handled and makes a persuasive argument for the role of the emerging historic preservation movement in the revitalization of this burial ground as a unique memorial site.

Readers more interested in the local history of the District of Columbia will also find much value in this study. The history of Congressional Cemetery, originally named the Washington Parish Burial Ground, is intimately connected with the evolving demographics of its locale. Its corresponding decline as the neighborhood around Christ Church and the cemetery changed led to its rise as a cause célèbre for those supporting historic preservation on

Capitol Hill. Together with the recent publication of Rebecca Boggs Roberts' and Sandra K. Schmidt's *Historic Congressional Cemetery* in the Images of America series (Arcadia Publishing, 2012), *In the Shadow of the United States Capitol* will provide renewed appreciation for the place of Congressional Cemetery in the memory of the nation.

Donald R. Kennon, Chief Historian
U.S. Capitol Historical Society
June 2012

ACKNOWLEDGEMENTS

In 1989, editor and historian David Thelen created a special issue of *The Journal of American History* entitled "Memory and American History." In the introductory essay, he declared that the function of history "is to recover the past and introduce it to the present," which he believed was "the same challenge that confronts memory." Thelen's statement captures well our effort in this study of Congressional Cemetery, which was initiated in 1992 when we made our first visit to the burial ground and began to explore and document the site.

Our efforts "to recover the past and introduce it to the present" were supported by a group of talented and dedicated members of the Association for the Preservation of Historic Congressional Cemetery (APHCC), established in 1976. They had expended considerable time and energy in rediscovering and reclaiming the old burial ground, and they shared information with us. We particularly acknowledge the substantial contributions of Patrick Crowley, Linda Harper, Jim Oliver, and Sandra Schmidt. Others also provided memorable commentary about challenges and achievements at the historic site, including C. Dudley Brown, George A. Didden III, and Chris Herman. We are indebted to all of them, as well as to others in the APHCC, for assisting us in our narrative focused on Congressional as a place of national memory.

In addition to the APHCC, we are grateful to Christ Church, Washington Parish, particularly Reverend Judith Davis, Reverend Cara Spaccarelli, and the late Nan Robertson, for giving us access to documents maintained in the congregational archives. They include vestry minutes, annual reports, financial records, selected sermons, and correspondence. The information given in these texts was critical to our commentary focused on the activities of Christ Church in assuming ownership of the cemetery in 1812, operating the burial ground until 1976, and laying the basis for establishment of the APHCC.

We thank the staff at the Washingtoniana Room in the District of Columbia Public Library for directing us to documents that proved essential to this study. They included city maps, historic images of the cemetery, and full runs of area newspapers, as well as memorable articles from individual issues. We are grateful as well to the reference librarians and circulation desk staff at the Library of Congress for their assistance in identifying and retrieving documents published by the federal government, particularly the *Congressional Record*. The personnel associated with the Library's Manuscript Division, as well as its Prints and Photographs Division, were also attentive to our many requests for materials. We are also grateful to the Special Collections staff at Georgetown University Library for identifying both archival holdings and historic maps that enriched our study of the burial ground.

Our thanks are extended as well to the staff of the Office of the Architect of the Capitol, particularly Barbara Wolanin and Pam McConnell, for giving us access to documents and images that proved key to this project. In addition, we are thankful to the staff of the National Capital Region of the National Park Service, especially Terry Carlstrom and Sally Blumenthal, for making materials relevant to Congressional Cemetery available to us. We also found significant documentation in the National Archives and want to thank Kara Newcomer for her support in this effort.

We are indebted as well to journal editors and professional organizations that provided us with outlets for our initial findings relevant to the history of the cemetery. Edited by Kathryn Smith, *Washington History: Magazine of the Historical Society of Washington, D.C.*, published Abby's "'The Memory of the Community': A Photographic Album of Congressional Cemetery" (spring/summer 1992). We were invited to present scholarly papers focused on the cemetery by the American Studies Association in 1995 and the

European Association of American Studies in 2000 and 2004. During fall 2005, the United States Capitol Historical Society invited us to present a paper focused on our research and then published "A Legacy in Stone: The Latrobe Cenotaphs at Congressional Cemetery" in *The Capitol Dome* (summer 2010).

We want to thank the Department of History at Georgetown University for funding Ron's 2001 spring sabbatical, which was instrumental in his research of documents maintained in various federal archives. In addition, we are grateful to the United States Capitol Historical Society, particularly Chief Historian Donald Kennon, for providing him with a fellowship in 2004-2005 so that he could complete his research at the Office of the Architect of the Capitol, the Library of Congress, and the National Archives.

We thank in particular historian David Nye for his support of this project and many words of encouragement. We are pleased as well that architectural historian Pam Scott took a special interest in our research and provided helpful comments as we proceeded with our study. Our Georgetown colleagues John Tutino and Sandra Horvath-Peterson offered insightful observations in response to our presentation at a 2007 History Department forum. Carole Sargent, Director of the Office of Scholarly and Literary Publication at the university, read an initial draft of the manuscript and provided helpful suggestions as we continued with our study.

Regarding our final efforts in preparing the monograph for publication, we want to thank David Hagen of Lauinger Library at Georgetown for his technical support in compiling our photographic file for publication. We are grateful as well to our publisher Anna Lawton, who recognized the significance of our topic and thus the value of our narrative focused on the first national cemetery in the United States.

Finally, we are thankful for the joy of collaboration and the pleasure we found in interpreting the rich history of the first national burial ground. Our collaborative effort will have a special place in our shared memories.

A.A.J.
R.M.J.

Washington, D.C.
July 2012

INTRODUCTION

THE FIRST NATIONAL BURIAL GROUND

Congressional Cemetery, founded in 1807 and located on thirty acres of land in southeast Washington, D.C., is singular in its status as a U.S. national cemetery. It is, to begin, the first national burial ground. As a national cemetery, it is in a category of its own. It is not a national military cemetery, like Arlington across the Potomac River, but a one-of-a-kind national public cemetery, accessible to the broad sweep of the American community, including members of Congress, veterans of all U.S. wars, and everyone else. The burial ground has been owned since 1812 by Christ Church on Capitol Hill, which was established in 1794 as the first Episcopalian parish in the original city of Washington, D.C. The church operated the cemetery for use by the broader community, including the federal government, until 1976, when the Association for the Preservation of Historic Congressional Cemetery (APHCC), a volunteer organization, assumed management of the site.

Affirmations of the Legacy

During the antebellum period, the burial ground was identified as the cemetery of Congress and Congressional Cemetery. In *A New Guide to Washington* (1842), for example, George Watterston, the first Librarian of Congress, provided a substantial section entitled, "Congressional Burial Ground." This publication, along with many others, was instrumental in formulating the name by which the cemetery is recognized to this day.[1]

The cemetery gained broader recognition as the first national burial ground in the decades following the Civil War. Two Quartermaster Generals of the United States Army—Montgomery C. Meigs (1816-1892) and Henry Gibbins (1877-1941)—acknowledged and enhanced this larger understanding of the site. In his 1881 annual report to the Secretary of War, Meigs, who was Quartermaster General during 1861-1882, observed that "the existing Congressional Cemetery is rapidly filling up" and recommended that Arlington be established as "the official national cemetery of the government," to be used as had Congressional "for the interment of soldiers" and "for the burial of officers of the United States, legislative, judicial, civil, and military, who may die at the seat of government or whose friends may desire their interment in a public national cemetery."[2] Henry Gibbins, Quartermaster General during 1936-1940, provided a more expansive assessment of the burial ground at the beginning of his 1939 "Memorandum on Congressional Cemetery" to Congress:

> In reality, the Congressional Cemetery was the first National Cemetery created by the Government. It was fostered and developed by the Congress of the United States, most of the major construction and improvements being made through appropriations from Congress. Many of the patriots who guided the destiny of the Nation or defended it on land and sea are interred there, and cenotaphs and monuments have been erected to the memory of many illustrious names. More early historic interest is contained within its confines than in any other cemetery in the nation.[3]

The statements by Meigs and Gibbins are of particular import because they were responsible as Quartermaster Generals for both Arlington and the other national military cemeteries.

Congressional leaders emerged during the nineteenth, twentieth, and twenty-first centuries as forceful advocates of federal support for the burial ground.[4] Among these legislators, Representative George Mahon (1900-1985) of Texas and Senator Byron Dorgan (1942-) of North Dakota offered particularly memorable observations. In testimony delivered in the House of Representatives on July 2, 1960, Mahon, a legislator in twenty-two consecutive congresses (1935-1979), identified Congressional as likely the only national cemetery in the United States:

> It is not surprising that this cemetery has been known almost from its establishment as Congressional Cemetery and is usually so designated in acts of Congress and by the public generally. It is often referred to as our first national cemetery and is perhaps our one true national cemetery due to the fact that Arlington and all other so-called national cemeteries are dedicated primarily for interment of the remains of those who have served in our Armed Forces, whereas Congressional Cemetery is primarily civilian.[5]

Senator Dorgan urged Congress to provide additional financial support for the burial ground in comments given in the Senate on June 27, 2003. In so doing, he presented his understanding of the site as a place of national memory:

> I think all recognize that this is something to which we should pay some attention. I know there are many other very big issues we deal with here in the Senate. But this is something that I think is important to the memory of who we are, who served our country, how we treat them in death, and how we respect their memories. We can and should do better to bring a sense of repair and majesty to Congressional Cemetery.[6]

These statements and many others by congressional leaders focus on the status of the cemetery as the first national burial ground and its chronic state of decline and disrepair. These conflicting realities surface large, important questions not only about Congressional as an historic site but also about public memory and the sites that do and do not become fixtures within that larger sense of national history.

Questions Relevant to Congressional Cemetery

Despite its historic significance, Congressional Cemetery does not have a clear and secure place in the broader public understanding of national historic sites. It is not part of the federal system of national cemeteries, as is Arlington, nor is it maintained by the National Park Service, as are the burial grounds at Gettysburg, Antietam, and Fredericksburg. It is not regularly featured in televised broadcasts of Memorial Day ceremonies in the national capital, nor is it generally considered a site that must be visited on initial tours of federal Washington, D.C. Why is this the case? What transpired over the preceding two centuries that excluded this "first national cemetery" from the galaxy of federal sites that are familiar to the general public and that are generally considered, in the words of Senator Dorgan, "important to the memory of who we are" as a nation?

In addressing these questions, the authors focused on the three primary stages in the history of Congressional Cemetery: (1) the years 1812 to the Civil War, when the burial ground functioned as the first national cemetery and was used by the federal establishment, particularly the U.S. Congress, and by the broader community; (2) the complicated, increasingly difficult period extending from the end of the Civil War into the 1970s, when the infrastructure of the cemetery continued to deteriorate as the burial ground lost status as a place of national significance; and (3) the current period, beginning in 1976, when the APHCC leased the burial ground from Christ Church and embarked upon ongoing efforts to restore, maintain, and preserve it as an historic site.

Each of the three stages in the long history of Congressional Cemetery raises fascinating questions relevant to its status as an historic site. During the initial stage, the hybrid identity of the cemetery posed numerous questions. Owned and operated by Christ Church on Capitol Hill, Congressional Cemetery served the federal government, as well as the parish and the broader community of Washington, D.C. Meanwhile, the federal government provided critical funding for key infrastructure developments at the burial ground. Viewed from the vantage point of the twenty-first century, this informal partnership between the church and the federal government might appear unusual, irregular, perhaps even a breach in the historic separation of church and state.

The establishment of the national military cemeteries during the Civil War raised profound questions about the very identity of Congressional Cemetery during the extended second stage of its long life. Arlington National Cemetery in particular challenged and ultimately overwhelmed the status of Congressional as the first national burial ground. To both legislators and the general public, national cemetery became synonymous with national military cemetery. This general shift in definition surfaced queries about the legacy of Congressional as not only a national public burial ground but as likely the only such cemetery in the United States. The singularity of Congressional constituted its problem in that it was not reducible to any one category of generally accepted U.S. historic sites. Thus, it was difficult to sort out the possible federal responsibilities for Congressional Cemetery. During its extended period of decline, the unanswered questions about the burial ground lingered as an important part of its historic legacy.

The third and ongoing period in the saga of Congressional Cemetery raises another set of intriguing questions. They focus, for example, on the respective responsibilities of the federal government and the APHCC in preserving the first national burial ground. How much can be expected over the long term of a volunteer organization in preserving the first national cemetery? What responsibility does the U.S. government have in helping to assure the continuation of the one burial ground in the United States directly linked by its very name with the U.S. Congress? The most important question of all is as follows: what gains will be realized by the preservation of Congressional Cemetery for future generations of Americans?

An historic burial ground, such as Congressional Cemetery, is a resonant text for various readings of the surrounding culture. Some studies present cultural analyses of gravestones, as does *Cemeteries and Gravemarkers: Voices of American Culture* (1992), edited by Richard E. Meyer. Others concentrate on the larger meanings associated with particular cemetery grounds. Blanche Linden offers one such reading in her *Silent City on a Hill: Landscapes of Memory and Boston's Mount Auburn Cemetery* (rev. ed., 2007). While this history of Congressional Cemetery provides commentary on the grounds and monuments,[7] it concentrates on the dominant narrative associated with the site: its legacy as the first national burial ground. Rich, powerful narratives are invariably associated with historic burial grounds. This is particularly so with Congressional Cemetery, situated as it is both geographically and figuratively in the shadow of the U.S. Capitol.

PART ONE

CREATION OF THE HISTORIC SITE

1

A NEW CEMETERY FOR
THE NEW FEDERAL CITY

This book begins and concludes with stories of state funerals. These ceremonies proved central to framing a larger historic narrative that examined how the federal government has buried Representatives, Senators, members of the military, Vice Presidents, and Presidents. In doing so, we sought to explain the origins and evolution of a national funereal tradition. The roots of this development originated in the colonial and early federal periods, became more elaborate during the antebellum era, and reached their full manifestation with the burial of Abraham Lincoln.

The founding and rise of Congressional Cemetery as a federal memorial site provide an ideal setting to explore the larger process of American state funerals. The origins of the cemetery playing this role started with the burial of Representative Levi Casey (ca. 1752-1807). His death on February 3, 1807, raised anew the challenge for the new federal government, now situated in the District of Columbia, of where to bury federal legislators who died while serving in office. Because no cemetery had been provided with the founding of Washington, members of Congress had to bury their deceased colleagues in church graveyards outside the city. In the case of Representative Casey, the chosen site was Georgetown Presbyterian Church's burial ground, located on the western edge of the new and as yet unformed capital.

As delineated in *The National Intelligencer* on February 6, 1807, the funeral procession formed in the following order at the U.S. Capitol: Marine Corps, chaplains of Congress, ministers, physicians, corpse, pallbearers (six generals), mourners, speaker and members of the House of Representatives, president and members of the Senate, heads and officers of federal departments, and citizens. The parade then proceeded in carriages down Pennsylvania Avenue, past the Executive Mansion, and then to Rock Creek, where the mourners walked in pairs to the prepared gravesite. The ride to the cemetery posed challenges at that time of the year. In 1804, one William Janson declared that the "boasted" Pennsylvania Avenue, which had been cut through thickets and brambles three years earlier, was "as much a wilderness as Kentucky, with this advantage, that the soil is good for nothing." In 1807, a congressman wrote this about a fall from his horse in the wilderness midway between Capitol Hill and the White House: "Figure to yourself a man almost bruised to death, on a dark, cold night, in the heart of the capital of the United States, out of sight or hearing of human habitation, and you will have a tolerably exact idea of my situation."[1]

Given the difficulties in staging a funeral procession across a raw landscape in late winter, the U.S. government supported development of a new graveyard on the eastern side of the city, virtually in what was then the backyard of the U.S. Capitol. This chapter delineates the unique partnership between Christ Church, an Episcopalian parish established in 1794, and the U.S. Congress in creating this burial ground.

The Missing Piece in the L'Enfant Plan

The burial ground emerged to fill a void left in the grand design for the new federal city developed by Peter Charles L'Enfant (1754-1825).[2] In his celebrated "Plan of the City Intended for the Permanent Seat of the Government of the United States" (1791), the French architect and engineer focused on elegant geometries, to be achieved by avenues that extended outward from the U.S. Capitol and the Executive Mansion, that were intersected by a rectangular network of streets, and that were bisected now and then by green spaces, including city parks. None of these green spaces was, however, to be a cemetery. L'Enfant proceeded to state in his plan that "no burying grounds will be admitted within the limits of the City, an appropriation being intended for that purpose without." While he did not expand upon this statement, he proceeded in agreement with contemporaries in both Europe and the United States who were concerned about the crowded conditions in many urban cemeteries and the possible health hazards associated with interring the dead among the living.[3] His prohibition of burial grounds within the city was nonetheless shortsighted, as became readily apparent after the federal government moved from Philadelphia to Washington, D.C., in 1800.

The cemeteries in Washington, D.C., during the late eighteenth and early nineteenth centuries constitute an intriguing, largely forgotten chapter in the early history of the federal city. Scattered in a haphazard fashion across the community, they included traditional church and family burial grounds, graveyards established to meet special requirements, and two public cemeteries. With one exception, the church cemeteries founded in the area during the eighteenth century have all disappeared, their contents having been removed to other burial grounds. Such was the case with St. Patrick's Catholic Cemetery, organized during 1797 in the northwest quadrant (on Boundary, now known as Florida Avenue, between North Capitol and Third Street NW). The remains preserved in this graveyard were reinterred at Mount Olivet Cemetery shortly after it was founded in Washington, D.C., during 1858.[4]

The one church graveyard that was established in Washington, D.C., during the eighteenth century and continues to the present is Rock Creek Cemetery. Rock Creek Church, an Episcopalian parish that was organized in 1712 and is both the oldest and the only surviving colonial church in the District of Columbia, owns and operates this burial ground. In 1719, Colonel John Bradford, a vestryman and a prosperous landowner, gave the parish one-hundred acres surrounding the church. The cemetery, created in the same year, has been in continuous operation ever since, providing a final resting place for some 100,000 people.[5]

The family graveyards, like most of the early church cemeteries, have disappeared, buried beneath successive layers of construction and rubble. At the turn of the nineteenth century, however, they proliferated across the area. Hoping in part to protect the deceased from grave robbers, many families buried their own within the family property. Christian Hines (1781-1875) identified a few such burial grounds, as well as other remarkable graveyards, in his *Early*

Recollections of Washington City (1866), which delineates his memories of the new federal city from 1796 to 1814. All of the cemeteries he discussed had been largely forgotten by the surrounding community or had disappeared altogether by the time his book was published. He noted, for example, the graveyard of the Pearce family on what is now Lafayette Square, directly across from the White House: "Part of it, I think, is covered by the brick pavement that lies along the south side of the square." The Pearce family, who had owned land in that area, once occupied a farmhouse on the northeast corner of the square, "long before the President's House was thought of," Hines added. He identified a couple of other burial grounds that had belonged most likely to families. One had been dug into the eastern slope of what is now Observatory Hill. When Hines chanced upon this once "tolerably large grave yard," "nothing remained but a small quantity of black dust," "a few bones," and a single gravestone. Another burial ground, positioned along F Street N., perhaps between Twenty-Second and Twenty-Third Streets, was surrounded by some "half dozen cedar trees" and included a marker "erected to the memory of Casper Yost."[6]

Hines identified a few other burial grounds, two of which fit into the category of graveyards established to meet special needs. The first of these cemeteries, which he said was located on Twenty-Fourth Street W., between H and I Streets N., was understood by some to have been the graveyard for soldiers housed in that neighborhood and by others to have been the burial ground for the slaves of one Robert Peter, who at that time owned much of the surrounding land. Situated on "a considerable hill," the cemetery was established sometime "previous to 1800." During the construction of Twenty-Fourth Street W., each side of the projected roadway was excavated about one foot beneath the graves, "leaving on both sides open graves and coffins projecting into the street." Hines went on to say that "I have myself seen pieces of skulls lying in the streets."[7] No wonder, one might add, many of the early visitors to the new federal city described the area as a veritable wasteland.

The next of these special cemeteries was "quite . . . small" but particularly unique. Located between E and F Streets N., near "Easby's ship yard," the site was said to have been used for the burial of "the drowned who were found floating down the river." The river was probably the Tiber, because Hines thought it had been covered over by the Washington Canal,[8] which in turn was covered by Constitution Avenue. No marker identifies the former site of this unusual burial ground or the others recalled by Christian Hines.

During most of the eighteenth century, the existing cemeteries met the needs of the surrounding community. These requirements changed substantially toward the end of the century, however, with the influx of population associated with initial construction of the new federal city during 1792-1800 and then with relocation of the federal government from Philadelphia to Washington, D.C., in 1800. Anticipating sizable growth across the broader community, the commissioners of the District of Columbia set aside two squares on February 28, 1798, for "public burial grounds for the use of all denominations of people": Square 109, which was on the western side of the city and designated as the Western Burial Ground, and Square 1026, on the eastern side and identified as the Eastern Burial Ground. The commissioners had selected sites "on the borders of the city," mindful as L'Enfant had been "of the numerous objections which have been made against burial grounds in other cities."[9]

With legislation passed on May 15, 1802, the U.S. Congress authorized the city of Washington to maintain the Western and Eastern Burial Grounds. City officials subsequently specified that three commissioners supervise each cemetery, that the mayor appoint these officials, and that the mayor also establish procedures for each burial ground to be enclosed by fencing made of "good and sufficient locust or cedar posts and chestnut rails. . . ." Signaling the racial divide in the new city, and following practices generally in effect at cemeteries across the United States, city officials also stipulated that a thorn fence, with all its attendant symbolism, separate the sites set aside for the burials of Washington's white and "colored" residents. They did not, however, make provisions for the development and maintenance of the two cemeteries until 1807, when funds were established to appoint sextons, erect fences, and establish burial sites.[10]

In his *Centennial History of the City of Washington, D.C.* (1892), Harvey Crew noted that the Western Burial Ground was "the most popular" cemetery "in Washington" up to the year 1816 but that it went into a decline in that year that extended to 1859 or 1860, when the last interment was made at the site. In 1879, the District of Columbia was given title to this land for the establishment of public schools. Beginning in 1880, the remains of the Western Cemetery were removed to other graveyards, including Rock Creek and Congressional Cemetery.[11]

The Eastern Burial Ground achieved neither the recognition nor the longevity of the Western Cemetery. The graveyard was, in fact, a singular disappointment from the start. While it was located advantageously for residents on the eastern side of the city, it was situated on swampy ground, generally considered unsuitable for burials. The end of this graveyard was clearly in sight by 1807, the year when the city first provided funding for the development and care of the public cemeteries.

On April 4, 1807, eight prominent citizens living on the eastern side contributed $200 from their own resources to purchase Square 1115, comprising about 4.5 acres of land encircled by E and G and by 18th and 19th Streets SW. They then requested permission from Thomas Munroe, Superintendent of the City of Washington, to establish a cemetery at this site. In approving their request, Munroe delineated provisions for an inclusive cemetery, open to everyone. He stated first, for example, that "all denominations of people" should have the right of burial at the site. In addition, he directed that "one-fourth part of the said square" should be used "for the gratuitous interment of those inhabitants who may die without leaving the means of purchasing grave sites or paying for the privilege of burial therein" and that the price of purchase for a grave site and burial at the site "shall in no case nor at any time hereafter exceed the sum of two dollars for each corpse, exclusive of the customary expense of digging a grave."[12]

On the same date, April 4, 1807, the purchasers signed their names to a preamble and articles of subscription for the burial ground. The preamble articulated the pressing need for this cemetery: "A great inconvenience has long been experienced by the citizens residing in the eastern portion of the city for want of a suitable place for a burying ground. It is well known that the one at the northeast boundary of the city, now occupied as such, is a low and watery situation and very unfit for a place of interment." Square 1115 met all requisites for the desired new cemetery in terms of location and topography. Positioned about one mile east of the U.S. Capitol, the site was readily accessible to those living on the eastern side. Located on high ground, the land was dry, and it offered an excellent place to look out over the emerging city, as well as the Eastern Branch of the Potomac River. George Watterston, first Librarian of Congress, thought the selection of Square 1115 could not have been better: "The site of this graveyard has been most judiciously chosen. It commands a fine view of the surrounding country and the Anacostia, which flows at a short distance below it, and, in a calm summer evening, when the water is still and placid, reflects from its polished bosom the beautiful landscape on the opposite side of the river."[13]

The April 4, 1807, articles of subscription comprised seven rules for governance of the new cemetery. These guidelines focused on practical matters, including policies regarding eligibility for interment at the site:

First. The ground shall be laid off in lots of 3 by 8 feet.

Second. Any person shall be at liberty to subscribe for lots from 1 to 15, at $2 each, the lots to be transferable.

Third. Any person applying at a future time to purchase shall be admitted at the same rate as the original subscribers.

Fourth. If there should not be a sufficient sum subscribed to carry into effect the object hereby contemplated and any citizen will advance a sufficient sum to complete the same, they shall be reimbursed with interest the sum so advanced out of the first money arising from the proceeds of said ground.

Fifth. When the graveyard, with its improvements, shall be unincumbered of debt, then the subscribers shall assign over all the right and title of the said ground not subscribed for to the vestry of Washington parish, subject to the restrictions of the third article.

Sixth. Immediately after the ground shall be properly inclosed [sic] and laid off, a sexton shall be furnished with a plan of the burying ground laid off in lots properly numbered, and each proprietor's name marked on his particular lot. No person shall be permitted to dig a grave but the sexton or his assistant.

Seventh. No person known to deny a belief in the Christian religion shall ever be admitted to a right in this burying ground.[14]

The founders most likely included the seventh article because they intended to transfer the cemetery when free of debt to "the vestry of Washington parish," as noted in the fifth article, and had concluded that such a statement would facilitate the transfer. The seventh article remained in place only until 1812, however, when the burial ground was free of debt and was transferred as intended to the vestry of Washington parish.

The following individuals signed the articles of subscription: George Blagden, Griffith Coombe, John T. Frost, Henry Ingle, Dr. Frederick May, Peter Miller, Samuel Smallwood, and Commodore Thomas Tingey. The key members within this group were Blagden, Coombe, and Ingle, whom the others chose in a meeting on May 6, 1807, to serve as trustees and to assume responsibility for cemetery care, including the provision of a sexton. Among the trustees, Ingle had the leadership role, for he was selected during the same meeting as agent for the committee. Ingle was accordingly responsible for securing all documentation required to establish a cemetery on Square 1115 and to formalize its eventual transfer to Christ Church.[15]

The founders were all parishioners of Christ Church, most of them members of the church vestry, all of them leaders in the broader community and in the development of the eastern sector of the city. For the most part, however, they seem to have vanished from public memory. With the exception of Thomas Tingey, who had been commandant of the Washington Navy Yard, their names have not appeared in histories intended for national audiences. Local historians have drafted occasional essays on selected individuals, as did Washington Topham in his article on "Dr. Frederick May," published in the *Records of the Columbia Historical Society* in 1930. On the whole, however, the commentary has been abbreviated and scattered and thus insufficient in conveying the contributions of these individuals in establishing critical infrastructure for the new federal city. The following paragraphs provide brief introductions to the cemetery founders.

Henry Ingle (1764-1822), prime mover within the committee of founders, came to Washington from Germantown, Pennsylvania, in 1799, lured by the opportunities he saw in the new city. He and his wife Mary, along with their four young children, established their residence first on Greenleaf's Point in one of the houses built by the early speculators. They later moved to a home virtually at the foot of Capitol Hill, on New Jersey Avenue, between B and C Streets. Ingle lived in this house, one of the first constructed in that area, to the end of his days.[16]

His resume, gleaned from vestry minutes, information provided in *The National Intelligencer*, and the published reminiscences of Virginia Campbell Moore, a descendant of the Ingle family, is impressive. Ingle was a successful businessman, establishing the first hardware store in the city. This enterprise, managed later by his sons and sons-in-law, including Virginia Campbell Moore's father, became a local landmark, situated on Pennsylvania Avenue near Sixth Street and recognized widely as Campbell and Coyle. In addition, Ingle was an prominent public servant, having served, for example, in the fifth and sixth councils of the city government and as one of three commissioners appointed by the City Council to "superintend the improvement of the Grave Yards in the city of Washington," as noted in *The National Intelligencer* of September 11, 1807. The available documentation does not indicate his tenure in this capacity, although it does identify his fellow commissioners as Thomas H. Gilliss and Robert Underwood, also prominent members of Christ Church.[17] Through all his long years of public service, Ingle remained a stalwart figure within the Christ Church community, participating variously as registrar and secretary of the vestry and in the increasingly weighty efforts attendant upon maintaining the new cemetery on Square 1115.

George Blagden (n.d.-1826), a native of Yorkshire, England, came to Washington from Philadelphia in 1793. He worked as both chief stonecutter at and superintendent of masons employed in the construction of the U.S. Capitol Building. He was also a member of the first school board in Washington, D.C., serving with President Thomas Jefferson, among others. In addition, he had been one of the directors of the Bank of Washington, an alderman in the city of Washington, a commissioner of the Columbia Manufacturing Company, which established a cotton mill in Washington, D.C., and a promoter of and a major stockholder in the Great Bridge Company, which constructed in 1808 the first Long Bridge over the Potomac River to an area north of Alexandria, Virginia. Blagden was also an active member of Christ Church, serving as contractor in the construction of a new building for the congregation in 1807.[18] While he was a significant figure in the formative years of Washington, D.C., he was remembered in the obituary published in *The National Intelligencer* on June 3, 1826, for the shocking circumstances of his death:

> About 6 o'clock on Saturday evening . . . he was standing beneath a bank of earth some six feet high, at the south West [sic] corner of the Capitol, inspecting a part of the old foundation which the digging had uncovered, when the bank caved in as he was going from it, and fell upon him, he falling on his face before it. His head was not covered, and he was soon dug out, and carried home, apparently not severely hurt, sensible, and directing himself how he should be placed. After arriving at his house, half a mile from the scene of the disaster, he was able to sit up in his bed and assist those about him in changing his clothing, but, in one short hour he was a corpse!

Griffith Coombe (1767-1845) was remembered in *The National Intelligencer* of September 15, 1845, as "one of the first and most active and enterprising founders of this city." A successful businessman, he owned and operated a lumberyard on Greenleaf's Point that flourished during the early decades of construction on the eastern side of the city. In addition to serving on the Christ Church vestry, he took an active role in the great civic projects. He was a director, for example, of the Washington Canal Company, launched by an Act of Congress in 1809 to establish a waterway that incorporated the Tiber River and that extended from the Potomac River to the foot of Capitol Hill and then south to Greenleaf's Point. Constitution Avenue now rests on the bed of the old canal. Coombe was also a commissioner of the Columbia Turnpike Company, organized to build thoroughfares connecting the new city with its surroundings.[19] Still bearing the company name, Columbia Pike, a busy thoroughfare in northern Virginia, is one of the surviving roads established by his firm.

Active in the affairs of the city, Coombe was also well-connected in his personal life. Married to Mary Pleasonton, aunt of General

Alfred Pleasonton who later emerged as a controversial leader of the Union cavalry during the Civil War, Coombe socialized with prominent residents in the area. They included Thomas Law, one of the early speculators, and Dr. Frederick May, fellow founder of the new cemetery. Historian Madison Davis noted that George Washington "dined and slept" in the fine old Coombe residence, built at what is now the corner of Georgia Avenue and Third Street SE before the government moved from Philadelphia to Washington, D.C. The location of the home must have been instrumental to the courtship and marriage in 1811 of daughter Juliana Coombe to James Barry, who was another of the early speculators and who lived on the opposite side of Third Street, in a house facing the Coombe home. The fruits of this union included a large family, descendants of whom lived in the city into the twentieth century.[20]

Dr. Frederick May (1773-1849) was the one professional man among the cemetery founders and a clear standout among other outstanding individuals in the city. A graduate of Dartmouth College and Harvard University, he came to Washington, D.C., from Boston in 1795. At an auction conducted on September 19, 1798, at Little Hotel on F Street near Fifteenth, he paid $667 for one of the lots that had originally been purchased by speculators James Greenleaf and Robert Morris for development and that did not, according to historian Washington Topham, "terminate satisfactorily." Located on Virginia Avenue, between Third and Fourth Streets SE, the lot was valued just three years later at $1,500. In 1800, Dr. May built a house at this location, where he lived until 1818, when he purchased the mansion of Thomas Law.[21] Samuel Smallwood, whom he knew well from work on the cemetery, then bought the home on Virginia Avenue.

Frederick May made a major contribution to the Washington community as a medical professional. In the late 1790s, he emerged, in the words of Washington Topham, as one of "the two outstanding physicians" in the city, the other being Dr. John I. Crocker. Proceeding on the strength of May's reputation, the U.S. government retained the young physician during spring 1798 to provide medical services to the construction crew, including slaves, working on the U.S. Capitol Building. A charter member of the Medical Society of the District, established in 1819, May served as president of the organization from 1833 to 1848. He was also a member of the city's first Board of Health, established in 1822. Among other activities, he emerged as a distinguished professor of medicine at Columbian College, now George Washington University, and in 1826 became one of the builders and owners of the Columbian Medical School Building, at the corner of Tenth and E Streets NW.[22]

Among the other cemetery founders, Samuel Smallwood (1770-1824) experienced the most dramatic rise in his career, proceeding from overseer of slaves working on construction of the Capitol Building to mayor of the city of Washington. He functioned in the former capacity during the late 1790s and perhaps the early years of the nineteenth century. The available records do not identify the factors leading to his selection for this task or his specific responsibilities. It is known that he felt unappreciated, underfed, and underpaid, having complained that his diet was "nothing more than salt meat for breakfast, dinner and supper which is neither palitabel [sic] nor constitutional and to bye tea sugar and other vegitables [sic] out of fifteen dollars [a month] you must reasonably suppose gentlemen will reduce that to a mear [sic] nothing. . . ."[23]

The available documentation about Smallwood's life, specifically essays by historians Madison Davis and Allen Clark, as well as coverage provided in *The National Intelligencer* upon his death, does not mention his work as overseer of slaves. The narratives focus instead on his contributions as a businessman and particularly as a civic leader. As noted, Smallwood had been a supplier of lumber and also the owner of a wharf along the Anacostia River. He was remembered primarily, however, for his leadership in a number of public ventures, particularly as a founder of the Washington Canal Company and of the Navy Yard Bridge Company, which constructed the first bridge over the Anacostia River after the British had destroyed the two existing structures in 1814. Smallwood also served as manager of the public lottery, sanctioned by the city government to raise funds for the construction of City Hall and public school buildings. The culmination of Smallwood's public career came in 1819, when he was elected to a four-year term as mayor of the city of Washington. Reelected to a second term, he served but four months (June to September) before his death on September 29, 1824. Smallwood was also a member of the Christ Church Board of Trustees, having participated in this capacity since 1816.[24]

Thomas Tingey (1750-1829) has been remembered best among the cemetery founders. Described by Constance Green as a "big bluff" individual, with "engaging good humor," he was a man of action. Born in London, England, the son of a Church of England clergyman, he served in the British Navy, becoming an officer before leaving the service sometime after 1771. He came to the United States through the Virgin Islands, where he had become involved in the West India trade, and via his marriage to the daughter of a Philadelphia merchant, whom he met and wed in Saint Croix. During the naval war with France, he served with distinction as a captain in the U.S. Navy. On January 22, 1800, Benjamin Stoddert, first Secretary of the Navy, directed Tingey to proceed posthaste to the city of Washington, where he was to supervise the planning and construction of a navy yard suitable for the young Republic.[25]

The compass of Tingey's career was set from that time forth. In 1804, he was appointed captain in the Navy and Commandant of the Washington Navy Yard. Serving in these capacities for the rest of his life, he oversaw the building of the Navy Yard, recommending early on that a company of Marines serve as guard of the facility, keeping close watch over the materials assembled for shipbuilding. "Wanting these," he observed, "the losses by pillage will no doubt be extreme." To make pillage impossible during the 1814 invasion of the British, Tingey personally torched the entire facility, which burned to the ground. Following the war, Tingey directed the reconstruction of the Navy Yard. The first naval officer to establish his permanent residence in the city of Washington, Tingey purchased a large house, forty-two feet square and two stories high, on 11th and G Streets, SE. He became a fixture in the community, participating in banquets, balls, and a host of other events. In addition, he was a faithful member of Christ Church, serving in the vestry from 1806 until his death in 1829.[26]

The surviving documentation provides the merest glimpse of the remaining two cemetery founders. During the early nineteenth century, John T. Frost served as a clerk at the House of Representatives and as registrar of Christ Church. Peter Miller was also a member of the Christ Church vestry, having been elected to that position with Thomas Tingey and six other men in 1806.[27] Thus placed, he was part of the group that not only established the new cemetery but also oversaw the construction of a new edifice for Christ Church, discussed below.

The committee of founders declared on April 4, 1807, that they intended to transfer ownership and operation of the new cemetery when free of debt to Christ Church. While their rationale for this decision is not specified in the extant records, it is likely that the plan originated with Henry Ingle and his fellow commissioners charged with supervising the cemeteries in the city of Washington. Responsible for "the improvement" of the municipal burial grounds, they understood that Square 1026, situated on "low and watery" terrain, was not a suitable site for a cemetery and that the most practical "improvement" involved the creation of a new burial ground at another location. In addition, they may well have had reservations about any involvement of the city government in the projected effort, given the significant errors made in selection of the site for the Eastern Burial Ground. In need of an organization to manage the new cemetery, they selected the institution they likely knew best—their church. In developing a model for this burial ground, they returned to a pattern familiar to many Americans at that time, the church cemetery.

Meanwhile, they arranged for burials at the cemetery that did not yet have a name. In so doing, they proceeded generally according to statements made in the April 4, 1807, articles of subscription to the effect that "any person" could purchase lots and thus be interred at the burial ground. During this early period in the history of the cemetery, "any person" came to mean both private citizens and federal officials. The first person to be interred at the new graveyard was William Swinton (1759-1807), an expert stonecutter who had been recruited by Benjamin Latrobe to participate in construction of the U.S. Capitol Building. Given Swinton's contribution to the development of key federal infrastructure, it is appropriate that his burial on April 11, 1807, was the first in the cemetery that would emerge during the antebellum period as the first national burial ground. The second burial was of Margaret Tingey, wife of Thomas Tingey, then much occupied with establishing the new graveyard. Dead at the age of fifty-six, she was interred on April 25, 1807, following "a long, lingering, and often excruciating illness," as noted in *The National Intelligencer* on May 1, 1807. The obituary was standard for the times in its praise of Margaret Tingey for her domestic accomplishments: "Her virtues in the relation of a wife, a parent and a friend were, perhaps, unsurpassed by any of her sex, and constitute a monument in the hearts of her kindred and friends, which will be imperishable."

The cemetery founders suffered a number of other losses close to the heart at about the same time. These constituted silent, grievous tragedies in that they involved infants and young children who died of causes that were not always specified in the local newspapers or other surviving documentation but that likely resulted from a number of ailments that would be readily manageable today. Henry and Margaret Ingle buried two children at the graveyard in the same site within a three-week period: their daughter Margaret, who died on August 15, 1807, at the age of one year and eight months, and her brother Henry, who expired on September 3 at the age of one month and three days. During the next two years, Samuel and Ruth Smallwood interred two daughters in adjoining lots: Martha Anne, who died on November 25, 1808, at an age not identified in the extant records, and Rebecca Addenson, who was two years old at the date of her death, May 16, 1810. After the passage of a few years, they lost four more infants, three of whom were placed in the same grave. By burying their own at the cemetery, the Smallwoods, Ingles, and the families of other cemetery founders committed themselves irrevocably to establishing the site on a lasting foundation.

During the years in which the founders buried members of their families at the graveyard, they also made arrangements for the interment there of federal representatives who died in the city when Congress was in session. The first of these individuals was Uriah Tracy, whose burial on July 19, 1807, constituted a new beginning for federal interments in the capital city. A Revolutionary War veteran and a U.S. senator from Connecticut, Tracy was the first public person buried in Square 1115. The obituary given in *The National Intelligencer* on July 22, 1807, summarized the accompanying ceremony, noting that "he was interred with the honors due to his station and character, as a statesman, and to his rank as a major general, his pall being supported by the heads of departments and officers of government." Congress subsequently authorized the placement of a substantial marker over his grave. This memorial in stone does more than identify the burial site of Senator Tracy. Viewed in hindsight, it signals the ex officio beginning of the cemetery as the first national burial ground.

In staging the funeral ceremonies for Uriah Tracy, Congress had the opportunity to test the accessibility of Square 1115 and the quality of the site itself. Clearly, the legislators were pleased with their findings, for they proceeded to the new graveyard for the interment of the next two congressmen to die in the city: Ezra Darby, a representative from New Jersey who expired on January 28, 1808, and Francis Malbone, a senator and previously a representative from Rhode Island who had "dropped down yesterday on his way to attend divine service at the Capitol and immediately expired," as noted in *The National Intelligencer* of June 7, 1809.

And thus a tradition was established. For the next half century, members of Congress proceeded over and again to the graveyard east of the Capitol Building to inter the remains of colleagues who died in the city. They accordingly had a critical role in the creation of what would become a singular institution—a cemetery that was owned by a local parish; that served the needs of the Capitol Hill community, including the federal government; and that periodically received federal funds for infrastructure development and maintenance.

Christ Church as Cemetery Owner and Operator

Both the local population and federal legislators in Washington, D.C., were taking a chance with the interments of beloved family members and respected national figures in a cemetery that from 1807 to 1812 had no formal name, was in debt, and had not yet been transferred to a reputable governing organization. They proceeded accordingly, however, because of the assurance provided in the fifth article of the April 4, 1807, articles of subscription, specifying that "title" to the graveyard, when free of debt, would be transferred to Christ Church on Capitol Hill. To the surrounding community, this church was an obvious choice as both owner and administrator of the cemetery. It was a fixture in the eastern part of the city, an established presence in the neighborhood when the federal government moved into Washington, D.C., at the turn of the century, accompanied by sizable numbers of professional men, merchants, military personnel, domestics, indigents, slaves, and others. To many of the newcomers, no matter their religion or lack thereof, this parish must have seemed a rock within a sea of enormous flux and uncertainty. A brief summation of its early history underscores its sizable presence within the city of Washington.

Proceeding under authority provided by the Maryland Vestry Act of 1794, Thomas John Claggett, the first Episcopal Bishop of Maryland, established Washington Parish in 1794 on land that was originally located in Maryland before the District of Columbia was created in 1791. At the first parish meeting, conducted on Easter Monday 1795, the local Episcopalians organized themselves into a congregation, which came to be known as Christ Church. The congregation initially met in a tobacco warehouse that was located at the intersection of New Jersey Avenue and D Street SE and that had been provided to the congregation by Daniel Carroll, one of the original landowners, for "a mere trifle." On June 14, 1795, James Greenleaf offered the following site for a new church building—lot 17 in Square 456, bordered by Sixth and Seventh and by E and F Streets NW. Following the lead of his friend and sometimes business partner, Samuel Blodget supplied timber for the frame of the building from Jamaica Farm, a plantation of his that extended from what is now LeDroit Park in northeast Washington, D.C., to about Twentieth Street NW. The vestry subsequently purchased lot 16, also in Square 456.[28]

Meanwhile, a number of other developments occurred within the parish. In 1798, the congregation elected Reverend Alexander T. McCormick, an Irish immigrant, as its second rector. Early in his pastorate, which extended to 1823, McCormick established a strong presence in the city, attracting members of the federal government to services he conducted at the tobacco warehouse on Sunday mornings and in the corridor of the War Office each Sunday afternoon, beginning at 4:00 p.m. Chief among the occasional attendees was Thomas Jefferson, who was widely viewed as a free thinker but was reputedly one of the most astute readers of the Bible ever to occupy the presidency. Reverend Ethan A. Allen, third rector of Christ Church, recalled this anecdote about the primary motivation propelling Jefferson to attend occasional services at Christ Church:

The President was coming to church one Sunday morning, crossing the fields with his large red prayerbook under his arm, when he was greeted by a friend. "Which way are you walking, Mr. Jefferson?" Jefferson replied, "To church, sir." "You going to church? Mr. Jefferson, you do not believe a word in it." "Sir," said the President, "no nation has ever yet existed or been governed without religion, nor can be. The Christian religion is the best religion that has been given to man; and I, as chief magistrate of this nation, am bound to give it the sanction of my example. Good morning, sir."[29]

In addition to his desire to set an example, Jefferson apparently liked the way McCormick read the lessons. He expressed his approval of both the rector and the work of the parish by contributing $50 annually to Christ Church for several years.[30] Based on the strength of his reputation within the federal establishment, Alexander McCormick was elected to two terms (1804-1805, 1807-1808) as Chaplain of the United States Senate.

At a congregational meeting conducted on April 7, 1806, Christ Church parishioners elected eight members to their vestry. They included Thomas Tingey and Peter Miller, both actively involved at that time in the establishment of the new cemetery; Thomas H. Gilliss, one of the three commissioners responsible for improvements to the city's two existing municipal cemeteries; and Robert Alexander, a rising young architect. Acting on the advice of Alexander, the vestry decided in a meeting on the following May 5 that the tobacco warehouse should not be repaired because it stood "on the publick ground" and that a permanent church building should be constructed on the eastern side of the city. Shortly thereafter, the vestry accepted land provided by William Prout (1758-1823), who was an active member of the parish. He offered this land, bounded by G Street, between Sixth and Seventh Streets SE, with the proviso that the new church building be completed "within a year." The involvement of William Prout was significant, given his prominence within the surrounding community. A wealthy landowner, he was also a dry goods merchant with a store near the Navy Yard. In addition, he participated in municipal affairs, serving in the first, fourth, fifth, eighth, eighteenth, and nineteenth city councils. Among other activities, he was a member of the Navy Yard Bridge Company in 1819, as was Samuel Smallwood, and was one of the commissioners appointed by the city council in 1820 to superintend the construction of City Hall.[31] His donation of land to the parish constituted yet another powerful endorsement of Christ Church as an important institution within the community.

Plans for the new structure proceeded apace. On June 16, 1806, the Christ Church vestry accepted the architectural design prepared by Robert Alexander, who was at that time a member of the vestry.[32] Ten days later, on June 26, an advertisement appeared in *The National Intelligencer* inviting all masons, no matter what their church affiliation, "to meet the Officers and Brethren of Washington Naval Lodge No 41, at their Lodge Room, on Tuesday next [August 3] at 10 o'clock A.M., to proceed from thence in Masonic order, for the purpose of laying the Corner Stone of the Protestant Episcopal Church."

During the rest of June and then July 1806, members of the vestry and the larger congregation apparently mulled over the architectural design provided by Robert Alexander. In a meeting on August 4, 1806, the vestry approved changes to this design, and Alexander promptly resigned from the vestry. Shortly thereafter, he left the city, proceeding to New Orleans, where he died of yellow fever on September 3, 1811, at the age of thirty. The vestry minutes provide no details about the modifications of Alexander's architectural plans or about his resignation, indicating only that two men were elected to fill the vacancy: Griffith Coombe, who had served as one of the three original trustees of the cemetery, and Judge William Cranch, who was a nephew of Abigail Adams and who served as chief justice of the U.S. Circuit Court of the District of Columbia from 1805 until his death in 1855 at the age of eighty-six.[33]

Cranch may have originally become acquainted with Christ Church through the involvement of James Greenleaf, brother of his wife Nancy. In a letter sent to his mother in 1800, when he and his wife were living in Georgetown, Cranch indicated his intentions of joining the church: "When we remove into the city I shall attend the Episcopalian Society under the instruction of Mr. McCormick, who appears to be an amiable man, and who has a good wife. They will be our next door neighbors. — And although I cannot subscribe to all the thirty-nine articles, yet I like their mode of worship better than that of any other sect, and shall not suffer small shades of difference in non-essentials to prevent me from frequent attendance on public worship."[34] Given his participation in a number of civic ventures, including as first vice president of the Washington National Monument Society, Cranch contributed in no small measure to the growing reputation of Christ Church as an institution that could be trusted as owner and operator of the new cemetery on Capitol Hill.

The congregation celebrated its first worship service in the new building on August 9, 1807. The edifice, by then widely recognized as "the new church by the Navy Yard," was brick and was thirty-eight by forty-five feet wide and two stories high. Thirty-nine of the forty-two pews on the first floor were rented, the revenues from which provided most of the church's income. The original group renting the pews comprised leading members of the congregation, including William Cranch and all cemetery founders but Samuel Smallwood and John Frost. The three remaining pews were reserved free of charge for William Prout, in gratitude for his gift of land; for the rector, to be available "forever"; and for the president of the United States,[35] in recognition of the occasional visits of Thomas Jefferson and to encourage ongoing attendance at services by both Jefferson and his successors. The upper level provided a U-shaped gallery, with seating available along the sides and back of the building. The diverse groupings occupying this gallery were the church choir; U.S. Marines, including instrumentalists who marched from the barracks to the church each Sunday; and the parishioners' slaves, the numbers and identities of whom are not identified in church records.

On August 20, 1807, the congregation formally adopted the name of Christ Church, which had been the informal appellation from the beginning of the congregation. Some two years later, on October 8, 1809, Bishop Thomas Claggett consecrated the new edifice, saying that "it is not large, but sufficiently elegant, and is the first building that hath been erected by the Protestant Episcopalians, for public worship, at the seat of government."[36] Viewed two centuries later, these words, particularly the reference to "the seat of government," signify more than originally intended, particularly as Christ Church came to preside over a burial ground that served in part as a federal cemetery.

The first interment at the new burial ground was that of stone-cutter William Swinton on April 11, 1807. During the next five years, the cemetery founders sold a sufficient number of burial sites to re-pay the debt incurred in both purchasing and then enclosing part of the land. On March 24, 1812, Henry Ingle accordingly informed his fellow trustees that "the burial ground was now unincumbered [sic] of debt." Proceeding with their approval, he prepared a deed of transfer for delivery of the burial ground to the Christ Church vestry for a sum of five dollars. The accompanying language in-cluded memorable phrasing, stating that "the said vestry of Wash-ington parish and their successors" were accorded the cemetery "to have and to hold . . . forever."[37] In a meeting conducted on Easter Monday, March 30, 1812, Ingle presented the deed of transfer to the vestry, which readily accepted ownership of the burial ground without extended debate over use of the word "forever" in the deed of transfer.

During the same meeting, the vestry adopted eleven regula-tions for operation of the Washington Parish Burial Ground, which they agreed should be the name of the new cemetery.[38] The most significant of these rules were the following, which despite pos-sible appearances to the contrary, particularly in connection with the seventh regulation, provided the basis for a cemetery that was truly public, in that it was accessible to everyone within the broader community

> First. *Resolved*, That in pursuance of a provision in the deed from Thomas Munroe, Superintendent [of the City of Washington], to Henry Ingle, for square No. 1115, the vestry do appropriate and set apart so much of the said square as lies south of the south fence (being one-fourth part) for gra-tuitous interments, subject, nevertheless, to the rules and regulations of the vestry.
>
> Second. *Resolved*. That the vestry do confirm and declare to be and continue in force the first, second, and third ar-ticles under which the subscribers did subscribe for sites in the burial ground.

Seventh. *Resolved,* That no person of color shall be permitted to be buried within that part of the burial ground which is now enclosed.

The vestry provided the first regulation in response to a requirement advanced by Thomas Munroe that one fourth of Square 1115 be reserved for the gratuitous interments of paupers. The city authorities clearly intended that this cemetery, which they saw as a replacement for the Eastern Burial Ground, would support the municipality in meeting the sizable needs of resident indigents. In his journals, Benjamin Latrobe talked about the causes of widespread poverty in the city, noting, for example, that laborers were recruited to the Capitol to work on construction, that they were given high wages "for a short time," and that they then proceeded for extended periods, "perhaps for a whole season," with no work and no wages. "Ruined in circumstances and health," the families of the poor were to be found, he observed, "scattered in wretched huts" across the city "or inhabiting the half finished houses, now tumbling to ruins which the madness of speculation has erected."[39]

Throughout the Jeffersonian years, a significant percentage of the municipal budget was directed toward meeting the needs of the impoverished living within the federal capital. By way of example, Constance Green noted that the city council appropriated a sizable forty-two percent of municipal revenues for relief of the poor in 1802, followed by twenty-eight percent in 1803, and seventeen percent in 1806.[40] While the numbers declined as the decade progressed, they nevertheless indicated that the municipality continued to appropriate sizable sums for relief of the poor. The Christ Church vestry accordingly agreed to provide "for gratuitous interments" at the new cemetery.

The second regulation announces a significant shift in policy by reaffirming only the first three of the seven articles of subscription issued in 1807: "First. The ground shall be laid off in lots of 3 by 8 feet; Second. Any person shall be at liberty to subscribe for lots from 1 to 15, at $2 each, the lots to be transferable; [and] Third. Any person applying at a future time to purchase shall be admitted at the same rate as the original subscriber." Missing from this list is the seventh article in the 1807 regulations, which had stated that "no person known to deny a belief in the Christian religion shall ever be admitted to a right in this burying ground." The second regulation adopted on March 30, 1812, is then highly significant in that the Christ Church vestry agreed to make its cemetery readily accessible to individuals affiliated with any Christian denomination, with any other religion, or with no religion at all.

The seventh regulation has frequently been misread, as exemplified by the interpretation given in the 1906 *History of the Congressional Cemetery*: "Among other provisions the [1812] regulations prohibited the interment of persons of color."[41] The seventh regulation states instead that persons of color were excluded only from the area then enclosed, not from the rest of the graveyard, including areas that could be enclosed in the future. With this regulation, the vestry reinforced segregated policies but only so far. From the very beginning of their administration of the new cemetery, the members allowed for the burial of both freed and enslaved blacks, perhaps thinking particularly of those working within their own homes, attending services at Christ Church, and living in the surrounding neighborhoods.

Two of the other regulations, identified below, focused in a cursory way on cemetery aesthetics:

> Sixth. *Resolved*, That the treasurer be authorized to have the burial ground ornamented with trees as near as he may think proper to the plan of the said ground.
> Ninth. *Resolved*, That no person shall be permitted to enclose their sites in the burial ground with any kind of fence or palisade of wood.

These standards anticipate in a general way the emergence of the rural/garden cemetery movement with the founding of Mount Auburn Cemetery outside Boston in 1831. Cemeteries established within this tradition were designed as garden sanctuaries in the Romantic tradition, offering the urban dweller a retreat for reflection on ultimate questions. While the vestry of Christ Church did not envision their new cemetery as a garden sanctuary, they did think that it was important to "ornament" the grounds with appropriate trees and to prohibit the types of lot enclosures that required ongoing care and that made it difficult to cut the grass and generally maintain the grounds. The vestry, however, minimized their emphasis on beautification of the grounds by giving the responsibility for meeting the sixth regulation to the treasurer, whose authority over the budget did not necessarily extend to either interest or expertise in horticulture.

One of the remaining regulations focused on the needs of the pastor of Christ Church and his family: "Fourth. *Resolved*, That sites Nos. 1, 2, 3, 4, and 5 in I west be, and they are hereby, appropriated and set apart for the exclusive privilege of the burial of Rev. Alexander T. McCormick and his family free of the stated charge for sites." This guideline related to the larger financial realities of life as a pastor/priest at the beginning of the nineteenth century. McCormick served twice as chaplain of the Senate perhaps in part to subsidize what has been described as "his meager clerical stipend," set in 1807 at $300 per year. When he resigned in 1823 from his pastorate at Christ Church, the parish still owed him $846 in back pay.[42] In donating burial sites to the McCormicks, the vestry may have intended to make the clerical salary seem a bit less "meager," even though the benefits of this largesse were to be realized after death. The more significant statement was their expression of gratitude to Alexander McCormick for his leadership in establishing the new church and the new cemetery on Capitol Hill.

The establishment of the cemetery was a remarkable accomplishment. The responsible parties—the founders, the Christ Church vestry, and supporting members of the congregation—likely shared prejudices of the times regarding race, class, and religion. Their sense of civic responsibility was more powerful, however, than any such prejudices and related concerns. They were committed to their community, they understood to their credit that the community needed a public burial ground, and they believed that Christ Church was the best institution to administer such a cemetery. At a time when slavery was still very much in effect and all kinds of newcomers were flooding into the city, the Christ Church vestry laid the foundations for a cemetery open to everyone—slaves, freed blacks, indigents, Christians, Jews, atheists, and the entire federal government.

The Partnership Between Christ Church and the Federal Government

In an appropriation dated August 10, 1846, the United States Congress provided $500 "for repairs to Congressional Burial Ground, rendered necessary by the late freshet," and $1,500 "for repairs to the road leading from the Capitol square to the congressional burial ground, rendered necessary by the late heavy rains, to be expended under direction of the commissioner of public buildings." The reference to "Congressional Burial Ground" indicates that the legislators had gone a long way in their thinking about the cemetery during the first half of the nineteenth century. In earlier appropriations, for example, Congress had identified the cemetery as "the burial ground of Christ Church, Washington Parish" (May 4, 1824), "Washington Parish Burial Ground" (July 14, 1832), and "the public burying ground" (June 30, 1834).[43] By 1846, Congress collectively believed that it had a claim on the graveyard and thereby had a responsibility to keep the road passable from the U.S. Capitol to the cemetery.

Meanwhile, members of the Christ Church vestry did nothing to discourage references to the "Congressional Burial Ground," even though the cemetery had been established as the Washington Parish Burial Ground. They actively pursued congressional involvement in the cemetery by making sites available for congressional burials and by requesting funding for cemetery repairs and improvements. Congress freely engaged in this partnership, raising no concerns in the extant documentation about issues relevant to separation between church and state.

Between the years 1824 through 1846, Congress provided $10,860 (rounded to the dollar amount) to Christ Church for cemetery development and repair, as indicated in Exhibit 1-1. This was a substantial contribution during a time of limited federal expenditures. Translated into the dollar values of the year 2012, the total comprised $274,940.[44] The federal government did not allocate comparable funding for the maintenance and expansion of any other cemetery during this same period. Clearly, the partnership between Christ Church and the federal government in the maintenance of Congressional Cemetery was unique.

While Christ Church made direct requests to Congress for most of the appropriations, Congress initiated some of the developments, such as the construction of a receiving vault for the temporary placement of deceased U.S. senators and representatives prior to their burial at Congressional or transfer to home districts for interment there. With all of the funded projects, Congress kept a careful eye on its own interests, as did Christ Church. Given the limitations in transportation and mortuary science during that time, Congress needed a cemetery close to the U.S. Capitol. Christ Church wanted to both meet this requirement and advance its own interests, particularly in the areas of infrastructure development and repair. And thus Christ Church and the U.S. Congress embarked upon an informal, undefined, evolving partnership that was advantageous to both parties during the antebellum period but that included unresolved, problematic issues that have extended into the present. The narrative that follows summarizes the history behind the appro-

Exhibit 1-1. Appropriations Provided by the U.S. Congress to Christ Church for Cemetery Development and Repair, 1824 to 1846.[45]

Construction of brick wall	$2,000.00	May 4, 1824
Construction of keeper's house and improvement of burial ground (e.g., planting trees, placement of boundary stones)	$1,500.00	May 31, 1832
Construction of receiving vault	$1,000.00	July 14, 1832
Completion of public vault, including railing	$1,600.00	March 2, 1833
Enclosure of public vault and improvement of burial grounds	$193.89	June 30, 1834
Repair of brick wall and construction of culvert and drain (made necessary by heavy rains)	$1,966.00	June 30, 1834
Completion of wall repair	$600.00	March 3, 1835
Repair of cemetery (made necessary by heavy rains)	$500.00	August 10, 1846
Repair of road from the U.S. Capitol to cemetery (made necessary by heavy rains)	$1,500.00	August 10, 1846
Total	$10,859.89	

priations provided directly to Christ Church by the U.S. Congress for the burial ground on Capitol Hill.

The Christ Church vestry encouraged the first congressional appropriation, given in 1824, by making two donations of burial sites to the U.S. Congress. As indicated in the 1906 *History of the Congressional Cemetery*, the members initiated procedures for the first donation during a meeting on April 15, 1816, when they designated a committee to select one-hundred burial sites "in the most eligible situation" within the cemetery "as a reservation for the interment of members of Congress." The minutes for the vestry meeting on April 7, 1817, Easter Monday, state that the sites had been selected and were accordingly reserved for congressional burials. During a meeting conducted three years later, on April 3, 1820, Christ Church extended the privilege of burial in those sites to the heads of departments within the government and to their families, as well as to the families of members of Congress.

The vestry deliberated during the same meeting on April 3, 1820, over the need to enclose the cemetery with a wall. Because income from the sale of burial sites was not sufficient to fund this project, the vestry appointed a committee to ask Congress for "a reasonable appropriation of money" to help Christ Church "inclose the Washington parish burial ground with a brick wall." The committee comprised three prominent individuals, all well known and respected on Capitol Hill: Reverend Ethan Allen, parish rector; Thomas Tingey, Commandant of the Washington Navy Yard; and Mayor Samuel Smallwood. The vestry had high hopes in pursuing the funding. As noted in the 1906 *History*, the members thought Congress would look favorably upon their request because of the previous donation of one-hundred sites to the government and because of the "prominent public officials" who had been buried there, including Senator Uriah Tracy of Connecticut, Senator Frances Malbone of Rhode Island, Vice President George Clinton of New York, and Vice President Elbridge Gerry of Massachusetts. "As a further inducement to secure this aid," the vestry decided during a meeting conducted on December 15, 1823, to donate an additional three-hundred burial sites, which were situated "in the vicinity of those previously donated for the use of the Government."

The U.S. Congress acted following this second donation of sites, passing legislation on May 4, 1824, that authorized the Secretary of the Treasury to provide $2,000 to the Christ Church vestry "for the purpose of aiding in the erection of a substantial wall around the burial ground of said parish. . . ."[46] As indicated by this transaction, the vestry seemingly felt no reservation in requesting funds directly from the U.S. Congress. Congress, in turn, apparently experienced no hesitation in accepting substantial donations of sites from Christ Church and then in providing $2,000 directly to the vestry for a brick enclosure. Through this appropriation, the U.S. Congress and Christ Church established a working relationship, a partnership in the development and maintenance of the cemetery that remained intact until the late 1850s.

The negotiations preceding the first appropriation from Congress are notable for another reason. The deliberations of the vestry over their own funding needs and associated site donations to Congress appear in vestry minutes beginning with the meeting on April 15, 1816. John P. Ingle, son of cemetery founder Henry Ingle, drafted and signed the minutes of that meeting as register. He proceeded to serve in this capacity almost to his death in 1863. Vestry records show that he was still register and still drafting and signing important vestry correspondence until at least the meeting conducted on March 30, 1857. John Ingle will emerge as one of the major figures in this chapter, as his father, Henry Ingle, was in the preceding narrative tracing the establishment of the burial ground.

Following emplacement of the brick wall, Christ Church neither requested nor received funding from Congress for the cemetery during the remainder of the 1820s. Substantial activity occurred during the first half of the 1830s, however, as indicated by the six congressional appropriations provided during that period.[47] After enclosure of the cemetery in 1824, the rate of burials continued to increase, requiring that the cemetery caretaker be employed at the burial ground "almost constantly." By the turn of the decade, the vestry had concluded that a house should be constructed at the cemetery for the caretaker. The members accordingly established a committee during their meeting on January 5, 1831, to ask Congress for financial support.

On May 31, 1832, Congress responded to the request advanced

by this committee, providing $1,500 for "the erection of a keeper's house, for planting trees, boundary stones, and otherwise improving the burial ground allotted to the interment of members of Congress and other officers of the General Government." The funds were "to be expended under the direction of the commissioner of public buildings," thereby underscoring the public status of the cemetery. The statute notes in addition that the funds were to be provided to the vestry of Christ Church to assist them in enhancing the burial sites reserved for federal officials. Clearly, the U.S. Congress continued to feel comfortable with burying its own in a cemetery that was operated by a local parish.

Meanwhile, at a meeting conducted on May 26, 1832, the vestry had appointed a committee of three to contract for and oversee construction of the caretaker's house and improvement of the burial ground. The membership of this committee is noteworthy, for it included Griffith Coombe, one of the cemetery founders; John P. Ingle, register of the Christ Church vestry and son of Henry Ingle, another cemetery founder; and Jonathan Prout, whose father, William Prout, had donated the land on which Christ Church was constructed. As the membership of this committee indicates, the administration of the church and cemetery had become in part a family affair, passed down from one generation to the next.

Congress initiated the next project at the cemetery, the installation during 1832-1834 of a receiving vault envisioned originally for the temporary deposition of congressmen who had died in Washington, D.C., and then later for use as well by the general public for a fee of five dollars per use. In addressing this project, the 1906 *History* noted that (1) by the beginning of the 1830s, the remains of some forty congressmen and government officials had been interred at the graveyard "by order of the Government," (2) the deceased officials who were occasionally buried elsewhere in the federal city "were afterwards removed and placed in the 'Congressional Cemetery,'" and (3) the cemetery "was generally recognized as the official burying ground of Congress." Anticipating continuing use of the cemetery, Congress appropriated $1,000 on July 14, 1832, for construction "of a substantial brick or stone vault in the Washington Parish Burial Ground, for the temporary interment of members of Congress." To complete the project, Congress provided an additional $1,600 on March 2, 1833, and $194 on June 30, 1834. The language accompanying the latter two appropriations acknowledged the larger use of the structure, calling it "the public vault."[48] Vent holes piercing the two iron doors that provide access continue to identify the structure in capital letters as "PUBLIC VAULT."

The placement of the vault near the geographic center of the cemetery was appropriate, given the generally acknowledged purpose of the burial ground by the early 1830s, which was to serve the needs of both the U.S. government and the general public. Use of the vault by the government, which had funded the structure, was to be without additional cost to the federal establishment. All others were to pay $5.00 per temporary use. Of this sum, $1.50 was to be given to the sexton for his services and the rest to the vestry "to be expended in the improvement of the grounds and in keeping the same in order." With this arrangement, Congress apparently intended to provide Christ Church with continuing funding for cemetery care.[49]

On June 30, 1834, the date when the final contribution was provided for the Public Vault, Congress also made the first of two appropriations ($1,966) to rebuild the brick wall, parts of which had been washed away by heavy rains, and to emplace a culvert and drain "at the burying ground," as stated in the accompanying legislation. The phrasing did not have to be more specific. About nine months later, on March 3, 1835, Congress provided an additional $600 to complete repair of the brick wall. For approximately the next ten years, the vestry neither requested nor received funding from Congress for the cemetery. Both public and private burials continued during this period, thereby providing the vestry with ongoing funding for cemetery upkeep. Moreover, the brick wall around the cemetery remained intact, as did the well-traveled road from the Capitol to the cemetery.

All this changed in the mid-1840s, when "unusually heavy rains had thrown down" approximately seventy-five feet of the south wall and one-hundred feet of the west wall of the cemetery, had "badly" damaged the roads within the graveyard, as well as those extending from the Capitol to the cemetery, and had also resulted in damage to the burial ground. On August 10, 1846, Congress appropriated $500 for unspecified repair of the cemetery and $1,500 for repair of the road leading from the U.S. Capitol to the burial ground.[50]

On September 16, 1847, President James K. Polk wrote a letter to Robert Clarke, then sexton of the cemetery. "Sir," he said, "you are hereby requested to set apart in the Congressional Burial Ground an appropriate spot for the interment of the body of the late Mr. [Henry Stephen] Fox, formerly Envoy Extraordinary and Minister Plenipotentiary of her Britannic Majesty to the United States." He signed himself simply as "Yours respectfully, James K. Polk."[51] This letter demonstrates once again that the lines of communication were wide open at that time between government officials at all levels of the federal bureaucracy and cemetery administrators. And thus the president of the United States issued an order directly to sexton Clarke. Moreover, he identified the cemetery as "the Congressional Burial Ground," using the all important definite article.

The letter from President Polk to Robert Clarke underscores the controlling idea of the preceding discussion. The road leading from the U.S. Capitol to the cemetery constituted a passageway etched in the collective thinking of the federal government, as well as the Christ Church vestry. When federal officials had to inter their own during the antebellum period, they turned regularly to the graveyard on Capitol Hill. During the first half of the nineteenth century, the linkage was accordingly clear and strong between the two partners in the cemetery that had gained recognition across the community as the Congressional Burial Ground.

Enlargement of the Cemetery

The original boundaries of the cemetery remained intact for approximately forty years, from the acquisition of Square 1115 in 1807 to the first purchase of additional land in 1848. By the early 1840s, however, the Christ Church vestry had realized that the burial ground needed to be expanded, given continuing use of the site by both the federal government and the general public. The action taken by the vestry to secure additional land constitutes another memorable narrative in the evolving, never fully defined partnership between Christ Church and the U.S. Congress in the development of the first national burial ground. The central actor in this effort was John P. Ingle, son of cemetery founder Henry Ingle.

During a meeting conducted on December 18, 1843, the Christ Church vestry appointed a committee to promote passage of a law by Congress that would enable the church to expand the size of the cemetery. As delineated in Exhibit 1-2, the parcels of land adjacent to Square 1115, except for city streets dividing the areas, were Square 1104 to the west, Square 1116 to the south, and Reservation 13 to the east. The vestry wanted in particular to purchase land on the western side of Reservation 13, located immediately to the east of Square 1115, and to incorporate into the cemetery the part of Nineteenth Street lying between Square 1115 and Reservation 13. It is likely that expansion into Reservation 13 seemed appropriate because this parcel of land had been set aside for use by the U.S. government and was at that time the site of the U.S. Marine hospital, as well as other federal facilities. As indicated in records of the commissioner of public buildings, then John B. Blake, Reservation 13 "was one of the original appropriations which, together with the streets, were reserved by President Washington's order [dated March 2, 1797] for the use of the United States forever."[52]

Exhibit 1-2: Parcels of Land Near Square 1115.[53]

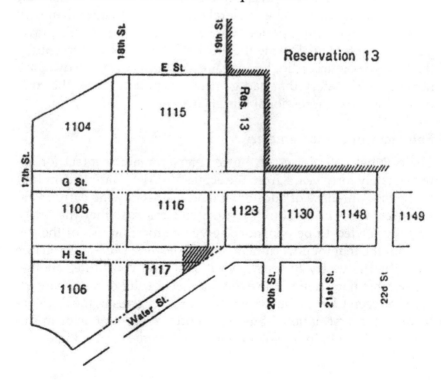

The committee from Christ Church petitioned Congress in late 1843 to pass the desired legislation. Congress, however, took no action on this request. The committee accordingly renewed its petition during the next four sessions of Congress, gaining a partial victory in 1847 when the U.S. Senate approved "A bill to authorize the sale of a part of public reservation No. 13 in the City of Washington, and for other purposes." To prompt corresponding action by the House of Representatives, the vestry adopted a resolution during its meeting of June 21, 1848, that allowed Congress to purchase up to one fourth of the unused land in the cemetery. The vestry pledged in turn to use the money realized from such purchase for "inclosing and graduating of the said burial ground." One month later, the House approved the desired legislation, which became law on July 25, 1848.

The statute authorized the following: (1) the commissioner of public buildings to sell to the vestry land within Reservation 13 as approved by the secretary of war and the secretary of the navy, (2) the vestry "to enclose, possess, and occupy" the part of Nineteenth Street lying between Square 1115 and land purchased within Reservation 13, as well as any street(s) between any other squares purchased in their entirety by the vestry for the cemetery, and (3) the vestry to enlarge the cemetery up to a limit of thirty acres. In addition, the act specified the following:

> That the Government of the United States shall be entitled to purchase from the said vestry, and to occupy as a burial ground for Members of Congress and such other members of the United States Government as the President shall deem expedient and proper to allow, a portion of the land hereinbefore authorized to be sold, not exceeing [sic] one-fourth part thereof, and which portion shall be laid out in some compact form and at such place as the Secretaries aforesaid shall select: *Provided*, That the ground so authorized to be purchased and used by the Government shall be paid for from time to time as it is actually used, at the price demanded by the vestry, for grave sites in other parts of the same ground: *And provided also*, That this reservation of the right to purchase to the extent aforesaid shall not be held

to subject the United States to any part of the expense of putting up or keeping up the enclosures of the said burying ground, or other expenses incident thereto.[54]

This statute conveys federal ambivalence about the cemetery. In the first part of the statement, the U.S. government recognized the graveyard as in part a federal cemetery, with twenty-five percent of the burial space to be reserved for federal officials and with the federal graves to be positioned "in some compact form," presumably in a designated area. In the latter part of the statement, however, the government distanced itself from responsibility for the burial ground by declaring that it would not accept responsibility for maintaining "enclosures" around the cemetery or for "other expenses incident thereto," which are not defined. The parties to this agreement, Christ Church and the U.S. federal government, could not have anticipated the future course of their unofficial partnership in Congressional Cemetery or the requirements for infrastructure maintenance over the following 150 years. The challenges that would emerge later in identifying their respective responsibilities for the federal sites originated in part, however, in the casual language used in agreements between the two parties, such as the law of July 25, 1848.

The vestry obtained additional land for the cemetery by purchasing lots within individual city squares. Upon securing all lots within one square, the vestry could then incorporate into the cemetery that square and any street enclosed between it and another square the church owned in its entirety. The existing records show that John P. Ingle purchased on his own initiative and with his own funds virtually all of the land added to the burial ground through this process. He was reimbursed by the vestry, which on April 19, 1854, established a trust fund, consisting of $1 from each burial, to raise money for cemetery expansion.[55] The following exhibit identifies the land secured by Ingle for inclusion within the burial ground.

Exhibit 1-3. Lots Purchased by John P. Ingle for the Incorporation of City Squares into Congressional Cemetery

City Square	Number of Lots Purchased	Dates of Purchase
1117	8	November 22, 1848–May 24, 1858
1116	20	November 29, 1848 – March, 12, 1849
1104	12	March 7, 1849 – May 3, 1851
1105	20	March 23, 1849 – December 8, 1851
1123	12	April 19, 1849 – May 24, 1858
1148	4	June 19, 1849 – October 13, 1853
1149	4	August 7,1851 – December 8, 1851
1106	23	March 7, 1849*
1130	12	**

* The available documentation regarding Square 1106 indicates only that Christ Church acquired the last of the twenty-three lots on April 11, 1876, thirteen years after the death of John Ingle on February 3, 1863. Subsequent to acquisition of the initial lot on March 7, 1849, Ingle likely made additional purchases within this square during the following years. With the addition of Square 1106, the burial ground comprised 31.098 acres and thus exceeded the thirty acres specified in legislation passed by Congress on July 25, 1848.

**Square 1130 was the last acquired for the cemetery. Ingle probably purchased the initial lots in this square. The last of the sites was not bought, however, until November 5, 1890. With this purchase, the cemetery comprised 33.437 acres.

The information given in Exhibit 1-3 underscores the sizable contribution made by John Ingle to Christ Church, the U.S. Congress, and the surrounding community in his efforts to expand Congressional Cemetery to its current size. He tracked the availability of all 115 lots over a twenty-year period, extending from 1843 to 1863, the year of his death. This was a daunting task, given the number of lots, the probability that he was acting alone on behalf of the vestry, and the possibility that other parties may well have been interested in some of this land, located in close proximity to the U.S. Capitol. He had to be certain that no other party purchased even a single lot in one of the targeted squares. If one lot was acquired by another party, Christ Church, as stipulated by the U.S. Congress, could not incorporate that square or any adjoining streets into the burial ground.[56]

Congressional Cemetery was not fashioned according to a coherent landscape design for the site but reflected instead the organization of Peter Charles L'Enfant's "classically-inspired plan" for the development of Washington, D.C., as noted by architectural historian Cathleen Breitkreutz. Upon its incorporation into the cemetery, each city square purchased by Christ Church was "laid out with roads, paths, and rows of gravesites in a closely-spaced grid pattern of straight lines and right angles." This pattern was followed even though the "trend in American landscape" design during the antebellum period had "moved away from the rational geometry of the Enlightenment to the romanticism of English picturesque landscapes."[57]

In "Cemeteries, Monuments and the Congressional Burying-Ground," published in *The National Intelligencer* on June 18, 1851, an unidentified writer accordingly observed that "despite continued growth and change at the cemetery, the grid-like arrangement of graves continued to be used in every new section." He proceeded to quote another author, also unidentified, who had observed earlier in 1851 that the layout "seems to have been fixed according to the old churchyard notions, and not at all in conformity with the liberal artistic conceptions to which Greenwood, Mount Auburn, Forest Hills, Laurel Hill, and Mount Hope owe their dimensions and arrangements."[58] The members of the vestry at Christ Church, who initiated and supervised developments at the cemetery, likely endorsed "the old churchyard notions" about burial grounds. The extant documentation of their deliberations, including the minutes of vestry meetings and other records accessible at Christ Church, does not indicate that they were familiar with or wanted to fashion Congressional according to "the liberal artistic conceptions" relevant to the rural cemetery movement. Their decisions were largely based on practical matters, which included arrangements that facilitated efforts to maintain the grounds, as did "straight lines and right angles."

National Memorials for the National Burial Ground

In 1815, the United States Congress commissioned Benjamin Henry Latrobe to develop plans for a monument to be emplaced at Congressional Cemetery in remembrance of each congressional representative who died in office. Latrobe completed his design during 1816-1817, and the monuments were fashioned thereafter according to his drawing.[59] The Latrobe cenotaphs at Congressional are the only monuments funded by the U.S. government in memory of individual members of Congress and by extension the legislative body of the U.S. government. Given the national significance of these memorials, they likely compounded difficulties later experienced by Robert Mills in his efforts to secure federal support for the construction of a national mausoleum in Washington, D.C.

In his journal entry for March 14, 1819, Latrobe addressed the purpose of funeral monuments, the underlying weaknesses of many contemporary memorials, and a way to remedy these problems. The purpose, he declared, "is assuredly to perpetuate the memory" and an understanding of the "merits" of the deceased. For this reason, the monuments had to be constructed for longevity. So many of the contemporary memorials were, however, "ingeniously contrived to last as short a time as possible." Latrobe noted that one such monument had been erected in a churchyard in New Orleans for William Charles Cole Claiborne, a congressman from Tennessee (1797-1801) and governor of Louisiana (1804-1816). Writing but sixteen months after Claiborne's death, Latrobe observed that his monument "is a miserable affair in task and construction, and is already tumbling to pieces."

The first problem with the Claiborne monument and so many

others was their placement on "ground newly dug, commonly called, *made ground*." Latrobe proceeded to identify a second and "worse" problem: "This ground contains a hollow wooden coffin. As the coffin decays, the ground gives way, the Slab, if horizontal, breaks; if perpendicular, it first leans over, and then falls & breakes [sic]." Even worse was "a new fashion" in monuments, whereby "a thin Slab is suported [sic] sometimes by 6 sometimes by only 4 balustres [sic], or small stone or marble posts." As the ground beneath the stone sank, the thin slab would fracture.

Given all the broken monuments he saw in church graveyards, Latrobe was ready with a solution, which he delineated in the same diary entry for March 14: "Whenever I have been consulted about a monument to be placed in a Church Yard, I have advised the foundation to be laid in rough stone, level with the bottom of the Grave and brought up in two Walls near to the surface and to be so arched as that any weight placed upon the arch cannot lose its position. The monument I always recommend to be made of as few blocks as possible & those of a[s] great weight as the form permits." In providing an example, Latrobe cited "the monument designed by me for Members of Congress who die in Washington and now adopted as marking their public character." Illustrated by Latrobe in the drawing given in Part Two of this study, the cenotaph is a "Cube block ... about eight hundred weight."[60]

Latrobe's monument was positioned over the graves at Congressional of congressmen who died in office and in Washington, D.C., into the 1830s. This practice began to evolve during the early part of the decade, however, when advances in transportation made it increasingly possible to arrange for the burials of congressmen in their home districts. The interment of Representative James Lent of New York signaled this shift. He died in the federal capital on February 22, 1833, was buried at Congressional Cemetery, and about one year later, at the wishes of his family, was reinterred in New York. Shortly thereafter, Latrobe's monument was placed over Lent's original grave, then empty, at Congressional Cemetery. During the next year and throughout the 1830s, the same marker was erected at the graveyard in memory of other congressmen who had died in office but had been interred at their home states.[61] Given this practice, the monuments came to be known in general as cenotaphs, meaning memorials emplaced in honor of persons whose remains are elsewhere.

With a resolution passed on March 3, 1839, the House of Representatives endorsed the emplacement of Latrobe's monument at Congressional Cemetery for each member who died while in office, no matter where the individual's place of burial." The Senate adopted the same custom. Latrobe's monument was accordingly placed at Congressional Cemetery through 1876 for each representative and senator who died in office. The respective branches of Congress financed the cenotaphs out of their contingency funds. According to extant records, they paid more in the early decades of the nineteenth century than later. During the 1820s, the price for a cenotaph could be as high as $170, while the cost fell to $125 by the 1840s, as indicated by receipts for payments to stonecutters who prepared the monuments. The average price was about $115 during the nineteenth century.[62]

The cenotaphs have not fared well in historical recollection, in part because of the materials used in their construction. While Latrobe had designed the memorials for longevity, Congress commissioned their construction out of local free stone and sandstone, which had been used in the U.S. Capitol Building. This stone, unlike granite, was readily damaged by weather and the passage of time. In A New Guide to Washington, published in 1842, George Watterston provided his assessment of the cenotaphs:

They are built of free or sandstone, painted white, have each four panels, on one of which are engraved, in black letters, the name, age, period of death, &c., of the deceased, and topped with a small pyramid. A brick wall is formed at the bottom of the grave, in which a splendid mahogany coffin, decorated with plated escutcheons, and containing the body of the deceased member, is deposited, and over which a brick arch is cast, and the whole surmounted by the very plain and rather tasteless tomb of which I have spoken. Some more beautiful design might be substituted without adding much to the expense; and the material should be marble, instead of the very ordinary sandstone of which they are now constructed.[63]

The 1859 Report of the Commissioner of Public Buildings focused on damage to the cenotaphs, noting in part that "the frost has caused the stone to shell off in some instances" and that "a number of the graves had settled under the monuments," which did not, however, "affect . . . their foundation. . . ."[64] Latrobe would not have been pleased to hear that many of the graves had settled under the weighty monuments. He would have been reassured, however, by the report that the foundations were secure, even though the Commissioner thought they "should be filled up, and newly sodded, to prevent water from running into them."

Robert Mills served as assistant to Benjamin Henry Latrobe during 1803-1808, beginning with the year in which President Thomas Jefferson had appointed Latrobe as Surveyor of Public Buildings. Mills felt fortunate in this apprenticeship, stating on one occasion that he was "the first native American that entered on the study of architecture and engineering in the United States—these he pursued under the celebrated Latrobe to whose talents and taste this country is so much indebted."[65] During his years with Latrobe, Mills gained detailed insight into the ongoing discussion about a monument for George Washington. He later proposed his own plan, involving the construction of a national mausoleum in the federal city.

On December 24, 1799, ten days after Washington had died, Congress unanimously passed a resolution to erect a memorial for him in the Capitol. After passage of the legislation, however, congressional unanimity rapidly dissolved as members vigorously debated the type of monument that should be constructed. The Federalists wanted something sublime, such as a design by Latrobe that featured a stepped pyramid one-hundred feet high. The Republicans preferred a relatively modest, understated memorial. When the question was called in the House on January 1, 1801, the vote divided along party lines, with the Federalists voting forty-five to three for the pyramid proposal and Republicans thirty-four to zero against the motion. The Federalist victory was short-lived. The Republicans assumed control of the presidency on March 4, 1801, with the inauguration of Thomas Jefferson, and the entire proposal suffered ultimate defeat when the two houses failed to agree on the details.[66]

The discussion about a possible memorial did not end, however. In the decades that followed, politicians said in one way or another that a monument really ought to be raised in the nation's capital for the founding father. John Quincy Adams and John Calhoun, for example, deliberated over this matter on December 27, 1820, when riding in a funereal cortege to Congressional Cemetery for the burial of Senator James Burrill of Rhode Island, who had died in Washington, D.C., on Christmas day. Adams wrote this in his diary entry for December 27:

> There is a resolution in Congress, existing ever since the death of Washington, that a monument in honor of his memory should be erected. I said to Calhoun that I thought, under that resolution, Congress ought to build a church of durable stone, equal in dimensions to Westminster Abbey or the Pantheon at Paris; that sheltered under this roof and within the walls of this church should be the sepulchral monument of Washington, and around it, suitably disposed, those of the statesmen and legislators of this Union. . . . Mr. Calhoun thought that Congress would not be supported in the expense of such a measure by the public opinion; of which I am well aware.[67]

During 1815-1829, Robert Mills oversaw the construction in Baltimore of a sizable monument in memory of George Washington. While working on this memorial, which would serve as a precedent for the monument he would later design for the National Mall, Mills concluded that a national memorial should be erected in Washington, D.C., for the interment of "the statesmen and legislators of this Union." On May 24, 1830, he wrote in his diary that he had "made a design for a Mausoleum" that would be located in Washington, D.C., in memory of U.S. presidents and members of Congress who died while in office. Situated at the intersection of what is now 9th and H Streets, the projected site for this memorial is currently the location of the National Portrait Gallery. Continuing his diary entry, Mills noted that he had shown his drawing to Representative Gersham Powers of New York, who was chairman of the congressional committee on the District of Columbia. His design was elaborate, in keeping with earlier federalist proposals. It featured a rotunda that was one-hundred feet in diameter and fifty feet high, that enclosed five-hundred catacombs, and that was crowned by an imperial seventy-six-foot column decorated with a sword and wreath motif.[68]

Mills continued to dream about a great mausoleum, even after he had prevailed in 1836 with his design for the Washington Monument. On July 31, 1852, he wrote a letter to R.M.T. Hunter, Chairman of the Senate Committee on Public Buildings, urging that a mausoleum be constructed at the Capitol in honor of U.S. presidents and congressmen who died in office. While his actual design is no longer available, he said that his scheme featured "a series of catacombs or niches in the interior . . . disposed on each side of a spacious elongated gallery, terminating in a Rotunda at each end. . . . Over each Rotunda rises an ornamental structure surmounted by appropriate symbols—on one a tripod—the symbol of immortality—and on the other the *facial* column—the symbol of authority." He also thought that both the Horatio Greenough statue of Washington, then positioned on the East Capitol grounds, and a statue of Jefferson in the White House could be placed prominently within the mausoleum.[69]

In presenting his design to the Chairman of the Senate Committee on Public Buildings, Mills addressed budgetary concerns. A mausoleum such as the one he proposed would be much less expensive, he observed, than the emplacement of cenotaphs at Congressional Cemetery, each of which he thought cost about $700. He understood that there were on average three deaths in Congress during each session. Reasoning from this number, which says much about the high mortality rates during the first half of the nineteenth century, Mills figured that $105,000 would be spent on cenotaphs over the following fifty years. His mausoleum, in contrast, would cost an estimated $80,000 and would serve, moreover, as a "Monument to *all the Presidents*. . . ."[70]

Nothing came of the Mills design for a national mausoleum, most likely because Congress could not achieve consensus regarding the projected memorial. Complicating factors likely included the increasing number of federal burials and federal monuments, particularly the Latrobe cenotaphs, at Congressional Cemetery.

Meanwhile, Congressional gained recognition as a place of national significance. Travel writer Jonathan Elliot, for example, identified the graveyard as "The National Burying Ground" in his *Historical Sketches of the Ten Miles Square*, published in Washington, D.C., during 1830.[71] A number of other contemporary travel writers, as well as journalists and historians, used similar terminology in characterizing the site. And thus the burial ground owned and operated by Christ Church became recognized during the first half of the nineteenth century as not only the new cemetery in the new federal city but more specifically as the national burial ground.

2

THE GRAND PROCESSION TO
THE NATIONAL BURIAL GROUND

On Easter Monday, March 30, 1812, the Christ Church vestry unanimously accepted the deed of title to the new cemetery on Square 1115 in Washington, D.C. Just three weeks later, on April 22, 1812, they oversaw the burial there of George Clinton, Vice President of the United States in the administrations of both Thomas Jefferson (1805-1809) and James Madison (1809 until Clinton's death). As characterized in *The National Intelligencer* on April 23, the events of that day had been "awful and impressive."

At 2:00 p.m. on April 22, the joint congressional committee in charge of arrangements for the funeral and a detachment of cavalry from the District of Columbia assembled at O'Neal's Hotel on Pennsylvania Avenue, which had been the former residence of the vice president when in the city. They left O'Neal's at 2:30 p.m., the cavalry providing an escort for the transfer of the vice president's remains to the U.S. Capitol under the supervision of the committee on arrangements. At 4:00 p.m., the funeral procession proceeded from the Capitol toward the new cemetery in the order that had been delineated in *The National Intelligencer* earlier that day:

The Cavalry
The Marine Corps
The Chaplains to both Houses of Congress
The Physicians who attended the deceased
The Hearse

Pall Bearers
Mr. [Benjamin] Tallmadge [NY] Mr. [Nathaniel] Macon [NC]
Mr. [Thomas] Sammons [NY] Mr. [Robert] Brown [PA]
Mr. [William] Butler [SC] Mr. [John] Sevier [TN]
Mr. [Matthew] Clay [VA] Mr. [Robert] Wright [MD]
The Family Mourners
The President of the United States (Madison)
The Sergeant-at-Arms of the Senate of the United States
President pro tempore and Secretary of the Senate
The Senate of the United States as Chief Mourners
The Sergeant-at-Arms of the House of Representatives
Speaker and Clerk of the House of Representatives
The House of Representatives of the United States
The Heads of Departments
The Officers of Government
Citizens and Strangers.

With the interment of Vice President Clinton, the United States government and Christ Church on Capitol Hill embarked upon a formative chapter in their collaborative efforts relative to the burial ground that became broadly recognized as Congressional Cemetery during the 1830s. For approximately the next half century, the U.S. government staged elaborate, dramatic funeral processions to the burial ground for leaders within all branches of the federal establishment, including three U.S. presidents. The staging of these events was unique, for never before or since has the U.S. government relied on a local congregation to function as a key participant, overseeing what was literally the last stop in the parade. The processions are historically significant because they articulated and shaped ceremonies integral to the U.S. state funeral parade, organized to the most dramatic effect upon the assassinations of President Abraham Lincoln and President John F. Kennedy.

Moreover, the processions defined a symbolic geography different from that found in contemporary Washington, D.C. Until the Civil War, the National Mall did not exist in anything resembling its current configuration. Even as late as 1860, it ended at the Washington Monument, which was only partially complete at that time. The central axis of the national capital extended along

Pennsylvania Avenue from the Executive Mansion to Capitol Hill. When funeral processions traversed that axis, they continued in a roughly straight line from the halls of Congress to what was then the national burial ground. The parades brought together a federal government often divided over partisan and sectional issues. In answering to the larger and unavoidable law of human mortality, the lawmakers made peace with one another, at least for the day of the funeral. The pall bearers came from all parties, and the funeral orations in Congress honored the passing of both enemies and friends. In short, the funerals of political leaders created opportunities for parades of unity that reaffirmed the structures of government and reassured onlookers.

Despite their historic significance, the funeral parades from Capitol Hill and/or the Executive Mansion to the cemetery have not secured a place in national memory. While they were delineated in notable detail by *The National Intelligencer*, they have never before been analyzed. The commentary that follows addresses this largely forgotten saga.

Participation by *The National Intelligencer*, U.S. Congress, and Christ Church

Three entities had major roles in the funeral processions to the cemetery during the first half of the nineteenth century: (1) *The National Intelligencer* (1800-1869), which functioned in part as the *de facto* voice of the federal government in these events, (2) the U.S. Congress, which moved swiftly in planning and orchestrating the ceremony, and (3) Christ Church, which exercised ultimate responsibility in maintaining the burial ground for use by the federal government.

The National Intelligencer, founded by Samuel Harrison Smith, was the first national political newspaper in the United States. The periodical was edited by Smith during 1800-1810, Joseph Gales, Jr., during 1810-1812, Gales and William Seaton until Gales death in 1860, and then Seaton until 1864. During those years, it "was considered the semiofficial organ of the federal government," providing "detailed congressional accounts" that were reproduced by newspapers across the nation, as noted by William E. Ames.[1] *The National Intelligencer* functioned in this capacity during the administrations it supported, particularly those of Thomas Jefferson (1801-1809), James Madison (1809-1817), James Monroe (1817-1825), William Henry Harrison (1841), and Zachary Taylor (1849-1851). Throughout its long life, the newspaper recorded the major events unfolding in the federal capital, including state funeral pageantry, with a special energy, diligence, and grace.

The schedule for funeral events was of necessity abbreviated during the first half of the nineteenth century, before advances in mortuary science made it easier to delay burial for a few days. The ceremonies for George Clinton, as narrated in *The National Intelligencer* on April 21, 1812, provide a case in point. Clinton, who had been ill for about one month, died at O'Neal's Hotel at approximately 9:00 a.m. on Monday, April 20. Informed shortly thereafter of Clinton's death, William Crawford, President of the Senate, announced to his colleagues the demise of "our venerable fellow-citizen," the Vice President of the United States. The Senate then unanimously approved this resolution, offered by John Smith of New York, Clinton's home state: "That a committee be appointed jointly with such as may be appointed on the part of the House of Representatives to consider and report measures proper to manifest the public respect for the memory of the deceased, and expressive of the deep regret of the Congress of the U.S. of a citizen so highly respected and revered." Congress then adjourned for the day, agreeing to reassemble at 9:00 a.m. on April 21 to consider and presumptively to approve the events planned by the joint committee. Thus, activities were set in motion that culminated in the interment of George Clinton on April 22.

The funeral parades to the burial ground staged in memory of Vice President Clinton and other federal officials were carefully scripted, as indicated by the published order of procession for George Clinton. The military marched at the front of the procession when the deceased had served in the U.S. military, as had Clinton, described in the April 23, 1812, *National Intelligencer* as "one of the brightest luminaries" of the "glorious revolution." Next came those who had stood watch over the soul and body of the deceased, the congressional chaplains and the attending physicians. The pallbearers, who followed the hearse, were chosen with care to make political statements, as will be discussed in connection with the elaborate funeral procession for John Quincy Adams. Representatives of the federal government customarily followed the family. For major figures, such as Clinton, the entire executive branch joined the procession—the U.S. President, U.S. Senate, and U.S. House of Representatives.

One of the most intriguing features of the Clinton procession, as well as the others considered in this chapter, is the place reserved at the end of the line for "citizens and strangers." Viewed in retrospect, the terminology poses all kinds of ambiguities because it was not defined in the official documentation of the parades or in accounts provided in the local press. Juxtaposed with the word "strangers," the meaning of "citizens" does not seem complex. The primary meaning was likely male residents of the federal city and surrounding communities, such as Georgetown and Alexandria. The definition of "strangers" is less certain and all the more fascinating. On one level, the word would have signified visitors to the nation's capital from other communities. "Strangers" is a large term, however, possibly incorporating other meanings. In his diary entry for April 7, 1841, drafted three days following the death of President William Henry Harrison, John Quincy Adams provided a tantalizing glimpse of those possibilities when he paused over the "floating multitude, male and female, of all ages and colors, [who] followed the procession" to Congressional Cemetery for the temporary placement of Harrison's remains "in the receiving vault—with some difficulty from the excessive crowd, but not the slightest disorder."[2] By reserving a place at the end of each procession for "citizens and strangers," the U.S. government made a large statement, democratic in the true sense of the word. Everyone, established residents as well as people living outside the structured system, was invited into the grand parade, celebrating the life of the deceased as well as the ideals of the new nation.

When the deceased had been the U.S. president at the time of his death, the parade proceeded from the Executive Mansion along Pennsylvania Avenue to the U.S. Capitol. Upon leaving the Capitol, it continued down Pennsylvania Avenue to E Street Southeast and then due east on E Street to the main entrance to the cemetery. When the deceased had been a member of Congress, the procession began at the U.S. Capitol and then followed the same route from there to the burial ground. Given the prominence of Pennsylvania Avenue in the drama, Samuel C. Busey observed in his *Pictures of the City of Washington in the Past* (1898) that "there is not another street in any city in this country that has suffered such distinguished affliction."[3]

Contemporary references to the cemetery underscored its key position as the last stop in the state funeral parades. The narratives provided in *The National Intelligencer*, for example, did not refer to the graveyard by its official name—Washington Parish Burial Ground—or by any other designation indicating that it was owned and managed by Christ Church. As the processions became increasingly elaborate and were given detailed coverage in *The National Intelligencer*, particularly beginning in the 1830s, the periodical regularly identified the site as Congressional Cemetery or a variant thereof, such as the Congress Burial Ground or the Government Burial Ground. Perhaps in part because of this terminology, numerous government leaders, as well as a substantial part of the general public, seemingly forgot or never realized that the so-called Congressional Cemetery was not property of the U. S. government.

This leads to one other notable characteristic of the funeral ceremonies—the loud and telling silence over the responsibility of Christ Church in the proceedings. In his diary entry for April 7, 1841, John Quincy Adams observed that "the corpse [of President William H. Harrison] was deposited in the receiving vault—with some difficulty from the excessive crowd, but not the slightest disorder." Like his congressional colleagues, Adams did not comment on the possible contributions of Christ Church in readying the cemetery for the planned ceremony or on the impact of that "excessive crowd" on the grounds, such as the boot marks that may have been left behind, the flowers possibly trampled, or the occasional gravestones perhaps nudged out of position.

The silence over these and related matters is somewhat surprising on the part of the astute Adams, who had participated in many funeral processions from the Capitol to the cemetery and was to be borne over the same way himself seven years later. He and his contemporaries had apparently grown accustomed to the personnel who supported the efforts of Congress and perhaps made arrangements with Christ Church. And thus Adams and his colleagues did not express concern or even occasional curiosity in the extant documentation about the work required to prepare the burial ground for ceremonies staged at the end of the grand funeral parades. The documentation maintained at Christ Church is no more informative about the possible involvement of congregational leaders in assuring the readiness of the cemetery or in overseeing in some capacity the cleanup activities after the crowds had left. It is likely that the contributions of the church were never recorded on paper but instead remained part of the institutional memory of long-time members of the vestry.

A Rich Weave of Pageantry

The parade to Congressional Cemetery for the interment of Vice President George Clinton on April 21, 1812, cited at the beginning of this chapter, was the most formal and elaborate funeral procession organized to that date by the U.S. government. It incorporated traditions formulated by New England Puritans, by Anglicans, especially in Virginia, and by the Masonic Order. The parade for Clinton influenced in turn the basic format of the funeral processions staged for members of the executive and legislative branches of the U.S. government throughout the antebellum period. Viewed in sum, the traditions associated with these parades shaped the funeral processions subsequently staged for Presidents Abraham Lincoln and John Kennedy, among others.

As fashioned by New England Puritans, the parade to the graveyard proceeded past central places within the community, particularly sites that had been important to the deceased. Samuel Sewall (1652-1730), a merchant and jurist who lived in Boston, provided details in his diary about funerals he had attended. In his entry for August 29, 1723, for example, he delineated the processional route to the graveyard for the burial of Dr. Increase Mather: "Was carried round the North-Meeting House, and so up by Capt. Hutchinson's and along by his own House and up Hull-Street, into the Tomb in the North burying place, and laid by his first wife."[4]

The processions of the seventeenth and early eighteenth centuries were primarily on foot. Because of the distances frequently involved, mourners sometimes arrived at the graveyard exhausted, thinking about their own mortality. Sewall captured a memorable example in connection with the interment of one Thomas Grove in 1697: "Mr. Morton is very short-breath, sat upon a Tomb in the burying-place, and said, for ought he knew he should be next." If he survived into the next century, Mr. Morton may well have joined those who rode to the graveyard in coaches. In the early 1700s, a scattering of such vehicles began to appear at the end of the more rigorous walks to the graveyard. As he grew older, Samuel Sewall increasingly chose this mode of transportation. In his diary entry for December 22, 1727, for example, he commented on his decision to see an old friend laid to rest: "I determined to go to the Funeral, if the Weather prov'd favourable, which it did, and I hired Blake's Coach with four Horses; my Son, Mr. Cooper and Mr. Prince went with me."[5]

The basic format of the processions was well established considerably before the time Sewall and others began to ride in coaches to the graveyard. The coffin invariably came first, supported by one set of casket bearers and assisted by an alternate set if needed during lengthy parades. Pallbearers walked beside the coffin in a purely ceremonial role, providing a type of honor guard. Following the coffin were family, beginning with those closest to the deceased, and then other mourners, walking in pairs. At the end of the line for the burial of distinguished citizens came the assemblage presaging the "Citizens and Strangers" of the later federal funeral processions. As noted by Sewall, the procession for Increase Mather in 1723 ended with "a vast number of Followers and Spectators."[6]

Sewall also delineated the elaborate procession that accompanied the body of Cotton Mather to the grave in 1728. One Reverend Gee, dressed "in deep Mourning," led the parade. He was followed by leaders within the local church, members of the congregation, "the Six first Ministers of the Boston lecture," the coffin and pallbearers, one of whom was Sewall, relatives dressed in mourning clothes, and a long line of dignitaries—Lieutenant Governor William Dummer, the Council, the House of Representatives, and "a large Train of Ministers, Justices, Merchants, Scholars, and other Principal Inhabitants both of Men and Women." Given Mather's prominence within the community, crowds of spectators lined the streets and looked from their windows as the procession made its way to the graveyard.[7] Cotton Mather received, in short, a grand sendoff, even though he had long been critical of the excesses he saw in Puritan funerals.

Given the ways in which they organized their funeral processions, the parades past places that had been important to the deceased, the inclusion of spectators, the eventual use of coaches, and the special pageantry for prominent individuals, the New England Puritans created new ways of burying their own. Over the years, these practices made their way into the larger culture, borne by witnesses to and participants in the ceremonies. And thus when the federal congresses staged their first burials in the 1790s, they, like the First and Second Continental Congresses (1774-1781) and the Articles of Confederation Congresses (1781-1788), drew upon traditions that had been shaped in part by the New England Puritans.

The federal congresses also incorporated burial customs formulated by New World Anglicans, particularly in Virginia. As political and social requirements dictated, Anglicans living in the colonies staged elaborate funeral processions that bore similarities in appearance to the Puritan parades for distinguished citizens but were decidedly different in intent. While the Puritan processions were formalized within a dissenting tradition, the Anglican pageantry was designed in part to affirm the authority of the crown during a period of increasing tension between England and the colonies. The ceremonies conducted in Williamsburg, Virginia, following the death of Norbonne Berkeley (Baron de Botetant) provide an example. Having been appointed governor of the colony by George III in 1768, he served in this capacity until his death on October 15, 1770.

As delineated in the *Virginia Gazette* of October 18, 1770, the events staged in memory of Berkeley included two processions, the first of which proceeded along Palace Street from the governor's mansion to the church, where the funeral service was conducted. The second parade went from the church to the College of William and Mary and then to the college chapel, where the governor's remains were placed in a vault as militia fired three volleys. The processions were carefully orchestrated to assert the authority of the crown over the colony, as illustrated by the printed format for the parade from the governor's mansion to the church:

The HEARSE,
Preceded by two mutes, and three on each side of the hearse,
Outward of whom walked the pall bearers,
Composed of six of his Majesty's Council,
And the Hon. the Speaker, and Richard Bland, Esq;
of the House of Burgesses.
His Excellency's servants, in deep mourning,
The Gentlemen of the Clergy, and
Professors of the College,
Clerk of the church, and Organist,
Immediately followed the hearse, the Chief Mourners.[8]

Following reference to "The HEARSE," the printed summation comprises two parts, each consisting of five lines and concluding with a period. The first of these passages begins with a reference to "mutes." Hired professional mourners, they were not part of any new funeral ceremony but were instead a transplantation of English mourning customs into the new world. The summation then references six representatives of "his Majesty's Council," who had been appointed by Berkeley to serve as his primary advisors. The two representatives of the House of Burgesses, the elected legislature, had a lesser position in the parade, having been placed after the representatives of "his Majesty's Council." The next five lines in the printed order of procession, also concluding with a period, identify those who followed the hearse, including Berkeley's servants, clergymen, and professors of the College of William and Mary. The remaining ten lines in the printed format for the parade specify other categories of participants, such as representatives of the city council and the courts, students of William and Mary, and then "the company," comprising the broad, undifferentiated general public, the "citizens and strangers" of the processions staged subsequently in Washington, D.C.

In terms of this study, the funeral procession for Governor Berkeley is significant because it was organized to make a clear political statement—that the power of the crown in Virginia came before all others, including the elected legislature. The first federal funeral processions, staged but two decades later, were also planned to make political statements. They bore a vastly different message, however, about the power of the general public, the citizens of a new land.

In orchestrating the first state funeral processions during the 1790s, the U.S. Congress drew upon Masonic traditions, as well as Anglican and to a lesser extent Puritan ceremonies. A significant number of the American revolutionary leaders were members of the Masonic order. Of those who signed the Articles of Confederation, for example, ten were Masons. In addition, the signatories of the Declaration of Independence and the Constitution included nine and thirteen Masons, respectively. These individuals would have been familiar with Masonic burial rituals, as delineated in William Preston's *Ilustrations of Masonry*, first published in England during 1754. According to these traditions, a Mason was expected to attend if at all possible the funeral of a brother; wear "decent," "uniform" mourning clothing, including "white stockings, gloves, and aprons"; and march in a structured procession to the graveyard. "From time immemorial," Preston observed, "it has been an established custom among the members of this respectable society, when requested by a brother, to accompany his corpse to the place of interment; and there to deposit his remains with the usual formalities." He delineated the standard Masonic funeral procession as follows:

The Tyler;
The Stewards;
The Music [Drums muffled, and Trumpets covered];
The Members of the Lodge;
The Secretary and Treasurer;
The Senior and Junior Wardens;
The Pastmaster;
The Bible and Book of Constitutions on
a cushion, covered with black cloth,
carried by a Member of the Lodge;
The MASTER;
The Choristers, singing an anthem;
The Clergyman;
The BODY,

Pall Bearers, with the regalia Pall Bearers,
placed thereon,
and two swords
crossed.
Chief Mourner;
Assistant Mourners;
Two Stewards;
A Tyler.[9]

Upon arrival at the burial ground, the lodge to which the deceased had belonged stopped at the entrance gate. Meanwhile, members of the other participating lodges formed a circle around the prepared grave, leaving an opening to receive the lodge of the deceased and other mourners. The lodge of the deceased brother and the other mourners then proceeded to the site, took their appointed places, and participated in the graveside service, conducted by a clergyman. Following the ceremony, the lodges marched out of the graveyard according to the order in which the members had entered the cemetery.[10]

President George Washington was interred at Mount Vernon in part according to Masonic ritual, as were a number of other leaders of the new republic. Washington Irving, who in 1859 drafted the first critical biography of Washington, described the ceremony, conducted on December 18, 1799:

About eleven o'clock the people of the neighborhood began to assemble. The corporation of Alexandria, with the militia and Free Masons of the place and eleven pieces of cannon arrived at a later hour. A schooner was stationed off Mount Vernon to fire minute guns.

About three o'clock, the procession began to move, passing out through the gate at the left wing of the house, proceeding round in front of the lawn and down to the vault, on the right wing of the house, minute guns being fired at the time. The troops, horse and foot, formed the escort; then came four of the clergy. Then the general's horse, with his saddle, holsters, and pistols, led by two grooms in black. The body was borne by the Free Masons and officers. Several members of the family and old friends followed as chief mourners. The corporation of Alexandria and numerous private persons closed the procession. The Rev. Mr. Davis read the funeral service at the vault, and pronounced a short address, after which the Masons performed their ceremonies and the body was deposited in the vault.

Such were the obsequies of Washington, simple and modest, according to his own wishes—all confined to the grounds of Mount Vernon which, after forming the poetical dream of his life, had now become his final-resting place.[11]

Free Masons, who had a lead role in the funeral procession staged at Mount Vernon, were a significant presence in many of the parades from the White House and/or the U.S. Capitol to Congressional Cemetery. In organizing these later processions, federal officials drew upon a rich and complex web of traditions. They did not intend to recreate ceremonies specific to any one religion or organization but instead to establish new, inclusive standards reflective of a nation won through bloody battle and established on democratic principles. They wanted to state, in short, that the crown had been banished from the new republic and that the new authority resided with the people and their elected representatives.

The Politics of Congressional Processions

During a visit to Washington, D.C., in 1828, English writer Frances Trollope observed the funeral parade staged in memory of Representative George Holcombe of New Jersey, which proceeded from the U.S. Capitol Building to Congressional Cemetery. In her *Domestic Manners of the Americans*, published in 1832, she declared herself "surprised by the ceremony and dignity of his funeral. It seems that whenever a senator or member of Congress dies during the session, he is buried at the expense of the government. . . . and the arrangements for the funeral are not interfered with by his friends, but become matters of State." She went on to delineate the order of the procession, finding it to be "rather grand and stately." Trollope had, however, no complimentary adjectives for the cemetery, identifying it as "an open 'grave yard,' near the city," or for Benjamin Latrobe's cenotaphs, describing them as "square blocks of masonry without any pretension to splendour."[12]

The U.S. Congress staged elaborate funeral processions from 1801, when the members relocated to Washington, D.C., through the 1850s, long after the visit of Trollope. In so doing, they incorporated ceremonial traditions shaped by Puritans, Anglicans, and Masons and also by the federal congresses in New York and Philadelphia during the 1790s.[13] The parades were in many ways astonishing spectacles. Shaped according to the evolving political climate, they made important statements about the history and survival of the new republic. For this reason, the various summations of the processions constitute "very resonant documents," to borrow phrasing provided by historian Mary Ryan.[14]

Exhibit 2-1 identifies the numbers of burials and temporary placements in the Public Vault at Congressional Cemetery during 1807-1867, the period extending from the establishment of the cemetery to the beginning of Reconstruction. In addition, the table specifies the number of congressmen who were reinterred at Congressional after having been buried at other graveyards preceding the establishment of Congressional Cemetery.[15]

According to standard congressional procedures, a traditional funeral procession preceded each burial and each temporary entombment in the Public Vault at Congressional as enumerated in Exhibit 2-1. During the first period of congressional burials, extending from 1807 through 1819, eleven congressmen died in Washington, D.C., when Congress was in session. Nine were interred at Congressional Cemetery. The body of Representative Jacob Crowninshield, one of the remaining two congressmen, was transported upon his death on April 15, 1808, to his home district for interment at Harmony Grove Cemetery in Salem, Massachusetts. Richard Brent, the other congressman, was buried at his home, Richland, in nearby Stafford County, Virginia, following his death on December 30, 1814.

Exhibit 2-1. Congressional Interments at Congressional Cemetery, 1807-1867

Years	Died in Washing-ton, D.C.	Buried at Congres-sional	Placed Temporarily in the Public Vault*	Reinterred at Congres-sional
1807-1819	11	9	0	0
1820-1829	12	11	0	1
1830-1839	16	12	4	5
1840-1849	18	9	7	1
1850-1859	13	4	4	0
1860-1867	6	1	1	0
Total	76**	46	16	7

*The Public Vault was not constructed until 1833.

**This number includes Senator Edward Dickinson Baker, who died in the vicinity of Washington, D.C., during the 1861 Battle of Balls Bluff, as discussed below.

The funeral processions conducted for congressmen during 1807-1819 were organized not only to honor the deceased and in so doing Congress but also to make larger statements shaped to the contemporary political climate. During this period, the new nation fought the "Second War of Independence" against England in hostilities extending officially from June 18, 1812, when the U.S. Congress declared war, until February 17, 1815, when President James Madison signed the Treaty of Ghent. The precipitating hostilities reached back to the beginning of the century, as British and French warships intercepted, often boarded, and sometimes confiscated

U.S. commercial vessels on the high seas. Organized against this backdrop, the funeral parades conducted by the U.S. government during the first two decades of the nineteenth century emphasized the power and confidence of the new nation as resident in both its military and political structures.

The procession arranged in honor of Representative Thomas Blount (1759-1812), who died in Washington, D.C., on February 7, 1812, provides a case in point. On February 11, 1812, two days following his interment at Congressional, *The National Intelligencer* provided an obituary that identified Blount as both a "statesman and warrior." It then summarized the format for his funeral parade, which featured military units, including a "Detachment from the Marine Corps" as well as a "Full Band of Martial Music," and the U.S. government, specifically both houses of Congress. Positioned toward the end of the procession was Vice President Clinton, who makes perhaps the most poignant statement upon viewing the parade in retrospect. Little did he or the other participants imagine that Clinton, seemingly at the apex of his political career, would be dead of pneumonia but ten weeks later and be borne over the same route to the burial ground.

In a letter drafted on New Year's Eve 1812, Representative Samuel Latham Mitchell of New York informed his wife Catharine about the death on the previous day of Representative John Smilie, "the old and respectable member from Pennsylvania." He noted that "to-day is appointed for his funeral" and then made this statement about death in the federal city: "With a grand interment at the public expense, and a monument in the great cemetery here, dying from home is so far from being thought a misfortune, that the sentiment seems to have gained considerable ascendancy that a member of Congress is very fortunate in coming to his end during his attendance here."[16] While this comment was surely offered in part as a wry observation, it underscored nonetheless the prominence at that time of "the great cemetery" in Washington, D.C.

The predominant themes of the funeral processions shifted in the 1820s and 1830s, the apex of congressional interments at the cemetery. As indicated in Exhibit 2-1, twenty-eight congressmen died in Washington, D.C., when Congress was in session during these two decades. Following formal processions from the U.S.

Capitol to the burial ground, Congress oversaw the interments of twenty-three of these individuals and the placement of four others in the Public Vault, completed in 1833. The remaining congressman was Representative James Johnson of Kentucky, who expired on August 13, 1826, and was interred in his family graveyard, located in his home district.

Also during the 1820s and 1830s, six members of Congress who had been buried at sites outside the federal capital were reinterred at Congressional. The first was Representative Theodorick Bland of Virginia (1742-1790), whose remains were buried at the cemetery near two of his original pallbearers on August 31, 1828, thirty years after his interment at Trinity Churchyard, New York City.[17] The remaining five, all of whom were reinterred at Congressional during the 1830s following initial burial at small cemeteries across Washington, D.C., were as follows: Representative James Jones (birthdate unknown-1801) from Georgia; Narsworthy Hunter (birthdate unknown-1802), a delegate from the Mississippi Territory; Representative James Gillespie (ca. 1747-1805) of North Carolina; Senator James Jackson (1757-1806) of Georgia; and Representative Levi Casey (ca. 1752-1807) of South Carolina.

The funeral parades to Congressional Cemetery during the first two decades of the nineteenth century underscored the strength and confidence of the new nation, then confronting threats beyond its borders. The processions of the 1820s and 1830s were staged against challenges from within, especially the partisan politics that increasingly threatened the stability of the republic. They stated in no uncertain terms that the U.S. government was united, operating according to established and consistent procedures. Congressmen fought in chambers over a host of divisive issues, particularly over the legitimacy and continuation of slavery, as well as the most appropriate ways to confront social upheavals caused by the economic panics of 1819 and 1837 and the resulting economic depressions. They always came together, however, to honor the life of a fallen colleague and to accompany his remains to the graveyard. Regardless of commentary provided in contemporary newspapers about partisan rancor on Capitol Hill, Congress was united in funeral ceremonies conducted on Capitol Hill and during the interments at Congressional Cemetery. The burial ground accordingly emerged during the 1820s and 1830s as a symbol of ultimate congressional unity and survival before the most implacable foe of all, death itself.

The funeral for John Galliard, senator from South Carolina, illustrates the standard procedures observed by Congress upon the death of a congressman during the 1820s and 1830s. Having served in the U.S. Senate for twenty-two years upon his demise on February 26, 1826, at the age of sixty, Galliard was remembered in *The National Intelligencer* of February 28 as "the oldest Member, for several years past," meaning the individual with the greatest longevity at that time in the Senate. On the day of his funeral, February 29, Congress conducted no other business, observing "the courtesy usually shewn to the memory of any member of either House." At 11:00 a.m., the funeral procession moved in this order, as delineated in the newspaper, from Senate chambers to the burial ground:

> The Chaplains of both Houses of Congress
> Physicians who attended the deceased
> Committee of Arrangements
>   Mr. Holmes
>   Mr. Berrien   Mr. VanDyke
>   Mr. Ruggles   Mr. Findlay
> Pall Bearers   B
>   Mr. Macon   O   Mr. Dickerson
>   Mr. Smith   D   Mr. Chandler
>   Mr. Lloyd   Y   Mr. Harrison
> Relatives of the deceased, and the Senator and Representatives
> from the State of South Carolina—as mourners
> The President of the United States (John Quincy Adams)
> The Sergeant-at-Arms of the Senate of the United States
> Vice President and Secretary of the Senate
> The Senate of the United States
> The Sergeant-at-Arms of the House of Representatives
> Speaker and Clerk of the House of Representatives
> The House of Representatives
> The Supreme Court and Bar
> The Heads of Departments
> Foreign Ministers
> Citizens and Strangers.

The National Intelligencer did not estimate the number of participants in the procession for Galliard or any of the other congressmen who died in Washington, D.C., during the antebellum period.
The importance of these parades did not, however, reside in the
numbers, which would have varied according to the reputation of
the deceased and the weather on the day of the funeral. Their significance was based instead on the intent of the legislators, which
was to honor the memory of a colleague and thus the institution
of Congress by accompanying his remains to Congressional Cemetery. The parades accordingly underscored the status of Congressional as the national burial ground.

The congressional interments at Congressional Cemetery declined progressively during the 1840s, 1850s, and 1860s, as indicated in Exhibit 2-1. Three primary factors brought about this change:
the expansion of the nation's rail system; advances in mortuary science, specifically in embalming and in new designs for caskets; and
the Civil War, with its enormous disruption of business as usual for
the United States Congress.

The national rail system began to take form in the 1820s and
1830s, during the apex of congressional interments at the burial
ground. The Baltimore and Ohio (B&O) Railroad, established in
1827, emerged first, followed shortly thereafter by other rail lines,
including the Mohawk and Hudson in 1830, Columbia Railroad of
Pennsylvania in 1834, and Boston and Providence in 1835. Washington, D.C., was initially linked to this expanding network in
1835, when the B&O Railroad constructed the first rail connection
from Baltimore to the federal city. Because the District of Columbia did not allow locomotives to enter into the municipality until
1851, teams of horses drew both passenger and freight cars from
city limits to the first rail depot within the city, located at Second
Street and Pennsylvania NW, two blocks west of the U.S. Capitol
Building. Over the next twenty years, the B&O and other rail companies linked Washington, D.C., to major cities in the north, including Philadelphia, New York, and Boston by the early 1850s, and to
the west, reaching St. Louis by 1857. Direct rail linkage between
Washington, D.C., and major points south, including Richmond,
Charleston, and New Orleans, was not established, however, until
after the Civil War.[18]

The development of the national rail system had a profound effect on the federal way of interment, beginning in the 1840s. During that decade, as indicated in Exhibit 2-1, nine of the eighteen congressmen who died in Washington, D.C., were buried at Congressional. The remains of an additional seven were placed temporarily in the Public Vault, pending removal elsewhere. The funeral ceremonies conducted for one of the other two, Senator Nathan Fellows Dixon of Rhode Island, illustrate changing patterns in federal burials. Following his death in Washington, D.C., on January 29, 1842, he was eulogized in a service conducted in Senate chambers on February 2. Upon conclusion of this event, the "remains of the honored dead were escorted, in procession, from the Capitol to the Railroad depot, where they were deposited in one of the cars appropriated for that purpose, and, with the evening train, were conveyed to Baltimore, on their way to Rhode Island for interment," as reported in *The National Intelligencer* for that day.

The delayed burials of U.S. congressmen at distant locations beginning in the 1840s depended not only on advances in transportation but also in embalming. One such development occurred during 1835 in France, with the publication by chemist Jean Gannal (1791-1852) of his *History of Embalming*. In this volume, Gannal traced the work of his predecessors, including Frederick Ruysch (1638-1731), a Dutch anatomist and botanist generally credited with developing the first successful system of arterial embalming, and William Hunter (1718-1783), a Scottish anatomist widely recognized as being the first to make effective use of arterial injection. Gannal made his own major contribution to the advancement of embalming by using sodium chloride for arterial injection, a process that dramatically slowed decomposition of the body.

Richard Harlan (1796-1843), an American educator with expertise in subjects including sanitation and public health, became acquainted with Gannal's book during a trip to Paris in 1839 to study methods of plague control. Viewing Gannal's research as an important advance in sanitation and as a means to prevent diphtheria, scarlet fever, small pox, and other epidemics in the United States, Harlan returned home with a copy of the *History of Embalming*, which he had translated into English and then published in Philadelphia during 1840. From the publication of this text into the

1860s, numerous specialists—including undertakers wishing to delay burial to facilitate funeral arrangements and pathologists interested in studying the human cadaver—drew on the work of Gannal and others in their efforts to enhance sanitation and preservation techniques.

In addition to advances in embalming, innovations in the design of coffins made it increasingly possible to transport the bodies of congressmen who had died in the federal city to their homes for burial there. One such development was the Fisk Metallic Burial Case, patented by its inventor, Almond D. Fisk, in 1848. Characterized by Robert Habenstein and William Lamers as "perhaps the most remarkable coffin ever patented and put into widespread use in America," it recalled in design "the ancient Egyptian sarcophagus, the iron torpedo, and the strong box." The top half of the two shells forming the case was designed to fit the shape of an individual lying on his or her back with arms folded over the chest. A glass plate made it possible for mourners to glimpse the face of the deceased.[19]

Almond Fisk made large claims about this invention, stating in part that "the air may be exhausted so completely as entirely to prevent the decay of the contained body . . . ." His comments were convincing to a number of congressional leaders, including John Calhoun, who was buried in a Fisk metallic coffin. During April 1850, shortly after the death of Calhoun on March 31 of that year, *The New York Tribune* published this testimonial under the heading of "Fisk's Metallic Burial Cases": "The entombment of John C. Calhoun in one of these cases has elicited the following letter, signed by many Hon. U.S. Senators—'Gentlemen: We witnessed the utility of your ornamental Patent Metallic Burial Case used to convey the remains of the late Hon. John C. Calhoun to the Congressional Cemetery. It impressed us with the belief that it is the best article known to us for transporting the dead to their final resting place.'" The signatories to this statement were a striking group, from the North, South, and West: Lewis Cass, Henry Clay, Jefferson Davis, Henry Dodge, and Daniel Webster. In addition to Calhoun, Clay was later interred in a Fisk metallic coffin.[20]

Divided over politics then, as they had been in previous decades, Calhoun, Clay, and Webster were united in their respective battles over age, sickness, and death and in their increasing interest in topics including coffin design. Their deaths all came in the early 1850s: Calhoun's on March 31, 1850; Clay's on June 29, 1852; and Webster's on October 24, 1852. The passing of Calhoun provides a vivid illustration of changing times for the nation, the leadership in Congress, and Congressional Cemetery.

On March 4, 1850, Calhoun made his last appearance in the U.S. Senate. He had come to deliver a speech opposing legislation advanced by Henry Clay that was designed to resolve the national debate over slavery in part by implementing popular sovereignty, whereby each new western state would make its own decision regarding this divisive issue. He was too weak, however, to read the statement, which was forceful in its support for the rights of slave owners and lengthy in its elaboration, comprising forty-two pages. Senator James Murray Mason of Virginia had agreed to read the text in his stead. As Calhoun sat nearby, wrapped in a black cloak, Mason delivered Calhoun's spirited rebuttal of any legislation that did not fully protect the rights of slaveholders or explicitly reject the arguments of northern abolitionists seeking to end slavery.

Calhoun returned to the Senate on March 7 to hear Daniel Webster's powerful statement in support of the Clay compromise. On March 27, Calhoun asked Andrew Pickens Butler, the other senator from South Carolina, to secure a one-week postponement in the scheduled debate over the legislation proposed by Clay. By that time, he expected to be strong enough to join in the deliberations. Calhoun died on March 31, reportedly saying at the end that "if I could have but one hour to speak in the Senate, I could do more good than on any previous occasion of my life." As it was, his final effort helped delay but not defeat the Clay compromise, which was voted into law as a series of separate measures during autumn 1850.[21]

Contentious during his life, Calhoun became a symbol of national unity in his death, as indicated by the comments of Clay and Webster upon the announcement in Congress of Calhoun's demise on April 1, 1850. Clay spoke first, saying that he was older than Calhoun and had expected to precede him in death, although he understood he would follow his old rival shortly thereafter: "I know that I shall linger here only a short time and shall soon follow him."

In keeping with his reputation as the Great Conciliator, Clay then declared that party politics paled before the certainty of death: "Sir, ought we not to profit by the contemplation of this melancholy occasion? Ought we not to draw from it the conclusion how unwise it is to indulge in the acerbity of unbridled debate? . . . How unbecoming, if not presumptuous, it is in us, who are the tenants of an hour in this earthly abode, to wrestle and struggle together with a violence which would not be justifiable if it were our perpetual home!"[22]

Daniel Webster, who spoke next, also sounded the theme of unity, saying that throughout his long relationship with Calhoun, which reached back to 1813, and "amidst all the strifes of party and politics, there has subsisted between us, always, and without interruption, a great degree of personal kindness." He drew to his conclusion by declaring that "however, sir, he may have differed from others of us in his political opinions, or his political principles, those principles and those opinions will descend to posterity under the sanction of a great name. . . . He is now a historical character."[23]

The funeral for Calhoun was orchestrated to emphasize national unity. Rev. Clement M. Butler, chaplain of the U.S. Senate, conducted the service, which began at noon on April 2, 1850, in the Senate chamber. He set the theme in his sermon, spoken to text given in Psalm 82: 6-7: "I have said ye are gods, and all of you are children of the Most High; but ye shall die like men, and fall like one of the princes."[24] Immediately upon conclusion of the service, a procession formed according to the standard congressional format to accompany the remains of Calhoun to Congressional Cemetery for temporary placement in the Public Vault. As was by then customary and as delineated in *The National Intelligencer* of April 3, 1850, the six pallbearers, all U.S. senators, occupied the fourth position in the parade, following the chaplains of the House and Senate (position 1), Calhoun's physicians (position 2), and the Committee of Arrangements (position 3). The committee had selected the pallbearers with care, intending to show a united front by balancing Whigs and Democrats. Aligned on the left of the coffin, from front to back, were three Whigs: Willie P. Mangum of North Carolina, Henry Clay of Kentucky, and Daniel Webster of Massachusetts. Positioned on the right of the coffin were three Democrats: Lewis Cass of Michigan, Rufus King of Alabama, and John Berrien of Georgia. Located near the center of the parade, following the Senate and the House of Representatives, was President Zachary Taylor.

The body of John Calhoun remained in the Public Vault for nearly three weeks, a tenure facilitated by the Fisk metallic coffin. On April 22, his remains were transported to the Washington docks on a hearse drawn by twelve black horses guided by black grooms. Thereupon, his body was placed on the steamer *Baltimore*, which was draped in black. Accompanying Calhoun on his final passage home were twenty-five leading South Carolinians selected by Governor Whitemarsh B. Seabrook (1795-1855); a congressional delegation consisting of five senators, including Jefferson Davis from Mississippi and James Mason from Virginia, as well as two members of the House of Representatives; and two of Calhoun's sons.[25]

The ceremonies staged in memory of Henry Clay, who died approximately two years after Calhoun, underscored new procedures in state funerals, thereby signaling changes for Congressional Cemetery in its status as the national burial ground. Prior to the funeral service, conducted in the Senate chamber on July 1, 1852, the remains of Senator Clay lay in state within the Capitol Rotunda for public visitation. He was the first person to be accorded this honor. Following the funeral, his body was escorted by the standard congressional procession not east to Congressional Cemetery but west to the rail depot at Second and Pennsylvania. And there began Clay's final passage home to Kentucky, which took nine days, was facilitated by advances in the linkage of rail and steam transportation systems, and was punctuated by ceremonies of remembrance at all major stops along the way. On July 10, he was buried in his Fisk metallic coffin at the Lexington City Cemetery.[26]

Daniel Webster died not in Washington, D.C., as had Clay and Calhoun, but at his home in Marshfield, Massachusetts. His preferences regarding his own funeral and interment provide another illustration of the changes in federal burials during the early 1850s. At the time of his death, October 24, 1852, approximately four months after the passing of Clay, he was Secretary of State in the administration of President Millard Filmore. The President wanted to honor Webster with a state funeral, similar to the pageantry accorded Clay and Calhoun. The family declined, in accordance with

Webster's wishes. He had stated in no uncertain terms in his will that "I wish to be buried without the least show or ostentation, but in a manner respectful to my neighbors, whose kindness has contributed so much to the happiness of me and mine. . . ."[27]

Despite his stated preference, Webster was honored in memorial ceremonies conducted across the nation, including a large service at Boston's Faneuil Hall on October 27. Two days later, approximately 10,000 people came to the Webster home in Marshfield to file past the open casket, positioned in the front yard to accommodate the crowd. Following the public viewing, the interment itself proceeded according to Webster's wishes. Six farmers from the immediate neighborhood bore Webster's coffin on their shoulders to a waiting carriage, which was drawn by two black horses to the ancestral burial ground and to Webster's interment there at home among family.[28]

The burials at home of Daniel Webster, Henry Clay, and John Calhoun during the 1850s underscored the challenges then confronting Congressional Cemetery. Following the establishment of the national cemetery system during the Civil War (see Chapter 3), Congressional no longer functioned in its special, albeit unofficial capacity as the national burial ground. As indicated by Exhibit 2-1, six congressmen died in Washington, D.C., during 1860-1867. Of this total, only two were interred at Congressional Cemetery, one in a designated congressional site and the other on a temporary basis in the Public Vault. These interments, while limited in number, were large in meaning, illustrative as they were of the larger political context.

Lemuel Jackson Bowden (1815-1864) was the one member of Congress buried at Congressional Cemetery during the Civil War. He was a recognized political figure in his home state of Virginia, having served in the Virginia House of Delegates from 1841 to 1846. As the national compromise of 1850 began to unravel during the autumn of that year, he hewed increasingly to unionist positions. Upon the secession of Virginia from the Union in 1861, Bowden worked with Republicans in northern Virginia to establish the Restored Government of Virginia, which was headquartered in Alexandria. In 1863, the Restored Government elected Bowden to the U.S. Senate, where he represented Virginia until his death from smallpox in 1864. A unionist from a secessionist state, Bowden could not easily go home again, even after death. He was accordingly interred at Congressional Cemetery, following a procession to the graveyard that included both houses of Congress and President Abraham Lincoln.[29]

Edward Dickinson Baker (1811-1861) was the sole member of Congress entombed in the Public Vault at Congressional Cemetery during the Civil War. He had a distinguished career, having been a lawyer, a skilled orator, a member of the House of Representatives from Illinois (1845-1846, 1849-1851), a veteran of the Mexican War, and a U.S. senator from Oregon (1859-1861). He is most remembered for his death, however. While a senator, he joined the U.S. Army as a colonel in the 71st Regiment, Pennsylvania Volunteer Infantry (1st California Regiment) and as major general of volunteers. He was killed on October 21, 1861, leading a brigade of 1700 troops at the Battle of Ball's Bluff, Virginia.

President Abraham Lincoln mourned Baker's death. Having been defeated by Baker for the Whig party nomination to the House of Representatives in 1844, he had come to view Baker in subsequent years with the warmest of regards, almost as a brother. He had even named one of his sons after his long-time friend. Lincoln had wanted the body of Baker to lie in state at the White House but was thwarted in this wish, perhaps by his wife, then involved in redecoration of the mansion. *The Washington Star News* of October 22, 1861, put it this way: "It was the desire of the President and Mrs. Lincoln that the body of Colonel Baker should be taken to the White House and placed in the East Room, but the house being just now in the hands of the upholsterers that course was not practicable." The remains of Colonel Baker were brought instead to the home of his friend Major J.W. Webb, at the corner of Fourteenth and H Streets.

The funeral was also conducted at the Webb residence, Congress not then being in session. As noted in *The Washington Star News* of October 24, 1861, the assemblage consisted "very largely of the most prominent men in the country," including President Lincoln, Secretary of State William Seward, General Winfield Scott, and Quartermaster General Montgomery Meigs. In addition, an "immense throng of people" congregated in the neighborhood of the Webb house, ready to join the funeral procession to Congressional Cemetery.

The parade began at the Webb residence, proceeded down Thirteenth Street to Pennsylvania Avenue, and then took the familiar course to "the Congressional Burying Ground," as delineated in *The Washington Star News*. President Lincoln was at the center of this procession, positioned immediately after the military units and personnel, among whom were officers of the Army, Navy, and Marine Corps, and at the head of the government departments and representatives, including the U.S. Supreme Court and both houses of Congress. Certainly, he wanted a grand parade to honor his old friend. He and the other participants probably wanted to make additional statements as well.

The U.S. Army had been significantly wounded in 1861 with losses in Virginia near the nation's capital. During the first Battle of Bull Run on July 21 in the proximity of Manassas, approximately 2,900 of the 13,000 federal troops were killed, wounded, or missing in action. Another 1,000 of 1,700 troops were killed, wounded, or missing in action during the October 21 Battle of Ball's Bluff in Loudoun Country. Given these among other losses, the U.S. government and military needed to affirm both to onlookers and perhaps also to themselves that they remained powerful and united. Thus, they participated yet again in the grand old tradition, the type of funeral processions staged in Washington, D.C., during the War of 1812, the Mexican War, and the years leading to the Civil War. They joined in the parade to Congressional Cemetery even though the body of Edward Baker was to remain in the Public Vault for less than one day before he began his long journey to San Francisco for burial there.

Viewed in their totality, the funeral parades to Congressional Cemetery for the interment of U.S. congressmen and senators constitute an important chapter in nineteenth-century American history. Conducted over and again along the same route, they punctuated political discourse, provided a pause for reflection on the passing of a colleague, on one's own future but certain demise, and on the course of the body politic, the Republic itself during times of both peace and war. They were elaborate, dramatic, seemingly unforgettable. Yet they have vanished from public and historical memory.

Other than the summations given in *The National Intelligencer*, Samuel C. Busey provided the only detailed commentary about the processions. While his observations proved useful, they comprised only twenty pages and appeared in a volume published in 1898: *Pictures of the City of Washington in the Past*. Busey found the ceremony fascinating, recognizing that "a complete history of the funeral pageantry of Pennsylvania Avenue would fill a large volume." He concluded, however, that the processions ultimately became "more spectacular and pretentious with each successive parade" and thus routine and meaningless. While he recognized their larger significance only in part, he nonetheless provided valuable summations of the pageantry.[30] Busey found the most compelling ceremony in the presidential processions to Congressional Cemetery.

Presidential Funeral Parades

Three sitting presidents died in Washington, D.C., during the period covered by this chapter: William Henry Harrison on April 4, 1841, Zachary Taylor on July 9, 1850, and Abraham Lincoln on April 15, 1865. In addition, John Quincy Adams, a former U.S. president and then a representative from Massachusetts in the U.S. Congress, died in the federal capital on February 23, 1848. All of these national figures had participated in many funeral processions to Congressional Cemetery, and all were accorded similar but much more elaborate parades upon their own deaths. Drawing upon formats refined through decades of congressional and military funerals, these processions were the most dramatic conducted in Washington, D.C., through the Civil War. The parades for Presidents Harrison, Adams, and Taylor took the familiar route to Congressional Cemetery, where the body of each was placed in the Public Vault while arrangements were made for the final journey home. The Lincoln procession was organized according to the formats of these earlier parades to Congressional Cemetery. It proceeded, however, from the Executive Mansion to Capitol Hill and then bypassed Congressional, going directly to the new train station on Second and New Jersey, NW.

The death of William Henry Harrison shocked the nation, coming but one month after he had secured the presidency by a landslide electoral vote. On March 4, 1841, he had ridden to his inauguration on horseback during a rainstorm; had spoken for perhaps too long—one-hundred minutes—on that raw, cold day without wearing either an overcoat or hat; and had thereafter attended three inaugural balls, during which he developed a chill that rapidly became pneumonia. His sudden death created a possible constitutional crisis, for never before had a sitting president died in office. Never before, then, had constitutional procedures for the transfer of presidential power been tested.

As it happened, the transfer of power was a quiet, almost humble ceremony. A few hours after Harrison's death, William Cranch, Chief Justice of the Circuit Court of the District of Columbia, administered the oath of office to Vice President John Tyler at Brown's Hotel in Washington, D.C., where Tyler had taken lodgings for the occasion. In his diary, John Quincy Adams identified the rationale behind the event: "The Judge certifies that although Mr. Tyler deems himself qualified to perform the duties and exercise the powers and office of President, on the death of President Harrison, without any other oath than that which he had taken as Vice President, yet, as doubts might arise, and for greater caution, he had taken and subscribed the present oath." Adams then penned the following supplication: "May the blessing of Heaven upon this nation attend and follow this providential revolution in its Government!"[31]

The funeral procession staged for President William Harrison on April 7 was similar in format to but much more elaborate than the parade conducted in memory of Vice President George Clinton. As delineated in *The National Intelligencer* of April 9, 1841, the parade comprised five sections, focused respectively on participation by the military, the fallen leader and his family, the federal government, civic organizations, and that "floating multitude" of citizens and strangers addressed earlier in this chapter. The first and the third of these sections made statements designed in part to reassure the larger public, then mourning the loss of a president only weeks after having celebrated his inauguration.

After identifying the many participating military units and organizations, *The National Intelligencer* underscored the statement given in the first part of the parade, which asserted in sum that the nation had been and would continue to be protected by its military force, no matter sudden loss at the top level of the U.S. government:

"Seldom has there been exhibited within a space so limited so many distinguished military men; the sight of whose well-known figures led back our thoughts to many a bloody field and many an ensanguined sea, on which the national honor has been well and nobly maintained." One of the participants was Major-General Alexander Macomb, General-in-Chief of the Army, who led the military part of the procession. Upon his death on June 25, 1841, approximately ten weeks later, his remains were escorted by an impressive military parade along the same route to Congressional Cemetery, where his body lies to this day beneath one of the most striking monuments at the burial ground (see Chapter 4).

The National Intelligencer continued with the federal part of the parade, observing that it "was not less striking than the military." The primary message articulated by this part of the procession, as well as the entire parade, was that there was continuity and coherence within the presidency. The primary conveyors of this statement were the new president, John Tyler, who rode in a carriage immediately behind the presidential hearse and family, and former president John Quincy Adams, who was positioned in his own carriage behind those of President Tyler and his cabinet.[32]

Seen in its entirety, the procession must have made a powerful impression on the crowds lining Pennsylvania Avenue. It was likely the most lengthy funeral parade conducted in Washington, D.C., to that date, extending as it did from the Executive Mansion to Congressional Cemetery and thus for approximately two miles. Along the way, it achieved dramatic effect in part through contrasts in the accompanying decor, particularly in the black and white surrounding the funeral car. Draped in black velvet, which extended over the wheels and nearly reached the pavement, it was drawn by six white horses, each of whom was led by an African-American groom dressed in white clothing, including a white turban and sash. Dressed in black, fifteen pallbearers, all of whom were white, walked on each side of the carriage, representing the various states and territories. The "effect" of all this was "very fine," according to *The National Intelligencer*, particularly when viewed against "the strong colors," the reds, blues, and yellows worn by the military personnel leading the parade.

Upon their arrival at Congressional Cemetery, the military

units formed a long line. The procession then advanced along this line, down the main avenue of the cemetery to the Public Vault. Sentries bearing arms had been stationed earlier around the Public Vault, keeping the crowds back during the service of interment, which was read by Reverend William Hawley, rector of St. John's, an Episcopalian church near the Executive Mansion. After the coffin had been placed in the Public Vault, and as reported in *The National Intelligencer*, a battalion of Light Artillery "fired a salute, which was immediately followed by several military bodies in line, who commenced firing from the left to the right, and continued the salute till it had thrice gone up the whole line." The parade then reformed and returned along the same route it had followed to the burial ground.

The body of William Henry Harrison remained in the Public Vault for two months, more than double the time he had served as president.[33] On April 28, three weeks after Harrison's death, a coffin bearing the body of Reverend Alexander McCormick was placed in the Public Vault, where it remained until burial at Congressional on June 8, 1841.[34] McCormick had been the rector of Christ Church from 1798 to 1823 and had provided leadership in establishing the cemetery. It seems appropriate that President Harrison and Rev. McCormick spent some time together in the Public Vault, for they represented the partnership—between the federal government and the Episcopalian parish on Capitol Hill—that had created the first national burial ground.

On June 26, Harrison began his long journey home. His son was in attendance as his casket was removed to the train station, where President Tyler, the congressional Committee of Arrangements, heads of various federal departments, and a reportedly large number of local citizens paid their last respects. A detachment of Marines then provided escort as the body was transported to North Bend, Ohio, and Harrison's final resting place on the banks of the Ohio River.[35]

The funeral ceremonies for John Quincy Adams seven years later were considerably different in emphasis from those conducted for Harrison, who died before he had the opportunity to secure his presidential legacy. Adams, in contrast, was celebrated upon his demise at the age of eighty as the grand old man of American politics, having persevered in public office for more than half a century. As narrated in *The National Intelligencer*, his death and funeral were extraordinary, bringing business as usual to a full stop in the nation's capital.

According to the account circulated on February 22, 1848, Adams had entered House chambers the preceding day in apparently "his usual health," voted on a pending motion "in an unusually distinct and emphatic manner," and collapsed a few minutes later: "Just after the yeas and nays were taken on a question, and the Speaker had risen to put another question to the House, a sudden cry was heard on the left of the chair, 'Mr. Adams is dying!' Turning our eyes to the spot, we beheld the venerable man in the act of falling over the left arm of his chair, while his right arm was extended, grasping his desk for support." Taken to the Speaker's chamber "in a state of perfect helplessness though not of entire insensibility," he partially recovered his speech and uttered what became his last words: "This is the end of earth; I am composed." Adams remained in the Speaker's chamber "in a state of apparent insensibility to all around him," as reported by *The National Intelligencer* on February 23. He died that evening just after 7:00 p.m.

On February 24, the House convened to initiate funeral arrangements. Speaker of the House Robert Winthrop of Massachusetts pledged at the outset that "the national sense" of Adams' "character and services should be fully commemorated." As directed by a House resolution, he appointed thirty congressmen, one from each state and territory, to the Committee of Arrangements. This strategy provided full sectional representation, the key requirement in antebellum efforts at national unity.[36] Speaker Winthrop also appointed members to the Committee of One for Each State and Territory, tasked with escorting the body of John Adams to his final resting place in Massachusetts. Intent again on achieving sectional balance, he included ten members from the Committee of Arrangements, along with twenty individuals representing the North and the South, Whigs and Democrats, as well as abolitionists and proslavery interests.[37]

The funeral staged in memory of President John Quincy Adams and then the procession to Congressional Cemetery took place on February 26, 1848. The events of that day were both "solemn" and "imposing," as recalled by William Seward, U.S. senator from New York during 1848-1860 and biographer of Adams.[38] The parade to the graveyard, which commenced upon conclusion of the midday service in the House of Representatives, had special resonance given Adams many prior visits to the cemetery. During his long years of service in the U.S. government, he had likely participated in more processions to Congressional Cemetery than had any other national political leader. It was fitting that he was remembered in an elaborate parade to the same site, even though his tenure there would be brief.

The procession had many remarkable features, the most memorable of which included the twelve pallbearers. They had been selected with care to convey national unity at a time of heightened sectional discord. Positioned immediately after the Committee of Arrangements, they proceeded in this order, as noted in *The National Intelligencer* of February 26:

Hon. James I. McKay, NC	C	Hon. Truman Smith, CT
Hon. Lynn Boyd, KT	O	Hon. Charles J. Ingersoll, PA
Hon. John C. Calhoun, SC	R	Hon. Thomas H. Benton, MO
Chief Justice Roger B. Taney	P	Hon. Justice John McLean
General George Gibson	S	Com. Charles Morris
Hon. William W. Seaton	E	Hon. Thomas H. Crawford.[39]

As arranged from the lead to the concluding pair, they represented the U.S. Congress, the Supreme Court, the U.S. military establishment, and the District of Columbia. Selected for their diversity, the six congressmen in the lead were a sometimes contentious group, comprising northerners and southerners, Whigs and Democrats, abolitionists, slave owners, and moderates over the issue of slavery. Engaged in divisive battles in Congress, they showed in this procession that they could on occasion rise above sectional politics.

Arguably the most intriguing pair of pallbearers was John Calhoun and Thomas Benton, who anchored the others, having been placed in their center. Calhoun, a slave owner, had long been on the opposite aisle in Congress from Adams. Through it all, however, they had been friends of sorts and had shared long memories, including those associated with a remarkable carriage ride to Congressional on December 27, 1820, for the burial of Senator James Burrill of Rhode Island (see the beginning of Chapter 4). John Calhoun must have had complicated emotions as he accompanied the body of John Adams to the graveyard. As for Thomas Benton, he was then a moderate on the issue of slavery, opposing both its abolition and extension and focused instead on preserving the union among states. Like Calhoun, he was a long-time political adversary of the deceased. He had agreed, however, to deliver a speech seconding a motion in the Senate to honor Adams. Later, in his autobiography, Benton recalled his personal struggle in formulating words of praise for the politician he had so consistently opposed.[40]

Upon reaching Congressional Cemetery, participants in the parade, specifically members of the immediate family and congressional representatives, gathered for a brief service conducted by Reverend Ralph Gurley, Chaplain of the House of Representatives. The body of John Quincy Adams was then placed in the Public Vault, where it stayed for approximately one week as preparations continued for the transport of his remains by train to Massachusetts.[41]

On March 5, 1848, the Adams family and the Committee of One for Each State and Territory oversaw the delivery of Adams' remains to the train station in Washington, D.C., and then accompanied the body of the former president on a five-day, five-hundred-mile journey to Quincy for burial there. The train stopped at both large and small towns along the way, where waiting crowds paid their final respects. In the countryside, the cortege passed through long lines of people standing silently with bowed heads. Reflecting over the elaborate ceremonies staged in memory of John Q. Adams, biographer Samuel Bemis declared that his sudden collapse and death while still on duty, at the age of eighty, "touched the imagination of his countrymen as nothing had since the deaths of John Adams and Thomas Jefferson" on July 4, 1826, the fiftieth anniversary of the Declaration of Independence.[42]

As with John Quincy Adams and William Henry Harrison, the death of President Zachary Taylor was quick and unexpected. He succumbed during the heat of a Washington, D.C., summer, after celebrating July 4, 1850, in apparent "full enjoyment of health and strength," as noted in *The National Intelligencer* of July 10, and after consuming large amounts of cherries and other fruit some thought suspect. The next day, he developed severe abdominal pains, diagnosed shortly thereafter as cholera morbus. He died during the evening of July 9, having served as president for less than two years.

The passing of Taylor, the second U.S. president to die in office, posed another test of constitutional procedures for the orderly transfer of executive power. As with the death of Harrison, *The National Intelligencer* captured the concerns of both Congress and the public over the sudden vacancy at the helm of the nation, which continued for more than twelve hours, as well as their pride in the effectiveness of constitutional procedures. Taylor died when Congress was in session, which had not been the case with Harrison, and thus the installation of Millard Fillmore took place in the House of Representatives on July 10 before a gathering "of deeply concerned spectators," according to the July 11 issue of the newspaper. The ceremony, the article went on to say, was "so brief and so simple, yet so important in its consequences, national, political, and personal." In short, the "scene [was] altogether American."

In contrast to the simple ceremony conducted within congressional chambers, the funeral procession was highly structured and elaborate, comprising both military and civic parades and extending, as had the Harrison procession, for nearly two miles—from the Executive Mansion, where the funeral service was conducted, almost to Congressional Cemetery, which was the end stop, at least for a while.[43] An estimated one-hundred-thousand people watched the grand show, clustered in part on front porches and at windows and on the roofs of houses along Pennsylvania Avenue, as noted by *The National Intelligencer* of July 15, 1850: "In some places the very roofs were almost literally tiled with human heads."

The civic procession underscored the orderly transfer of power in that the new president, Millard Fillmore, was positioned immediately behind the family of the former president. The rest of the civic parade was much like that staged for John Quincy Adams, as exemplified by the twenty pallbearers. As a group, they represented the U.S. Congress, the U.S. military, and the local jurisdiction. Considered individually, they were a diverse, remarkable assemblage of political friends and foes, representing a broad range of positions regarding the issue of slavery, in addition to other complex matters.

The first three pairs of pallbearers, all of whom were U.S. senators, provide a sampling of this complexity:

Hon. Senator Henry Clay, VA   Hon. Thomas H. Benton, MO
Hon. Lewis Cass, MI   Hon. Daniel Webster, MA
Hon. John M. Berrien, GA   Hon. Truman Smith, CT

As might have been expected, the pairings incorporated a demographic mix, with half of the pallbearers from free and the other half from slave states. In addition to providing commentary about political balance, four of the lead pallbearers recalled the high drama surrounding the 1848 presidential election. The victorious Whig candidate, Zachary Taylor, was the fallen commander-in-chief, lying in a casket surrounded by those he had defeated in life but who survived him after death: Henry Clay and Daniel Webster, whom he had defeated for the Whig nomination to the presidency, and Lewis Cass, unsuccessful candidate of the Democrats for the office. Positioned to the right of the casket, immediately behind Daniel Webster, was Truman Smith, who had figured among the first to promote Taylor's candidacy and who had directed his successful campaign. The united front exhibited by these players in the presidential drama of 1848 was arguably the greatest show of political cohesiveness in the entire procession. Joseph Gales, who owned *The National Intelligencer* with William Seaton, was perfectly positioned toward the end of the twenty pallbearers to recognize this statement and to ensure its inclusion in newspaper coverage of the event.

While the civic procession had its large moments, the energy, pomp, and real show came with the military parade and the celebration of Taylor first and foremost as a military hero. Leading the procession were a long line of military units from Washington, D.C., Maryland, Virginia, Delaware, and Pennsylvania, followed by the Marine Band attached to the Navy Yard and then additional military units. This first, lengthy part of the parade culminated in the imposing figure of Major General Winfield Scott, who was "mounted on a spirited horse, and shadowed by the towering plume of yellow feathers which marks his rank," as narrated in *The National Intelligencer* of July 15, 1850. The newspaper went on to say that "it is at once an elevating and a moving sight to behold such a Hero as TAYLOR followed to the grave by such a Hero as SCOTT." Taylor and Scott had their own personal history, with Scott having supported the advancement of Taylor during the Mexican War and having been subsequently defeated by Taylor in his own bid for the Whig candidacy in the 1848 presidential election.

The heart of the procession was, of course, the catafalque, decorated with traditional emblems of mourning. Draped in black and trimmed with festoons of white silk, the bier was surmounted by the figure of an American eagle, shrouded in black crepe. The car was drawn by eight white horses, each of whom was led by a groom dressed in white. Positioned immediately behind the hearse, in the place traditionally occupied by the family of the deceased, was Taylor's famed horse, Old Whitey, wearing an empty saddle with reversed spurs. So placed, he seemed an extension of "Old Rough and Ready," a symbol of glorious victories shared on the battlefield, which had been the great theater in Taylor's life. Taylor's immediate and extended family were located directly behind Old Whitey in the grand parade.

As the procession had begun with the military, so did it come to its conclusion, but not with the fresh faces of young recruits. Placed toward the end, and surely riding in carriages, were veterans of the Revolutionary War. They were followed, further down the line, by veterans of the War of 1812 and the Mexican War.

Upon reaching Congressional Cemetery, the military units formed a double line, through which passed the clergy, the pallbearers surrounding the coffin, and the family. They proceeded to the Public Vault, which was decorated with black ribbons, and into an open space amidst a pressing crowd, kept back by sentries. Reverend Smith Pyne, who had conducted the funeral earlier that day in the East Room of the Executive Mansion, read the burial rites, after which the remains of Zachary Taylor were placed in the Public Vault. According to cemetery records, they stayed there for more than three months, until October 24, 1850. The body of the former president was then transported by train and steamer to Louisville, Kentucky, for burial in a site that has since become the Zachary Taylor National Cemetery.[44]

During his tenure at Congressional Cemetery, Taylor shared

the Public Vault with Dolley Madison, who was to remain there for approximately 2.5 years (July 16, 1849, to February 11, 1852), after which she spent nearly six years (February 11, 1852, to January 12, 1858) in another vault before her remains were transported home for burial beside her husband at Montpelier, Virginia, the family plantation. This unexpected pairing in the Public Vault of Zachary Taylor, the famed general of many a bloody campaign, and Dolley Madison, one of the grand hostesses in federal Washington, D.C., recalls the old adage that politics can indeed make strange bedfellows. It also serves as a reminder of the historical oddities as well as the pomp and drama attendant upon the elaborate funeral parades that were staged for three U.S. presidents during an approximately ten-year period (1841 to 1850) and that proceeded down Pennsylvania Avenue to Congressional Cemetery and the Public Vault. These presidential processions, along with the congressional parades, illustrate in no uncertain terms the prominence of this graveyard as the first national burial ground.

Abraham Lincoln and the Processional Legacy

As a congressional representative from Illinois and then as U.S. president, Abraham Lincoln had prominent places in several high-profile funeral processions staged from the Executive Mansion/U.S. Capitol to Congressional Cemetery. Following his assassination on April 14, 1865, he was remembered in the largest, most elaborate funeral parade conducted to that date in Washington, D.C. This procession was based directly on the general format of those organized in the federal capital during the antebellum period, and it provided a standard for all subsequent funeral parades for U.S. presidents, particularly that conducted for John F. Kennedy.

As noted previously, Representative Lincoln served on the Committee of Arrangements that had planned the ceremonies staged in Washington, D.C., following the death of former President John Quincy Adams. Given their responsibilities, the members of this committee had a prominent place in the procession to Congressional Cemetery. As indicated in *The National Intelligencer* of February 24, 1848, they were located at the beginning of the parade, having been placed behind the lead units, including military companies and a marching band, and directly in front of the pall-bearers, who were arranged on both sides of the coffin. While serving as president, Lincoln had been at the center of high-profile processions to Congressional Cemetery for the burial of these individuals: Major General George C. Gibson (1775-1861), who had served as the eleventh Quartermaster General of the U.S. Army during 1816-1818 and then as Commissary General of Subsistence until his death at the age of 86; Edward Dickinson Baker (1811-1861), U.S. senator from Oregon; and Lemuel J. Bowden (1815-1864), Senator from the Restored Government of Virginia. In addition, President Lincoln and Secretary of State Edwin Stanton were identified as "chief mourners" at the funeral for the victims of the Arsenal disaster in Washington, D.C., on June 17, 1864 (see Chapter 4). So designated, they rode at the front of the approximately one-mile parade to the graveyard.

Following his death, the remains of Abraham Lincoln were brought to the Executive Mansion for public viewing. On April 19, his body was transported to the U.S. Capitol in a procession based directly on formats articulated in the parades to Congressional Cemetery during the preceding half century. The official "Order of the Procession," delineated below, was distributed on the day of the Lincoln funeral:

FUNERAL ESCORT IN COLUMN OF MARCH
One regiment of Cavalry.
Two batteries of Artillery.
Battalion of Marines.
Two regiments of Infantry.
Commander of Escort and Staff.
Dismounted Officers of Marine Corps, Navy, and Army in the order named.
Mounted Officers of Marine Corps, Navy, and Army in the order named.

CIVIC PROCESSION
Marshall.
Clergy in Attendance.
The Surgeon General of the United States and Physicians of the Deceased.

HEARSE.
Pall Bearers (Senate). Pall Bearers (House).
Pall Bearers (Army). Pall Bearers (Navy).
Pall Bearers (Civilians). Pall Bearers (Civilians).
THE FAMILY.
Relatives.
The Delegations of the State of Illinois and Kentucky as mourners.
THE PRESIDENT.
The Cabinet Ministers.
The Diplomatic Corps.
Ex-Presidents.
The Chief Justice and Associate Justices of the Supreme Court.
The Senate of the United States, preceded by its officers.
The House of Representatives of the United States, preceded by
its officers.
Governors of the several States and Territories.
Legislatures of the several States and Territories.
The Federal Judiciary, and the Judiciary of the several
States and Territories.
The Assistant Secretaries of State, Treasury, War, Navy, and
Interior;
And the Assistant Postmaster General and the Assistant
Attorney General.
Officers of the Smithsonian Institution.
The members and officers of the Sanitary and
Christian Commissioners.
Corporate Authorities of Washington and Georgetown, and other
cities.
Delegations of the several States.
The Reverend Clergy of the various denominations.
The Clerks and employees of the several Departments and
Bureaus, preceded
By the Heads of such Bureaus and their respective Chief Clerks.
Citizens and Strangers.[45]

The procession of April 19, 1865, that conveyed the remains
of President Abraham Lincoln from the Executive Mansion to the
U.S. Capitol Building has long been remembered as one of the most

elaborate and evocative of the funeral parades staged by the U.S. government.[46] The historical antecedents of this ceremony had two primary elements, the latter of which was the more definitive: (1) the funeral parades conducted in the colonies by Puritans, Anglicans, and Masons, discussed in the first part of this chapter, and (2) the half century of increasingly complex processions staged in Washington, D.C., from the Executive Mansion/U.S. Capitol to Congressional Cemetery. The basic organization of the Lincoln procession is clearly visible in the funeral parade staged in 1812 for Vice President George Clinton, the first member of the executive branch of the U.S. government to die in office and within the federal capital. Delineated at the beginning of this chapter, the primary elements were a military parade followed by a civic procession featuring the hearse, the family of the deceased, the U.S. president, both houses of Congress, and other officers of the federal government. The processions to Congressional Cemetery for the temporary interments of President William Henry Harrison (1841), former President John Quincy Adams (1848), and President Zachary Taylor (1850) comprised elaborations of this same basic structure.

Following the death of her husband in 1963, Jacqueline Kennedy decided to pattern major funeral events on ceremonies conducted in memory of President Lincoln, who had been assassinated some one-hundred years earlier.[47] The unforgettable procession that began at the U.S. Capitol Building and concluded at Arlington National Cemetery for the interment of President John F. Kennedy was thus structured after the elaborate format used in the parade bearing the coffin of President Lincoln to the U.S. Capitol. The Lincoln procession, in turn, was based on some fifty years of grand funeral parades conducted along Pennsylvania Avenue to Congressional Cemetery for the interment of leaders within all branches of the U.S. federal government, as well as military officers in confrontations extending from the Revolutionary War through the Civil War.

The remains of Lincoln's predecessors who died in office—Presidents William Henry Harrison (1841) and Zachary Taylor (1850)—were placed on a temporary basis in the Public Vault at Congressional Cemetery, as was the body of John Quincy Adams (1848), formerly president of the United States. Had Lincoln's death come some ten years earlier, it is likely that he, too, would have had a temporary stay in the Public Vault as arrangements were made for the transfer of his remains to his home district.[48] Given recent advances in both mortuary science and transportation systems, as delineated previously, the body of the fallen president could, however, be transported without significant delay to Springfield, Illinois, for burial there. So, too, could the remains of other federal leaders be returned to their home districts. And thus an era drew toward a close for Congressional as the first national burial ground and as the last stop in the great funeral processions staged in Washington, D.C., during the antebellum period.

3

CIVIL WAR MEMORIES
AT CONGRESSIONAL
AND ARLINGTON CEMETERIES

On February 8, 1899, the remains of John A. Rawlins (1831-1869), Secretary of War in the cabinet of President Ulysses S. Grant, were removed from Congressional Cemetery, where they had been for thirty years, and reinterred at Arlington National Cemetery. John A. Rawlins Post Number 1, Grand Army of the Republic, Washington, D.C., initiated the transfer. As had been announced in *The Evening Star* on February 1, 1899, the $500 expense for this effort was covered through a joint resolution of Congress, which was approved by President William McKinley and expended under the authority and supervision of the Secretary of War, Russell Alexander Alger.

The remains of Rawlins were transferred to Arlington in a parade that was reminiscent in its organization of the funeral processions staged from the Executive Mansion/U.S. Capitol to Congressional Cemetery during the antebellum period. Led by a battalion of the 4th Artillery from the Washington, D.C., barracks, it included eight noncommissioned officers of the artillery who served as pallbearers. They were followed by a long line of carriages transporting the immediate family, congressmen, government officials, and members of John A. Rawlins Post Number 1. In a reversal of the historic processions that went in an easterly direction toward Congressional, the parade proceeded west on Pennsylvania Avenue to Georgetown and then across the Aqueduct Bridge to Arlington National Cemetery in northern Virginia. By presidential directive, the flags on all public buildings flew at half mast along the processional route. Following the reinterment, the monument that had marked Rawlins' grave at Congressional was removed to Arlington and placed over the new burial site. According to *The Evening Star* of February 8, 1899, the reinterment of General Rawlins was appropriate in that his remains "now rest in the nation's cemetery at Arlington alongside those of the distinguished soldier's companions in arms of equal rank and distinction."

Viewed in hindsight, the reinterment of Rawlins at Arlington is emblematic of a much larger narrative. Part of this story has been told in various sources, as in summaries about the creation of Arlington National Cemetery. Other key elements of the narrative have not previously, however, been examined. They include the inspiration Quartermaster General Montgomery C. Meigs found in Congressional Cemetery for the development of Arlington National Cemetery, the differing definitions of what was considered "national" in relation to Arlington and Congressional as burial grounds, and the high drama of Memorial Day celebrations at the two cemeteries. This chapter focuses on these topics.

General Montgomery C. Meigs and His Vision of a National Public Cemetery

Various histories outline the establishment of Arlington as a national military cemetery during the Civil War. In so doing, they acknowledge the contributions of Montgomery Meigs, who as Quartermaster General during 1861-1882 was responsible in part for assuring sufficient and appropriate burial space for the Union dead. None of the documents, however, addresses the eventual connection in the mind and heart of Meigs between Congressional Cemetery, the old national burial ground he knew so well, and Arlington, the new cemetery with so much potential. As he shaped a future course for Arlington, Meigs came to envision not simply a national military cemetery but "a national public cemetery" modeled on Congressional Cemetery. It took him several years, however, to articulate this view and to proceed accordingly.

Accounts vary regarding the specific event initiating the creation of Arlington as a national cemetery. Among the differing narratives, the summation by journalists Karl Decker and Angus McSween is the most compelling. Their *Historic Arlington* (1892) is the first history of the burial ground. It was based on records provided by the War Department, on "the personal recollections of men now living who were connected with some of the different phases of Arlington history," on "historical documents" made available by Dr. Joseph M. Toner (1825-1896), a local historian, and on the material assistance of Richard N. Batchelder, who served as U.S. Quartermaster General during 1890-1896.[1]

Decker and McSween recalled that Meigs took a walk during "the late afternoon" on May 13, 1864, from the "old War Department building," where his office was located, into the "grounds surrounding the White House." He was preoccupied, even burdened that day, for he was mulling over the need to provide more burial space for Union troops in and around Washington, D.C. In addition, he was reportedly thinking about persistent rumors circulating in the northern states to the effect that the interment of Union troops was frequently done in a careless, even irreverent, manner. As he passed the White House portico, he was "hailed by a familiar voice," that of President Abraham Lincoln. Upon observing that the Quartermaster General "looked tired and worn out," Lincoln invited him for a drive in his carriage: "The President threw open the low door and the Quartermaster General entered the vehicle. A moment later the team clattered down the driveway and the carriage whirled rapidly away toward Georgetown."[2] Lincoln and Meigs proceeded across the Potomac River via the Acqueduct Bridge and then along a rough, unpaved road to Arlington Mansion, the gracious and by then vacated home of Confederate General Robert E. Lee.

As they stood on the terrace of Lee's mansion, looking out over the surrounding terrain, the President and the Quartermaster General saw the bodies of some twelve troops who had died in hospital tents on the grounds and were being removed for interment at Soldier's Home Cemetery in Washington, D.C. Meigs thereupon ordered the burial of these troops in graves to be prepared immediately in an area about a dozen yards south of the mansion, bordering Mary Lee's then famous rose garden.[3] By this action, he not only took the first step toward the transformation of the Arlington plantation into a cemetery, but he also brought the bloody conflict to the very door of the Custis-Lee estate.

During the prewar period, Meigs had admired the leadership and integrity of Lee, whom he had assisted upon graduation from the U.S. Military Academy in 1836 in a survey of the Mississippi River near St. Louis. He never forgave Lee, however, for his service to the Confederacy and for bringing the war into his own home, which was divided by the conflict.[4] Meigs' brother was then serving in the Confederate Army. Later, his son was killed by Confederate troops.

On June 15, 1864, approximately one month after he had ordered the first burials at the Custis-Lee estate, Meigs wrote to Edwin Stanton, Secretary of War, recommending "that the land surrounding Arlington Mansion, then understood to be the property of the United States, be appropriated as a National Military Cemetery, to be properly enclosed, laid out, and carefully preserved for that purpose. . . ." Stanton replied by letter that day, stating that "the Arlington Mansion and the grounds immediately surrounding it are appropriated for a Military Cemetery" and that Meigs was to execute "this order." And thus the Arlington estate became part of the U.S. national military cemetery system, which had been initiated by War Department General Orders Number 75, issued on September 11, 1861, and Number 33, dated April 3, 1862. General Order Number 75 made the commanding officers of military organizations responsible for the interment of troops and officers who died within their areas of responsibility. They were accordingly directed to fulfill all regulations promulgated by the Quartermaster General for this purpose. General Order Number 33 included the combat zone in the burial program, thereby providing for much needed additional land.[5]

On July 17, 1862, the U.S. Congress enacted and President Lincoln approved legislation directed toward establishment of a national cemetery system. The act specified "that the President of the United States shall have power, whenever in his opinion it shall be expedient, to purchase cemetery grounds and cause them to be securely enclosed, to be used as a national cemetery for the soldiers who die in the service of their country." Twelve national military cemeteries were established in 1862 under this legislation, including Alexandria National Cemetery in northern Virginia, because of the concentration of Union troops around Washington, D.C., and

Soldiers' Home Cemetery, which had been operational in the nation's capital since 1861.[6] In 1864, Battleground National Cemetery, the last of the three national military cemeteries established in Washington, D.C., was founded near Walter Reed Medical Center on what is now 6625 Georgia Avenue NW. This cemetery provided burial space as needed for quartermaster employees who had served under Meigs in the successful defense of the national capital during an encounter with Confederate troops on July 11-12, 1864. Some one-hundred Union troops, as well as fifty Confederate soldiers, were also interred at Congressional Cemetery, which continued to meet the needs of the military community.

During and immediately following the Civil War, Meigs enforced the prevailing understanding of the July 17, 1862, legislation—that burial in the national military cemeteries was to be restricted to "soldiers who die in service of their country," meaning Union troops who died during the Civil War in any capacity related to participation in the United States military. He did not extend this privilege to veterans of the Civil War or any other conflicts involving the United States or to family members of the deceased. Not everyone agreed with this interpretation. In 1868, for example, General George Henry Thomas, Commander of the Department of the Cumberland, reserved a section in the Chattanooga National Cemetery for the interment of Civil War veterans and their families. Meigs reversed that action, believing it in conflict with federal policies.[7]

Meanwhile, Secretary of War Edwin Stanton, drawing upon the authority vested in his office by the February 22, 1867, Act to Establish and to Protect National Cemeteries, expanded the national military cemetery system to include camp cemeteries that had been established earlier. They included Fort Smith, Arkansas, and Fort Gibson, Oklahoma, which had been organized in 1817 and 1824 and were incorporated into the network of national military cemeteries in 1867 and 1868, respectively. The camp cemeteries allowed for the burial not only of military men but also of family members. William W. Belknap, who succeeded Stanton as Secretary of War, supported the reinterment of soldiers and members of their families from camp cemeteries to the national military cemeteries. He accordingly made arrangements in 1872 to transport the remains of his father, General William G. Belknap, from the Fort Washita post cemetery in Oklahoma to the Keokuk National Cemetery in Iowa, the latter of which had been created in 1862.

Shortly thereafter, on March 3, 1873, Congress enacted legislation that extended eligibility for burial in national military cemeteries to all Union veterans of the Civil War who had been honorably discharged.[8] With the passage of this legislation, Meigs secured for himself the right of burial at Arlington. As founder of this cemetery, it is understandable that he desired eventual burial there. It is also understandable that he, like so many other Civil War veterans, wanted the right of interment extended to his family. The decisions made previously by Secretaries of War Stanton and Belknap created precedence for actions he took to establish Arlington not simply as a national military cemetery but as a national public cemetery, according to the model realized by Congressional Cemetery over its long history.

The evidence that Meigs wanted to proceed in this manner is given in his (1) reinterment at Arlington of a son killed during the Civil War and other family members who had never served in the military, (2) emplacement of a cenotaph in the family plot at Arlington that was identical in every way to the monument designed by Benjamin Latrobe for use at Congressional, (3) repeated statements about the connection he saw between Arlington and Congressional Cemetery in his final three Annual Reports to the Secretary of War, and (4) comments in the same documents calling for the types of road repair that would facilitate public access and thereby make it possible for Arlington to function as a national public cemetery.

Meigs reinterred the remains of seven family members at Arlington in two stages: during an undocumented day in July 1878 and on November 23, 1880. The burial sites were choice, located in Section 1, Lot 1, and thus just south of the Custis-Lee mansion. The July 1878 reinterments were of his grandfather Josiah Meigs (1757-1822) and his uncle Samuel Williams Meigs (1788-1818), whose remains had been in adjacent lots at Holmead's Cemetery in Washington, D.C., for more than fifty years. Neither had served in the U.S. military. Josiah, for example, had been a lawyer, educator, and public official, appointed as surveyor-general of the United States in 1812 and commissioner of the General Land Office in 1814. The

reinterments on November 23, 1880, were of Meigs' entire immediate family: his three young sons, his stillborn daughter, and his
wife Louisa. All of them had been interred originally at Oak Hill
Cemetery: Charles D. Meigs (September 3, 1853), eight years old;
Vincent T. Meigs (October 8, 1853), two years; a stillborn daughter
(December 12, 1856); Major John Rodgers Meigs (October 3, 1864),
twenty-three years; and Louisa Rodgers Meigs (November 21,
1879), sixty-three years.

The monuments over the graves of Major John Rodgers Meigs
and Josiah Meigs are particularly arresting, the first for the quality
and poignancy of the sculpture, the second, which was a cenotaph,
for the concrete, direct linkage it established between Congressional Cemetery and Arlington.

A bronze effigy created by Theophilus Fisk Mills marks the
grave of John Rogers Meigs, who had been killed by Confederate
troops within Union lines near Harrisonburg, Virginia. Proceeding
according to the wishes of Montgomery Meigs, Mills fashioned the
monument to John Rodgers as he had been found by Union troops
in the field: bareheaded, lying on his back, the sides of his body
marked by hoof prints, and with his pistol positioned several inches from his right hand. Only thirty-nine inches in length, this image
conveys the youth, innocence, and vulnerability of the young John
Rodgers and suggests even to this day the great loss suffered by
Montgomery and Louisa Meigs.[9]

The cenotaph marks the grave of Montgomery Meigs' grandfather Josiah. Emplaced at an unknown date, this cenotaph is identical in design, size, and composition (sandstone) to the monument
created by Benjamin Latrobe for the graves and memorial sites of
U.S. congressmen interred at Congressional Cemetery. It is not
known if Meigs commissioned a sculptor to create a cenotaph according to the Latrobe design or if he perhaps found one of the
monuments in a storage area at Congressional or at the studio of a
local sculptor. What is clear is that the cenotaphs at Congressional
comprise the most immediately visible symbol of its role as the first
national burial ground. The placement of an identical marker over
the grave of Josiah Meigs at Arlington is emblematic of both the
linkage Montgomery Meigs desired between Congressional and
Arlington National Cemetery and the historic connection between
the two burial grounds.

Meigs delineated the relationship he saw between Arlington and Congressional in his last three Annual Reports of the Office of the Quartermaster-General to the Secretary of War for the Fiscal Years Ending June 30, 1879, 1880, and 1881. Issued prior to his retirement from the position of Quartermaster General in 1882, these statements constitute a summation of his vision for Arlington. In the first of these documents, as in those that followed, he suggested that Arlington become a new Congressional Cemetery:

> There are 208 acres in this cemetery [Arlington], and a very large space is and will remain unoccupied by military interments. I suggest, therefore, that the attention of Congress be invited to the propriety of making this the National Public Cemetery, and authorizing the interment therein of any public officer, Senator or Member of Congress dying in office in the vicinity or elsewhere, whose friends may desire such a place of burial for him. The present Congressional Cemetery is, I understand, a private burying ground, in which the government owns some lots. The city is moving towards it, and the practice of modern civilization is to restrict interments of the dead within the limits of a city and near the habitations of the living.[10]

In his Annual Reports for 1880 and 1881, Meigs refined this recommendation, saying in 1880 that Arlington "be declared by law a national public cemetery" and in 1881 that space "not needed for the interment of soldiers, be used for the burial of officers of the United States, legislative, judicial, civil, and military, who may die at the seat of government or whose friends may desire their interment in a public national cemetery."[11] With these statements, he expressed his desire that Arlington would be responsive to the requirements not only of the military but also of all branches of the U.S. government, as had Congressional since its creation in 1807.

In the same three Annual Reports, Meigs stressed the urgent need for repair of the old Georgetown and Alexandria Road, which had been constructed in 1808 and led directly from the Aqueduct Bridge[12] to Arlington Cemetery and then to Alexandria. He presented this commentary in the paragraphs immediately preceding or following those focused on his vision of Arlington as a national public cemetery. By so doing, Meigs emphasized the essential connection he saw between accessible public roads and the establishment of a national public cemetery. He introduced this theme in his 1879 report, saying that the Georgetown and Alexandria Road, which had been built as a turnpike but never fully upgraded to a hard-surface road, "is badly constructed" and requires improvement that could be achieved by a "small expenditure," of about $10,000. In his 1880 and 1881 reports, Meigs asserted that this road was in places "almost impassable," thereby providing an assessment repeated by his successors to the position of Quartermaster General and by Secretaries of War to the end of the century.[13]

The condition of the primary road to Arlington had to have been an important factor in the ongoing prominence of Congressional Cemetery in the federal capital during the decades immediately following the Civil War. To some, Congressional may have seemed the more attractive alternative during extended periods of rain in the spring and cold in the winter, particularly when they were planning a relatively elaborate funeral procession to the graveyard. Congressional on Capitol Hill was not only the first national burial ground but also familiar terrain, readily accessible via Pennsylvania Avenue and other well-traveled roads.

By both his words and actions, Meigs demonstrated over and again that he had the Congressional model in mind when working to establish Arlington as a national public cemetery. He was intimately familiar with Congressional, where the following members of his family were buried: his prominent father-in-law, Commodore John Rodgers; his mother-in-law, Minerva Rodgers; his brother-in-law, Frederick Rodgers, who drowned at the age of seventeen near Norfolk, Virginia; and his uncle John Forsyth, who served as Secretary of State during 1834-1841 in the administrations of Presidents Andrew Jackson and Martin Van Buren. In addition, numerous professional associates and friends had been interred at Congressional.

In his Annual Reports for 1879, 1880, and 1881, Meigs had suggested that the right of burial at Arlington be given not only to military personnel but also to "any public officer, Senator or Member of Congress dying in office in the vicinity or elsewhere, whose friends may desire such a place of burial for him." Congressional Cemetery provided burial sites for all such persons. Standing there at the graves of John and Minerva Rodgers, Meigs was but a short distance from the burial sites of two powerful generals who served in consecutive order as Commander of the United States Army: Jacob Brown during 1821-1828 and Alexander Macomb in 1828-1841. In addition, he could have seen rows of the Latrobe monuments emplaced in memory of U.S. congressmen. He also had a view of the substantial monuments marking the graves of Vice Presidents George Clinton (1804-1812) and Elbridge Gerry (1812-1814), located near the brick wall in the northeastern side of the cemetery (see Chapter 4). In all directions, Meigs would have recognized the graves of many other distinguished individuals and their families. In Congressional Cemetery, Meigs found a compelling model for the development of Arlington as a national public cemetery.

Civil War Interments at Arlington and Congressional

In his Annual Reports for the years 1879, 1880, and 1881, Quartermaster General Meigs had recommended that Arlington be developed as "a national public cemetery" and thus in the model of Congressional Cemetery. It was too late by that time, however, to fashion the burial ground according to the suggested pattern. Created during the Civil War, Arlington became emblematic of the price paid in human blood to preserve the Union. The cemetery accordingly became a national shrine, a place of public visitation and remembrance. Along with Gettysburg and other prominent Civil War cemeteries, it thereby became associated with a new and exclusive definition of "national cemetery," which generally became synonymous in federal legislation, congressional appropriations, and the public imagination with "national military cemetery." The creation of the national military cemetery system had a significant impact on Congressional, which was national according to other terminology, having always been accessible as a national public burial ground to everyone in the surrounding community, civilians and military alike. While it was overshadowed by Arlington during and in the decades following the Civil War, Congressional nonetheless remained prominent, serving as the burial ground of choice for a sizable number of both officers and enlisted men and thus as a significant site for Civil War memories.

As for Arlington, the numbers of military interments were suffi-cient alone to establish the cemetery as a national shrine. Montgom-ery Meigs summarized the rapid rise in the figures he provided in his Annual Reports to the Secretary of War. On June 30, 1864, ap-proximately six weeks after he had ordered the first burials at the site, he reported that a total of 2,619 Union troops had been interred at Arlington. By June 30, 1865, the number had doubled, reaching 5,291 burials. The figures continued to escalate in the following years, totaling 15,547 by June 30, 1868, and 15,932 by June 30, 1870.[14]

The burials at Arlington during and immediately following the Civil War consisted largely of troops who had died of their wounds in hospitals in and around Washington, D.C., and of soldiers who had been recovered within an approximately thirty-five-mile radius of the federal city. The identities of many of these troops remained unknown. In April 1866, Meigs accordingly directed construction of the Tomb of the Unknown Dead of the Civil War, built approximately one-hundred feet from the former Lee-Custis mansion. Placed in this tomb, which was dedicated on September 20, 1866, were the remains of 2,111 soldiers, approximately 1,800 of whom had been recovered from the battleground at Manassas, located twenty-five miles west of Washington, D.C. The others had been found along the road to the Rappahonnock River, over which federal troops had passed enroute to the Battles of Fredricksburg (December 1862) and Chancellorsville (May 1863).[15]

The number of Civil War interments at Arlington during the ini-tial period of burials, extending from 1864 to approximately 1870, overwhelmed the totals at the other national military cemeteries in the Washington, D.C., area. Among these cemeteries, the United States Military Asylum, better known as Soldiers' Home, had the largest number, totaling 5,488 by the year 1870. For the same year, Battleground National Cemetery had 40 such burials. The figure for Alexandria National Cemetery, positioned across the Potomac River and south of Arlington, was 3,635.[16]

According to the same denominator, focused on the number of Civil War burials, Arlington ranked third among national military cemeteries. By the year 1870, the total at Vicksburg, Mississippi, was 17,012 and at Nashville, Tennessee, 16,529. Within the broader region around Washington, D.C., the total numbers of interments by the same year were 15,156 at Fredericksburg, 4,423 at Antietam, and 3,246 at Gettysburg.[17]

During the initial stage of burials at Arlington, conducted during 1864-1870, the overall public focus was not so much on specific individuals, most of whom were unknown to the larger community, but on the collective remains. While the community at rest was essentially faceless at that time to the surrounding population, it was powerful symbolically in terms of size. This community of the dead realized even greater symbolic import as it gained a public face during the next decades with the interment of prominent Civil War officers. The most celebrated of those heroes were Philip H. Sheridan (1831-1888), General of the Army of the United States at the time of his death, and Admiral David Dixon Porter (1813-1891), a distinguished naval commander. They were interred at sites that remain prominent to this day, located as they are on the terrace in front of the mansion.

Subsequent to the burials of Sheridan and Porter at Arlington, increasing numbers of Union senior officers were interred at the cemetery. While four generals and two admirals had been buried at Arlington prior to 1888, thirty-eight generals and thirteen admirals were interred there during the next eleven years, through 1899. One of the generals was Green Clay Smith, who died on June 29, 1895. As noted in his obituary, published in *The Evening Star* on June 30, 1895, he "had asked to be interred" at Arlington: "Not long ago the family purchased a lot in a city cemetery, but Gen. Smith believed that every soldier should sleep in a national cemetery, and it was in obedience to this preference that the beautiful site across the river was chosen." The families and friends of many other senior officers agreed with this sentiment. During 1890-1899, the remains of twelve generals and two admirals, including such prominent figures as Generals George Crook, James Haskin, Samuel Sturges, and John Rawlins, were accordingly reinterred at Arlington.

In addition to the prominence of the officers buried at Arlington, as well as the numbers of interments in general, another factor contributing to the cemetery's preeminence among national military cemeteries was its unique location: on Arlington Heights across the Potomac River from federal Washington, D.C. So situated, the cemetery was in a direct line of vision from the White House.

Standing at the back of the building and looking to the southwest, President Lincoln, President Grant, and their immediate successors could have seen the old Custis-Lee mansion, then incorporated into the still new national military cemetery. Located across the river from federal Washington, D.C., Arlington National Cemetery represented a deep and abiding wound within the heart of the nation. Its particular poignancy and symbolic import lay largely in that extraordinary proximity.

Congressional Cemetery also had an extraordinary location, arguably superior in some respects to that of Arlington. In sum, a river did not lie between the federal establishment and the Congressional burial ground. Positioned virtually in the backyard of the U.S. Capitol, Congressional was readily accessible to all branches of the federal government; to key military installations in the southeastern part of the city, including the Marine Barracks and the Navy Yard, as well as the U.S. Arsenal and fortifications at Greenleaf Point; and to local hospitals. The U.S. government accordingly purchased sites at the cemetery for the interment of Union troops, many of whom died in area hospitals of wounds incurred during battles near Washington, D.C.

Information on the numbers and identities of the Civil War troops and veterans interred at Congressional is available primarily in these sources: the estimates provided in 1896 by the Department of the Potomac, Grand Army of the Republic (GAR); the lists of burials maintained by the Association for the Preservation of Historic Congressional Cemetery (APHCC); and obituaries published in *The Evening Star*.[18] The Department of the Potomac concluded in 1896 that six- to seven-hundred Civil War veterans had been interred at Congressional, as noted in an article published in *The Evening Star* on October 27, 1896. The organization accordingly established a committee to locate the burial sites and to identify the names of the interred, the military units to which they had been attached, and their responsibilities during the war. Once this information had been collected, it was "expected that in the near future" the graves would "be marked with appropriate slabs." Follow-up articles on this initiative have not, however, been located in *The Evening Star* or elsewhere.

Documentation maintained at Congressional Cemetery is in

general agreement with the figures provided by the GAR Department of the Potomac in 1896. As indicated by the archived records, 577 Union and 50 Confederate troops were interred at Congressional. The bodies of thirty-four troops were later removed for reinterment elsewhere. The military personnel remaining at Congressional include the following Union senior officers: Generals Henry W. Benham (1813-1884), William Helmsley Emory (1811-1887), Andrew A. Humphreys (1810-1883), Robert B. Mitchell (1823-1882), Alfred Pleasonton (1824-1897), Augustus J. Pleasonton (1808-1894), Albin Francisco Schoepf (1822-1886), and Joseph G. Totten (1788-1864); Admirals Thomas H. Patterson (1820-1889), John Jay Almy (1815-1895), and Louis M. Goldsborough (1805-1877); as well as Commodore Richard Wainwright (1817-1862). General John A. Rawlins (1831-1869) was not, then, an isolated example of a Union senior officer interred at Congressional. While he was reinterred at Arlington during 1899, many other distinguished officers remained at Congressional Cemetery, including a sizable number who passed away long after the Civil War.

The ceremonies attendant upon the death of John Rawlins were particularly memorable. A confidant of President Ulysses S. Grant throughout the Civil War, he had moved swiftly through the ranks from lieutenant in 1861 to brigadier general and chief of staff of the Army in 1865. *The Evening Star* of September 6, 7, and 9, 1869, provided detailed, dramatic coverage of his death from consumption, the procession that bore his remains to Congressional, and his interment at the burial ground. These narratives not only captured the attention of countless readers but were also instrumental in shaping public understanding of Rawlins as a national figure. In addition, they underscored the continuing national significance of Congressional, which President Ulysses S. Grant selected as the place of burial for the individual who had been his trusted confidant during the Civil War and had then served in his cabinet as Secretary of War.

As elaborated in *The Evening Star*, the following question framed the high drama surrounding Rawlins' death: which would come first, the demise of Rawlins, who was in the last stages of consumption, or the arrival at his bedside of President Grant, who had been in upstate New York. Having been informed by Secretary of the Navy George Maxwell on September 5 about his friend's critical condition, Grant responded with this telegraphed message: "Tell Secretary Rawlins I leave here within an hour for Washington." Grant left Saratoga on September 5 on the 5:50 p.m. train and arrived in Washington, D.C., as scheduled, at 5:20 p.m. the next day. He was too late.

Upon reaching the home on Grant Street of General Giles A. Smith, the president proceeded into the room in which Rawlins had died. After looking "long and mournfully upon the face" of his friend, Grant wrote a brief, decisive telegram to Mrs. Mary E. Rawlins, who was at that time in Danbury, Connecticut. As quoted in *The Evening Star* of September 7, 1869, the message read as follows:

> Your beloved husband expired at 4:12 o'clock this afternoon, to be mourned by a family, friends who loved him for his personal worth and services to his country, and a nation who acknowledge their debt of gratitude to him. On consultation with friends, it is determined that he shall be buried in the Congressional burying ground as the most appropriate place, unless you have other suggestions to make. The time of the funeral is not arranged but will probably take place on Thursday next.

As indicated by the forceful tone of this telegram, Grant clearly believed that the decision about the place of burial was his to make. He was not only president of the United States but also one of two executors of the will appointed by Secretary Rawlins. The other executor was Mary Rawlins, whose authority in this matter Grant seemingly dismissed with his summary reference to any "suggestions" she might have about a burial site.

Grant also dismissed the wishes of Rawlins' parents, who had asked that their son be interred in the city of his birth, Galena, Illinois, and of Illinois Governor John M. Palmer, who requested burial near the state capital, Springfield. As directed by Grant, General John E. Smith telegraphed the following statement to Governor Palmer on September 7. It was reproduced on the same day in *The Evening Star*: "Your telegrams of this day were submitted to the President, who directs me to say that it has been decided to bury

General Rawlins in the Congressional Burying Ground, whence he can be removed, if desirable, hereafter. With this view, his body has been embalmed." A similar telegram was sent to Rawlins' parents.[19]

Grant clearly understood that it was appropriate to inter Rawlins at Congressional because it was the burial site of other prominent individuals who had served in presidential cabinets, as well as top military officers. Given its prestige on both local and national levels, Congressional outdistanced potential competitors in the area, particularly historic Rock Creek Cemetery (established during 1712 in western Prince George's County, Maryland) and the relatively new (founded in 1848) and prominent Oak Hill Cemetery in Georgetown. It also outpaced its emerging rival, Arlington Cemetery, which was not then an option for Rawlins in that the right of burial at the site was not extended to Civil War veterans, no matter their stature, until 1873.

In keeping with the wishes of President Grant, William Tecumseh Sherman planned the funeral events. He accordingly orchestrated the last of the great processions to Congressional Cemetery. Staged on September 9, 1869, the parade began at Seventeenth Street and Pennsylvania, just outside the War Department, where the funeral had been conducted. It then proceeded along the historic route: down Pennsylvania Avenue to the U.S. Capitol, around the Capitol to E and Eleventh Street East, and then along E Street to the burial ground. Drawing upon patterns formalized on the streets of Washington, D.C., over the preceding sixty years, Sherman arranged a very good show, as indicated by the summation given that day in *The Evening Star*. Providing the lead was the Marine Corps Band, which was followed by military units in full dress uniform, including an artillery battalion that wore "light blue pants, dark blue coats, and slouch hat(s), with black plumes trimmed with red." The heart of the procession was, of course, the hearse, which was followed by Rawlins' riderless white horse, draped in black. The sixteen pallbearers, all but one of whom were generals, included Quartermaster General Montgomery Meigs, the central figure in the creation of Arlington Cemetery. President Ulysses S. Grant rode in a carriage following the pallbearers and the Rawlins family.

Upon reaching the primary entrance to Congressional Cemetery, the procession was met by a large crowd, most of whom the

police had kept from streaming into the burial ground. Eight cav-
alrymen removed the coffin from the hearse, proceeded through
the main entrance, which was draped in black, and moved slowly
to the vault of George Blagden, who had been one of the cemetery
founders. Following a reading of the burial services of the Methodist Episcopal Church, the coffin was placed in the Blagden Vault.
When space was available five months later, the remains of John
Rawlins were transferred to the Public Vault, where they stayed for
nearly four years. After transfer to yet another site at Congressional
during October 1873, Rawlins was reinterred at Arlington National
Cemetery on February 8, 1899, thirty years after his death.[20]

Among the other Union senior officers interred at Congressional, General Henry Benham and Admiral Thomas Patterson are
notable for their connections to the Navy Yard which, like Congressional Cemetery, was located in southeast Washington, D.C. Benham had supervised its construction during 1852, while Patterson
had been commandant of the Navy Yard during 1873-1876. Having
worked in the neighborhood where the graveyard was located, it
was fitting that they were interred at the site, where many Navy
Yard personnel had been buried. General Joseph Totten, another
of the Union senior officers interred at Congressional, had been
responsible during the Civil War for supervising special projects,
including the development of a substantial defensive network
around Washington, D.C.

Given their service, all of the Union senior officers identified
above could have been buried or reinterred at Arlington. Commodore Richard Wainwright and General Joseph Totten, who had died
respectively on August 10, 1862, and April 22, 1864, qualified for reinterment at Arlington after it had opened for burials during summer 1864. The others became eligible after Congress passed legislation in 1873 that allowed for the interments of Civil War veterans at
Arlington and the other national cemeteries. Few Union senior officers were, however, interred at Arlington prior to the late 1880s and
the burial there of General Sheridan in 1888. Thus, it is not unusual
that the following were not interred at Arlington: General Benham,
who died in 1884; General Emory, 1887; Admiral Goldsborough,
1877; General Humphreys, 1883; Admiral Patterson, 1883; and General Schoepf, 1886. Their families and/or others could, however,

have removed them to Arlington later, as happened with General Robert Mitchell in 1895 and General John Rawlins in 1899. Instead, these officers remained where they had been originally buried.

The obituary for Admiral John Almy, published in *The Evening Star* on May 16, 1895, stated that "the interment will be made at Congressional Cemetery, instead of at Arlington, as it might have been had the family so elected." In their choice of Congressional, the Almy family, as well as the families of the Union senior officers cited above, opted not for a national military cemetery but for a national public cemetery that allowed for the burials of extended families in adjoining sites, even in family vaults, as discussed later in this chapter.

Arlington, as a national military cemetery, could not be so inclusive in its extension of burial rights. Beginning in the late nineteenth century, wives were, however, frequently interred beside their officer husbands, as was Irene Rucker Sheridan (1856-1939), widow of General Philip Sheridan (1831-1888) and daughter of Brigadier General Daniel H. Rucker (also buried at Arlington). In addition, dependent children, adult children who had served in the U.S. military, and occasionally other relatives could be interred at Arlington. For example, the burial site of General Romeyn Beck Ayres (1825-1888), chief of artillery and infantry commander in the Army of the Potomac, also includes the remains of his son Charles Greenleaf Ayres (1854-1909), who had been a colonel in the U.S. Army; his daughter-in-law Mary Elizabeth Fairfax Ayres (1859-1909); his grandson Henry Fairfax Ayres (1885-1979), who had been a lieutenant colonel in the U.S. Army; and his mother-in-law Juliet Opie Hopkins (1818-1890), who was regarded as the Florence Nightingale of the South because of her service to Confederate hospital systems during the Civil War.[21]

It was, then, possible for wives, children, and other relatives to be interred at Arlington beside officers and occasionally enlisted men following the Civil War. Nonetheless, numerous military men were buried at Arlington without the subsequent interment there of family members, as was General Gabriel R. Paul (1813-1886), the first senior officer buried at Arlington. Despite Meigs stated desire that Arlington become a national public cemetery, it continued to be a national military cemetery.

All of the Union senior officers who were buried at Congressional were preceded in their interments by relatives except for General Rawlins, who was buried there by presidential directive, and General Robert Mitchell, who apparently had no family ties to the cemetery. While both Rawlins and Mitchell were later removed to Arlington, the other officers remained at Congressional, surrounded by relatives. A few of the officers followed distinguished parents to the burial ground. Others were laid to rest alongside their children, a number of whom had died in infancy. Still others were interred within extended, memorable family groups.

General Andrew Humphreys and Admiral Louis Goldsborough, for example, were both preceded in their burials at Congressional by notable family members. The Humphreys presence was established by the general's father, Samuel, who had been interred at the cemetery in 1846. As Chief Naval Constructor from 1826 to his death in 1846, Samuel designed ships for the U.S. Navy and was reportedly a master of his craft. He had been trained by his father, Joshua Humphreys, who as the first United States Naval Constructor designed *Old Ironsides* and her five sister frigates, including the *Constitution* and *United States*. While Joshua was not buried at Congressional, his son Samuel and his grandson Andrew, along with their families, were interred at the site, which was appropriate given its proximity and historic connection to the U.S. Navy Yard.

The bodies of Admiral Louis Goldsborough and his immediate family—wife, son, and daughter—were placed in the family vault of William Wirt, famed prosecutor in the Aaron Burr trial, U.S. Attorney General from 1817 to 1829, candidate on the Anti-Masonic ticket for U.S. president in 1832, and author of *Letters of the British Spy* (1803) and *Sketches of the Life and Character of Patrick Henry* (1817). The connection between the Goldsboroughs and the Wirts was through Admiral Goldsborough's wife Elizabeth, who was the daughter of William Wirt. Given the prior interment of their son and daughter in the Wirt vault, during 1863 and 1866, respectively, they must have elected years before their own deaths (Louis in 1877 and Elizabeth in 1885) to rest into eternity beside the Wirts rather than Goldsborough's parents, who had been interred in adjoining sites at Congressional (his father in 1843 and his mother in 1851).

The other Union senior officer interred in a family vault was Commodore Richard Wainwright. The Wainwright vault includes the remains of the commodore's mother and wife, among several other family members. Richard Wainwright's wife was Sally Franklin, great-granddaughter of Benjamin Franklin, and thus another significant family is represented at Congressional.[22]

The Generals Alfred and Augustus Pleasonton were the last of seven family members interred at Congressional in adjacent sites within two contiguous rows of graves. In one row are the graves of their parents, Mary (who died in 1851) and Stephen (1855), and of their sister Mary (1858). In the next row are their sisters Clementine (1888) and Laura (1893) and then General Augustus (1894) and General Alfred (1897). Contemporaries of the Pleasontons may well have paused over this family grouping, remembering the dramatic Civil War tales about bravery and cowardice that General Alfred used to share with fellow veterans at Charlie Godfrey's "all night" saloon. They surely would have recalled the remarkable stories, then current, about the actions of Stephen Pleasonton, who had been the fifth auditor of the U.S. Treasury at the time of his death. As British troops had advanced upon Washington, D.C., during the War of 1812, Stephen reputedly saved key federal documents by transporting them in "coarse linen bags" to a "vacant stone house" some thirty-five miles from the capital city, where they remained until the enemy withdrew from the area. They included the original Declaration of Independence, the Articles of Confederation, and the federal constitution.[23]

For the Pleasontons, as well as the families of the other Union officers identified above, Congressional offered unique advantages—the prestige of the first national burial ground and the inclusivity of a national public cemetery. In short, Congressional replicated many times over and in considerable variety the family groups Quartermaster General Meigs had attempted to establish through his own example at Arlington.

In addition to the senior officers and their families interred at Congressional, the burial ground is the resting place for many more junior officers and enlisted men who had fought for the Union during the Civil War. A number of these individuals were remembered in obituaries that are remarkable in several ways, including on occasion for information about their contributions to Congressional Cemetery. One such narrative was provided in *The Evening Star* on October 2, 1912, upon the death in nearby McLean, Virginia, of Reverend Nelson H. Miller. He had been a junior vice commander of the G.A.R., Department of the Potomac, and then a clerk within the Presbyterian Synod of Baltimore, which comprised the presbyteries of Washington, D.C., Baltimore, and New Castle, Delaware. As noted, he was instrumental in the development of Memorial Day observations at Congressional, which are subsequently addressed in this chapter:

> He was for several years in charge of the Decoration day [sic] exercises held annually in Congressional Cemetery under the auspices of the Grand Army. His choice of orator for the occasion in that cemetery last May was former Representative Harvey S. Irwin of Louisville, who in preceding years had made addresses at Stone River and other historic battlefields of the civil war [sic]. At the close of the exercises Dr. Miller was widely congratulated on the program he had supervised.

The obituary also provided a significant statement regarding his place of burial, noting that "no arrangements have been made for the funeral" but that Adjt. General O.H. Oldroyd of the G.A.R., Department of the Potomac, had "said today that the Grand Army would participate, and that the burial may be in Arlington, if Dr. Miller's family acquiesces." The family clearly did not acquiesce, most likely because of Miller's long association with Congressional Cemetery.

The fifty Confederate troops interred at Congressional included ten officers and comprised eight percent of the total number of Civil War military personnel buried at the site. The imbalance in numbers between Confederate and Union troops is not surprising in that Congressional was generally viewed during the antebellum period as the U.S. national burial ground. The Confederate troops that were interred at the site had established residences in the city of Washington, having worked previously in the U.S. government and/or military. In addition, many of them had extended families living in the surrounding area.

Among the ten Confederate officers, two are particularly interesting. Only one of the officers—Admiral French Forrest (1796-1866)—had senior status. He had an extraordinary career, having served in the U.S. Navy for five decades. During that period, he participated in the War of 1812 and the Mexican War, as well as served as commandant of the U.S. Navy Yard during 1855-1856. After all his long years in the U.S. military, he joined the Confederacy in 1861 upon the secession of his home state of Virginia. Among his subsequent assignments, he was commander of the Norfolk Navy Yard in 1861-1862 and of the James River Squadron during 1863-1864. After the war, he returned to his home in Alexandria, Virginia. Following his death on November 22, 1866, this officer of the Confederacy was remembered in *The Evening Star* as "a kind and affectionate husband and father, and a true and sincere friend, beloved and respected by all who knew him."

The other particularly memorable Confederate officer interred at Congressional Cemetery is Colonel Charles F. Henningsen (1815-1877), who was born in England to Swedish parents. He was remembered in the obituary published in *The Evening Star* on the day of his death, June 14, 1877, as a dashing military figure, who had fought with the Carlists in Spain and Kossuth in Hungary and had "command of the defenses of Richmond" during the Civil War. Henningsen was a prolific author, having published a couple of novels, as well as studies of Hungary and Russia, among other works; an accomplished linguist, having "the fluency of a native" in French, German, Italian, Russian, and Spanish; and an individual of "striking appearance, being tall, erect and soldier-like in his bearing."[24]

In addition to the ten Confederate officers, forty Confederate troops were interred at Congressional. As with the Union enlisted men, most of them have not been remembered in historical monographs. *The Evening Star* did, however, provide obituaries for individuals who had families living in the surrounding community. These narratives are important in part because of insights they provide into life in Washington, D.C., during the years following the Civil War, when Union and Confederate veterans resided in some of the same neighborhoods and participated in some of the same organizations.

The obituaries addressed below focus on three individuals who had volunteered for the Confederate Army when in their teens and who returned to Washington, D.C., following the war and were later interred at Congressional. One was William Prince Lipscomb, who died on June 8, 1932, and was remembered in a lengthy obituary published the following day in *The Evening Star*. As noted, he had joined the Confederate Army when he was seventeen and "remained in service" until the end of the Civil War. During the post-war period, he was well-respected, having been the "first vice president of the District National Bank for many years," an officer at the Vermont Avenue Christian Church, as well at "other organizations," and a "prominent Washington contractor." As president of the William P. Lipscomb Company, he had "built many of the outstanding embassies, homes, churches and office buildings in the city." Viewed in retrospect, the detail provided in this summation underscored the healing, the general acceptance within the surrounding community following the Civil War of individuals who previously had differing political allegiances.

The next two veterans—William H. Smoot and Jeremiah De Bell Wilson—were remembered with remarkable anecdotes. Smoot, who died in Washington, D.C., on December 1, 1885, at the age of forty-five, had enlisted in the Confederate Army at the age of sixteen, along with "his entire class" at a school in Blacksburg, Virginia. At the end of the war, he proceeded to his grandmother's home in Maryland:

> And as he was coming up the path to the house, his mother, who was on the porch, saw an unkempt, emaciated man with several weeks' growth of beard and bare-footed. She became alarmed and started to return to the house when he cried, "Mother, don't you know me?" Her first remark was, "But where are your boots?" "I ate them before I left Richmond."[25]

As indicated by the obituary published in the July 13, 1908, issue of *The Evening Star*, Jeremiah De Bell Wilson was remembered within the surrounding community primarily for his remarkable horse, described as "the famous black mare referred to repeatedly by Col. [John Singleton] Mosby in his memoirs as the finest mount in the Confederate Army." "Many a Confederate officer" had sought unsuccessfully to purchase the mare, and federal troops had tried repeatedly to capture the horse. At the end of the war and upon his return to Washington, D.C., Wilson reportedly sold his famed mare "for a good figure." The purchaser was not a fellow veteran but the priest at St. Dominic's Catholic Church in the federal capital.

Few visitors to Congressional pause these days over the graves of the Civil War officers and enlisted men. They were remembered, however, during the Memorial Day observances delineated in the final section of this chapter.

The Larger Meaning of General Philip Sheridan's Interment at Arlington

The burial of General Philip Sheridan at Arlington on August 11, 1888, was a pivotal event for both Arlington National Cemetery and Congressional Cemetery. The attendant ceremonies, particularly the transfer of his remains via train to Washington, D.C., the sizable funeral staged there, the elaborate parade to the burial ground, and the accompanying narratives given in *The Evening Star*, secured the status of Arlington as not only a preeminent national shrine but also as the most prominent national cemetery in the Washington, D.C., area. In so doing, the pageantry underscored the decline in status of Congressional Cemetery. While it remained a place of national memory and meaning, Congressional was not part of the national military cemetery system, which was the only officially sanctioned network of U.S. national burial grounds.

Sheridan died on August 5, 1888, in Nonquitt, Massachusetts, where he had been constructing a vacation home.[26] The transfer of his body to Washington, D.C., via train and steamer was carefully orchestrated to achieve maximum dramatic effect. The train crew, for example, had been "selected from among those who had seen service in the field with the dead general," as noted in *The Evening Star* of August 9, 1888. Among the crew members, conductor Charles A. Thompson had served under Sheridan's command during the Shenandoah Valley Campaign and had participated in the victory at Winchester inspired by Sheridan's call to "face the other way, boys! face the other way!" Flagman Pearson had been with

Sheridan at Five Forks on April 1, 1865, and at Appomatox when Robert E. Lee surrendered eight days later.

The funeral train arrived in Washington, D.C., on August 9 at 3:20 p.m. As narrated in *The Evening Star* the following day, the journey ended in silence among a large gathering of citizens: "The crowds of people in the depot received their first notice of the approach of the train from the movement and murmuring of the crowd outside on 6ᵗʰ street, who could see the train as it rounded into 6ᵗʰ street from Maryland Avenue. It was recognized by the black crape with which the forward car was draped and the black flags flying in front of the engine. The crowd remained in perfect silence as the train rolled into the depot."

Thereafter ensued a period of confusion, focused first on the place of interment. Given Sheridan's status at the time of his death as General of the Army of the United States, the immediate family wanted the burial to be in or near Washington, D.C., and at a national military cemetery. In addition, they wanted to assure their right to eventual interment beside the general. The family hoped originally that these requirements could be met at Soldiers' Home National Cemetery, as noted in *The Evening Star* of August 6, 1888: "The interment will be made at the grounds of the Soldiers' Home in Washington if . . . assurance can be obtained that his wife and children may be given a resting-place beside him."

The reasons for the family's initial focus on Soldiers' Home is not clear from information provided in either newspaper accounts or subsequent biographies of Sheridan. While family members learned shortly thereafter that they could be buried beside Sheridan at Arlington, their concern illustrates the advantage that led other Union senior officers to Congressional—the ready assurance that they could be buried within family groups, no matter the size and without special application.

Other questions surfaced within the U.S. Senate regarding its responsibilities for the funeral and interment. *The Evening Star* of August 6, 1888, captured the uncertainty:

> In regard to what action the Senate ought to take respecting the death of the commanding-general of the armies, there was some question. There was no precedent to follow.

General Sheridan was the first commanding-general to die while in active service. General Washington was in retirement when he died, and General Scott had been retired prior to his death. General Grant was also on the retired list, but with his full rank at the time of his death. Gen. Rawlins, who held the position of Secretary of War under President Grant, died on the 6th of September, 1869, when Congress was in recess. The Senate leaders determined to announce the death and adopt resolutions expressive of the appreciation of Gen. Sheridan's services and sense of their great loss. On the day of his funeral Congress will probably adjourn.

In terms of this narrative about Congressional Cemetery, the key line in the above passage is this: "There was no precedent to follow." As indicated in Chapter 2, "The Grand Procession to the National Burial Ground," there were detailed guidelines to consult in preparing for the Sheridan interment. They had been shaped and refined over sixty years of federal interments at Congressional, including the burial there of two commanding generals of the U.S. Army, Jacob Brown (1775-1828) and Alexander Macomb (1782-1841), both of whom had died in office. The misinformation in the newspaper coverage illustrates the surprisingly rapid disappearance from public memory of the large role Congressional Cemetery had in national funeral events. In terms of the Sheridan funeral and interment, however, the legislators soon regained their collective memory and followed procedures that had been in place for decades.

The funeral for General Sheridan was a dramatic, well-orchestrated event conducted on August 11, 1888, at St. Matthews, then located on the corner of Fifteenth and H Streets. The approximately 1,500 invited guests at the cathedral included top leaders within all branches of the federal government and the U.S. military, including President Grover Cleveland and members of his cabinet, nearly every member of the U.S. House of Representatives and Senate then in the city, Associate Justice John Marshall Harlan and the other Supreme Court justices, and General William Tecumseh Sherman, along with other military heroes. Also in attendance were representatives of foreign legations and distinguished local citizens. The overall emphasis was on national unity, as illustrated by the former Union and Confederate officers who gathered around the open coffin before the service and by the sermon delivered by James Cardinal Gibbons, Archbishop of Baltimore from 1877 to 1921. The Archbishop declared that "the death of General Sheridan will be lamented not only by the North, but also by the South. I know the Southern people; I know their chivalry; I know their magnanimity, their warm and affectionate nature, and I am sure that the sons of the Southland, especially those who fought in the late war, will join in the national lamentation and will lay a garland of mourning on the bier of the great general."[27]

The final stage in the funeral events was the procession to Arlington. As recounted in *The Evening Star* of August 11, 1888, "the scenes were like those of decoration day," inspired by the larger than life reputation of the general and also by the weather, which for that Saturday in the nation's capital was "ideal." Photographers worked to capture those scenes, while vendors situated in the neighborhood of St. Matthews and all along the parade route hawked pies, cakes, and lemonade. Long before the procession began, crowds lined the parade route, stretching from Pennsylvania Avenue, across the Aqueduct Bridge, and along both the Fort Meyer road and "the lower road"[28] to the cemetery, where numerous onlookers, many of whom shared picnic baskets, waited for the arrival of General Sheridan.

The parade was based on the general format of the processions conducted previously from the U.S. Capitol to Congressional Cemetery. Beginning with elite military units, it continued with a caisson bearing the remains of Sheridan, Sheridan's horse Guy, Sheridan's family, President Grover Cleveland and his family as well as cabinet, members of the Supreme Court, congressional representatives and, at the end of the procession, citizens. One of the features of this parade was the preeminence accorded Sheridan's horse, who was positioned closer to the general than were his wife and family. Guy had been a favorite of Sheridan because of his resemblance to Rienzi, the old war horse he had ridden to victory at Winchester.[29] Given his location in the procession, Guy recalled the identical placement of the famed "Old Whitey" in the funeral parade bearing the remains of President Zachary Taylor to Congressional Cemetery on July 9, 1850.

Sheridan was accorded a prime burial site, in front of the Lee mansion. The account of the interment given in *The Evening Star* of August 11, 1888, focused on this location, highlighting the unique placement of Arlington on a hill clearly visible from across the river in federal Washington, D.C.: "As seen from the city, there is a dense green bank, then a sudden break and opening, with a mellow spot of light in the center. This marks the vicinity of the dead general's grave, which is located a short distance to the southeast, in the midst of a little grove of trees. If a monument should ever be erected over the grave, as is very likely, it may be seen from almost any point in the city." The burial ceremony concluded as bugler Charles Kimball, who had served with Sheridan in Mexico, played Taps. "That was the end," the reporter declared.

The Sheridan interment marked the beginning of another stage in the evolution of Arlington, characterized by the interment there of many more Union senior officers, including General William Belknap in October 1890, Admiral David Dixon Porter in February 1891, and Quartermaster General Montgomery Meigs in January 1892. While their funerals and burials were not so elaborate as Sheridan's, in part because the officers were retired when they died, the ceremonies were nonetheless remarkable. The funeral procession for Admiral Porter, for example, was witnessed by a crowd estimated at "more than one-third of the city's population," according to *The Evening Star* of February 17, 1891. The parade for General Belknap included some six-hundred individuals affiliated with local posts of the Grand Army of the Republic. The walk to Arlington had, however, become increasingly arduous for some of these veterans, as noted in *The Evening Star* of October 16, 1890:

> At the northern end of the [Aqueduct] bridge several of the Grand Army veterans fell out; it was a long march for the aged, some of them crippled to a distressing degree by their wounds. One old, white-haired man who could barely walk remarked to a comrade who asked him to return: "No, sir; I'm going to see the general to his grave. My old wound hurts like the devil, but I got it fighting with the man whose body's back there in the hearse, and I'm going to be with him to the end," and the battered veteran shook an empty sleeve at the deserter while he tramped on.

Such narratives not only reflected actual events but also created a new reality, expressive of the preeminence of Arlington as a national military cemetery, a shrine on a hill across the river.

Meanwhile, funeral processions continued to wend their way toward Congressional Cemetery. Compared to those directed toward Arlington, however, they were modest parades, featuring organizations based in the southeastern section of the city and in neighborhoods around the cemetery. The participants, including Masons, local G.A.R. units, and representatives of the Oldest Inhabitants Association, frequently rode in carriages to Congressional, thereby providing scant copy for *Evening Star* reporters. Clearly, the heyday of the great processions to Congressional had ceased. With this ending, however, the burial ground began another stage in its long history, as exemplified by the Memorial Day ceremonies addressed in the next section. Congressional accordingly gained renewed recognition as a cemetery that offered a special, inclusive definition of the word "national."

Memorial Day Celebrations on Both Sides of the Potomac River

Viewed in sequence, the Memorial Day observances at Arlington National Cemetery and Congressional Cemetery document a broadening understanding of national debt first to the Civil War dead and then to all Americans who had died on the battlefield. The ceremonies began at the two burial grounds at approximately the same time—1868 at Arlington and 1869 at Congressional. They diverged thereafter, reaching their peak at Arlington in the mid-1870s, when large crowds assembled on the grounds for commemorative events. In the late 1870s, when the ceremonies attracted diminishing numbers of attendees at Arlington, they found new life and definition at Congressional Cemetery, which was in turn reinvigorated by these celebrations.

The observances at Arlington and Congressional had their antecedents in exercises conducted during and immediately after the Civil War in a number of northern and southern communities, including Boalsburg, Pennsylvania; Columbus, Mississippi; and Waterloo, New York. As noted by historian David Blight, "the first collective ceremony" occurred on May 1, 1865, when approximately 10,000 people, most of them former slaves, decorated Union graves at a cemetery that had been established on the grounds of the former Washington Race Course in Charleston, South Carolina. Additional events included some thirty speeches by Union officers and abolitionist missionaries, among others, and a drill by a full brigade of Union infantry, including the 104th U.S. Colored Troops. With these observances, Blight concluded, African Americans established "a ritual of remembrance and consecration" that was originally recognized as Decoration Day.[30]

General John Logan, national commander of the Grand Army of the Republic, officially instituted this day of remembrance with General Order Number 11, issued on May 5, 1868. With its blend of religious and patriotic imagery, the order directed Union veterans to decorate the burial sites of their fallen comrades, to "guard their graves with sacred vigilance," and "to let no neglect, no ravages of time, testify to the present or to the coming generations that we have forgotten as a people the cost of a free and undivided republic." The first official Decoration Day was celebrated on May 30, 1868, when observances were conducted at 183 cemeteries in twenty-seven states and Washington, D.C., and were attended by thousands of people.[31]

The Evening Star provided informative narratives focused on the annual ceremonies of remembrance at Arlington and Congressional.[32] During the first stage of this coverage, extending from 1868 to about 1878, the periodical concentrated primarily on events conducted at Arlington, noting in the May 30, 1871, issue, for example, that "Arlington was of course the central point of attraction" and in the May 30, 1876, issue that "while the scope of these arrangements were [sic] intended to embrace all cemeteries in which had been deposited the remains of Union soldiers, the great center of attraction, as hitherto, was the National [sic] cemetery at Arlington, where there are 15,585 graves." Given this emphasis, the documentation of ceremonies at Congressional, Oak Hill, Mount Olivet, and other area cemeteries was relegated to third level headings and a couple of summary statements. This focus contributed substantially to the eminence of Arlington.

The ceremonies of remembrance at Arlington, Congressional, and other well-established cemeteries in the Washington, D.C., area began with decoration of the graves, usually early in the morning,

and then continued with exercises that quickly became standard-
ized in overall format, including musical presentations, prayers,
orations, and poems, often written for the occasion. The most elaborate of the local observances were at Arlington, as illustrated by the
Order of Exercises for May 30, 1873, summarized below[33]:

- National Artillery Salute, by 3" Ordnance Rifle (Cannon)
- Presentation of Colors and Banners of Societies and Orders
- Patriotic Music, by the United States Marine Band
- Calling the Assembly to Order
- Prayer, composed by The Rev. O.H. Tiffany, D.D.
- Anthem: *To Thee, O Country*, by J. Eichberg
- Poem, written by E.A. Duncan, M.D.
- Anthem: *Peace on Earth*, by J. Lowell
- Oration, delivered by The Rev. T. DeWitt Talmage, D.D.
- Anthem: *Comrades in Arms*, by A. Adam
- Procession of the Assemblage to the Tomb (Memorial) of
  the Unknown Dead of the War Between the States
- Anthem: *God Save Our Union*, by P.S. Gilmore
- Prayer, by Ralph R. Miller, Jr.
- Anthem: *Soldiers' Memorial Day*, by W.O. Perkins
- Poem [Title Unknown], by J.P. Irvine
- Anthem: *America*, by H. Carey
- Floral Decorations Placed with Honor at the Tomb of the
  Unknowns
- Roll Call of Societies and Orders
- Artillery Salute
- Dismissal Remarks
- Retiring of the Colors.

Given the length not only of the agenda but also of the original poems and prayers, the Memorial Day crowds needed staying
power.

Viewed in retrospect, selected exercises at Arlington have particular resonance. In 1869, for example, the special guests seated
at the stand erected immediately behind the Arlington mansion
included Secretary of War John Rawlins, who would be buried
at Congressional Cemetery but three months later, and President

Ulysses Grant, who would decide that Rawlins should be buried there. Other guests included General William Emory, who would join Rawlins at Congressional in 1887, and General William Tecumseh Sherman, who had been "brought to a dead stop" by the dense crowd as he proceeded toward the stand, as reported in *The Evening Star* for May 29, 1869. Shortly thereafter, "some person called out, 'Don't hinder Gen. Sherman on his March to the Sea.' The crowd thus being notified who the distinguished individual was, immediately gave way with cheers, and the General speedily made his way to the stand."

On that second Decoration Day at Arlington, the crowd was indeed large, comprising an estimated twenty-five thousand people. They crossed the Potomac River via the Aqueduct Bridge, as well as by the Long Bridge (at the location of the present Fourteenth Street Bridge). The reported rate of passage was notable, comprising an estimated six-hundred vehicles ("carriages, omnibuses, and ambulances") and two-thousand pedestrians per hour over the Aqueduct Bridge alone between 10:00 a.m. and 1:00 p.m., when the ceremonies began.[34]

The celebrations at Arlington were particularly memorable in 1871, for that was the year when Frederick Douglass delivered his powerful oration in commemoration of "those unknown heroes" who had died to preserve the Union. In poetic, periodic sentences, he brought the crowd to his conclusion: "If now we have a united country no longer cursed by the hell-black system of human bondage; if the American name is no longer a bye word [sic] and a hissing to a mocking earth; if the star spangled banner floats only over free American citizens in every quarter of the land . . . we are indebted to the unselfish devotion of the noble army who rest in these honored graves all around us." Douglass recognized the high quality of this address, which was the only one he selected for publication with his autobiography.[35]

During the first several years, Decoration Day/Memorial Day at Arlington and elsewhere was generally viewed as an occasion for remembrance and reverence. With the passage of time, however, the general public became familiar with the ceremony, developed some distance from their Civil War memories, and began increasingly to view the occasion as a holiday, a time to visit the graves but also to enjoy the day at the cemetery and elsewhere with family and friends. A shift in tone is visible in the coverage of Memorial Day events in *The Evening Star* beginning as early as 1873. The narrative for that year, published on May 30, began as usual by declaring that "Memorial Day has come to be regarded as one of the most sacred of American commemorative holidays." It continued with summaries of the formal exercises and identifications of distinguished guests, including President Grant, Frederick Douglass, and Generals Sherman and Meigs, both of whom were regularly in attendance at Arlington. Along the way, the article provided vignettes of picnics in "shady nooks" and other convivial times on the grounds: "On the west side of the mansion house and strung along the carriageway were a line of stands, where soda water, confectionery, sheets of ginger cake, cigars and oranges were sold—the scene reminding one of an old-time country militia muster. One man had a stereoscopic show, and gave views of battle scenes, which attracted considerable attention."

As the years rolled by, the public began increasingly to enjoy the day elsewhere, as indicated by the following statements:

There were not as many persons on the grounds as on previous years, owing probably to the fact that there were several excursions and pic-nics down the river, up the river, and across the country, which were participated in by a large number of our citizens (*The Evening Star*, May 29, 1875).

The streets at an early hour were filled with people, many of them with lunch baskets, fishing tackle, &c., wending their way to the railroad depots, the steamboat wharves, and country roads. This with the warm sunshine, made it look and feel like a 4th of July morning. . . . A large crowd attended the ceremonies at Arlington to-day. The attendance was, however, much smaller than in the year previous (*The Evening Star*, May 30, 1878).

On their arrival at Arlington the people distributed themselves over the grassy hills, and sat in groups chatting or making an early raid on the dinner baskets. Whole families came. The sultry day and the threatening weather in the morning doubtless kept a number away who wished to participate in the ceremonies. There were fewer present than last year, in fact the attendance was comparatively slim (*The Evening Star*, May 30, 1897).

The Grand Army of the Republic, which continued to view the day as a sacred event, as "the festival of our dead," disapproved of the "excursions and pic-nics." As noted by Stuart McConnell in his *Glorious Contentment: The Grand Army of the Republic, 1865-1900*, some G.A.R. orators even chastised President Grover Cleveland for fishing during one fine Memorial Day.[36] In 1880, the local G.A.R. posts, including John A. Rawlins Post No. 1, instituted Memorial Day parades to Arlington, probably in part as an attempt to refocus attention on the original import of the day and to bring back the crowds. These parades were a new kind of funeral procession in the nation's capital in that they focused not on the death of one eminent leader but on the collective dead. While they provided a feast for the eyes and ears, they did not bring back the crowds, as indicated by very readable copy provided in *The Evening Star* on May 30, 1881.

The unidentified writer clearly intended to focus first on "The Procession," which is the initial heading within the piece. He was distracted, however, by all those Washingtonians having other plans for the day, summarizing their activities immediately before and after his description of the parade to Arlington. The paragraph preceding "The Procession" reads as follows:

At an early hour the streets were full of excursionists and picnickers bound to Harper's Ferry, to Richmond, down the Potomac, and to various points in the surrounding country, while fishing parties were numerous. At Whitfield (near Lanham's, some ten miles out), on the B.& P. R.R., the Sunday school at that place, with those of Parker's Chapel, Bladensburg and Benning's, picnicked. The Midland train took about 150 excursionists to Luray, the Washington Excursion Co. took nearly 400 to Richmond, Ryland Chapel about 180 to Carlin's Spring, Va., and about 1,500 went to Harper's Ferry.

The reporter also thought that the crowds at Arlington were insufficiently attentive to the occasion: "There were many more people at Arlington to-day than those who paid any attention to the ceremonies. The grounds, romantic and picturesque in the extreme, make [it] one of the best places in the neighborhood of Washington for purposes of outdoor enjoyment. Many parties went over to-day simply to picnic and have a good time."

Irritated though he was by the "picnickers" both at Arlington and elsewhere, The Evening Star reporter provided a lengthy and very readable summation of the Memorial Day events at Arlington. He began by delineating the parade to the cemetery, which proceeded from select military units to the Marine Corps Band under the direction of John Philip Sousa, other regular and volunteer military divisions, and then local posts of the G.A.R., led by John A. Rawlins, Post Number 1. The various units reportedly attracted considerable attention, as did the West Washington Zouaves, who were "uniformed in red pants, white leggings, blue jacket [s] and red cap [s]" and made "a brilliant appearance." The aging G.A.R. veterans also "made a fine show," dressed in uniform, including "McClellan caps[37] and blue blouses," and carrying bouquets of flowers for placement on the Arlington graves.

The Memorial Day parades to Arlington continued until 1899, when they were disbanded in acknowledgement of both old and new realities. The old realities included poor roads. The Evening Star of May 30, 1881, provided an example of the difficulties: "The dust was pretty bad early in the day. In the afternoon too much traveling had made it fearful. A team raised dust enough to last a month; and every time one walking put a foot down a little cloud of the same delightful substance arose. There was not much laughing coming back. The heat and burdens of the day had about taken all the fun out of those who went to Arlington."

The new realities involved differing understandings of Memorial Day as memories of the war began inevitably to fade. Speakers at Memorial Day services conducted at Arlington and Congressional noted an accompanying shift in public focus, conveying both concern and wistful regret in summations provided in The Evening Star. In his address delivered at Arlington on May 30, 1885, General Samuel Swinfin Burdett (1836-1914) observed that "since the close of hostilities a new generation had arisen. The war was to them but as a tale that is told. . . . Only a few more years and the hand of the stranger (not of the comrade) will bring the annual offering of flowers, if flowers be brought at all." Speaking at Congressional nine years later, on May 30, 1894, General S.S. Yoder remarked that "the forms and faces of these stirring times, and the events of the great war in which we bore a part, after thirty years seem unreal and shadowy, like the remembrances of a dream."

As sharp, clear memories of the Civil War faded into "shadowy" dreams, Memorial Day observances became broader in focus, acknowledging the debt owed to the veterans of each U.S. war and to all those who had passed away, extending from national political leaders to families and friends. As noted in his oration at Congressional on May 30, 1896, which was summarized that day in *The Evening Star*, Rev. W.E. Parson, D.D., observed that the meaning of the occasion had been expanded so that it incorporated the memory of "all the dead" and thus functioned as "a Decoration day for all graves."

Congressional Cemetery offered an ideal setting for the more encompassing celebration of Memorial Day because of its uniquely inclusive community at rest, which included not only Civil War troops but also veterans from all other U.S. wars, as well as top federal leaders and citizens within the broader community. Memorial Day orators repeatedly acknowledged this unusual assemblage at Congressional, terming it "historic," as did Colonel William McLean, Deputy Commissioner of Pensions, in his address on May 30, 1885, which was covered that day in *The Evening Star*.

Recognizing the special significance of Memorial Day at Congressional, the general public came to observances there in increasing numbers, as noted in successive editions of *The Evening Star*. While figures are not available for the years 1869 through 1879, the estimates proceeded from "quite a large assemblage" in 1880, to "three or four thousand" in 1884, to crowds apparently too large to estimate, as on May 30, 1893, when the "numbers seemed to include the entire population of East Washington," and on May 30, 1897, when "an endless stream of humanity passed along all the streets leading to this city of the dead." Meanwhile, public transportation was taxed to the limit, as on May 30, 1899: "Street car lines and omnibuses could not transport the throngs that sought the city of the dead in remembrance. . . . Every street and avenue leading to the place was the scene of a steady stream of people making their way there. . . ."

As the crowds increased in size, so did the newspaper coverage of Memorial Day observances at Congressional Cemetery. Commentary in *The Evening Star* on May 31, 1869, about the first ceremonies of remembrance at the burial ground was tucked into one sentence: "Yesterday the committee who had visited Oak Hill and Glenwood . . . sub-divided at the last named, one portion going to Mount Olivet, and the other to Congressional Cemetery where the graves of the fallen brave were decorated." Until the late 1870s, press coverage remained minimal, focused largely on decoration of General Rawlin's grave. When the crowds began to expand at Congressional, so too did the copy in *The Evening Star*. On May 30, 1882, for example, the summary of Memorial Day activities at Congressional Cemetery was the equivalent of 6.5 pages typed single-space.

Memorial Day celebrations began at Congressional as they did at Arlington, with decoration of the graves in the morning. This event, as with other activities of the day, was organized by local G.A.R. posts, with the particular involvement of the Women's Relief Corps. Starting with a few hundred people, several thousand citizens eventually participated in "strewing" flowers on the Congressional graves. The ritual had special interest in particular years, as illustrated by a few examples from narratives given in *The Evening Star*. In 1886, for example, the assembling crowd found that nature had already provided decorations in that "roses and honey-suckles were in bloom upon the graves." In 1889, "a squad of Marines" proceeded into the cemetery "with several baskets of flowers" to decorate the graves of fallen comrades. For Memorial Day 1898, children and their parents brought to the cemetery flowers from their home gardens and from fields passed enroute to the burial ground. Upon their arrival at Congressional, they placed them in the center of the cemetery. At noon, the flowers were distributed to the children, who spread out across the burial ground to decorate every grave. By 1899, merchants had recognized commercial possibilities in the ceremonies and had positioned stands at the cemetery gate where visitors could purchase bouquets before entering the graveyard.

The Women's Relief Corps introduced a dramatic new element in 1904 to honor members of the U.S. Navy and Marine Corps who had been lost at sea and had not, according to many citizens at the time, been remembered sufficiently in Memorial Day exercises. Upon conclusion of the ceremonies at Congressional, they proceeded to the bridge on Pennsylvania Avenue that spanned the Anacostia River. They then set afloat a raft that was covered with flowers and flew an American flag in remembrance of the dead.[38]

As at Arlington, processions were a major part of the Memorial Day celebrations associated with Congressional Cemetery. Viewed together, they provided both a continuity with and a contrast to those that proceeded west on Pennsylvania Avenue. The peak period for the Congressional parades extended from 1891, when they were instituted, through 1899, after which they went into decline and were then discontinued in 1905. During the final years, 1900-1904, participants convened at the usual meeting place, on Pennsylvania Avenue between Third and Fourth Streets. Instead of then marching to the old cemetery, as was customary during 1891-1899, they proceeded via carriages and buses. The enthusiasm for the traditional ceremonies ebbed in these years.

Organized by the Farragut Post of the G.A.R., based in southeast Washington, D.C., the parades to Congressional focused during the 1890s on youth and traditional values in relation to nation, church, neighborhood, and family. They emphasized the participation of children "in the service of their country, thus instilling into their minds sentiments of patriotism and reverence for the memory of the nation's heroes that they will never forget, no matter how many Decoration days they may live to see," as noted in *The Evening Star* of May 30, 1891. The format for this first Memorial Day parade to Congressional was as follows:

- Carriages with Distinguished Participants
- Comrade Weber's Band
- National Rifles, Juniors (nineteen members)
- Sunday Schools, totaling 1125 children from ten Baptist, Christian, Congregational, Episcopal, Methodist Episcopal, and Presbyterian congregations in the surrounding area
- Junior Fraternal Orders, representing (1) Mount Vernon

Council, Number 10, Order of United American Mechanics (O.U.A.M.); (2) Empire Council, Number 14, Sons of Jonadab; (3) Capital Commandery, Number 323, United Order of the Green Cross; and (4) Cammack Tent, Number 42, Order of Rechabites

- Farragut Post, Number 10, G.A.R. (one-hundred members in full uniform).

Representatives of the Farragut Post provided the framework for the parade, riding with other "distinguished participants" in the lead carriages and marching "in full uniform" at the end of the line. They and the participating children made for a memorable procession, characterized in *The Evening Star* of May 30, 1891, as "a beautiful sight this, of a great band of children marching with the veterans to the old cemetery to help decorate the graves of the dead heroes of the great war."

The Memorial Day events at Congressional concluded year after year with a program conducted at what was then a symbolic center of the graveyard, an area next to the site that until 1899 constituted the grave of General John Rawlins. The monument emplaced in memory of Rawlins invariably caught the eye, draped as it was for the occasion in American flags and emergent from a bank of flowers. The ceremony underscored the unique status of this burial ground through the inclusion of program elements that were standard for the occasion, such as speeches, readings of the Gettysburg Address and original poems, and musical performances by organizations based in the area, such as the Marine Corps Band. The keynote speakers were invariably members of Congress, thereby demonstrating the historic connection between this cemetery and the federal government. Representing states from across the nation, they included Senator J.M. Gallinger of New Hampshire in 1892, Senator Frank J. Cannon of Utah in 1897, and Senator W.B. Heyburn of Idaho in 1910.

In speeches made at Congressional on Memorial Day, two Civil War veterans provided comments that offer differing ways of viewing the burial ground. On May 29, 1880, one Comrade Turell said this about the cemetery, as cited in *The Evening Star* for that day: "Here, within this beautiful place, under the shadow of their nation's Capitol, a peaceful river at their feet, rest the remains of many brave comrades. . . ." Three years later, on May 30, 1883, Comrade W.W. Granger declared that as he stood among the historic graves at Congressional, he was "almost in sight of Arlington," as quoted in *The Evening Star*. Viewed together, these two observations convey more than they did when first stated. Granger saw Congressional in relation to Arlington, while Turell posited the U.S. Capitol as the most appropriate referent point. Both comments are meaningful.

The history of Congressional Cemetery in the second half of the nineteenth century is best understood in connection with the emergence of Arlington National Cemetery. Over the full length of its long life, however, Congressional is most appropriately viewed in relation to the U.S. Congress. It has always been in the metaphorical "shadow" of the U.S. Capitol, given the differing meanings of that word. Positioned in the protective shadow of Congress in the first half of the nineteenth century, the cemetery went into a slow decline during the next fifty years as Congress generally lost sight of the old burial ground in its increasing focus on Arlington National Cemetery. During the same period, Congressional emerged as the final resting place for a notably diverse population. The cemetery is, for example, the final resting place of important Native Americans as well as of those who defeated them in conquest of the American West. Given the diversity of the community at rest, Congressional is a national cemetery in ways that Arlington could never be.

PART TWO

THE COMMUNITY AT REST

4

A TRULY NATIONAL ASSEMBLY

The route had become all too familiar, John Quincy Adams observed as he rode with John Calhoun in a carriage from the U.S. Capitol to Congressional Cemetery. The date was December 27, 1820, and they were part of the funeral cortege orchestrated in memory of James Burrill, a U.S. senator from Rhode Island who had died in Washington, D.C., on Christmas Day. The approximately one-mile procession to the burial ground began at noon, upon conclusion of the memorial service in the Senate chamber.

As they moved along Pennsylvania Avenue, Adams, then Secretary of State, and Calhoun, Secretary of War, talked about death and burial. They were thinking about the cemetery, which Adams characterized in his diary entry for that day as "the spot where all the members of Congress dying here, and not removed by their friends, are interred." And they were remembering former colleagues buried at the site: "We were remarking upon the number of members of Congress already mingling with the dust of this region, among whom are the two successive Vice-Presidents George Clinton and Elbridge Gerry." As he drew toward his conclusion, Adams grew increasingly somber: "We are obliged to live from hand to mouth, to provide for the day that is passing over us, and to leave posterity to take care of itself."[1]

The observations Adams provided in his diary underscored the status of Congressional as the federal burial ground during the antebellum period. In addition to operating in this capacity, Congressional was the cemetery of choice for other significant constituencies and individuals. George Watterston (1783-1854), who served as the first Librarian of Congress and was himself buried at the site, provided this memorable characterization of the community at rest: "Here repose the statesman, the orator, and the warrior; the illustrious and the obscure, 'and all that beauty, all that worth e'er gave,' alike crumble into dust, and mingle with the common elements from which they sprang."[2] As delineated in this chapter, Congressional has provided a final resting place for individuals from all sectors of the broader society and has thereby operated over the long years as follows:

- A Cemetery for the Federal Government
- The First National Military Cemetery
- A National Cemetery Open to Everyone
- A Native American Memorial Site
- A Resting Place for Explorers of the West and Beyond
- A Gathering Place for Other Notable Individuals.

This chapter identifies and analyzes the congregation at rest, which currently totals about 55,000 individuals. In so doing, it provides a text for the multiple readings of the burial ground given in the other chapters of this monograph.

In *The Last Great Necessity* (1991), David Sloane described the cemetery in general, without specifying any one site, as "a location for the memory of the community" and as "an excellent source" for the study of American culture.[3] The biographies of those interred at Congressional underscore its singularity in that the burial ground holds the memory of the entire American community, extending from U.S. presidents and commanding generals of the Army to former slaves and to homeless individuals living along the margins of the American experience. Viewed together, the first three sections delineate the broad range of the community at rest, while the rest of the chapter elaborates upon this theme.

A Cemetery for the Federal Government

Beginning with its establishment in 1807, Congressional functioned in part as the cemetery used by the U.S. government for the interments of federal officials who died in Washington, D.C., during the decades preceding the Civil War. They included U.S. presidents and first ladies, vice presidents, members of presidential cabinets and the U.S. Congress, as well as architects and builders of the U.S. Capitol. This section provides abbreviated information about selected individuals within these categories.

The bodies of three U.S. presidents—William Henry Harrison, John Quincy Adams, and Zachary Taylor—and of first lady Dolley Madison were placed temporarily in the Public Vault at Congressional, with Harrison remaining from April 7, 1841, to June 26, 1841, Adams from February 26, 1848, to March 6, 1848, Taylor from July 13, 1850, to October 25, 1850, and Madison from July 16, 1849, to February 10, 1852. Constructed with federal funds, the Public Vault was designed for interment of the deceased until the body could be transferred to a permanent site, often at a distant location. As indicated by the name of this structure, it was available to everyone, regardless of a person's status within the broader community. Over the years, the Public Vault has served as a station along the way for some 4,600 people, a number of whom had national reputations in the federal government and the military, among other areas. Various commentators have accordingly suggested that Congressional qualifies as a national landmark on the basis of the Public Vault alone.[4]

Official Washington was in no hurry to relinquish the remains of Dolley Madison, who by all accounts had been a hostess of exemplary charm and diligence from the time her husband became Secretary of State in 1801 to her last public appearance at a White House reception in February 1849. On February 10, 1852, her body was removed from the Public Vault to the family vault of James Causten, husband of her niece. Her remains stayed there for approximately six more years.[5] Meanwhile, Dolley Madison was joined by Louisa Adams, wife of John Quincy Adams. The body of Louisa, who died on May 18, 1852, was transferred the next day to the Causten Vault. On December 14, 1852, her remains were removed from this site for transport to Quincy, Massachusetts, and burial there beside her husband. In 1858, the body of Dolly Madison was conveyed to Montpelier, Virginia, where she was laid to rest beside her husband, the fourth president of the United States. Her son from her first marriage, John Payne Todd, who nearly reduced her to poverty in her declining years, remains at Congressional Cemetery, where he was buried without fanfare in January 1852.

Three U.S. vice presidents were also interred at Congressional: George Clinton (1739-1812), Elbridge Gerry (1744-1814), and John Calhoun (1782-1850). While the bodies of Clinton and Calhoun were later removed elsewhere, Elbridge Gerry remains at Congressional. The fifth U.S. vice president, he served in the administration of President James Madison from March 4, 1813, to November 23, 1814. The only signatory of the Declaration of Independence buried in Washington, D.C., Gerry had been a member of the Continental Congress during 1776-1780 and 1783-1785, a delegate to the Constitutional Convention of the United States held in Philadelphia in 1789, a member of Congress from Massachusetts during 1789-1793, and governor of Massachusetts during 1810-1812. During his term as governor, he supported an unpopular bill to redistrict the state in favor of the Republicans, an action that resulted in coinage of the term gerrymander. Gerry rests at Congressional beneath a monument that bears his own admonishment: "It is the duty of every citizen, though he may have but one day to live, to devote that day to the good of his country."[6]

It is certainly significant that three U.S. presidents and two U.S. vice presidents were laid to rest on a temporary basis at Congressional and that the body of another U.S. vice president remains at this site. The burial ground has long been known as Congressional Cemetery, however, and the number of congressional interments makes it unique among U.S. burial grounds, as do the cenotaphs emplaced in memory of congressmen who died in the federal capitol prior to 1876. Among the 806 burial sites owned by the federal government at Congressional, eighty-four have been used for congressional interments. Of those interred, sixty-five were members of the House of Representatives, fourteen were U.S. senators, and five had been members of both the House and the Senate. Uriah Tracy, delegate to the House from Connecticut during 1793-1796 and a U.S. senator during 1796-1807, was the first congressman buried at Congressional. Reinterred from Rock Creek Cemetery in Georgetown, his burial took place on July 19, 1807. The most recent congressional burial was that of Representative Tilman Bacon

Parks, a Democrat from Arkansas who served in eight successive Congresses (March 4, 1921 – January 3, 1937) and was interred at the site on February 14, 1950.

In addition to members of Congress, many officers of Congress are buried at the cemetery, including secretaries of the Senate, Senate sergeants-at-arms, clerks of the House, House sergeants-at-arms, doorkeepers of the House, chaplains, and pages. Reverend Alexander McCormick figures among the notable personalities in these groups. A familiar figure on Capitol Hill during the early nineteenth century, he was both the rector of Christ Church (1798-1823) and chaplain of the U.S. Senate (1804-1805 and 1807-1808). As rector of Christ Church, he presided over the establishment of the cemetery. Building upon his contacts within the Senate, he was then instrumental in developing this burial ground as Congressional Cemetery. Having been interred initially in the Public Vault (April 28 – June 8, 1841), Reverend McCormick was buried at a site that is near the main entrance to the cemetery.[7]

Among the many officers of Congress interred at the cemetery, Isaac Bassett (1819-1895) was a particularly compelling figure. He served in the U.S. Senate for sixty-four years, having been appointed by Senator Daniel Webster as a Senate page in 1831 and having functioned in this capacity until he became an assistant doorkeeper prior to the Civil War. In a memorable profile published on December 10, 1895, *The Evening Star* recalled that Bassett had been "to the Senate what an executive officer is to the man-of-war," that he knew the history of "every desk in the Senate," and that he had "exchanged pinches of snuff with many of the most famous men in the history of the country." He was "a familiar figure" in the halls of Congress: "For a generation he has been one of the sights of the building as little to be overlooked as would be the marble room adjoining the Senate, or the echo stones in the Old House of Representatives." As noted in an historical profile provided in the *Congressional Cemetery Association Newsletter* of January 1997, Bassett had "embodied the tradition and institutional memory of the Senate."

The prominent members of presidential cabinets interred at Congressional Cemetery include John Forsyth (1780-1841), Secretary of State (1834-1841) in the administrations of both Andrew

Jackson and Martin Van Buren; William Pinkney (1764-1822), Attorney General of the United States (1811-1814) in the cabinet of President James Madison; William Wirt (1772-1834), Attorney General of the United States (1817-1829) in the administrations of Presidents James Monroe and John Quincy Adams; and Samuel Southard (1787-1842), Secretary of the Navy (1823-1829) during the second administration of James Monroe and through the entire administration of John Quincy Adams.[8] While it is the rare person who now visits their graves at Congressional, these individuals were large figures in their times.

William Wirt, for example, was the candidate of the Anti-Masonic Party for the U.S. presidency during 1832. While he did not prevail over Andrew Jackson in the larger campaign, he did participate through this effort in three large firsts achieved by the Anti-Masonic Party. Organized in 1826 to combat the perceived secrecy of the Masons, the Anti-Masons emerged as the first third party in American politics, the first party with an official political platform, and the first political party to convene a national convention, during which it selected Wirt as its presidential candidate. With this gathering, conducted in Baltimore during September 1831, the party originated the convention system in American politics.

In connection with its role as the cemetery used by the federal government during the antebellum period, Congressional also served as the final resting place for the architects and builders of the U.S. Capitol and other structures that characterize the landscape of federal Washington, D.C. The most prominent architects in residence at Congressional are William Thornton (1759-1828) and Robert Mills (1781-1855).

Robert Mills, who was Architect of Public Buildings from 1836 to 1851, designed the Washington Monument and three of the most prominent nineteenth-century buildings within the capital city: the Treasury Building, Patent Office, and Post Office. Given his many contributions to the architectural landscape of the federal district, it is notable that his grave at Congressional lay unmarked, without any gravestone, for approximately eighty years following his death in 1855. In 1936, a group of architects, along with members of the Mills family, redressed this inexplicable omission by positioning a monument over his grave that echoed in design the cenotaphs emplaced in memory of the congressmen who had died while serving in office.

William Thornton is generally recognized as the first Architect of the Capitol, although he also designed a number of other prominent buildings in the federal city, including the Octagon House, Tudor Place, and Brentwood Mansion. While he submitted his design for the U.S. Capitol Building after the competition of 1792 had ended, President George Washington selected it nonetheless because of its "grandeur, simplicity and convenience." On September 12, 1794, Washington appointed Thornton as one of three federal commissioners of the District of Columbia, who were responsible for overseeing construction of the initial government buildings in the new city, including the U.S. Capitol. The interment of William Thornton at Congressional following his death on March 28, 1828, has particular resonance, given his role as first Architect of the Capitol. As is discussed in the final chapter of this study, it was the Architect of the Capitol in the late 1990s who articulated the formula now in place—a public/private partnership—for the preservation of Congressional Cemetery.

The immediate successors to William Thornton as Architect of the Capitol were Benjamin Latrobe and Charles Bulfinch, who served in this capacity during 1803-1817 and 1817-1830, respectively. While neither was buried at Congressional, they both interred children who had died in Washington, D.C., at this site. Latrobe buried his stillborn daughter Louisa there in September 1808. Later, he designed the signature cenotaphs positioned at the cemetery in memory of congressmen who died in Washington, D.C., prior to 1877. In May 1829, Bulfinch interred his only daughter, Susan Apthorp Bulfinch Hall, at Congressional following a protracted illness. Latrobe himself was interred at St. Louis Cemetery No. 1 in New Orleans, having died in the city during a yellow fever epidemic. Bulfinch, who was originally interred in King's Chapel Burial Ground in Boston, was reinterred at historic Mount Auburn Cemetery, established in 1831 as the first garden cemetery in the United States.

Other notable architects and builders are interred at Congressional, including George Blagden and George Hadfield, both of whom died in 1826. Blagden was chief stonecutter at and superintendent of the masons employed in construction of the U.S. Capitol Building. In addition, he was one of the founders of Congressional Cemetery and is accordingly profiled with the other founders in Chapter 1 of this history. Hadfield supervised construction of the U.S. Capitol Building from October 1795 to May 1798, when he was dismissed over differences with Thornton regarding architectural plans for the structure. He remained in Washington, D.C., for the rest of his life, providing designs for other landmark buildings. They included the Old City Hall, completed in 1820, and Arlington House,[9] which became the residence of Robert E. Lee and is now surrounded by Arlington National Cemetery.

As noted in this section, Congressional functioned in part during the antebellum period as the burial ground of choice for all branches of the U.S. federal government. Operating in this capacity, it emerged in the years prior to the Civil War as the most prestigious cemetery in the federal city. For this reason, as well as its advantageous location, it became the burial ground of choice for other populations within the broader community, including the United States military.

The First National Military Cemetery

Prior to the Civil War and the establishment of the military cemetery system, Congressional functioned in part as the first national military cemetery. The numbers of confirmed interments of U.S. military personnel are 33 for the Revolutionary War, 6 for the Tripolitan and Algerian Wars, 124 for the War of 1812, and 44 for the Mexican War. In addition, Congressional was the burial site for 545 veterans of the Grand Army of the Republic, of whom 12 were senior officers. Fifty Confederate soldiers, including ten officers, were also interred at the cemetery.[10] The significance of these interments does not reside in the total numbers but in the identities of those buried, as well as in the associated narratives.

General Philip Stuart, who died in Washington, D.C., on August 14, 1830, was among the last high-ranking Revolutionary War veterans interred at Congressional. In addition to identifying his home on "Greenleaf's Point" in southeast Washington, D.C., the obituary in *The National Intelligencer* of August 16, 1830, included this statement: "He was, we believe, almost the last relick of the Revolutionary worthies in our immediate community, and we should think it a proper tribute of respect to his memory . . . for our military companies to unite in paying the honors of war to his remains, at their interment today." While Stuart was not the last of the Revolutionary War veterans interred at Congressional Cemetery, he was the last of the generals, who also included, in chronological order according to the dates of their deaths, General Thomas Hartley (1748-1800), General Daniel Hiester (1747-1804), Major General Uriah Tracy (1755-1807), Major General William Blount (1759-1812), and General Peterson Goodwyn (1745-1818). General James S. Jackson (1757-1805), who was originally buried at Rock Creek Cemetery, was reinterred at Congressional on August 10, 1832.[11]

Among the six confirmed interments of Tripolitan and Algerian War veterans at Congressional, three also served in the War of 1812 and are discussed below. The remaining three include two successive U.S. consul-generals to Algeria: Commodore Richard Henry O'Brien (1758-1824), who served in this capacity from 1797 to 1803, and Tobias Lear (1762-1816), consul-general during 1803-1812. The most compelling narratives are associated with Tobias Lear, who was a casualty of the Tripolitan War after his return to the United States. Lear had been private secretary to George Washington (1785-1793 and 1798-1799), U.S. consul to Santo Domingo (1801-1802), and U.S. consul-general to Algiers (1803-1812). He spent nearly two years in Algiers trying to secure the release of Americans captured on October 31, 1803, from the U.S. *Philadelphia*. Then, on July 3, 1805, Lear suddenly agreed to pay $60,000 in ransom for their return. The Algerians, who had originally demanded $200,000, accepted. This agreement, which was ratified by the U.S. Congress, became the defining moment in Lear's career. Opponents of the Jefferson administration roundly criticized the agreement as hasty and ill-advised. The ensuing controversy eventually brought Lear's diplomatic career to an end. Upon his return to the United States in 1812, he became an accountant in the War Department, serving in this capacity until his suicide on October 11, 1816.

Lear spent his last evening as he had spent many others, in the company of his wife Fanny, his friend Commodore John Rodgers, who had been one of those prisoners freed by the ransom payment, and Rodgers' wife Minerva. Ann Minerva, one of the Rodgers' ten children, later described the occasion:

My father and mother had been making a late visit to the Lears one evening, and, as they were bidding good-bye, Mr. Lear said, "I will walk with you, Commodore, a little way." He accompanied them, slowly strolling and talking; at last they were near home, he stopped and said, "Goodbye, Mrs. Rodgers! Goodbye, Commodore!" pressing my father's hand warmly. The very next morning my parents were sent for. Something terrible had happened at Mr. Lear's. . . . My mother always fancied that he wished to say something to my father, which her presence prevented; and they both remembered his farewell to them had been more tender and lingering than usual.[12]

After breakfast on the morning of October 11, Lear walked into his garden and shot himself with a pistol. His body was discovered by his son Benjamin, who had heard the report of the gun. Lear left no farewell note and gave no reason for his suicide, which some thought might have been occasioned by depression, caused by lingering criticism over the Treaty of Tripoli, the subsequent collapse of his political career, and/or his sometimes violent headaches, which could have been the sign of a serious illness. As noted in *The Washington City Gazette*, a "long train of coaches" accompanied the remains of "the much respected Col. Lear" to Congressional Cemetery,[13] where he was interred in close proximity to the grave of Elbridge Gerry, the monument of which urges each citizen, "though he may have but one day to live, to devote that day to the service of his country."

While Congressional was a significant burial ground for veterans of the Revolutionary and of the Tripolitan and Algerian Wars, it has a more direct and powerful connection with the War of 1812, which was conducted during 1812-1814 and has been subsequently viewed by many historians as the "Second War of Independence." Given the surviving documentation, it is reasonable to conclude that Congressional, among all other cemeteries in the District of Columbia and elsewhere, is the one most fully connected with this conflict.

The British army entered Washington, D.C., during the evening of August 24, 1814, following their victory at the Battle of Bladensburg, just north of Washington, D.C. That night, they set fire to the U.S. Capitol Building, the Executive Mansion, all departmental buildings with the exception of the Patent Office, and several private homes. In addition, they destroyed the offices of *The National Intelligencer*, which Admiral George Cockburn believed had slandered him personally. Meanwhile, William Jones, Secretary of the Navy, ordered Commodore Thomas Tingey, Commandant of the Navy Yard, to burn the facility so that it could not be used by the British. Tingey, who proceeded according to orders, had been one of the founders of Congressional Cemetery, which was at the very perimeter of these events.

Among the veterans of the War of 1812 interred at the burial ground, Major General Jacob Jennings Brown (1775-1828) was "the most successful," having prevailed over the British in four of the nine primary confrontations (Sackett's Harbor, Chippawa, Lindy's Lane, and Fort Erie).[14] Upon the conclusion of the war, Brown was one of only two major generals retained by the Army, the other being Andrew Jackson. In 1821, the U.S. Congress created the position of commanding general of the Army and appointed Brown to serve in this capacity, in which he was the primary military advisor to the president and the secretary of war. Brown was interred at Congressional following a state funeral and an impressive procession down Pennsylvania Avenue. He was succeeded by Alexander Macomb, who served as commanding general until he was interred at the burial ground in 1848.

Brown and Macomb provide the nexus for a memorable cluster of graves at Congressional Cemetery. Brown's burial site, which is marked by a broken column on top of a pedestal, is located in Range 57, Site 151, which is about fifteen feet from that of Macomb, in Range 55, Site 149. Macomb rests beneath a conspicuous neoclassical monument[15] positioned next to memorials marking the graves of two other prominent veterans of the War of 1812: Commodore John Rodgers (1773-1828), buried in Range 56, Site 152, and Commodore Todd Patterson (1786-1839), located in Range 55, Site 151. Rodgers made four cruises in the *U.S. President* that resulted in the seizure of twelve ships from the British West Indies Squadron. In addition, he was instrumental in the June 1814 defense of Baltimore, Maryland, providing key naval support in the Battle of North

Point and in the attack on Fort McHenry. Patterson emerged as a hero in the Battle of New Orleans. In a decisive confrontation on New Year's Day 1815, his naval batteries destroyed British artillery that had continuously bombarded the U.S. position all that morning. General Andrew Jackson later said to President James Monroe that "too much praise cannot be bestowed on those who managed my artillery."[16]

This remarkable grouping of the graves of General Jacob Brown, General Alexander Macomb, Commodore John Rodgers, and Commodore Todd Patterson constitutes a compelling memorial to the veterans of the War of 1812 buried at locations scattered across the cemetery. It is not, however, designated as such by a special marker at the site or in tourist guides to Washington, D.C. The four monuments are perhaps all the more powerful for their quiet statement about the contributions made to the nation by the veterans of the War of 1812 interred at Congressional.

In addition to providing a final resting place for veterans of the War of 1812, Congressional is a significant memorial site for participants in the Mexican War. The significance does not reside in the sum of such interments, which totals forty-four and thereby comprises a very small number of the American troops who died in that conflict. In *The Mexican War, 1846-48*, K. Jack Bauer identified the total as 12,876, of whom 1,192 were killed in action, 529 died of wounds, and the majority—11,155—died of disease. Most of these troops were interred in unmarked graves on the battlefield or near Army encampments. Efforts were later made to identify the burial sites of some troops, primarily officers, whose remains were recovered and returned to the United States for reinterment in home communities. Because the U.S. government did not provide this service at that time, families and friends assumed the associated costs, which was not possible in most cases. As noted by Richard Bruce Winders in *Mr. Polk's Army: The American Military Experience in the Mexican War*, "thousands of soldiers in Mr. Polk's army did not come home."[17]

The interments at Congressional of participants in the Mexican War are significant in part because of the involvement of the Polk administration in the ceremonies. Top officials in the U.S. federal government and the military recognized these burials as an occasion to honor the contributions of those who died at Cerro Gordo, Contreros, Tuspan, Vera Cruz, and other storied battlegrounds. The individuals celebrated were not the generals and admirals who later served in the Civil War but three junior officers: Colonel Truman Cross, who was killed on April 10, 1846, by Mexican bandits near Fort Brown, Texas, and reinterred at Congressional on November 10, 1846; Colonel William Montrose Graham, who died on September 8, 1847, from wounds inflicted at Molino del Rey and was reinterred at Congressional on January 24, 1848; and Captain Charles Hanson, who fell before enemy fire at the Battle of Contreras on August 19, 1847, and was reinterred at Congressional on March 20, 1848. *The National Intelligencer* was instrumental in disseminating their credentials as heroes by narrating tales of their courage in battle and by delineating the funeral processions associated with their burials at Congressional Cemetery. On January 24, 1848, for example, the newspaper provided this summation of Graham's death at Molino del Rey:

> While leading his regiment to this tremendous and daring assault Col. Graham received ten wounds, three of which were mortal, and he expired on the field a few minutes after receiving them. His last words, while reclining wounded on the ground, were 'Charge on the enemy—charge!' And then he lay quietly down and breathed his last.

On the following November 9, *The National Intelligencer* delineated the procession that conveyed Graham's remains to Congressional Cemetery. As noted, President James K. Polk was located at the center of this parade, which also included officers of the Army, Navy, and Marine Corps in dress uniform, as well as members of both houses of Congress. Certainly, funeral processions that involved the U.S. president and both houses of Congress were not staged in any other U.S. city at that time for military men who died in the Mexican War.[18] The military processions to Congressional during the antebellum period, as well as the interments there of both officers and enlisted men, established its status as being in part the first national military cemetery.

A National Burial Ground Open to Everyone

In its totality, the community at rest at Congressional Cemetery provides a challenging, ultimately profound text for exploring national memory. A standard reading of this text concentrates on the many "illustrious" figures interred at the site, to recall terminology provided by George Watterston in 1842. While such a perusal is compelling, it neglects the thousands of others buried at Congressional, identified as "the obscure" by Watterston. Having worked in various capacities within the broad middle class, as well as having been former slaves, domestic servants, and day laborers, they were the "anonymous Americans" and have thus "largely escaped traditional historical inquiry," to borrow the phrasing of historian Tamara K. Hareven.[19]

While these individuals are critical to the definition of Congressional as the first national burial ground, they pose challenges in that documentation about their lives and deaths is generally accessible in only two sources: the index of burials compiled by Jim Oliver and the obituary database prepared by Sandra Schmidt,[20] which includes as available summations provided in *The National Intelligencer* and *The Evening Star*. Drawing upon this information, the narrative that follows delineates representative categories within the larger community at rest, proceeding from an alphabetical subset of burials to groups identified according to their shared manner of death, organizational affiliation, racial identification, and economic status.

The alphabetical subset consists of the individuals interred at Congressional who had the last name of Martin, which was selected because it is a common American name and thus incorporates a sizable sampling of the larger population. According to the index of burials, 249 Martins were interred at Congressional, primarily during the nineteenth century. The list of these Martins, which includes several families, begins with forty-six entries identified simply as "MARTIN, (CHILD)." The accompanying information is sparse, generally identifying the date of the child's death, the location of the burial site, and the name of the father. In addition, the age of the child at the time of death and the cause of death are sometimes specified. In their brevity, these details convey the grievous losses experienced by some of the families, including that of William Martin and his wife, who is not identified in the index of burials. During the first half of the 1830s, they lost four children: a son who "died in measles" on May 11, 1830, at the age of one; a child identified only according to the date of death, which was August 30, 1831; another child who died of measles on June 9, 1835, at the age of two; and still another child who succumbed to "inflammation in lungs" on July 5, 1835, at the age of three. All of these children were interred in the same site, R50/151, as was their father, William, who died on September 2, 1855.

The obituary database generally provides the same types of information about the many children interred at Congressional. The exceptions are for those who died from injuries sustained in accidents. In notifying the surrounding community, area newspapers delineated the unfolding events in headings immediately preceding abbreviated narratives. On June 13 and 14, 1900, for example, *The Evening Star* announced the demise of Lottie Martin at the age of one year and seven months with the following summation: "Policeman's Little Daughter Overturns Kettle of Boiling Preserves" and "The Injuries Fatal." The obituaries for children sometimes included familiar poems, as did that for Charles A. Martin, who succumbed to an unspecified "short illness" on September 2, 1902, at the age of six. The announcement in *The Evening Star* on the same day included verses attributed to "His Loving Grandma," "His Mother," and "His Aunt Maggie." The stanza from "His Mother" read as follows: "Oh, Charlie, must I give you up,/ You whom I loved so well?/ How can I drink this bitter cup/ And say a long and last farewell." The lines were powerful because they were conventional and familiar, having been replicated but for the name in announcing the deaths of many other children who succumbed to ailments that could have been readily treated at a later date.

In connection with the Martin adults interred at Congressional Cemetery, the obituary database includes abbreviated death notices as well as occasional lengthy narratives for eighty-five individuals, comprising about thirty-five percent of the total number of Martins buried at the graveyard. As indicated by these summations, they constituted a cross-section of the surrounding municipality, including volunteers who served in the U.S. Army during the Civil War; federal and municipal employees, among whom were teachers at the D.C. public schools; entrepreneurs, such as a businessman who manufactured bricks for nearly fifty years at a factory he and his brother operated at the base of South Capitol Street; and many others who had productive lives in the surrounding community. The obituaries were abbreviated for all of these individuals. In contrast, they included arresting detail, sometimes at considerable length, for those who experienced unusual or violent deaths.[21]

The most extensive and memorable of the narratives was given in *The National Intelligencer* following the murder of Tobias Martin on June 28, 1826. The summation of this tragedy, published in installments on June 29, June 30, and July 1, 1826, as well as on May 9 and June 23, 1827, portrayed Martin, who was a whitesmith (tinsmith) by trade, as a respected individual within the surrounding community and as "our neighbor," having lived with his family in a home "near to the office of the *National Intelligencer*" and having been working at the time of his death on a new power press for the newspaper.[22] His murderer, in stark contrast, was identified as "a person living on the borders of this city" who had the last name of Devaughn.

The coverage provided on June 30, 1826, focused first on the burial of Martin, "whose mortal remains were yesterday attended to the grave [at Congressional] by a great concourse of indignant and sorrowing townsmen, and with military and Masonic honors." The article then delineated his murder, noting that "several boys," one of whom was Martin's son, had "strayed" into fields owned by Devaughn looking for blackberries. Devaugh thereupon "pursued" and "roughly handled" the youths, seizing both the basket and hat of young Martin and informing him that they would not be returned "until some money was paid for their redemption." The parents of the boy subsequently walked to the house of Devaugh and "very civilly requested" the return of these items, whereupon Devaugh loosed "his sharp and furious dogs":

> Mr. and Mrs. M. were endeavoring by flight to escape from them, when, one of the dogs having seized Mr. M's coat, he had turned around to defend himself . . . and at that moment received a load of slugs in his breast from a musket deliberately aimed and fired at him by Devaugh. He turned

to his wife, who by this time reached the fence, exclaiming, "I am a dead man!" and, taking her hand, bidding her affectionately "Farewell!" he soon breathed his last.

Joseph Devaugh was apprehended and charged with murder on June 30, 1826. Chief Justice William Cranch presided over his trial, which concluded in May 1827 when he sentenced Devaugh to death by hanging. The execution was conducted on June 22, 1827, at a site about "half a mile north" of what is now the city of Alexandria, Virginia, "in the presence of an immense concourse of people," as noted the following day in *The National Intelligencer*. For all its drama, this saga has been long forgotten by the surrounding community. So, too, have compelling stories about thousands of others at Congressional Cemetery. As for Judge William Cranch, he was interred at the burial ground on September 4, 1855, some three decades after Tobias Martin.

Congressional Cemetery is the locus for many other compelling summations. One of these accounts focuses on the Arsenal tragedy, which was the largest civil disaster in Washington, D.C., during the Civil War. It occurred on Friday, June 17, 1864, in one room of a four-room wooden building at the facility, located at the end of Four and One-Half Street SW. During the morning, trays of explosive materials had been placed in the yard adjacent to the building. The heat of the sun subsequently ignited these materials, and a piece of fuse floated through an open window into a room where twenty-nine young women were making cartridges for small arms to be used by Union troops. The fuse landed on loose powder, causing a "terrific explosion," as reported that day in *The Evening Star*. Within seconds, the interior of the building was in flames. Only eight of the young women and the chief clerk, Hosea B. Moulton, escaped with their lives.

The Evening Star narrated the disaster in special editions of the newspaper issued at 2:30 and 4:00 p.m. on the afternoon of June 17. In so doing, the newspaper characterized the accident as a tragedy experienced by the entire community, extending from the families of the victims to President Abraham Lincoln. The first of these issues, distributed under the heading of "Frightful Explosion at the Arsenal," noted that "the news of the accident spread like wild fire" and that "hundreds of anxious parents, brothers and sisters" appeared at the "scene of the disaster" shortly thereafter, as did U.S. Secretary of War Edwin Stanton and General Henry W. Halleck, Chief of Staff of the U.S. Army. The 4:00 p.m. edition provided details under this heading: "Further Particulars of the Terrible Explosion at the Arsenal." The specifics were indeed "terrible," as exemplified by details about the bodies, which "were in such a condition that it was found necessary to place boards under each one in order to remove them from the ruins . . . ."

The funeral and then the service of interment at Congressional were conducted on Sunday, June 19. As delineated the next day in *The Evening Star*, the funeral was staged in an outdoor forum at the Arsenal among an assemblage totaling "several thousand" people who had "pushed" their way through the gates of the facility. Following the service, they and thousands of other Washingtonians witnessed the funeral procession to Congressional for the interment there of sixteen of the victims, fourteen of whom were buried in a mass grave. The parade was more than a mile in length, including participants who rode in some 150 carriages, as well as on horseback, along with countless others who walked to the cemetery. The "chief mourners" were President Lincoln and Secretary of War Stanton, who were in a hearse at the front of the procession. As it made its way to the burial ground, the parade proceeded along streets that were lined with people and past houses with spectators sitting on the rooftops.

The service of interment was conducted at Congressional among "a dense crowd" that included many who had arrived earlier to secure a place near the burial site. One year later, a monument that had been prepared by sculptor Lot Flannery and funded by the local citizenry was emplaced over the mass grave. This memorial, which can be seen at a considerable distance across the burial ground, features a neoclassical statue of a grieving woman standing atop a twenty-foot pedestal with head bowed and hands clasped. A depiction of the Arsenal fire and the names of the victims—Helissa Adams, Emma Baird, Kate Brosnahan, and all the others—are carved into the base of the monument.[23]

Another unique burial site, small in size compared to the Arsenal Monument but large in its commemorative significance, is the one for Leonard Matlovich (1943-1988). Made of the same black marble used in the Vietnam Veterans Memorial, the monument is dedicated to "A Gay Vietnam Veteran." The monument also contains Matlovich's powerful testimony that "When I Was in the Military They Gave Me a Medal for Killing Two Men and a Discharge for Loving One." Over the years since his burial, the Matlovich grave site has emerged as the key monument in the development of a larger LGBT community at rest in the cemetery.

Born into a military family, Matlovich joined the Air Force in 1963, serving twelve years. By the early 1970s, he had become actively gay after years of ambiguity on his part. As a decorated war hero, he now came forth to challenge the existing ban on homosexuals openly serving in the military. On March 6, 1975, in a letter to his commanding officer, he strongly affirmed both his sexual orientation and desire to stay in the military. The request was rejected but a legal battle resulted in his reinstatement. In the end, he left the Air Force to fight for gay rights. 24

Matlovich became an activist just as the HIV/AIDS epidemic hit the United States. He fought for expanded medical treatment to fight the growing impact of the disease. In the early 1980s, he first envisioned the need for a gay veteran's memorial. Becoming infected with AIDS himself, he oversaw the construction of the monument. His funeral on July 4, 1988 with full military honors led to his burial in a setting he had often visited and preferred to Arlington National Cemetery.

No such easy affirmation is applicable to the African Americans interred at Congressional before and during the Civil War. As noted in Chapter 1 of this study, the original rules and regulations for the cemetery, adopted by the Christ Church vestry on March 30, 1812, stated "that no person of color shall be permitted to be buried within that part of the burial ground which is now enclosed." These standards said nothing, however, about such interments outside the enclosed area, which at that time comprised approximately three-quarters of the original Square 1115. Cemetery records identify the burials of seventeen "colored" persons at Congressional before and one at the start of the Civil War within the sites extending from 113 to 140 in Range 24, which was just beyond the enclosed area. The first such burials were of Henry Windsor Linney, who reportedly died of "asma" and was interred on May 25, 1829, and of Letty McPherson, interred on September 20, 1833, without nota-tion in the records of the contributing condition. When conducting research for this book, the authors chanced upon a gravestone that had been emplaced in memory of one Emma Lewis and has since disappeared from the cemetery. The simple inscription stated that she was "coloured" and that she had died on December 7, 1860, in her twentieth year. The one identified burial of an African-Ameri-can during the Civil War was of Lucy Bell, who died at the age of ninety-nine and was interred on June 10, 1862.[25]

The legal status cannot be determined for all of the identified persons of color interred at Congressional before and during the Civil War. Some were clearly slaves, as indicated by these sample notations from cemetery records: "(Child), (Slave)"; "James Young's Colored Woman, Aunt Jenny"; "Vina. I. P. Chase's Colored Girl"; and "Colored Boy of Joshua Morsell." Others, including the follow-ing, may have been free African Americans working as servants for some of the prominent families in Christ Church: Kitty Kaw and Lucy Kaw, who died on December 12, 1851, and August 3, 1855, respectively, and were interred in the same site; Louisa (April 17, 1855) and Susanna Gordon (December 18, 1855), also buried in one lot; and Jenny Walker, who was interred on May 21, 1856.[26]

Cemetery records identify the burials of four African-Ameri-cans in the decades immediately following the Civil War: Annie Bell (May 3, 1873), who was interred in the same site used for Lucy Bell (June 10, 1862) and may have been her daughter; Eliza Riv-ers (March 15, 1877); Mocca Brown (July 12, 1884); and Theopolus Howard (April 1, 1891). As indicated in the minutes of a meeting conducted on June 16, 1868, the Christ Church vestry had agreed to "allow" Mocca Brown, identified as a "black communicant," to buy eight sites at the cemetery; Elisa Rivers, another "black com-municant," to buy a lot next to Brown's sites; and Theopolus How-ard, identified as the "black Sexton" of the church, to purchase five sites.[27] They now rest in near proximity, Rivers in Site 22/250, Brown in 23/250, and Howard in 22/253. The purchase of these sites by Rivers, Brown, and Howard probably coincided with removal of the old sanction prohibiting the burial of "people of color" within the enclosed area at Congressional Cemetery.

Indigents, the most obscure of all the obscure at Congressional, the most forgotten of all the unknown, were accorded burial rights officially denied to African Americans until Reconstruction. In a document dated March 25, 1808, Thomas Munroe, then Superintendent of the City of Washington, transferred Square 1115 to Henry Ingle, who served as agent for the committee working to establish the new cemetery. This deed of transfer included the following provision: that "one-fourth part of the said square" be reserved for "the gratuitous interment" of paupers. This proviso was attached because indigents posed a significant financial burden for the new city. In his *Journal*, Benjamin Latrobe detailed the problems of laborers and craftsmen brought to the city to work on federal projects and then left penniless when Congress failed to appropriate funds for these efforts. In providing relief for these and other indigents, the city expended substantial sums, comprising forty-two percent of its revenues in 1802 and twenty-eight percent the following year.[28]

Statistics are not available showing the numbers of paupers interred at Congressional over its long history. Marginal in life, they are marginal people in death, buried without ceremony, with no markers identifying names and dates, along the cemetery roadways and pathways. Perhaps more than any others interred at Congressional, these people convey, in the words of Kenneth Jackson, "the transitory nature of human existence, the fragility of social bonds and the power of death."[29]

The top federal and military leaders are a vital but not the only part of the equation that makes Congressional a unique national burial ground. The remaining part includes everyone else, representing the other socio-demographic segments within the larger population.

They comprise the forgotten people, including those in the Martin subset of burials, the victims of the Arsenal disaster, former members of old Ebenezer Methodist Church, the black slaves and servants interred during the nineteenth century, and the many homeless people buried without markers along the walkways threading across the cemetery.

Congressional is both the first and a unique national burial ground because it has provided a place from its very beginning for everyone in the broader American community.

A Native American Memorial Site

On September 26, 1971, representatives of the American Indian Society (AIS) and the Apache Nation gathered at Congressional Cemetery to dedicate a monument emplaced over the grave of Taza (ca. 1835-1876), who was the first-born son of Cochise and his successor in 1874 as an Apache chief. During summer 1876, Taza had traveled to Washington, D.C., as part of an Apache delegation to conduct peace negotiations with the U.S. government. He died of pneumonia on September 26, 1876, and was buried the next day at Congressional in a grave that remained unmarked for nearly one-hundred years, until the dedicatory ceremony in 1971. His gravestone is one of the most arresting monuments at Congressional. Based purportedly on a photograph of Taza, its power lies in the sculpted image of his head and upper shoulders.

Representatives of the American Indian Society returned to Congressional Cemetery on Memorial Day 1972, as they have in subsequent years, to visit the graves of the Native Americans interred at the site. As indicated by this and other events conducted at the burial ground, Congressional has special meaning as a place of remembrance for Native Americans.[30] The significance does not reside in the number of interments, which totals thirty-five, but on these factors: the diverse origins of those interred, who came to the U.S. capital as representatives of thirteen Native American tribes; the prominence of these individuals within their home communities, where they served variously as tribal chiefs, diplomats, jurists, and warriors, as well as in other capacities; and their reasons for coming to Washington, D.C., which were largely to negotiate treaties with the U.S. government focused on terms associated with their withdrawal from tribal lands.[31]

The Native American community at rest at Congressional comprises representatives from these tribes, with the number of burials associated with each given in parentheses: Apache (one interment), Cherokee (fourteen), Chippewa (three), Choctaw (six), Creek (two), Dakota (one), Kiowa (two), Lakota (one), Nez Perce (one), Pawnee (two), Sac and Fox (one), and Winnebago (one). The historical record of their activities in Washington, D.C., as well as their deaths in the city, is the most complete in connection with the Cherokee and the Choctaw.

As characterized by Herman J. Viola, the Cherokees were particularly "blessed" as negotiators. Educated and bilingual, they engaged in detailed, extended deliberations in English with U.S. officials. Calvin Colton (1789-1857), a journalist and the author of many books, observed that the Cherokees he met in Washington, D.C., were "well-dressed gentlemen of good manners—themselves good society for any sensible man—sitting at the publick [sic] tables throughout the City—undistinguished from the common man except it be in superior delicacy of feeling." Among other observations, he provided this assessment of William Shorey Coodey, who was later buried at Congressional, and John Ridge, another skilled Cherokee negotiator: "They actually know more of the institutions, laws, and government of the United States than a large fraction of those, who occupy a seat in the House of Representatives."[32]

Among the fourteen Cherokees interred at Congressional, four individuals—William Coodey, Ezekiel Starr, John Looney, and John Rogers, Jr.—had notable roles in events driven by deliberations over the 1835 Treaty of New Echota, which resulted in the forced relocation of the Cherokee to territory west of the Mississippi in 1838. Of the Cherokees who represented the tribe in negotiations with the U.S. federal government, Coodey was the most accomplished in that he was both a diplomat and a skilled writer.

While he had originally supported the 1835 Treaty of New Echota, as had a number of other prominent Cherokees, Coodey subsequently joined thousands of others in their opposition to this agreement, which resulted in the removal of the Cherokee Nation to designated territory in 1838. On August 28, when the first of thirteen staged removals began, Coodey drafted several letters to friends, one of whom was John Howard Payne (1791-1852), the actor and playwright who had written "Home Sweet Home" (1822). The most memorable part of the letter to Payne focused on the beginning of the enforced relocation, when nature itself seemed to participate in the unfolding tragedy: "The sun was unclouded—no rain fell—the thunder rolled away and sounds hushed in the distance. The scene[s] around and before me . . . were peculiarly impressive & singular" and were "looked upon as omens of some future event in the west."[33]

Subsequent to the relocation of the Eastern Cherokee, Coodey drafted the 1839 Act of Union Between the Eastern and Western Cherokee, which became the formative document in the reunification of the Cherokee Nation. The phrasing of this act recalls in part the U.S. Declaration of Independence, as exemplified by this statement: "We, the people composing the Eastern and Western Cherokee Nation, in national convention assembled, by virtue of our original unalienable rights, do hereby solemnly and mutually agree to form ourselves into one body politic, under the style and title of the CHEROKEE NATION."[34] During the decade that followed, Coodey held significant positions within the reconstituted Cherokee Nation, serving as president of both the Cherokee Senate and Supreme Court, as well as in other capacities. In addition, he was a prominent member of the Cherokee delegations that met regularly in Washington, D.C., with U.S. officials to negotiate in part payment for land ceded under the 1835 Treaty. He died in the federal capital on April 16, 1849, when participating in one such delegation.

The available documentation, including the narrative given in *The National Intelligencer* on April 17, 1849, provides only abbreviated commentary about his untimely death. As noted, Coodey contracted an unspecified illness when enroute to Washington, D.C., during late 1848 with his wife and their infant daughter, Charlotte. Upon hearing shortly thereafter that her father was ill, his daughter Henrietta Jane, who was at that time a music teacher at Patapsco Female Institution in Ellicott City, Maryland, visited him in his lodgings at the boarding house of one Mr. Shackelford, which was opposite the Willard Hotel in Washington, D.C. While in the city, she too became ill and then died on March 4, 1849. She was interred at Congressional Cemetery in Range 43, Site 49. Just one week later, on March 12, the baby Charlotte died and was buried with her sister in Range 43, Site 49. William Coodey expired during the following month, on April 16, 1849, and was interred next to his two daughters in Range 43, Site 50. In their proximity, the Coodey graves constitute a poignant memorial site.

The graves of three other Cherokee negotiators, John Looney, John Rogers, Jr., and Ezekiel Starr, constitute another memorial site at Congressional. They all had participated in negotiations conducted in Washington, D.C., relevant to implementation of the

1839 Act of Union Between the Eastern and Western Cherokee. Given their presence in Washington, D.C., during 1846, it is likely that they subsequently engaged in deliberations over the Cherokee Treaty of 1846, the focus of which was on realizing unification by providing, among other measures, amnesty to all fugitives if they returned to the nation by December 1, 1846, equal protection for all Cherokees under the Cherokee legal system, and trial by jury. All of them died of unknown causes in Washington, D.C., shortly before the treaty was signed on August 6—Starr on April 6, Looney on May 16, and Rogers, Jr., on June 12. They were interred at Congressional in Range 40, with Starr and Rogers in adjacent sites (90 and 91) and Looney some fifty feet distant in Site 44.

The biographies of three other Cherokees interred at Congressional—Richard Fields, James McDaniel, and Thomas Pegg—are reflective of the substantial fissures within the Cherokee Nation during the Civil War. While they all initially supported the Confederacy, McDaniel and Pegg reversed themselves in 1862 and joined the Union Army, serving as captains in Company A, 2nd Indian Home Guards. Fields, however, remained loyal to the Confederacy, affiliating himself with a unit that became the 1st Cherokee Mounted Volunteers.

Following the Civil War, representatives of both Union and Confederate factions among the Cherokee came to Washington to press their interests before the federal government. At issue was the status of the Cherokee Nation, specifically whether it should remain unified or whether it should be split into two separate nations, comprising the constituencies that had supported the Union and the Confederacy. Central among these negotiators were James McDaniel and Thomas Pegg, both of whom supported a unified Cherokee Nation. On January 15, 1866, McDaniel, Pegg, and John Ross, principal chief of the Cherokees, met with President Andrew Johnson in the White House to discuss the factors that had caused the Cherokee Nation to align itself initially with the Confederacy and then with the Union. Pegg, who was the lead negotiator, gave Johnson a lengthy handwritten document entitled "Memorial of the Delegates of the Cherokee Nation to the President of the United States and the Senate and House of Representatives in Congress." He then urged the president to read the text, which delineated the support provided by the Cherokees to the United States during the Civil War. In his concluding remarks, Pegg asked that "the Government do its duty to us" by supporting the preservation of a unified Cherokee Nation. Following this presentation, President Johnson said that he would read the "Memorial" and that the U.S. government would fulfill its responsibilities to the Cherokee. Pegg died shortly thereafter, on April 22, 1866, and was buried at Congressional Cemetery.[35]

On July 19, 1866, Cherokee representatives in Washington, D.C., including James McDaniel, signed the Cherokee Reconstruction Act of 1866, which the U.S. Senate approved the following August 11. This treaty repealed the earlier alliance with the Confederacy, abolished slavery, and, among other provisions, offered a general amnesty, thereby inviting the Confederate Cherokees, including Richard Fields, to join a united Cherokee Nation. McDaniel and Fields died in Washington, D.C., on February 1, 1868, and March 11, 1873, respectively. They were buried at Congressional in sites that were not in close proximity to each other or to the burial site of Thomas Pegg. So situated, their graves seem expressive of the large issues that had separated constituencies and threatened the existence of the Cherokee Nation during the Civil War.

Among the six Choctaws interred at Congressional, two were particularly impressive figures: Pushmataha (ca. 1764-1824), a prominent chief, warrior, and negotiator, and Peter Parker Pitchlynn (1806-1881), who was also an important chief and negotiator, as well as an educator. The monuments on their graves underscore their stature within the federal community of Washington, D.C., as well as among the Choctaw. The memorial for Pushmataha is similar to the cenotaphs emplaced at Congressional in remembrance of the congressmen who died during the nineteenth century. Pitchlynn's grave is marked by the imposing figure of an angel who is positioned atop a pedestal and who appears to be recording the names of the dead.

Inscriptions are carved in capital letters on three sides of Pushmataha's monument, which was "erected by his brother chiefs" who had participated with him in negotiations with the U.S. government in 1824, as stated on one side of the marker. The inscription on another side reads as follows: "Push-ma-ta-ha was a warrior of great distinction. He was wise in council, eloquent in an extraordinary degree, and on all occasions, and under all circumstances, the white man's friend." The first sentence in this epitaph acknowledges in part his valor during the War of 1812, when he participated with the U.S. Army in twenty-four battles, including Talladega, Holy Ground, and Pensacola.[36] He later accompanied General Andrew Jackson, who had become one of his great admirers, to New Orleans, where he was present at the decisive defeat of the British on January 8, 1815. The assertion that Pushmataha was "on all occasions . . . the white man's friend" is expressive of the politics sometimes associated with gravestone inscriptions, as will be noted below.

In 1824, the U.S. federal government had invited a Choctaw delegation to Washington, D.C., to forge an agreement that would address problems attendant upon the 1820 Treaty of Doak's Stand. This delegation included Pushmataha as well as John Pitchlynn, who served for more than four decades as a U.S. government interpreter. The new treaty they negotiated, which was ratified by Congress on January 14, 1825, established the current boundary between Oklahoma and Arkansas, directing the Choctaw Nation to relinquish to the United States all territory east of that boundary and specifying that the United States provide the Choctaw with $6,000 per annum for sixteen years and an annuity of $6,320.

Pushmataha did not witness the conclusion of this treaty, for he died at his lodgings in Tennison's Hotel shortly after midnight on December 24, 1824. According to a statement from the Quartermaster General's office, he succumbed to croup after but one day of illness and "in spite of the best medical care employed on his behalf." On his deathbed, Pushmataha had reportedly asked to see his friend General Jackson, who arrived at the hotel shortly before Pushmataha died. Just before his death, Pushmataha made this request of Jackson: "When I am dead, let the big guns be fired over me." Jackson assured that this final ceremony was accorded to his friend, whom he had described on many occasions as the "greatest Indian" of his acquaintance.[37]

Pushmataha was interred at Congressional Cemetery on Christmas Day 1824, following a funeral procession that was led by the United States Marine Band and that included members of the Choctaw delegation, as well as federal officials and "citizens of Washington." According to the December 28 issue of *The National Journal*, "at least 2,000" people joined the parade to the burial ground. During the service of interment, Marines, as directed by the Secretary of the Navy, fired "three volleys" over the new grave. Following a subsequent visit to Congressional Cemetery, John Randolph (1773-1833) of Virginia, who had served in both the House of Representatives and the Senate, said that his "attention" had been "arrested by" the monument emplaced in memory of Pushmataha: "He was, I have been told by those who knew him, one of nature's nobility, a man who would have adorned any society. He lies quietly by the side of our statesmen and high magistrates in the region" where "the Red Man and the White Man are on a level."[38]

The most expressive and durable memorial for Peter Pitchlynn is likely the portrait delineated by novelist Charles Dickens in his *American Notes*, published originally in 1842. In this two-page portrayal, Dickens said that he had met Pitchlynn by chance on the Pike steamboat when traveling along the Ohio River from Cincinnati to Louisville. The conversation that followed was open and frank, possibly in part because it occurred on what could be viewed as neutral terrain, free from everyday boundaries. Dickens was initially surprised by the sophistication of Pitchlynn, who *"sent in his card* to me," "spoke English perfectly well," "had read many books," enjoyed in particular the poetry of Sir Walter Scott, and "appeared to understand correctly all that he had read." He was also impressed with his appearance, noting that Pitchlynn "was a remarkably handsome man; some years past forty I should judge; with long black hair, an aquiline nose, broad cheek bones, a sunburnt complexion, and a very bright, keen, dark, and piercing eye."[39]

As for Pitchlynn, he seemed free on that steamboat to express doubts about the possible outcome of ongoing treaty negotiations with federal officials in Washington, D.C., and about the very continuation of the Choctaw Nation. Among other comments, he said that he had been in the federal capital during the previous seventeenth months and that the discussions between his nation and the U.S. government "were not settled yet . . . and he feared never would be." As their conversation came to an end, Dickens recalled that Pitchlynn "took his leave; as stately and complete a gentleman of Nature's making as ever I beheld; and moved among the people in the boat, another kind of being."[40]

Pitchlynn was of mixed heritage, having a father who was Scottish and a mother who was Native American. Situated between two cultures, he did not fit easily into either. Drawing upon the ambiguity of this situation, he fashioned a remarkable career, navigating the boundaries between tribal and U.S. national interests. Among other accomplishments, he participated in drafting the Choctaw constitution of 1826, established the Choctaw national school system, served as Principal Chief of the Choctaw Nation during 1864-1866, and functioned as the foremost Choctaw delegate in negotiations with the U.S. government from the early 1850s until his death in Washington, D.C. Pitchlynn's major focus as a negotiator was on the "net proceeds" claim, whereby the Choctaws alleged that the U.S. government owed the tribe $3 million for the purchase of ten million acres of Choctaw territory that had been incorporated into the State of Mississippi. He died on January 17, 1881, before this claim was resolved. Following a memorial service at the Masonic Temple in Alexandria, Virginia, his body was placed in the Public Vault at Congressional Cemetery, followed by interment at the burial ground on April 22, 1881.

While Pitchlynn did not live to see resolution of the net proceeds claim, his death propelled action on the measure. On March 1, 1881, the Senate voted in favor of the pending legislation after Augustus Hill Garland of Arkansas (1832-1899) provided recollections about Pitchlynn's long support of this action. Following an additional five years of negotiations, the United States Supreme Court determined on January 25, 1886, that the Choctaw be granted approximately $3 million for settlement of the net proceeds claim. Of this sum, Pitchlynn's family received his share, totaling approximately $107,311.[41]

In addition to the historical record associated with the Cherokee and Choctaw interred at Congressional, powerful narratives relate to other Native Americans buried at the cemetery. They focus on large matters, beginning with the causes of death, which were particularly compelling in relation to the three Chippewa and the one Santee Sioux Indian interred at the site. In abbreviated death notices published on March 19, 20, and 23, 1866, *The Evening Star* announced that the Chippewa had succumbed to black measles at the "quarters of the delegation" (B Street, near Third) on consecutive days: A-Moose, identified as "head chief of a tribe of Chippewa Indians," on March 18; St. Germain, another Chippewa chief, on March 19; and Shawbo-Wis, a member of the negotiating team, on March 20. The only additional information was given in the commentary about A-Moose, which noted in part that he had been given medical care by one Dr. Dove and a consulting physician and then stated that "the disease, it is said, is not a dangerous one when properly treated, and not likely to attack whites." Having died of the same disease, at the same boarding house, and on successive days, the Chippewa negotiators were buried together at Congressional: A-Moose in Range 53, Site 211, and St. Germain and Shawbo-Wis in 210, the adjacent site in that range.

The Santee Sioux Indian interred at Congressional was Kan-Ya-Tu-Duta (Scarlet Crow), a tribal chief who had traveled from Minnesota as part of a negotiating team. He disappeared during the evening of February 24, 1867, whereupon the Bureau of Indian Affairs offered a $100 reward for his return. A couple of weeks later, two residents of Alexandria, Virginia, discovered his body in a wooded area close to nearby Arlington. While it initially appeared that he had hung himself, the subsequent investigation indicated that he had likely been murdered. The federal government, in addition to providing the reward to those who had found the body, gave $500 in goods to the family of Scarlet Crow. In 1916, Congress appropriated $100 for a monument to be placed over his grave, which had remained unmarked during the approximately fifty years following his death. According to Edgar B. Merrit, then Commissioner of Indian Affairs, the funding was given in recognition of his service as a scout for the United States during the 1862 uprising of Sioux in Minnesota.[42]

The narratives given in *The Evening Star* also underscored the high drama associated with some of the interments of Indian negotiators at Congressional. An article published on April 6, 1863, for example, noted that O-Com-O-Cost (Yellow Wolf) was dressed for his burial by other members of the Kiowa delegation during the last minutes of his life: "About half an hour before the breath left deceased, his companions commenced to paint his face, hands and feet with red paint, and then securing new clothes and new blankets, they arrayed the dying chief in them." O-Com-O-Cost was buried at Congressional with a selection of his personal effects, including his bow and arrows, which other members of the delegation had broken in half immediately following his death. In addition, "a large silver medal" was placed in the grave. The journalist thought this action "almost ridiculous" in that President Thomas Jefferson had given this medal to "the ancestors" of the deceased and it had "been handed down from father to son since that time." It thus constituted "a connecting link between the present and the past which should be placed in charge of the Government." The Kiowa delegation had insisted otherwise, however, "and the agents do not desire to offend them by a refusal."

The Evening Star also provided memorable coverage of ceremonies attendant upon the death of Tuck-a-Lix-Ta (Owner of Many Horses) on March 29, 1858, when in Washington, D.C., as part of a Pawnee negotiating team. Narratives published on March 30 and 31 indicated that the funeral procession to Congressional was "very long and striking" and that it was inter-tribal and also included "white guests," such as the Acting Commissioner of Indian Affairs. In speeches given at the cemetery, both Pawnee and federal spokespersons addressed suspicions that people back home in tribal territory might have regarding the cause of death. Charles E. Mix, Acting Commissioner of Indian Affairs, observed that "I wish to impress upon their minds that the death of their brave was the act of the Great Spirit" and that "the Great Father will set a mark on this grave, so that if any of their braves ever come here and wish to see the spot where the young brave sleeps they can find it."

The marker emplaced by the U.S. government over the grave of Tuck-a-Lix-Ta contributes to a larger statement conveyed by the memorials positioned over the graves of the other Native Americans interred at Congressional, by commentary about their lives and deaths as given in *The National Intelligencer* and *The Evening Star*, and by Memorial Day observances conducted at the site by the American Indian Society. Viewed together, they assert that Congressional Cemetery constitutes in part a unique, important Native American memorial site.

A Quiet Harbor for Magnificent Voyagers

The winter 1985/1986 newsletter of the Association for the Preservation of Historic Congressional Cemetery included "A Quiet Harbor for Magnificent Voyagers," an article that delineated the substantial accomplishments of the U.S. Exploring Expedition of 1838-1842 conducted by the U.S. Navy in the Pacific basin. The narrative addressed in part the contributions of two individuals who were later interred at Congressional: William M. Walker (1798-1877), who was commanding officer of the expedition and captain of *Flying Fish*, one of six participating ships, and William Rich (1800-1864), the principal botanist. The title of this article, which was based on an exhibition then current at the Smithsonian Institution,[43] provides a memorable summation of Congressional Cemetery as a final resting place for both Walker and Rich and for a number of major explorers of the American frontier, foremost of whom were Henry Rowe Schoolcraft (1793-1864) and Joseph Nicollet (1786-1843).

During 1818-1819, Schoolcraft participated in an expedition down the White River into territory that is now Arkansas. He presented his observations of the surrounding terrain as well as the mineralogy in *A View of the Lead Mines of Missouri* (1819), which was the first published account of an exploration into the Ozarks. In 1821, he was the geologist in an expedition led by General Lewis Cass into the Upper Great Lakes to find in part the source of the Mississippi River. Schoolcraft published his record of this trip, which did not result in discovery of the headwater of the river, in *A Narrative Journal of Travels . . . from Detroit through the Great Chain of American Lakes to the Source of the Mississippi River* (1821). In an expedition conducted during 1832, he determined that the headwater of the Mississippi was a lake he named "Itasca," which is an adaptation of the Latin expression for "true source." Schoolcraft chronicled this journey in his *Narrative of an Expedition through the Upper Mississippi to Itasca Lake* (1834).

A critical juncture in Schoolcraft's life came a decade earlier, when President James Monroe appointed him in 1822 to the position of Indian agent in the area of Sault Ste. Marie, Michigan. He embarked there on research into Native American history and culture that eventually resulted in his six-volume *Historical and Statistical Information Respecting the History, Condition, and Prospects of the*

Indian Tribes of the United States (1851-1857). Funded in this effort by the U.S. Congress, Schoolcraft completed these volumes during his residency in the federal capital, which extended from 1847 to his death in 1864. Given his extensive, valuable research on Native American culture, it is appropriate that Schoolcraft is interred in the cemetery that serves in part as a final resting place for Native American negotiators who came to the city during the years when he was compiling his seminal study.

It is appropriate for the same reason, among others, that Joseph Nicollet was interred at Congressional. Nicollet died in Washington, D.C., on September 11, 1843, four years before Schoolcraft established his residency in Washington, D.C. The surviving documentation about the lives of these two great explorers does not indicate that they had ever met or that they corresponded. Nicollet was, however, familiar with Schoolcraft's journey to the headwaters of the Mississippi River shortly after this expedition had been concluded. During late summer or early fall 1832, for example, General Alexander Macomb, who was then commander in chief of the U.S. Army and who would himself be interred at Congressional in 1842, asked Nicollet to read a manuscript documenting Schoolcraft's 1832 expedition to Lake Itasca as drafted by Lieutenant James Allen, a young civil engineer who had participated in this journey.[44]

During 1836-1837, 1838, and 1839, Nicollet conducted his three signature expeditions, focusing primarily on territory later incorporated into Minnesota, while also proceeding into what is now North and South Dakota. In the first of these journeys, he retraced in part the course followed by Schoolcraft to the headwaters of the Mississippi. During 1838, he surveyed terrain in what is now southwestern Minnesota and southeastern South Dakota. Following the last of his great surveys, which was an exploration of the region between the Mississippi and Missouri Rivers, Nicollet proceeded to Washington, D.C., where he consolidated the data he had collected into his Map of the Hydrographical Basin of the Upper Mississippi. This map, which was published in 1843 after his death, provides exacting detail about the river channel, as well as features along the banks, including locations of Native American villages. Maintained in the Manuscript Division of the Library of Congress, Washington, D.C., this document served as a foundational chart for subsequent maps of the Midwest.[45]

The obituary published in *The National Intelligencer* on September 15, 1843, identified Nicollet as "the distinguished stranger," adding that "we regret that we know so little of the history of this distinguished man." While he was not widely recognized within the surrounding community, Nicollet was honored by his colleagues. Following a memorial service conducted on September 13, 1843, officers of the Corps of Topographical Engineers in full dress uniform provided escort as his remains were brought to Congressional Cemetery.[46]

While Schoolcraft and Nicollet mapped the upper Mississippi, four other individuals interred at Congressional had major roles in the exploration of the far western part of the United States: Charles Ludwig Preuss (1803-1854), Thomas Fitzpatrick (ca. 1799-1854), William Helmsley Emory (1811-1887), and Joseph Goldsborough Bruff (1804-1889). They are introduced below in connection with these efforts, beginning with Preuss and the great exploring expeditions led by John C. Fremont during the 1840s.

Charles Preuss, who emigrated to the United States from Germany in 1834, worked at the U.S. Coast Survey in Washington, D.C., until 1838. He subsequently secured employment as a cartographer with John C. Fremont. In his maps of 1845, 1846, and 1848, Preuss delineated the routes taken as well as geographical and cultural data collected during Fremont's expeditions of 1842, 1843-1844, and 1848. According to Carl Wheat, an authority on U.S. western maps, these documents constitute "a monument of modern cartography," given their topographical detail and exactitude, as well as their impact on westward migration.[47]

The first of these documents, entitled *Map of an Exploring Expedition to the Rocky Mountains in the Year 1842 and to Oregon & North California in the Years 1843-44*, traced the routes of Fremont's first and second expeditions. Among other information, it provided critical geographic and topographic linkage with data collected by the U.S. Exploring Expedition of 1838-1842. The Preuss map was presented in the inside back cover of Fremont's 693-page narrative of the expedition. The publishers of this document were Joseph Gales and William Seaton, who were the editors of *The National Intelligencer* and were later interred at Congressional Cemetery (see the next section of this chapter).[48]

Drawing on data collected during Fremont's expedition to Utah, Oregon, and California in 1843-1844, Preuss created his *Topographical Map of the Route from Missouri to Oregon Commencing at the Mouth of the Kansas in the Missouri River and Ending at the Mouth of the Wallah-Wallah in the Columbia*, published in 1846. This document, comprising seven sections, was detailed, printed at the scale of ten miles per inch. On the face of the map, Preuss provided notations that were directed at the anticipated needs of travelers into this new land and that focused on subjects including the topography of particular areas, sources of fuel, and water supplies. "Aimed at the wants of emigrants," this "authoritative" and "well drawn" map constituted one of the "greatest contributions to the development of the American West," noted historian William Goetzmann.[49]

Preuss completed his third map during summer 1848, shortly after news had spread from the Pacific to the Atlantic about the discovery of gold in California. Entitled "Map of Oregon and Upper California," this document delineated territory west of the Rocky Mountains. It was likely the first to provide information, abbreviated though it was, on the gold fields in California. Correctly anticipating the gold rush of 1848, the U.S. Senate ordered the printing of some 50,000 copies of this map.[50]

While Preuss has been remembered primarily for his monumental maps of the American frontier, he was also a notable diarist and artist. Erwin G. and Elisabeth K. Gudde, who translated and edited his diaries, declared that they constitute "a primary document in an important phase of our national history." Preuss wrote his diaries "on the scene," providing candid assessments on a range of topics, including the food and weather, both of which he frequently found wanting. He also sketched memorable portraits of people met along the way, including Native Americans and the so-called mountain men, one of whom was Tom Fitzpatrick, who is introduced below. Focused on these drawings, the Guddes observed that Preuss was "one of the outstanding artists of early western exploration."[51]

Thomas Fitzpatrick, who was also interred at Congressional Cemetery, was preeminent among the famed mountain men, who made significant contributions to the exploration of the American frontier from the 1820s through the 1850s. They were denizens of the white spaces on then current maps, working as fur trappers, traders, and guides in uncharted areas of the Rocky Mountains. Functioning in these capacities, they were the first line in the westward expansion of the new nation. Upon the death of Jedediah Smith (1799-1831), Fitzpatrick emerged as "chief" of the mountain men.[52] An Irish immigrant, Fitzpatrick had arrived in St. Louis, Missouri, in 1823 at the age of nineteen. He thereupon responded to an advertisement placed in the *Missouri Gazette and Public Advertiser* and the *St. Louis Enquirer* by General William H. Ashley (1778-1838) and Major Andrew Henry (ca. 1775-1832), who sought "to engage ONE HUNDRED MEN, to ascend the river Missouri to its source, there to be employed for one, two, or three years" as trappers. Retained by Ashley and Henry, Fitzpatrick worked in the area of the upper Missouri River from 1823 to the collapse of the Rocky Mountain Fur Company in 1826. During this period, he participated in an exploratory party that found an opening through the mountains that became known as the South Pass and was used by emigrants bound for Oregon and California over the next twenty years.

Fitzpatrick worked for the next four years with the successor enterprise and then beginning in 1830 with the Rocky Mountain Fur Company. Upon the demise of this firm in 1834, Fitzpatrick served as a guide during 1835-1846 for emigrant groups and government expeditions traveling across the continent. The latter included John Fremont in his second passage over the mountains to California during 1843-1844 and the Army of the West, led by General Stephen W. Kearney, in its five-hundred-mile journey from Kansas to New Mexico at the start of the Mexican War in 1846. In November 1846, President James Polk appointed Fitzpatrick as Indian agent for the Upper Platte and Arkansas Rivers and thus for tribes including the Arapaho, Cheyenne, and Shoshone. He continued in this capacity until his sudden death from pneumonia on February 7, 1854, when "on business connected with his agency," as noted by *The Evening Star* on February 8. While the writer thought that he "must have been approaching seventy years," given his appearance, Fitzgerald was then fifty-five years old.[53]

William Helmsley Emory had a major role during the 1840s and 1850s in exploring and charting new terrain along the U.S. borders. A graduate of West Point in 1831, he worked as a civil engineer with the Corps of Topographical Engineers, established in 1838. Functioning in this capacity, he conducted pioneering surveys along the Texas-Mexican border in 1844, the U.S.-Canadian border during 1844-1846, and the U.S.-Mexican border in 1848-1853, as well as for the Gadsden Purchase during 1854-1857. During the Mexican War of 1846-1848, Emory served as chief topographical engineer under General Stephen W. Kearney and traveled with the Army of the West, guided by Thomas Fitzpatrick, in its march of some five-hundred miles from Fort Leavenworth, Kansas, to Sante Fe, New Mexico, and beyond. The journey proceeded into "singular," hitherto unmapped terrain and was ultimately more important as "a geographical and scientific achievement" than as a military exercise, as noted by historian Robert Utley. Emory deserves major credit for this achievement in that he and his team made use of the "opportunity" to survey and chart a landscape that at that time was "virtually unknown to Americans."[54]

During this march to the west, Emory made daily entries in his journal about the surrounding terrain, including details about the landscape, animal and plant life, prehistoric ruins, fortifications, and Mexican settlements, primarily in areas that are now New Mexico, Arizona, and the southern part of California. He subsequently used the information to prepare his *Notes of a Military Reconnaissance from Fort Leavenworth in Missouri to San Diego in California*, which was published by the U.S. Congress in 1848. This document, as characterized by William Goetzman, is "one of the landmarks in western American cartography" in that it was the first accurate map of the area and "the final piece needed to complete the early outline of trans-Mississippi geography."[55]

Joseph Goldsborough Bruff worked as a draftsman and cartographer in Washington, D.C., for the U.S. Corps of Topographical Engineers, where William Emory was employed as an engineer. While he was likely familiar with Emory's *Notes of a Military Reconnaissance*, Bruff was particularly inspired by the reports of John C. Fremont and the accompanying maps by Charles Preuss. In his journal, he noted that he had "made duplicate drawings of all of Fremont's Reports, maps, plates, &c. for the two houses of Congress." This effort, he recalled, "revived the Spirit of adventure So long dormant [sic], and I was anxious to travel over" and visit the charted terrain, "more particularly when a golden reward appear'd to be awaiting us at the nether end of the route."[56] He thereupon resigned from his position at the Corps of Topographical Engineers to lead the Washington City and California Mining Association Expedition of 1849-1851.

During spring 1849, Bruff and sixty-three men from the greater Washington, D.C., area traveled by stage coach, train, and steamboat to St. Joseph, Missouri. From there, they proceeded west across the established central route through South Pass, along the Humboldt River through Nevada, and then across the Black Rock Desert in northwestern Nevada to the northern Sacramento Valley, which they reached in November 1849. Bruff remained in California until July 1851, during which time he found no "golden reward." His expedition was a lasting success, however, because of his drawings, which are maintained in part at the Library of Congress and Yale University Library, and his journals, which were published in 1949 and thus one-hundred years after the start of the Washington City and California Mining Association Expedition. In his monograph on the California Gold Rush, J.S. Holliday underscored the value of both the drawings, observing that they "provide a unique depiction of life on the [wagon] train and in California," and the journals, noting that they figure among "the most detailed of all 1849 diaries."[57]

Bruff, Emory, Fitzpatrick, and Preuss experienced notable success as explorers, even though their journeys were not invariably triumphant. Another of the explorers interred at Congressional—William H. Cross—is in a category of his own, in that he participated in the enormous tragedy of the Lady Franklin Bay Expedition of 1881-1884, generally remembered as the Greely (Arctic) Expedition. Its purpose was to establish a circumpolar weather station at Fort Conger in the northern part of Ellsmere Island, northeast of the Arctic Archipelago. The successes of this journey, which included the mapping of a sizable geographic area, were largely forgotten in the disaster that unfolded when supply ships failed to reach the party during the frigid summers of 1882 and 1883. When help finally did arrive during summer 1884, eighteen of the twenty-five members of this party had died of starvation and exposure. The first was machinist Sergeant Cross, who had expired on January 18, 1884, at a new base camp the group had established near Cape

Sabine in the southern part of the island. He was interred twice, once in the Arctic wilderness and later at Congressional Cemetery.

In a series of memorable articles published from July 31 through August 11, 1884, *The Evening Star* announced the death of Cross, the transport of his body and those of the other "Arctic Dead" to New York City via ship and their arrival in the harbor on August 8, the transfer of the remains of Cross via rail to Washington, D.C., on August 9, and then the funeral, conducted on August 10 at his home on 374 2nd Street SE. Beginning at 6:00 a.m. on the day of the ceremony, "there was a constant stream of people passing in and out of the house to view the casket," which was covered with an American flag and elaborate floral arrangements. At 3:30 p.m., when the service was scheduled to begin, the doors "of the little house" were closed to contain "the large number of persons who pressed for admittance." The officiating minister was Rev. C. D. Andrews of Christ Church, who spoke about Cross "as a hero of duty" who died in service to his country. Following the ceremony, the funeral procession, which was led by the Marine Corps Band and included "a long line of carriages," proceeded to Congressional Cemetery. A "large concourse of people" was waiting there to "witness the final rites" and then the second and final interment of William Cross at a site that was within walking distance of both his former home and the Washington Navy Yard, where he had worked as a machinist prior to his participation in the Greely Expedition.

In addition to the individuals profiled above, Congressional is the final resting place for others who participated in continental and oceanic expeditions. They include Frederick D. Stuart, Sr. (1811-1878), who took part in the U.S. Exploring Expedition of 1838-1842 as the personal secretary of Charles Wilkes, leader of the expedition. Wilkes was "blunt, highly opinionated and always self righteous," as characterized by Rear Admiral John D.H. Kane, Jr., in his introduction to the *Autobiography of Rear Admiral Charles Wilkes, U.S. Navy, 1798-1877*. While Wilkes wrote scathing comments about some members of the crew, he consistently praised Frederick Stuart, observing that "he had been with the Expedition on its first starting & was equal to many duties." Among other tasks, Stuart "acted as my clerk and kept the accounts and a Journal of the various employments of those engaged with me."[58] Upon conclusion of the U.S. Exploring Expedition, Stuart served as secretary of Admiral Wilkes until 1853 and then as a hydrographer in the North Pacific Exploring Expedition (1853-1856), which had been commissioned by Congress to chart the Bering Straits, North Pacific Ocean, and China Seas. Stuart was interred at Congressional following his death in Washington, D.C., on January 25, 1878.

Wilkes was interred at Arlington National Cemetery, which is the final resting place for other late nineteenth- and twentieth-century Arctic and Antarctic explorers, including Robert E. Peary and Matthew Hensen, who together discovered the North Pole, and Richard Bryd, the first to fly over both the North and South Poles. The explorers interred at Congressional made their contributions earlier, largely before the Civil War. While they included a few oceanic explorers, as noted above, they concentrated primarily on surveying and mapping the trans-Mississippi Basin and uncharted terrain extending across the continent to the Pacific Ocean. They each made singular contributions: Henry Schoolcraft, in discovering the source of the Mississippi River; Joseph Nicollet, in charting the trans-Mississippi River system as a "point of departure," he said, for future exploration westward; Charles Preuss, in mapping the overland trail from Missouri to Oregon; Thomas Fitzpatrick, in discovering with Jedediah Smith the South Pass in the Rocky Mountains and then leading the first emigrant wagon train across the continent to Oregon; Joseph Goldsborough Bruff, in providing his unique narrative and drawings of the 1849 Gold Rush; and William Emory, in delineating the topography of the southwest and surveying the trail that would become the primary route from Santa Fe to California. To retrieve the metaphor introduced earlier, these individuals were indeed "magnificent voyagers" who found at long last a "quiet harbor" in Congressional Cemetery.[59]

A Gathering Place for Other Notable Individuals

Congressional is the also final resting place for many others who made substantive contributions on the national level. They constitute an eclectic assemblage, including journalists, artists, and political activists. Working in their various capacities, they established the first national newspaper in the new federal city, campaigned to secure equal rights for women, and captured indelible images of the nation in various artistic media, among other accomplishments. This section focuses on the contributions of journalists Joseph Gales, Jr. (1786-1860), William Seaton (1785-1866), and Anne Royall (1769-1854); photographer Mathew Brady (1822-1897); lawyer and activist Belva Lockwood (1830-1917); sculptor Adelaide Johnson (1859-1955); and maestro John Philip Sousa (1854-1932).

Joseph Gales and William Seaton have long been remembered in connection with *The National Intelligencer*, the first national political newspaper published in the United States. Founded by Samuel H. Smith in Washington, D.C., during 1800, the periodical was owned and edited by Gales during 1810-1812, Gales and Seaton from 1812 until Gales death in 1860, and then by Seaton until 1864, when he sold the newspaper. *The National Intelligencer* supported the administrations of Thomas Jefferson (1801-1809), James Madison (1809-1817), and James Monroe (1817-1825) and was widely viewed as "the semiofficial organ of the federal government during those years," as noted by historian William E. Ames. Given their understanding that Gales and Seaton had special access to the U.S. government, the editors of some six-hundred newspapers across the nation provided verbatim reproductions of articles that had originally appeared *The National Intelligencer*.[60]

As guided by Gales and Seaton, *The National Intelligencer* offered detailed coverage of major congressional debates, the deliberations of successive U.S. presidents and their respective cabinets, and significant events in the federal city, including ceremonies attendant upon the deaths of national figures. Alexander K. McClure, who established *The Philadelphia Times* in 1875, addressed the quality of the publication in his "Random Recollections of Half a Century," published in *The Washington Post* on July 28, 1901: "It was the most delectable of all the great papers ever published in this country. It had all the dignity of the *London Times*, tempered and embellished with a degree of vigor and progress which made it quite as highly respected in the New World as the *London Times* in the Old World...." Given its singular coverage of life and death in the federal capital during the antebellum period, *The National Intelligencer* constituted an invaluable resource for this study of Congressional Cemetery.

Anne Royall was also a pioneering, albeit a controversial journalist in Washington, D.C., during the antebellum period. In the two newspapers she established in the federal city — *Paul Pry* (1831-1836) and *The Huntress* (1836-1854) — she vigorously exposed corruption and waste in the U.S. government and elsewhere. While she published her periodical using type provided by *The National Intelligencer*, she did not share the ready access Gales and Seaton had to government officials. Royall was, in sum, an accomplished and unconventional woman who was born considerably before her time, as indicated by abbreviated commentary given in *The Evening Star* of October 2, 1854, in announcing her death the preceding day at her residence on Capitol Hill. The lead statement identified her as "eccentric," noting that "to the hour of her death she preserved all the peculiarities of thought, temper, and manners, which at one time rendered her so famous throughout the land."

Following her burial at Congressional on October 2, 1854, the grave of Anne Royall remained unmarked until May 12, 1911, when a monument was emplaced in her memory. The coverage of this event, as given the next day in *The Evening Star* and *The Washington Post*, revealed that Anne Royall had found an appreciative audience at long last. *The Evening Star* noted, for example, that she had been "known as the pioneer woman publicist, a newspaper writer and author of books of travel in the United States" and that "several scores of men and women mindful of her sterling qualities" had gathered around her grave to dedicate "a rugged granite monument to her memory." The memorial was inscribed with this statement: "Anne Royall, Pioneer Woman Publicist, 1769-1854." The dedicatory ceremony included several speeches, one of which was delivered by Sarah Harvey Porter, author of *The Life and Times of Anne Royall*, which was published in 1909 as the first biography of the deceased. As noted in *The Evening Star* of May 13, 1911, this volume had "aroused an interest in her life and writings," thereby creating momentum for the ceremony conducted at the grave of Anne Royal fifty-seven years after her death.

Mathew Brady, who was interred at Congressional on January 18, 1896, provided concise images in his black and white photographs that complemented the discursive portrayals of people and events given in the narratives drafted by Joseph Gales, Jr., William Seaton, and Anne Royall. In his *Reading American Photographs* (1989), Alan Trachtenberg accorded him high praise, identifying Brady "as a founding figure in American photography" and asserting that "more than any other American, Brady shaped the role of the photographer as a national historian." He stated as well that Brady's *Gallery of Illustrious Americans* (1850) was "the first ambitious photographic project to take America itself as a subject and a theme" and that the volume made a significant "national gesture" at a time of deepening sectional divide by presenting images of both Democrats and Whigs.[61] The daguerrotypes included portraits of national leaders who had participated in numerous funeral processions to Congressional Cemetery, such as Presidents Zachary Taylor and Millard Fillmore; Senators John Calhoun, Henry Clay, and Daniel Webster; as well as General Winfield Scott.

The Civil War images captured by the Brady Studio, particularly by Alexander Gardner and Timothy O'Sullivan, had a powerful impact on the broader American public, as exemplified by reactions to photographs taken at Antietam on September 17, 1862. On October 18, 1862, *Harper's Weekly* published engraved versions of selected pictures, which constituted "the first graphic battlefield images, with bodies, published in this magazine," as noted by historian Mary Panzer.[62] *The New York Times* observed on October 20 that these images brought "home to us the terrible reality and earnestness of war" and that Brady, "if he has not brought bodies and laid them in our door-yards and along the streets . . . has done something very like it."

Two days after his death in New York City on January 16, 1896, Brady was interred at Congressional Cemetery which, as noted previously, served in part as the place of burial for many Civil War veterans. He was buried next to his wife, Juliette Handy Brady, who had died in 1887, and in close proximity to the graves of other members of the Handy family. Levin C. Handy, a prominent photographer based in Washington, D.C., had a large role in preserving the photographic legacy of Mathew Brady. Upon Brady's death, Handy became owner of a substantial number of Brady's negatives, which he maintained until his own death and burial at Congressional Cemetery in 1932. Thereupon his daughters, Alice H. Cox and Mary Evans, preserved the negatives until 1954, when they sold what became known as the Brady-Handy Collection to the Library of Congress. As identified by the Library of Congress, this collec-

tion comprises some 10,000 "original, duplicate, and copy negatives" of images captured by Brady during and following the Civil
War, as well as a limited number of photographs depicting life in
Washington, D.C. The National Archives also maintains a total of
6,176 Brady photographs, including Civil War images. It is fitting
that these substantial collections are maintained at federal archival
facilities located within walking distance of Brady's grave at Congressional Cemetery.

Among the images of other notable Americans, the Brady-
Handy Collection at the Library of Congress includes the original
of a photograph taken by Mathew Brady of Belva Lockwood (1830-
1917), who was interred at Congressional twenty-one years following the burial of Brady. Born and educated in New York, Lockwood
moved to Washington, D.C., in 1866. She subsequently became one
of the first women to study law in the United States, gaining admission to the National University Law School in 1870 after rejections
on the basis of gender from Columbia College (later George Washington University), Georgetown University, and Howard University. Thereafter, she became one of the first women admitted to
the Bar of the Supreme Court of the District of Columbia, securing
this privilege on September 14, 1873; the first woman admitted to
the U.S. Supreme Court Bar, a right she gained on March 3, 1879;
and the first female candidate for president of the United States,
serving as nominee of the Equal Rights Party in 1884 and 1888. In
both campaigns, Lockwood promoted female suffrage, observing
in 1884, for example, that "there are only 10,500,000 male voters in
the country to 12,500,000 adult women tax-payers" and that "this
country is supposed to be governed by the will of the majority." Of
her two presidential campaigns, Lockwood was more successful in
1884, securing 4,149 votes in six states. In addition, Indiana's elec-
tors requested and were subsequently denied the right to transfer
to Lockwood the votes they had originally given to Grover Cleveland. Lockwood declared that she was more pleased with this request than by anything else in her 1884 presidential bid.[63]

In 1906, when she was seventy-six years old, Lockwood waged
one of her last battles on behalf of the Eastern and Emigrant Cherokees, who had not received financial compensation from the U.S.
government for land ceded in North Carolina, Georgia, and Ten-

nessee. In statements before the Supreme Court, she declared in part that she had "personal knowledge of these people, having visited them in their homes, and represented about six thousand of them by individual or family powers of attorney." She prevailed in her argument, securing a settlement of approximately $5 million for her clients[64] and thereby realizing an end pursued by Cherokee negotiators interred at Congressional in 1846.

Following her death in Washington, D.C., on May 19, 1917, Lockwood was eulogized by prominent suffragists on May 22 at Wesley Methodist Episcopal Church, where she had long been a member.[65] She was buried at Congressional Cemetery next to her second husband, Ezekiel Lockwood, who had been interred on May 26, 1877. In "My Efforts To Become a Lawyer," published in *Lippincott's Monthly Magazine* during February 1888, Lockwood had observed that "I have not raised the dead, but I have awakened the living," a statement that could well serve as her epitaph.

A similar statement could have been inscribed on the tombstone of sculptor Adelaide Johnson (1859-1955), who had much in common with Belva Lockwood. While Lockwood had campaigned for female suffrage, Johnson memorialized prominent suffragists in weighty stone monuments. She has been remembered most for her *Memorial to the Pioneers of the Women's Suffrage Movement* (1921), later known as the *Portrait Monument to Lucretia Mott, Elizabeth Cady Stanton, and Susan B. Anthony*. The National Women's Party commissioned this memorial to commemorate ratification on August 18, 1920, of the nineteenth amendment, stating that "the right of citizens of the United States to vote shall not be denied or abridged by the United States or by any State on account of sex." The monument features portrait busts of Mott, Stanton, and Anthony emerging from a 7.5-ton block of white Carrara marble. The portraits are copies of individual busts Johnson had sculpted for the Court of Honor of the Women's Building at the 1893 World's Columbia Exhibition in Chicago.[66]

The presentation ceremony for the monument was conducted in the Rotunda of the U.S. Capitol on February 15, 1921, the centennial anniversary of the birth of Susan B. Anthony. Representatives from more than seventy-five women's groups attended the event, which was presided over by Jane Addams, founder of Hull House.

Frederick H. Gillett, Speaker of the House of Representatives, accepted the monument on behalf of Congress, declaring that the sculpture was "symbolic of a change of tremendous significance which has just occurred, the admission of women into our electorate as equal partners in the great business of government." Two days later, the monument was removed to the Capitol Crypt, where it remained for the next seventy-five years. In September 1996, following decades of pressure exerted by the Woman Suffrage Statue Campaign, the U.S. Congress adopted House Concurrent Resolution 216, directing the relocation of the memorial at long last to the Capitol Rotunda. On May 11, 1996, which was Mother's Day, Johnson's monument was returned to the Rotunda, where it remains. The event was commemorated in a rededication ceremony conducted on the following June 26.

Adelaide Johnson died in Washington, D.C., on November 10, 1955, some forty years before the return of her sculpture to the Capitol Rotunda. The obituary provided in *The Evening Star* on November 11, 1955, noted that the vestry of Christ Church had given a burial plot at Congressional Cemetery to the Adelaide Johnson Foundation "in honor of Mrs. Johnson." As indicated, the foundation "had planned to buy the land there as a final resting place for Mrs. Johnson because they felt this cemetery," which is the burial place of "many great Americans who were alive during her" long life, "was the 'one she belonged in.'"[67]

This section draws toward a close with John Philip Sousa (1854-1932), who was the last and most prominent of the seven leaders of the U.S. Marine Corps Band interred at Congressional Cemetery.[68] A native son of Capitol Hill, he was born at 636 G Street SE in a house that was in the same city block as Christ Church (third home east of the church) and that was two blocks from the Marine Barracks and nine blocks from the burial ground. During 1880-1892, Sousa directed the Marine Corps Band, which had been established in Philadelphia by an Act of Congress signed into law by President John Adams on July 11, 1798, and then moved to Washington, D.C., with the federal government in 1800. In 1892, he organized the Sousa Band, which he directed for the next forty years, until his death while on concert tour.

The Marine Corps Band gained recognition early on as The

President's Own, having been created to provide music for presidential functions. When Sousa began his tenure as director, he stated that "the Marine Band is virtually the National Band and the band that should be great among bands as America is among nations."[69] He proceeded to compose and then lead The President's Own in playing the great marches that established its reputation as the national band. Among these compositions are "Semper Fidelis" (1888), the official march of the U.S. Marine Corps, and "The Stars and Stripes Forever" (1896), which became the national march of the United States on December 11, 1987, when President Ronald Reagan signed legislation providing it with this status.

Sousa died of a heart attack on March 6, 1932, a few hours after presiding over a band rehearsal in Reading, Pennsylvania. The last piece he conducted during that rehearsal was "The Stars and Stripes Forever." In addition to this signature composition and "Semper Fidelis," Sousa wrote 133 other marches, 70 songs, and 15 operettas. In his essay "John Philip Sousa and the Culture of Reassurance," Neil Harris focused on the significance of the Sousa marches, observing that they "remain a major national treasure, disciplined statements of national exuberance as unmistakably American as the Strauss waltz is Viennese" and that Sousa as the originator and the famed conductor of these compositions "was an authentic cultural hero."[70]

Sousa was eulogized in a funeral that underscored the alliances he had cherished throughout his life. From 3:00 to 10:00 p.m. on March 9, his body lay in state at the Marine Band Auditorium, Marine Barracks, where his funeral began at 3:00 p.m. the next day with Reverend Edward Gabler, rector of Christ Church, and Sidney K. Evans, Chief Chaplain of the U.S. Navy, as the officiating clergy. After the service, as eight white horses drew the black caisson to Congressional Cemetery, the Marine Band played Sousa's "Semper Fidelis" in dirge tempo, along with other of his compositions. Following a brief graveside ceremony, which concluded with a salute by a Navy firing squad and "Taps" offered by a Marine bugler, Sousa was laid to rest in a site that is now marked by a tablet inscribed with a familiar phrase from "The Stars and Stripes Forever."[71] Every November 6, the date of his birth, a delegation from the Marine Corps Band plays a selection of Sousa marches at his grave.

Sousa is surrounded at Congressional Cemetery by many members of both his family[72] and the U.S. Marine Corps Band. Pre-eminent among the other six band leaders interred at the site is Francis Maria Scala (1819-1903), who enjoyed the longest tenure as conductor, serving for sixteen years (1855-1871). Among his other achievements, Scala increased the size of the organization from ten to approximately thirty-five musicians, balanced the traditional brass instrumentation by incorporating woodwinds, and established close relationships with various U.S. presidents, particularly with "my friend" Abraham Lincoln.[73] In addition to the seven leaders of the U.S. Marine Corps Band, twenty-one musicians within the organization are interred at Congressional. A participant in the Sousa Band – cornetist Herbert L. Clarke (1867-1945) – is also buried at the site. A brilliant technician and stylist, he was a commanding presence within the organization for nearly twenty-five years, serving as premier soloist and assistant conductor. Shortly before his death, he asked that he be buried as close as possible to Sousa. His grave, about thirty feet from that of his friend, is marked by a monument bearing this inscription: "World's Premier Cornetist and Bandmaster."[74]

Viewed in sum, across the entirety of the community at rest, Congressional Cemetery is not only the first but also a unique national burial ground. Commentators, including Quartermaster General Henry Gibbins, have long accorded it national status by focusing on the top federal and military figures interred at the site. In his 1939 report to Congress, Gibbins observed, for example, that Congressional was the final resting place not only "of the patriots who guided the destiny of the Nation" but also of the military men who "defended it on land and sea."[75] The prominent federal and military leaders are a vital but not the only part of the equation that makes Congressional a unique national burial ground. The other part comprises everyone else, including prominent Native Americans, western explorers, and artists, as well as individuals who have not been remembered in historical studies. Congressional claims our attention not only because it was the first national cemetery or because it is the final resting place for many prominent individuals. Congressional is a national cemetery because the community at rest represents all sectors within the broader population.

IMAGES OF
THE HISTORIC SITE

Main Entrance to the Burial Ground
The main gate to Congressional Cemetery in Washington, D.C., provides
entrance to an historic site that was established by a local congregation in
1807 and that is rich in national memory and meaning extending from the
early nineteenth century to the present.
Photograph Courtesy of Abby Arthur Johnson

Christ Church, 1918
Christ Church, an Episcopalian parish on Capitol Hill, was founded in 1794. The congregation owned and managed Congressional Cemetery from 1812 to 1976, when it transferred operation of the burial ground to the Association for the Preservation of Congressional Cemetery.
Photograph Courtesy of Christ Church

Architectural Drawing of a Monument for Vice President George Clinton, 1812
In this first image of the burial ground, Benjamin Henry Latrobe included memorials in the background that prefigure the monuments he later designed for placement at the graves of the members of Congress interred at Congressional Cemetery.
Watercolor Drawing: Courtesy of the Prints and Photographs Division, Library of Congress

Benjamin Henry Latrobe, Ca. 1815
Born in England during 1764, Latrobe came to the United States in 1796 to pursue a career in architecture. After establishing his reputation in this field, he served as Architect of the Capitol from 1815 to 1817. During that time, he designed memorials for members of Congress that became known as the congressional cenotaphs.
Rembrandt Peale Portrait: Courtesy of the Maryland Historical Society

Captain Thomas Tingey
Tingey was one of the founders of the cemetery who purchased land for the burial ground in 1807 and then transferred control of the site to Christ Church in 1812. He became the first Commandant of the Washington Navy Yard in 1804 and served with distinction in this capacity until his death in 1829.
John Trumbull Portrait (1820): Courtesy of the Art Gallery Collection, Naval Historical Center

Iron Fence and Walkway to the Public Vault
The iron fence along the northern boundary of the cemetery replicates the fence that originally encircled the U.S. Capitol grounds. Christ Church purchased the fence in 1857 and added it to the existing brick wall around the cemetery. Today, the gate shown here opens to the same walkway used to reach the Public Vault during the funeral processions for Presidents William Harrison, John Quincy Adams, and Zachary Taylor.
James W. Rosenthal Photograph: Courtesy of the Prints and Photographs Division, Library of Congress

Public Vault
During 1833-1834, Congress funded construction of the Public Vault for temporary interments. In its century of use, the remains of an estimated 4,600 individuals, including U.S. presidents, senators, and representatives, were placed there until arrangements were made for permanent burial sites.
Photograph Courtesy of Abby Arthur Johnson

Vice President
George Clinton

The first state funeral procession to Congressional Cemetery was staged following the death of Vice President George Clinton on April 20, 1812. The parade included representatives from all branches of the federal government, foremost of whom was President James Madison. Military units as well as numerous local citizens also joined the procession.

John Chester Buttre Portrait: Courtesy of the Prints and Photographs Division, Library of Congress

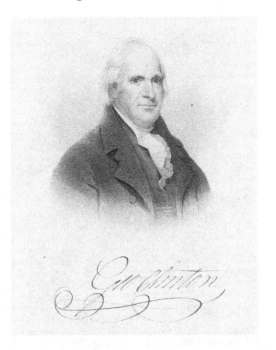

Vice President
Elbridge Gerry

Elbridge Gerry, the fifth vice president of the United States, died on November 23, 1814. The ceremonies attendant upon the interments of Vice Presidents Gerry and Clinton contributed to the emerging status of Congressional Cemetery as the national burial ground.

James Bogle Portrait, after John Vanderlyn, 1861: Courtesy of Independence National Historical Park, Philadelphia

PRESIDENT HARRISON'S FUNERAL DIRGE

As performed on the occasion of his burial at

Washington City,

April, 1841.

Composed by

HENRY DIELMAN.

Price 25 Cts. Nett.

Philadelphia. OSBOURN'S MUSIC SALOON, 30 S. Fourth St.

President Harrison's Funeral Dirge

The first U.S. president to die in office, William Henry Harrison was remembered in an elaborate state funeral and a lengthy procession to Congressional Cemetery for temporary interment at the site. Shown above, the cover of the Henry Dielman dirge dramatizes the departure of the funeral parade from the White House on the way to the burial ground.

Sinclair's Lithography, Philadelphia: Courtesy of the Franklin D. Roosevelt Presidential Library, Hyde Park, New York

The Death of John Quincy Adams
In this Currier & Ives lithograph, the former U.S. president and member of the House of Representatives is surrounded by fellow legislators after collapsing on the House floor during the afternoon of February 21, 1848. He remained in the Capitol, unable to be moved, prior to his death two days later.
Lithograph, N. Currier: Courtesy of the Currier & Ives Foundation

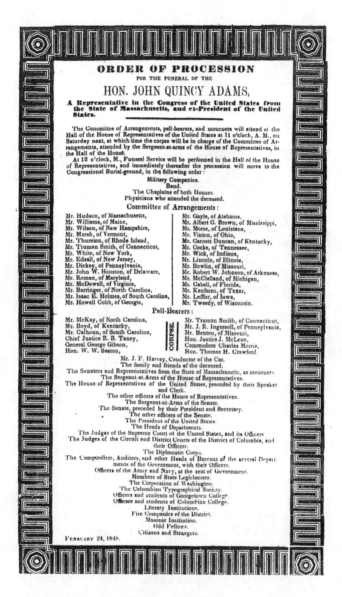

ORDER OF PROCESSION
FOR THE FUNERAL OF THE
HON. JOHN QUINCY ADAMS,
A Representative in the Congress of the United States from the State of Massachusetts, and ex-President of the United States.

The Committee of Arrangements, pall-bearers, and mourners will attend at the Hall of the House of Representatives of the United States at 11 o'clock, A. M., on Saturday next, at which time the corpse will be in charge of the Committee of Arrangements, attended by the Sergeant-at-arms of the House of Representatives, in the Hall of the House.

At 12 o'clock, M., Funeral Service will be performed in the Hall of the House of Representatives, and immediately thereafter the procession will move to the Congressional Burial-ground, in the following order:

Military Companies.
Band.
The Chaplains of both Houses.
Physicians who attended the deceased.

Committee of Arrangements:

Mr. Hudson, of Massachusetts,	Mr. Gayle, of Alabama,
Mr. Williams, of Maine,	Mr. Albert G. Brown, of Mississippi,
Mr. Wilson, of New Hampshire,	Mr. Morse, of Louisiana,
Mr. Marsh, of Vermont,	Mr. Vinton, of Ohio,
Mr. Thurston, of Rhode Island,	Mr. Garnett Duncan, of Kentucky,
Mr. Truman Smith, of Connecticut,	Mr. Cocke, of Tennessee,
Mr. White, of New York,	Mr. Wick, of Indiana,
Mr. Edsall, of New Jersey,	Mr. Lincoln, of Illinois,
Mr. Dickey, of Pennsylvania,	Mr. Bowlin, of Missouri,
Mr. John W. Houston, of Delaware,	Mr. Robert W. Johnson, of Arkansas,
Mr. Roman, of Maryland,	Mr. McClelland, of Michigan,
Mr. McDowell, of Virginia,	Mr. Cabell, of Florida,
Mr. Barringer, of North Carolina,	Mr. Kaufman, of Texas,
Mr. Isaac E. Holmes, of South Carolina,	Mr. Leffler, of Iowa,
Mr. Howell Cobb, of Georgia,	Mr. Tweedy, of Wisconsin.

Pall-Bearers:

Mr. McKay, of North Carolina,		Mr. Truman Smith, of Connecticut,
Mr. Boyd, of Kentucky,		Mr. J. R. Ingersoll, of Pennsylvania,
Mr. Calhoun, of South Carolina,	CORPSE	Mr. Benton, of Missouri,
Chief Justice R. B. Taney,		Hon. Justice J. McLean,
General George Gibson,		Commodore Charles Morris,
Hon. W. W. Seaton,		Hon. Thomas H. Crawford.

Mr. J. F. Harvey, Conductor of the Car.
The family and friends of the deceased.
The Senators and Representatives from the State of Massachusetts, as mourners.
The Sergeant-at-Arms of the House of Representatives.
The House of Representatives of the United States, preceded by their Speaker and Clerk.
The other officers of the House of Representatives.
The Sergeant-at-Arms of the Senate.
The Senate, preceded by their President and Secretary.
The other officers of the Senate.
The President of the United States.
The Heads of Departments.
The Judges of the Supreme Court of the United States, and its Officers.
The Judges of the Circuit and District Courts of the District of Columbia, and their Officers.
The Diplomatic Corps.
The Comptrollers, Auditors, and other Heads of Bureaus of the several Departments of the Government, with their Officers.
Officers of the Army and Navy, at the seat of Government.
Members of State Legislatures.
The Corporation of Washington.
The Columbian Typographical Society.
Officers and students of Georgetown College.
Officers and students of Columbian College.
Literary Institutions.
Fire Companies of the District.
Masonic Institution.
Odd Fellows.
Citizens and Strangers.

FEBRUARY 24, 1848.

Adams Funeral Procession, February 24, 1848
The funeral for John Quincy Adams took place in the U.S. Capitol and was followed by a formal procession to Congressional Cemetery for the temporary interment of his remains. His casket was accompanied to the burial ground by, among others, President James K. Polk, members of Congress, Supreme Court justices, military leaders, and civic organizations, as well as residents of and visitors to Washington, D.C.
Broadside Courtesy of the Architect of the Capitol

A Visit to the Cemetery, ca. 1850
Memorial cards, like funeral procession broadsides, were circulated
frequently during the nineteenth century as a way of honoring the
deceased. The individuals depicted in this card are pausing near the
cenotaph emplaced in memory of John Quincy Adams.
Memorial Card, ca. 1850: Courtesy of the D.C. Public Library, Washingtoniana Division

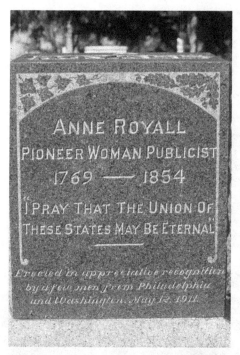

Anne Royall Headstone
Anne Royall (1769-1854) was a travel writer, a journalist, and the publisher of two newspapers issued in Washington, D.C.: *Paul Pry* and *The Huntress*. Her interview of President John Quincy Adams was the first conducted by a female reporter of a U.S. president. She was criticized, however, for her sharply worded critique of Adams, as well as other political leaders.
Photograph Courtesy of Abby Arthur Johnson

Robert Mills Memorial
Mills designed the Washington Monument, Treasury Building, and U.S. Patent Office Building. He did not, however, gain due recognition for these accomplishments during his life. In 1936, eight decades after his death, this tombstone was emplaced at his gravesite. President Franklin D. Roosevelt endorsed this initiative as a "belated tribute" to Mills architectural legacy.
Photograph Courtesy of Abby Arthur Johnson

Mathew Brady Headstone

Brady (ca. 1822-1896) had a major role in documenting Civil War battles and in advancing the development of photography in the United States. Buried at Congressional Cemetery, his remains lie in close proximity to the substantial collections of his prints at the Library of Congress and National Archives.

Photograph by James W. Rosenthal: Courtesy of the Prints and Photographs Division, Library of Congress

Emma Lewis Headstone

The African Americans buried at Congressional Cemetery are limited in number. The headstones for Emma Lewis and others offer moving testimony, however, relevant to the lives of those who lived in the shadow of slavery and racial segregation.

Photograph Courtesy of Abby Arthur Johnson

Taza, Son of Cochise; Headstone
Taza is one of thirty-five Native Americans interred at Congressional Cemetery. Representing twelve tribes, their presence contributes significantly to its status as a burial ground for all Americans.
Photograph Courtesy of Abby Arthur Johnson

General Alexander Macomb Monument
Alexander Macomb succeeded Jacob J. Brown as general-in-chief of the U.S. Army, serving in this capacity from 1828 until his death in 1841. Like his predecessor, he was interred at Congressional Cemetery with full military honors. His tombstone is a reminder that Congressional Cemetery functioned in part as the first military cemetery during the antebellum period.
Photograph Courtesy of Abby Arthur Johnson

The Arsenal Monument
This monument honors the lives of twenty-one young women who died in an explosion at the Washington Arsenal in 1864. Following a funereal parade to the burial ground led by President Abraham Lincoln and other federal officials, thousands crowded into the cemetery. The memorial was emplaced during the following year.
Photograph Courtesy of Abby Arthur Johnson

CONGRESSIONAL CEMETERY.

Monuments at Congressional Cemetery
This illustration, which appeared in John B. Ellis' *The Sights and Secrets of the National Capital* (1869), reflects public understanding of the burial ground as a site of national memory.
Engraving by Harper and Brothers

Victorian Motif: The Comforting Hand

A number of the monuments and headstones at Congressional Cemetery are decorated with Victorian motifs. The above image shows a hand holding a basket of flowers, an image associated with both the beauty and the frailty of life.

Photograph Courtesy of Abby Arthur Johnson

John Philip Sousa Memorial

Among the 136 marches composed by John Philip Sousa (1854-1932) is "The Stars and Strips Forever," the official march of the United States. Every year on the date of his birth, November 6, the Marine Corps Band convenes at Sousa's grave and plays a selection of his compositions.

Photograph Courtesy of the Carol M. Highsmith Archive, Prints and Photographs Division, Library of Congress

Myra Summers Gravestone
In the late afternoon sun, this dignified statue marking the grave of Myra Summers (1893-1910) makes a quiet statement with her eyes closed, head bent slightly to the ground. The inexorable passage of time is evident in the statue's condition, especially in the blurred facial features.
Photograph Courtesy of Abby Arthur Johnson

Angelic Recorder
The angel in this Victorian monument inscribes the name of the deceased in the Book of Life where all who are destined for heaven are listed. Impressed by monuments such as the above, architectural historian James M. Goode observed in 1974 that Congressional Cemetery had the "most historic collection of funeral sculpture" in Washington, D.C.
Photograph Courtesy of Abby Arthur Johnson

Elbridge Gerry Tomb
This photograph by E.B. Thompson features the tombstone for Elbridge
Gerry, Vice President in the administration of James Madison. The epitaph
provides Gerry's admonition that "It is the duty of every citizen, though he
may have but one day to live, to devote that day to the good of his country." Thompson took this and the following two photographs in 1913.
Photograph Courtesy of the D.C. Public Library, Washingtoniana Division

William Wirt Memorial
William Wirt (1772-1834) served as U.S. Attorney General during 1817-1829, thereby establishing a record for the longest tenure in this position. In 1832, he was the unsuccessful candidate of the Anti Masonic Party for the U.S. presidency. In the above photograph of the Wirt memorial, E.B. Thompson also provided a view of the old slate walkway to the Public Vault.
Photograph Courtesy of the D.C. Public Library, Washingtoniana Division

The Oldest Cenotaphs
Benjamin Latrobe designed the cenotaphs in 1817. The date of their initial emplacement at the cemetery is not known, although the first documented sightings occurred three years later. In this image, E.B. Thompson shows the deterioration of some of the older memorials.
Photograph Courtesy of the D.C. Public Library, Washingtoniana Division

Original Gatehouse
This structure was both the residence of and the office for the cemetery keeper from 1832 to 1923, when it was replaced by the current gatehouse. Among other features, the photograph shows the bell tower that was originally tolled for every burial at the cemetery.
Photograph Courtesy of the D.C. Public Library, Washingtoniana Division

Burial Site for Victims of the Wawaset Disaster, 1913
On August 8, 1873, the steamboat Wawaset, with about 110 passengers on board, caught fire and sank in the Potomac River south of Washington, D.C. As reported in *The Evening Star* on August 9, "the steamer was entirely destroyed" and some "fifty lives" were lost. Among the deceased were "Policeman Reed of South Washington" and "his entire family," all of whom were interred at Congressional Cemetery.
Photograph Courtesy of the D.C. Public Library, Washingtoniana Division

Monuments of National Memory
Beginning in the 1830s, increasing numbers of congressional cenotaphs
were emplaced at the burial ground in memory of individual members
of Congress who died in office. This 1913 photograph by E.B. Thompson
documents the imposing presence of the federal government at Congressional Cemetery.
Photograph Courtesy of the D.C. Public Library, Washingtoniana Division

The Chapel

Constructed in 1903 at the central nexus of the cemetery, the chapel provided a compelling site for funeral services and gatherings. This 1913 photograph by E.B. Thompson documents the presence of horse-drawn hearses at that time. A sign on the Main Gate stated that automobiles were not allowed inside the burial ground.

Photograph Courtesy of the D.C. Public Library, Washingtonian Division

General Montgomery C. Meigs
As Quartermaster General of the Army during 1861-1882, Meigs had a primary role in the establishment of Arlington National Cemetery. He envisioned a national burial ground for the interments of both civilians and military personnel and urged that Arlington be modeled on Congressional Cemetery
Photograph Courtesy of the Prints and Photographs Division, Library of Congress

Major General Henry Gibbins
Henry Gibbins, Quartermaster General of the Army during 1936-1940, ordered a study of Congressional Cemetery to identify military personnel interred at the site. In the preface to the report, which he presented in Congress in 1939, Gibbins stated that "in reality, the Congressional Cemetery was the first National Cemetery created by the Government."
Photograph Courtesy of the U.S. Army Quartermaster Foundation, Fort Lee, Virginia.

Vandalized Monument
The general decline of Congressional Cemetery after World War II, particularly during the 1960s and 1970s, led to increased vandalism at the cemetery. This statue of a young girl exemplifies the damage done to individual monuments and to the cemetery as a revered historic site.
Photograph Courtesy of Abby Arthur Johnson

Standing Watch
In 1979, the Association for the Preservation of Historic Congressional Cemetery hosted an exhibit of Elise Forbes Pachter's photographs of the burial ground. In this image, Pachter captured both the beauty of selected monuments and the deterioration of the landscape.
Photograph Courtesy of Congressional Cemetery

Shadow on the Monument
The photography of Elise Forbes Pachter made a compelling statement that Congressional Cemetery had priceless funereal art but that this legacy was jeopardized by deterioration of the burial ground. The shadow on the obelisk conveys a powerful message in this image.
Photograph Courtesy of Congressional Cemetery

Cemetery in Crisis
In 1978, journalist Brian C. Kates visited Congressional Cemetery and later published "Forgotten Heritage" in the June 1978 issue of *American Cemetery*. His article, accompanied by photographs, delineated in stark terms the challenges confronted by the Association for the Preservation of Historic Congressional Cemetery.
Photograph Courtesy of American Cemetery Magazine

Volunteers in Action, 2005
Led by professional conservators, volunteer members of the Conservation Task Force repair, clean, and reset headstones at Congressional Cemetery. Volunteers from this organization and others have made substantial contributions to restoration projects at the burial ground.
Photograph Courtesy of Congressional Cemetery

John P. Saylor
In 1973, John P. Saylor, Representative of the 12th District of Pennsylvania, introduced legislation in Congress that would require the federal government to assume ownership of Congressional Cemetery. While this effort failed, it helped build momentum in Congress to increase funding for the restoration of federal monuments at the burial ground.
Photograph Courtesy of Special Collections and Archives, Indiana University of Pennsylvania

Corinne Claiborne (Lindy) Boggs
Lindy Boggs was an energetic advocate of federal support for Congressional Cemetery during 1973-1991, when she was a member of the House of Representatives, and she continues to support the burial ground. The above photograph shows Lindy Boggs holding a photograph of her grandaughter Rebecca Roberts, who is now an active member of the Association for the Preservation of Historic Congressional Cenetery.
Photograph Courtesy of the Roberts Family

A Cenotaph for Representative Hale Boggs
On May 19, 1981, Representative Lindy Boggs and her family, along with federal officials, dedicated a cenotaph in memory of her husband, who died in 1972 when traveling in Alaska. This cenotaph, the most recent of those emplaced at the burial ground, underscores the legacy of Congressional Cemetery as the first national cemetery in the United States.
Photograph Courtesy of the Architect of the Capitol

PART THREE

PRESERVATION OF THE LEGACY

5

KEEPERS OF THE LEGACY

John Clagett Proctor (1867-1956) contributed a series of articles to *The Evening Star* that focused on the historic legacy of Congressional Cemetery and on the parties responsible for preservation of that legacy. In "Congressional Cemetery Long Used for Official U.S. Memorials," published on March 17, 1929, he criticized the U.S. Congress for neglecting "its responsibility to care for its holdings" at the burial ground and for depending on Christ Church to maintain the federal graves and monuments "for so many years . . . without making any appropriation to cover the necessary expense." Proctor understood that while Christ Church had ultimate responsibility for Congressional Cemetery, it could not be expected to maintain the federal monuments, as well as other memorials, without support from Congress and other interested parties.[1]

This chapter focuses on the organizations and individuals who shared this understanding and who contributed to the preservation of Congressional Cemetery from the end of the Civil War to approximately 1950. The narrative continues after the great funeral parades were over, when Christ Church was left with an historic site undergoing continuing deterioration. While lacking the high drama associated with earlier periods, the surviving documentation is nonetheless compelling, centered as it is on the frustration, disappointment, courage, and commitment of organizations and individuals intent on preservation of the old burial ground. The narrative proceeds from Christ Church as keeper of the burial ground to many others who believed in the legacy, including members of the United States Congress, the Daughters of the American Revolution, and the American Institute of Architects.

Federal Decisions About an Iron Fence, Cenotaphs, and City Streets

Deliberation over concrete matters, specifically an iron fence, the cenotaphs, and parts of city streets, brought definition of sorts to the relationship between Christ Church and the U.S. Congress in the development and maintenance of Congressional Cemetery. The related discussion was not timely, beginning some fifty years after Congress had made its first burial in the new cemetery—of Senator Uriah Tracy of Connecticut in 1807. Moreover, it did not emerge according to a planned agenda but almost by happenstance, over issues that surfaced along the way. And when this stage of definition was over, at about the centennial anniversary of the cemetery in 1912, the partnership between Christ Church and the U.S. Congress in terms of the cemetery had more clarity but was still problematic.

The Christ Church vestry and the U.S. Congress discussed the iron fence, the cenotaphs, and parts of city streets in consecutive order, beginning with the fence during the 1850s. The deliberations centered on two key questions: (1) Could the cemetery be defined as "public grounds" and thus be eligible for public funding? and (2) What were the respective responsibilities of Christ Church and Congress in preserving this historic graveyard for future generations? The conversation about the iron fence was pivotal in that it resulted in the first formal decision by the federal government that Congressional Cemetery was not public land, meaning that it was not owned and managed by the U.S. government.

The discussion, conducted during 1850-1856, originated from the desire of the vestry to enhance security at the cemetery by erecting an iron fence along its northern boundary. Because Christ Church could not fund this project, it proceeded as it had in the past by offering the federal government burial sites, in this instance five-hundred lots, in exchange for the required support. The vestry depended on the negotiating skills of John Ingle, who was assisted by another member of Christ Church, Marine Corps General Archibald Henderson. They communicated directly with Dr. John B. Blake, Commissioner of Public Buildings in Washington, D.C.[2] Blake, who supported the vestry in their attempt to secure federal funding, forwarded their requests to consecutive U.S. Secretaries of the Interior, the most important of whom in this matter were Robert McClellan (March 8, 1853 - March 9, 1857), who served during the administration of President Franklin Pierce, and Jacob Thompson (March 10, 1857 - January 8, 1861), appointed by President James Buchanan.

As a result of these efforts, Congress appropriated $5,000 on August 18, 1856, "to enable the Secretary of the Interior to purchase five hundred burial lots in the Congressional burying ground . . . *Provided*, That the same be expended in the construction of an iron fence on the north side of said burial grounds." In the months that followed, Ingle and Henderson secured designs and estimates from local contractors for the iron fence. Meanwhile, Congress passed legislation on March 3, 1857, that authorized the Secretary of the Interior to remove the iron fence then encircling Capitol Square, to use part of this fence in enclosing Judiciary Square, and to apply the rest in enclosing "such of the public grounds as the President may direct."[3]

Proceeding from this ruling, the Christ Church vestry suspended their efforts to obtain estimates for an iron fence, hoping instead to purchase "for a lower price" part of the fence targeted for removal from Capitol Square. On March 16, 1857, Ingle and Henderson wrote to Commissioner Blake asking "whether this cemetery may be regarded as public grounds, to which the President may grant a part of the old fence, and if so, that you would please to ask the President for authority to apply so much as may be necessary for the front of it. It is true that the whole of this ground does not belong to the United States, but they own a large part of it and many expensive monuments on it."

While supportive of the vestry, Blake could not himself decide on the case. On March 18, 1857, he accordingly forwarded the March 16 letter to Secretary Thompson. In an accompanying letter, Blake observed that while Christ Church owned the cemetery, the U.S. government had "a large interest" in the burial ground, having erected approximately one-hundred cenotaphs "to the memory of members of Congress," appropriated funds for construction of the Public Vault, and tasked Blake himself with the recent purchase of an additional five-hundred burial sites. Given these actions, the commissioner concluded that the cemetery "may be considered public ground."

Secretary Thompson spent little time reflecting on the historic, complex nature of the alliance between the federal government and Christ Church in the development of Congressional Cemetery. Three days later, on March 21, 1857, he sent Blake a terse reply stating that "the cemetery (the title to which is not in the Government) can not be regarded as 'public grounds'" and that "your proposition to sell the fence cannot be entertained." During their meeting on March 30, 1857, the Christ Church vestry accordingly authorized the purchase of 1200 feet of iron fencing at the projected cost of $6.50 per foot.

Timing was significant in this narrative. Previously, Commissioner Blake had directed his correspondence about Congressional Cemetery to Secretary McClelland, who seemed generally supportive. McClelland's tenure as Secretary of the Interior ended, however, on March 6, 1857. When Secretary Thompson penned his response to Blake, he had been in office for only fifteen days. His summary dismissal of the request would have critical importance in the long history of Congressional Cemetery in that it was the first statement in the public record that the graveyard was not "public grounds." As such, it established precedent for subsequent determinations about the cemetery by the Department of the Interior and other federal agencies from the mid-nineteenth century into the 1970s (see Chapter 6).

Congressional decisions about the cenotaphs also underscored the change in status of the burial ground following the Civil War. Over a period of forty-two years, extending from 1833 to 1875, the U.S. Congress emplaced cenotaphs at Congressional Cemetery in memory of individual members who had died while in office. The legislators discontinued funding for these memorials in 1875 for two primary reasons, the first of which was that "the cemetery was gradually losing its semiofficial character of a Government institution," as noted in the 1906 *History of the Congressional Cemetery*. The second was that the lawmakers seemingly had no historical understanding about the origin of these monuments. On May 23, 1873, they accordingly approved legislation that provided for congressional memorials but allowed for a different type of monument.

This decision proceeded from commentary delivered in Congress by Representative George Hoar of Massachusetts:

> It is certainly adding new terrors to death to propose that in any contingency, whatever may be the poverty or degradation of any Member of Congress, his body should be put under a structure similar to the cenotaphs now there, which are only excusable on the ground that nobody is buried under them. I can not conceive of an uglier shape to be made out of granite or marble than those cenotaphs now there. To propose gravely to require by law that for all time structures of that fashion shall be placed over deceased Congressmen seems to me a little too bad.

Regarding the origin of the cenotaphs, the 1906 *History* states that "just who selected the form of these monuments is not known."[4] From this statement and that of Representative Hoar, as well as the general congressional approbation of his comment, it appears that the U.S. Congress in 1906, as well as in 1873, had no recollection that the distinguished Benjamin Latrobe had designed the cenotaphs (see Chapter 1).

As it was, discussion of the cenotaphs resulted in congressional recognition that "the cemetery was gradually losing its semiofficial character of a Government institution." The earlier debate over the iron fence had resulted in the determination that Congressional Cemetery was not "public grounds." Deliberations over the use of city streets, which did not conclude until the beginning of the twentieth century, had perhaps the most difficult ending for Christ Church in that it resulted in a dissolution of the historic, albeit unofficial alliance between church and state in the development and maintenance of the old cemetery. Congress would provide occasional financial support to Congressional Cemetery during the twentieth century, but its most active period of involvement was coming to an end.

The discussion about the city streets focused on the most appropriate use of sections that had been incorporated within the cemetery as Christ Church purchased additional land for the burial ground. With legislation approved on July 25, 1848, Congress authorized the vestry "to enclose, possess, and occupy" parts of streets lying between city squares purchased in their entirety.[5] Representative William Breckinridge of Kentucky acted on this precedent when he introduced a bill in Congress on July 19, 1890, that allowed the congregation to use the sections of Eighteenth and Nineteenth Streets East and of South G and South H Streets that had by that time been enclosed within cemetery boundaries. The proposed legislation authorized the church to divide this land into burial lots, to sell those lots, and to use the proceeds "solely to the improvement and adornment of the cemetery," as stated in *The Evening Star* of July 19, 1890.

The ensuing debate focused not only on the Breckinridge bill but also on statutes introduced in Congress through 1906. As the discussion of these proposals gained focus and intensity, it honed in on two overriding concerns: who was the primary owner of the cemetery and who had primary responsibility for maintaining the grounds. The parties to the debate comprised Christ Church, the federal government, and a sizable group of concerned lot owners, who became increasingly assertive about their perceived rights regarding the burial ground. The participation of the lot owners is of particular interest as it demonstrated powerful community support for the cemetery, revealed at the same time some suspicion of the vestry in their management of cemetery funds, and underscored the general confusion regarding the meaning of "lot ownership."

The thirteen protesting lot owners were respected citizens within the surrounding community. They included Edmund F. French, a trustee of the East Washington public schools and the brother of the late Benjamin Brown French, who had been a confidant of President Abraham Lincoln; Stilson Hutchins, proprietor of *The Washington Post*; and Mary Gunton Temple, an active participant in both benevolent and religious groups within the city. The lot owners had a personal stake in the cemetery, most of them having burial sites awaiting them there. Through letters sent to Congress and a series of well-orchestrated public hearings, they sought to protect a cemetery they considered a legacy according to both national and personal measures. In a statement submitted to Congress in April 1892, for example, the lot owners asserted that "the occupation of these avenues for burial purposes would, in our opinion, greatly detract from the natural beauty and desirability of the cemetery as a resting place for the dead, and would be an injustice to those who have bought lots therein, under the belief that it would be perpetuated by Congress in its present condition."[6]

As the debate continued, the lot owners sharpened their public critique of the vestry and made their own claims on the cemetery more specific and encompassing. A hearing conducted before the D.C. Board of Commissioners on March 16, 1898, provides a case in point. O.B. Hallam, register of Christ Church, represented the vestry, and W.W. Eldridge spoke for the lot owners. As summarized in the minutes of this hearing, Eldridge asserted that the series of proposed bills focused on use of the city streets "had been repeatedly introduced at the instance [insistence] of the vestry of Washington parish in order to increase and perpetuate the profits it receives from Congressional Cemetery." He then declared that "the lot owners were the owners of nine-tenths of the cemetery" and that "the cemetery should be turned over to the control of the lot owners."[7]

In response to these claims, which he clearly found outrageous, O.B. Hallam explained that the vestry wanted to incorporate the identified sections of streets into the cemetery not to increase its supposed profits through the sale of additional burial sites but in large part to raise funds for a "much-needed chapel" on cemetery grounds. In addition, he explained that the so-called "lot owners" had not actually purchased burial sites but had bought instead "the right for burial purposes and not the title to the ground." Christ Church, in short, remained the proprietor of the burial ground, including all burial sites.[8]

The debate over the use of the city streets in question came to an official end on March 2, 1907, when President Theodore Roosevelt approved legislation that became Public Law 207. This law gave Christ Church "the right to sell burial sites" in "portions of G and H streets [sic] and also of Eighteenth and Nineteenth streets SE which are located within the limits of the Congressional Cemetery." The number of projected sites totaled approximately 2,000, which expanded the size of the graveyard to 31.68 acres. The previous size, established by an 1848 act of Congress, was thirty acres.[9]

Documents from both houses of Congress accompanied legislation that became Public Law 207: the 1906 *History of the Congressional Cemetery*, which was "presented" to Congress by Senator Elmer Burkett (see note 2 in this chapter), and *Burial Sites in Congressional Cemetery*, a report submitted to Congress by Representative Samuel W. Smith of Michigan, who was then serving on the House Committee on the District of Columbia. Both documents delineated the conditions attached to "the right to sell burial sites" in the specified sections of city streets. The "most important" of these conditions, as identified in the report submitted by Smith, were that "the proceeds of sales" were "to be devoted exclusively to cemetery purposes" and "the vestry [was] to perpetually care for and protect and preserve in good order the Government ground, monuments, gravestones, and cenotaphs. . . ." In addition, the document reserved one of the streets, having five-hundred burial sites, for use by the United States government.[10]

Public Law 207 is a pivotal piece of legislation for two primary reasons, the first of which is that it made Christ Church, a private institution, responsible for the perpetual care of federal infrastructure within the cemetery, including the cenotaphs and all other federal monuments. It signaled thereby the withdrawal of the federal government from its historic alliance with the parish in developing and maintaining the burial ground. The legislation indicated at the same time, however, that the government contemplated significant future use of the cemetery, thus its reservation of an additional five-hundred burial sites. As the documented history of Public Law 207 suggests, the federal government and the Christ Church vestry accepted the terms of this statute without deliberating over some weighty issues, particularly the following: (1) the emerging and differing interpretations of perpetual care and (2) potential problems associated with transferring the responsibility for providing this care to a private institution consisting almost exclusively of unpaid volunteers and struggling with an ongoing effort to balance its budget.

Chronic Debt and Perpetual Responsibility for Christ Church

The period extending from the end of the Civil War to 1912, the centennial anniversary of Congressional Cemetery under Christ

Church management, was uniquely challenging for the congregation. During these years, the once prosperous parish experienced
chronic debt. At the same time, Congressional Cemetery realized
increasing profits. To manage its debt and thereby assure its survival as a congregation and as the owner and operator of the burial
ground, the church transferred carefully specified, limited sums as
required from cemetery to parish accounts. During the same period, the vestry established three trust funds as well as a so-called
Bequest Fund to secure the future of the cemetery at such time as
it might no longer be profitable. The commentary given below addresses issues relevant to the transfers and trust funds. The narrative accordingly focuses in part on the meaning of some particularly thorny terms, such as lot ownership and the perpetual care of
burial sites. In addition, this section identifies key infrastructure developments at the cemetery during the years under consideration.

The Christ Church vestry, which was invariably a discreet as
well as a dedicated group of local citizens, rarely made public comments about their increasingly heavy burden in maintaining the
cemetery. A memorable statement surfaced nonetheless in an article about the burial ground that was written by Mark L. Olds,
rector of Christ Church, and published in *The Washington Star* on
August 24, 1867:

> The history of Christ Church and that of the Congressional
> Burial Ground are intimately connected, though the present
> rector of the church would be well pleased if they were less
> so, as the "ground" has given the "church" much trouble
> and no profit. "If Congress would only take it in charge,"
> said the rector. And why shouldn't Congress? They call it
> by their own name, much of the space is filled with the dis-
> tinguished dead of the nation, and the cemetery is always
> spoken of and written of as the property of the Union.

This statement, which is unusual for its candor, underscores
both the challenges and the occasional frustration of Christ Church
in its management of Congressional Cemetery in the decades following the Civil War.

For Christ Church, budgetary issues were a major concern during this period, as indicated by periodic snapshots in vestry minutes of sizable deficits. A contributing factor was probably the demographic shift at that time within the surrounding neighborhood. During the latter part of the nineteenth century, middle-class neighborhoods emerged to the north and east of the U.S. Capitol. Some members of Christ Church likely relocated into these areas and transferred their church memberships accordingly. Meanwhile, skilled laborers were moving into southeast Washington, D.C., to work at the Navy Yard, which had expanded its operations.[11] While this development brought new vitality to the surrounding community, there is no evidence indicating that it also resulted in increased membership at Christ Church.

From the Civil War to 1912, Christ Church had two standard sources of revenue: offerings collected during Sunday services and funds received from pew rentals. These resources were not always sufficient, as indicated by statistics for the quarter beginning on October 1 and concluding on December 31, 1887. The church ended that period with a deficit of $2503.38, after accounting for the receipt of $78.22 in Sunday offerings and $233.48 in pew rentals. For the same quarter, Congressional Cemetery realized a profit of $2368.24. To help manage its debt, Christ Church transferred $350 from cemetery funds to the church. This transfer lowered the deficit to a still sizable $2153.38.[12]

During a meeting conducted on March 27, 1869, the vestry had initiated transfers as required from cemetery to church accounts. The history of these transfers constitutes a complex narrative that was not well understood within the surrounding community, particularly among lot owners who were not parishioners. The church, which was the sole owner and operator of the cemetery, was chronically in debt, while the burial ground regularly realized profits in the decades following the Civil War. To maintain solvency, and thus its capacity to operate the burial ground, the church transferred documented sums from cemetery to church accounts. While the usual figure was $350 per quarter, the total was periodically increased as the vestry deemed necessary.[13] On November 16, 1886, for instance, the vestry raised the quarterly transfer to $500 and added an additional transfer of $500 for that one period, as specified in the meeting minutes.

During a pivotal monthly meeting on March 8, 1887, the vestry reversed their decision of November 16, 1886, and reaffirmed the earlier resolution specifying quarterly transfers of $350, totaling $1400 per year. The discussion leading to this decision was apparently part of the public discourse, as indicated by the minutes for the March 8 meeting: "After considerable discussion through the medium of the newspapers and committees of the parish and lot owners, an agreement was reached by which the Vestry were to retain for their supervisory and administrative services $1400 per annum and the remainder of the income was to be applied to the care and maintenance of the cemetery . . . ."

The same minutes underscore the continuing financial problems of Christ Church, which then had annual expenses of about $3,600 and an annual income of about $3,050, of which an average of $1200 was derived from pew rentals, $450 from Sunday offerings, and $1400 in transfers from the cemetery fund. As indicated by these numbers, the church realized a deficit at that time of about $550 per year. The minutes do not show that the vestry deliberated during this meeting over possible plans for eliminating the chronic and accumulating debt. Given their own scruples and the ever watchful eye of lot owners, it seems likely that they felt uncertain regarding the next steps.

Through the first decade of the twentieth century, the vestry made quarterly transfers of $350 and additional transfers as needed. The concerned lot owners, meanwhile, knew that transfers continued to be made from cemetery to church accounts, but they did not have specifics regarding either the reasons for these transfers or their frequency and amount. In 1906, they accordingly took action, as indicated by the minutes of a particularly significant vestry meeting on March 12. During this session, the vestry deliberated over two brief letters from representatives of a committee of five that had been appointed by concerned lot owners to examine both church and cemetery financial accounts. The first, dated March 6, 1906, and signed by T. Edward Clark, made this request: "I ask whether you will allow us [himself and another committee member] to examine the books of the Cemetery or Vestry of Christ Church for such facts as are wanted by the Com. [sic]. What we want generally speaking is receipts and expenditures of Cem. [sic] for the past ten years, to what purposes the surplus, if any, was applied. . . ." The second letter, drafted by Judson T. Cull, committee chairperson, and dated March 12, 1906, supported the request made by Clark, asking the vestry to "give them as our sub committee all the aid and information you can to enable them to properly perform their duties in the premises, that we may be able to make a true and fair report to the lot owners."

During a meeting conducted on the same day, the vestry passed a series of resolutions. As summarized in the meeting minutes, the most significant of the decisions directed that a lawyer be retained to communicate with the lot owners, that Christ Church receive two-thousand dollars per annum for its management of the cemetery, and that the vestry establish a trust fund to ensure the preservation of the burial ground after it "ceases to be self supporting." The vestry proceeded according to each of these resolutions. As in the past, they acted to assure the survival of the parish through specified transfers from cemetery to church financial accounts. At the same time, they worked to ensure the preservation of the historic cemetery through the establishment of a trust fund, which became the second of three such funds created by the church for the cemetery.

The saga of the trust funds is long and complicated. It began in 1854, when the vestry decided during their April 19 meeting that one dollar from each burial site sold after May 1 "should be invested in some safe stocks in the name of the vestry of Washington Parish as a Trust fund the interest of which should be used for keeping in order and improving the cemetery." While the related documentation does not indicate where the original investment was made, it does suggest that the vestry felt secure in this undertaking, agreeing during their meeting on June 28, 1862, to increase the price of each burial site by one dollar and to invest the capital realized through this increase in the trust fund beginning on September 1, 1862. The trust fund grew accordingly, totaling $4950 in April 1863 and $11,240 in August 1873.[14]

In August 1873, the first trust fund was on deposit at Merchants National Bank, where it had been placed by the treasurer of the vestry, who was a cashier there. In September 1873, Merchants National Bank collapsed, a casualty of the banking crisis then sweeping across the country.[15] The vestry made repeated, unsuccessful attempts to secure "Books, Papers, or Vouchers" from their then erstwhile treasurer. The end of this particular narrative was summarized as follows in the October 13, 1873, vestry minutes by the vestry register, who had the memorable name of E.B. Bury: "It therefore appears that the trust fund together with all the other monies of the vestry were lost by the failure, excepting four thousand dollars ($4000) afterward realized by Deed of Trust" in the former treasurer's farm.

Shortly thereafter, the vestry established another trust fund. While this effort ended well, it had a difficult beginning. As recalled in the minutes of the vestry meeting on March 8, 1887, lot owners who were "alarmed at the failure" of the vestry to provide for the cemetery over the long term had convened "for the purpose of compelling" the church "to make such future provision." Proceeding from their understanding that Congressional Cemetery was a national burial ground, they considered making an appeal to Congress "to interfere in their and its behalf, as Congress had a large interest therein." Christ Church parishioners, meanwhile, were apparently concerned about possible "Congressional interference" and created a second trust fund. The goal for this fund, which was managed by the National Safe Deposit Company, was to reach a total of $50,000, at which time the interest would be used "for the perpetual care and protection of these grounds under the supervision of the Vestry of Washington Parish." The minutes track the steady growth of this fund, which realized a total of $14,647 by March 8, 1887, $41,394 by October 12, 1893, and then the goal of $50,000 by March 12, 1906.[16]

During their meeting on March 12, 1906, the vestry decided to establish a third trust fund. As stated in the meeting minutes, the members understood that the current fund of $50,000 was "insufficient" for the proposed task—of maintaining the cemetery "in proper condition and repair"—and they agreed to invest fifty percent of the receipts from the sale of burial and vault sites after April 1, 1906, in "first mortgage securities." In addition, the members agreed that they would not draw upon any interest from that fund until it reached $50,000, at which time the income realized would be transferred to the church treasurer "to be used by the Vestry for the care and maintenance of said Washington (Congressional) Cemetery and for no other purpose."

Christ Church was confronting a daunting task as it proceeded toward the year 1912, which marked its centennial anniversary as the owner and manager of Congressional Cemetery. Experiencing chronic debt, the church had assumed perpetual responsibility for an historic cemetery serving the needs of Congress and the surrounding community, including its own members. In an additional effort to meet this responsibility, the vestry had resolved on January 8, 1889, "that a special fund be created from voluntary contributions and requests, from such Persons as wish special care taken of their lots, monuments, etc, in the Wash. Cemetery, to be known as the Bequest Fund." The accompanying resolutions remained in force through the centennial anniversary of 1912.[17]

Developed with the best of intentions, the guidelines for the Bequest Fund were problematic because the language was too general. The lead sentence stated, for example, that "any person who desires special care of any lot in the Cemetery may donate or bequeath any sum for that purpose." The subsequent guidelines did not, however, qualify either the type(s) of "special care" available or the period during which this service would be offered. They suggested instead that this service would be provided "forever," including this word in the receipt given by the vestry to the contributor: "Received from _____, _____ dollars, to have and to hold, in trust forever, to be invested under the direction of the Vestry of Washington Parish, and the proper proportion of the income derived from the total investment of the 'Bequest Fund' to be applied to the care taking of Sites numbered _____ in Ranges numbered _____ in the Washington Cemetery."[18] Given the unqualified reference to "forever," a lot owner could not be faulted for thinking that the "special care" would somehow continue in perpetuity.

The surviving documentation of contributions made during the 1890s and the first decade of the 1900s suggests that lot owners generally had unrealistic expectations of the "special care" possible at Congressional Cemetery. Their gifts were relatively modest, ranging from a low of about $45 to $50 to a high of approximately $200 to $300.[19] Their expectations, however, were considerable, as indicated by this statement from the vestry minutes of November

10, 1892: "The committee on [the] cemetery reported that it had received from Mrs. Sarah Utermehle $300 & had caused the register to give her a certificate or contract that in consideration thereof the Vestry was to keep in repair sites 141 to 144 Range 42 clean the monument and coping and sod the graves when necessary cut the grass and rosebushes and fill the vases with growing flowers in the spring of each year." Mrs. Utermehle provided this donation approximately seven months after her husband had been buried at Congressional and four months before she herself would be interred there, next to her husband and their son. They are still there, more than a century after she had given her gift in full expectation that the family monuments would be cleaned, the graves sodded, the grass and rosebushes cut, and even the vases filled with flowers "in the spring of each year" — all for a donation of $300 made in 1892.

In connection with the Bequest Fund and additional efforts to secure the future of Congressional Cemetery, the vestry kept its own counsel. According to available documentation, particularly vestry minutes, the members did not exchange information with other organizations managing cemeteries, and they did not participate in the annual meetings of the Association of American Cemetery Superintendents (AACS), established in 1887.[20] The vestry caught, nonetheless, echoes in the wind, phrases and concepts then current within cemetery management circles, such as "perpetual care" and "special care." So, too, did lot owners and the U.S. Congress, all of whom referred loosely to perpetual care without deliberating over its possible meanings. On December 13, 1887, the vestry agreed, for example, that the interest gained from the second trust fund "shall be used for the perpetual care and protection of these grounds," as documented in the minutes for that meeting. Commenting on the expected interest from the same investment, an article in *The Evening Star* of September 11, 1891, stated that this fund, upon reaching $50,000, "is to be held perpetually and the income applied to the care and ornamentation of the grounds. This will insure the perpetual care of the grounds after the sale of lots shall have ceased and there will be no further income from this source." The federal government joined this indiscriminate chorus about perpetual care when requiring the vestry to "perpetually care for and protect and preserve in good order the Government ground, monuments, gravestones, and cenotaphs" in exchange for "the right to sell burial sites" in the parts of city streets identified previously. Clearly, none of these parties—the vestry, lot owners, or federal government—had any precise understanding about the meanings or the probable costs of perpetual care.

Neither did the AACS at that time, although members recognized the importance of deliberating over possible definitions, as they did during their annual meetings in the 1890s and the first decade of the twentieth century. For example, during their twelfth annual meeting, conducted in 1898, one George M. Painter spoke at the request of the association's executive committee about "The Importance of Placing Our Cemeteries Under Perpetual Care." The ensuing discussion focused in part on problems in defining the terminology, as indicated by this statement: "Perpetual care in some cemeteries applies to the care of grass only, in others to grass, shrubs and trees, etc., and in some instances it is made to cover the care of the monumental work as well as everything on the lot. . . ."[21]

The AACS continued the conversation during their meeting in 1899. One Mr. Floyd framed the discussion when he said this: "I would like to hear views on the questions, 'How far should perpetual care be expended to get the best results? How best to ascertain rates?'" The transcript of the ensuing conversation makes for an interesting read in that the participants voiced substantially different views. A Mr. Ross stated, for example, that the administrators in his cemetery "take perpetual care of the grass, trees, shrubbery and also . . . keep the monumental work clean." He added that "we charge 33 1/3 cents a square foot for the perpetual care, but we are not getting enough for what we agreed to do." A Mr. McCarthy followed with this observation:

> You are too liberal; you take care of everything. . . . to take care of everything is a dangerous custom; at present there may be only a few monuments or a few headstones, but as time goes on the headstones and monuments have increased; but the fund has not proportionately. My idea is to separate the items for which the money is left—a certain amount for grass, another for the cleaning or preservation

of headstones and monuments. We care for the grass only —
cutting, fertilizing or top dressing and resodding if necessary. . . .[22]

Had the superintendent of Congressional Cemetery and members of the Christ Church vestry participated in such discussions,
they might well have paused before agreeing to "perpetually care
for and protect and preserve in good order the Government ground,
monuments, gravestones, and cenotaphs. . . ."

The vestry minutes do not indicate why Christ Church did not
send representatives to the annual AACS meetings. The reasons can,
however, be surmised. To begin, the parish was managing a cemetery considerably different from those maintained by members of
the AACS. From the time of its founding in 1887, the AACS had
espoused the superiority of the "landscape lawn plan," which focused on expansive areas of lawn with clusters of trees and shrubs.
Adolph Strauch proceeded to implement this approach at Spring
Grove Cemetery in Cincinnati beginning in 1855, as well as at other
garden cemeteries he designed or worked to re-design as a consultant. Given the unique history and appearance of Congressional
Cemetery, with its imposing rows of cenotaphs, the vestry would
not have participated in discussions focused on the maintenance of
cemeteries fashioned according to the landscape lawn plan, just as
it did not take part earlier in the rural cemetery movement.

Then, too, the members of the vestry were not cemetery pro-
fessionals but dedicated public servants, many of them spending
their working hours in various business and professional fields.
They oversaw Congressional Cemetery during their own time, and
they, not the superintendent of the burial ground or any landscape
architect, made the critical decisions about cemetery development
and maintenance. Given these factors, the insularity of the vestry in
relation to deliberations among cemetery managers is understandable. Their relative isolation was nonetheless problematic, exacer-
bating mounting difficulties they were experiencing in securing a
future for the first U.S. national burial ground.

Christ Church did, nonetheless, initiate infrastructure developments at the burial ground in the years extending from the end of
the Civil War to the centennial anniversary of the burial ground at

the beginning of the twentieth century. These efforts, identified below in chronological order, included installing an ornamental water fountain, renovating the gatehouse, naming streets within the burial ground, and constructing a chapel.

The vestry initiated the first of these developments in May 1868, when the members established a fund for the emplacement of a water fountain, which was a popular feature at other burial grounds at that time, including Green-Wood in Brooklyn, Laurel Hill in Philadelphia, and Mount Auburn in Boston. Approximately one year later, a fountain was positioned at the intersection of Eighteenth and G Streets within the burial ground. This initiative, which had been facilitated by the completion of a public water supply system for the municipality during the early 1860s, was removed during construction of the chapel at the same site in 1903. The image of the fountain remains in at least three extant stereo-views.[23]

During the early 1870s, the Christ Church vestry determined that the superintendent's house at the cemetery, which had been constructed in 1832, had to be replaced. In May 1873, the members accordingly engaged Emile S. Friedrich, a prominent architect based in Washington, D.C., to design a new building. The vestry ultimately concluded, however, that they could not meet the projected cost for the structure, estimated at $6,000. They proceeded to renovate the existing structure, which was completed by July 1874 at a cost of $1,650. The rehabilitation of the gatehouse, as the building came to be called, was the last substantial project undertaken by Christ Church at Congressional Cemetery during the nineteenth century.[24]

Upon completion of the gatehouse restoration, the vestry named nine of the eleven streets that had been incorporated into the burial ground after long-time, faithful members of the Christ Church vestry. They included Coombe Avenue, which recalled the service of Griffith Coombe, who had been a vestryman for thirty-nine years (1806-1845), and Henderson Avenue, named after General Archibald Henderson, who served for thirty-six years (1823-1859). Ingle Avenue memorialized the invaluable contributions of both Henry Ingle, who had been a vestryman for sixteen years (1806-1822), and his son John P. Ingle, who was a member of the vestry for thirty-four years (1828-1862) and register of the parish for forty-nine years (1813-1862). McCormick Avenue was named after Rev. Alexander McCormick, rector of Christ Church during 1807-1823.[25] These and other individuals remembered in the naming of the roadways had been important in the establishment of the burial ground. As delineated in the preceding chapters, the U.S. Congress also had a significant role in the development of the cemetery, and thus it is appropriate that the primary avenue in the graveyard, the one that leads in a straight line from the gatehouse, positioned at the entrance, to the chapel, is Congress Road.

The chapel, designed by architect Arthur M. Poyton and built by J.H. Gibbins at a cost of approximately $4,500, won high praise upon its completion during summer 1903. The September 1903 issue of the *Architects and Builders Journal*, for example, identified the new structure as "one of the most complete mortuary chapels in Washington," replete with both "crypts and modern appointments for disposing of the remains": "It stands in the central part of the cemetery in a circular plot of ground and is Gothic in style. The exterior is of pebble dash, a slate roof covers it, while the windows are of stained glass, surmounted by a gilt cross." Positioned within a "circular plot of ground," the chapel offered relief from the grid-like pattern of monuments and roads within the cemetery that echoed the pattern of Charles Pierre L'Enfant's design for the federal city.

In the history of Congressional Cemetery, the years extending from the end of the Civil War to 1912 do not include the high drama associated with the antebellum period, such as the dramatic funeral processions to the burial ground. They nonetheless comprise an extraordinary chapter in its long history, surfacing the challenges faced and the gains realized as Christ Church and supporters within the surrounding community worked to preserve and extend the legacy of the first national burial ground.

Summations of Congressional Cemetery at Centennial Milestones

Two centennial milestones are significant in the long history of Congressional Cemetery: 1907, which marked the passage of one-hundred years following the first burial at the site, and 1912, the centennial anniversary of Christ Church's ownership and management of the graveyard. Publications by diverse organizations underscored the historical significance of the cemetery at these milestones. This section focuses on the summations given in the 1906 *History of the Congressional Cemetery*, articles by veteran journalist James Crogan on "Old Washington" that were published in *The Evening Star* during 1912, and *Washington Parish Burial Ground (Congressional Cemetery), 1807-1913*, issued by Christ Church in 1913. While these documents advanced differing perspectives, they each characterized Congressional as a national burial ground.

In developing the *History of the Congressional Cemetery*, the committee chaired by Senator Elmer Burkett accessed documents available in federal and church archives, including records focused on the establishment of the cemetery in 1807, the transfer of ownership to Christ Church in 1812, and the operation of the burial ground from 1812 into the 1870s. The committee then wrote the first extended history of the cemetery, establishing its credentials as a national burial ground beginning with the title page and opening paragraphs. The abbreviated title made a large statement in its reference to "the Congressional Cemetery," rather than to the Washington Parish Burial Ground. The title alone conveyed the larger legacy of the cemetery to legislators who received copies of the publication, even if they did not read beyond the cover page.

The initial page addressed the message given in the title. The second paragraph, for example, noted that the burial ground had been recognized from the beginning as the Congressional Cemetery rather than by its official name "because when the cemetery was first established in 1807 it was chosen by the United States as the place of interment for nearly every member of Congress or executive officer who died while holding office, and the custom was adhered to by the Government for many years afterward." The following paragraph elaborated on the same theme:

During the earlier years of holding sessions of Congress in Washington, Christ Church was the place of worship for many men prominent in Government affairs. President Thomas Jefferson attended there. Some of the descendants of President Washington were members of the vestry, and a pew in the church was set aside by the vestrymen for the perpetual use of the President of the United States and his family. Hence it was but natural that the Government should select for the interment of deceased Government officials the burying ground owned by Christ Church. Monuments have been erected therein for nearly 200 members of Congress and other public men.

The particularly memorable phrasing in the above statement is the comment that "it was but natural that the Government" would inter deceased federal officials in this cemetery. Christ Church used similar phrasing in characterizing federal use of the cemetery, as will be explained below. Subsequent passages in the *History of the Congressional Cemetery* focused on connections between the burial ground and the government, identifying "the burial sites acquired therein by the Government through donation and purchase," "the appropriations made by Congress for its care, improvement, and repair," and the "interments made and monuments erected therein by the Government."[26]

In his contributions to *The Evening Star*, James Croggan, a native Washingtonian, focused on the inclusivity of the community at rest at Congressional Cemetery. In 1912, when he published his three articles on the burial ground, he was seventy-seven years old and likely the most senior active journalist in Washington, D.C. While he had officially retired from *The Evening Star* in 1894, he continued to write special pieces for the newspaper until July 1915. As noted in his obituary, which was published in the periodical on August 22, 1916, "the best known" of these contributions was probably his series on "Old Washington," which included his retrospectives about Congressional Cemetery. The articles, published on May 11, May 18, and June 1, 1912, delineated the history of the site from 1807 to 1850. In so doing, they characterized Congressional as a national burial ground because it was open to everyone: the federal government, the local community, and people who had nowhere else to go. "It may be said," Croggan observed in the last of these publications, that "every condition" of the community "is represented in the interments here—warriors, statesmen, professional men, merchants, mechanics, etc. But here there are also some who occupied the lower positions in life."

Croggan organized his articles so that they generally proceeded from identification of those at the top of the social strata to those at the bottom. Thus, in his narratives of May 11 and 18, he emphasized the federal connection noting, for example, that the first interment at the cemetery was of Senator Uriah Tracy of Connecticut and that "practically every deceased senator or representative who [had since] died in office was buried here." In addition, he stated in the article published on May 18, as well as in the last of this series, that the federal government regularly referred to the cemetery as "the Congressional Burial Ground" in legislation providing funding for the graveyard.

In his second (May 18) and third (June 1) articles, Croggan noted its preeminence as a community cemetery. "Although other cemeteries had been established, St. John's Episcopal Foundry Methodist among them, the Congressional Ground was the leading one of Washington," he observed on May 18. In the June 1 article, he sharpened the definition: "As a burial ground for the old families of the District it grew in the popular estimation, and it may be said that this with the Methodist ground opposite [Old Ebenezer Methodist Church] was used by nearly every family of the eastern part of the city . . . ."

Croggan reserved the concluding part of his third article to address the burial at Congressional of someone occupying one of the "lower positions in life":

> In one case there is interred the body of a woman whose career was a short one before she was enforced to take up her residence in the workhouse. She was committed there for drunkenness when the Washington Asylum was on the square bounded by M, N, 6th and 7th streets northwest. The inmates were removed therefrom to the Washington Asylum, north of the cemetery, in 1846, and she was included. She was allowed to make her home there, with the privilege of walking out during the day, but she seldom availed herself thereof, and then went but a short distance from her home, which she occupied for nearly fifty years. Early she resolved not to be buried as other inmates in the potter's field, and in a few years she had saved money with which to buy a lot, and when the end came her body was given a Christian burial, but the lot bearing her real name, the place where Becky Smith lies, cannot be identified.[27]

The reference by Croggan to a fifty-year residence at the Washington Asylum that began in 1846 indicates that "Becky Smith" was probably Rebecca F. Smith, who was interred at Congressional on March 22, 1898. By concluding his 1912 articles with commentary on someone occupying one of the "lower positions in life," Croggan emphasized the inclusivity of Congressional, thereby underscoring his understanding of the special legacy of this cemetery. Impressed with this legacy, Croggan decided that he too would be buried at Congressional, as he was on August 24, 1916.[28]

Christ Church published its history of the cemetery in 1913 and thus approximately one-hundred years after the congregation had assumed ownership of the site. James Berry, who was at that time a member of the three-person Cemetery Committee, drafted this sixteen-page document, entitled *Washington Parish Burial Ground (Congressional Cemetery), 1807-1913*. The publication is notable in part because it identifies the philosophy of Christ Church in operating what it saw as an inclusive burial ground, open to everyone. The introductory section, entitled "A Paragraph of Reminiscence," states in part that the vestry "gives the same thought and bestows the same care" in the preservation of all burial sites, extending from those with "beautiful" and historic markers to "the humblest unmarked grave." Underscoring this approach to maintenance of the first national burial ground, the initial section ends as follows: "In the democracy of death, there can be no distinctions."[29]

The 1913 history also summarizes efforts undertaken by Christ Church to assure long-term preservation of the cemetery, notably the trust funds previously discussed. Buoyed by progress made to that date, Berry stated in his conclusion that "this generous endowment guarantees for all time, the proper preservation, further beautification and improvement of the Burial Ground."[30] As delineated below, events unfolded in the following decades that challenged this confident statement about ongoing stability and prosperity for the old burial ground.

A Rediscovery of the Legacy during the 1920s and 1930s

National organizations rediscovered the historic legacy of Congressional Cemetery between World Wars I and II. They proceeded thereafter to sponsor federal legislation and host events of national import to rescue the graveyard from the effects of time, which were by then all too evident. The Daughters of the American Revolution provided the lead, recalling the U.S. Congress to its responsibility for the graveyard that continued to be recognized in public parlance and national deliberations as the Congressional Cemetery. They were joined by the Association of Federal Architects, who focused the attention of President Franklin D. Roosevelt on the cemetery, and the U.S. Quartermaster Corps.

In their respective efforts, these organizations reflected broader national interest in the American historical legacy, as evidenced by elaborate commemorative celebrations staged during the 1920s upon the 150th anniversary of the signing of the Declaration of Independence, among other events, and by numerous ceremonies organized in the 1930s. In his *Remaking America: Public Memory, Commemoration, and Patriotism in the Twentieth Century,* John Bodnar noted that these celebrations "had made a definite impact on the public mind by 1930 and reinforced the notion that the past was indeed glorious and a source of inspiration." During the 1930s, this understanding was reinforced in particular by the George Washington Bicentennial Commission, which encouraged the staging of more than 4.7 million events in 1932 that celebrated the legacy of the first U.S. president.[31]

The federal government continued to expand its role in historical commemoration and preservation during the administration of President Franklin Roosevelt. On June 10, 1933, for example, Roosevelt signed Executive Order 6166, which incorporated all national parks, all national monuments, and the eleven national cemeteries into a National Park System. Two years later, Congress passed the Historic Sites Act, which authorized the Department of Interior, through the National Park Service, to pursue a national policy focused on the preservation of historic sites for public use.[32] While these initiatives did not directly affect Congressional Cemetery, they did help create a climate conducive to restoration of the burial ground.

Meanwhile, the Daughters of the American Revolution emerged as a forceful advocate for the preservation of Congressional Cemetery. Founded on October 11, 1890, to honor the legacy of the Revolutionary War and enroll women who could trace their ancestry to participants in that conflict, the organization had embarked upon "an incessant campaign to revitalize the past," as noted by Margaret Gibbs, author of *The DAR* (1969). By way of example, she cited the focus on historic cemeteries:

Hundreds of newly awakened amateur historians began roaming the countryside to ferret out the half-forgotten graves of Revolutionary soldiers. They not only supplied appropriate markers for them but also, if necessary, had stones repaired and dutifully tabulated the names of the deceased in DAR archives. Other zealous Daughters spent days in musty back rooms and cellars of town halls, churches, and libraries and often rescued early records from the trash barrel.[33]

The initiatives undertaken by the DAR in support of Congressional Cemetery are noteworthy because they were advanced by the national leadership of the organization, they challenged the U.S. Congress to act upon its historic responsibility for the burial ground, and they established a solid foundation for future actions in support of the cemetery.

The initial DAR effort was the publication of "Cenotaphs and Epitaphs in Congressional Cemetery," by Nelson McDowell Shepherd, in the April 1921 issue of *Daughters of the American Revolution Magazine*. In this article, Shepherd articulated themes recalled by DAR leaders in subsequent initiatives designed to secure federal support for the burial ground. He underscored first its historic significance, saying that "the burying ground of the century-old Christ Church, known nationally as Congressional Cemetery, is rich in the interest it holds for students of the Revolutionary and succeeding periods of American history." In support of this claim, he noted the many interments of historic figures: "It is said that more patriots whose names are linked with the early periods of our history are buried along this river slope, perhaps, than in any other single cemetery in the country. . . ." Shepherd also commented on the special importance of the cenotaphs, which he had highlighted in the title of his article: "In these surroundings are to be found the only group of cenotaphs – a memorial customary in Europe – ever erected by the U.S. Government in honor of deceased Senators and Representatives."[34]

These statements resonated with the top leadership of the DAR, specifically Grace H. Brosseau, who was president general during 1926-1929, and Margaret C. Gregory, national chairman of legislation in the same period. They collaborated in their efforts to secure federal support for Congressional Cemetery. Powerful in their respective roles, they also had other important connections. While Grace Brosseau was the wife of Alfred Brosseau, president of Mack Trucks, Gregory was the daughter of Lee Slater Overman, longtime (1903-1930) senator from North Carolina and a man much interested in the preservation of Congressional Cemetery.

The North Carolina connection became prominent in DAR efforts to secure federal support for Congressional Cemetery. On March 22, 1928, Charles L. Abernethy, a congressman from that state, delivered a speech in the House of Representatives recalling Congress to its historic responsibility for the maintenance of Congressional Cemetery. Approximately one month later, on April 24, 1928, he introduced H.R. 11916 at a hearing before the House Subcommittee on Military Affairs. H.R. 11916, identified as "A BILL To provide for the care and preservation of certain land and monuments in the Washington Parish Burial Ground (Congressional Cemetery)," offered a substantial revision of arrangements put in place by Public Law 207, which President Roosevelt had approved on March 2, 1907. As noted previously, Public Law 207 allowed Christ Church to incorporate specified sections of city streets into the cemetery conditioned in part upon agreement by "the vestry to perpetually care for and protect and preserve in good order the Government ground, monuments, gravestones, and cenotaphs." H.R. 11916 specified for the first time a federal keeper for the federal property at Congressional Cemetery:

> *Be it enacted by the Senate and House of Representatives of the United States of America in Congress assembled,* That the Secretary of War is authorized and directed to care for and preserve the land and monuments owned by the United States in the Washington Parish Burial Ground (Congressional Cemetery). The Secretary of War is authorized to make such

expenditures, including expenditures for personal services at the seat of government, as he deems advisable to carry out the provisions of this act. There is authorized to be appropriated such sums as may be necessary to carry out the provisions of this act.[35]

This proposed bill, which did not become law, was the first of a number of other efforts to secure federal support for the federal graves at Congressional that extended until 1973, as will be delineated in the next chapter.

The hearing on H.R. 11916 featured statements by Margaret Gregory and Representative Abernethy. Their commentary and the subsequent discussion were well intended but also notably confused, largely because neither the speakers nor the subcommittee as a whole had communicated with Christ Church as owner and operator of the burial ground, secured historical documentation regarding the cemetery, or even visited the grounds, as indicated by their remarks about the location of the federal graves.

Representative Abernethy acknowledged the contributions of the DAR, "this great patriotic organization," and its representatives who "have come here and shown us what our duty is, to care for and preserve one of the most historic spots in America." He credited in particular the efforts of Grace Brosseau, who had presented him with a letter, dated April 24, 1928, advocating federal support for the preservation of Congressional Cemetery, and Margaret Gregory, who had focused his attention on "this matter." He then asked that Brosseau's letter be made part of the official record of the hearing in that she was "anxious to make a statement" about the burial ground.[36]

After commending the efforts of the DAR and its representatives, Abernethy read extracts from the speech he had delivered in Congress, noting in particular the "long list of distinguished men" who had been buried in "the part [of the cemetery] that belongs to the Government." This statement fueled a remarkably confused exchange of comments among Abernethy, Representative B. Carroll Reece of Texas, and Representative James P. Glynn of Connecticut:

Mr. REECE. To whom does the cemetery belong. [sic]

Mr. ABERNETHY. The part that I am talking about belongs to the Government.

Mr. REECE. It belongs to the Government?

Mr. ABERNETHY. Absolutely.

Mr. GLYNN. That is, a part of this cemetery was deeded to the Government, as I understand, as a burial place for Government officials.

Mr. ABERNETHY. Yes, sir.[37]

And thus the dialogue continued with occasional queries about budgetary matters pertinent to preservation of the burial ground—"You have no estimate as to the cost, I assume?" [Representative Glynn]; statements of regret—"It is a shame that something has not been done to take care of" the cemetery [Representative Abernethy]; and remarks about responsibility—"Since the Government accepted that ground it should assume responsibility for the burials there" [Representative Reece].[38]

Representative Abernethy then introduced Margaret Gregory, who began her comments with a brief personal recollection: "Mr. Chairman and gentlemen, I have taken an interest in this matter because my father, Senator Overman, took me there one afternoon and said he thought it was one of the most perfect pieces of patriotic activity we could engage in." Following this statement, she engaged in dialogue with members of the committee, this time also including Representative Daniel E. Garrett of Texas. The conversation focused as before on ownership of and responsibility for Congressional Cemetery, demonstrating again a surprising lack of knowledge about the primary role of Christ Church in all matters relevant to the burial ground and about the locations of the federal sites, which were situated in various parts of the cemetery:

Mr. REECE. And could the Government take that part over as a National Cemetery without reference to the rest of the cemetery?

Mrs. GREGORY. Oh, yes.

Mr. REECE. It is so arranged that that could be done?

Mrs. GREGORY. Yes. As I understand, it is just one corner
of the cemetery.
Mr. GLYNN. It is under the direction of some Washington
parish, as I understand.
Mrs. GREGORY. Yes, I think it is an Episcopal parish. . . .

The rest of this particular narrative appears in the official report
issued by the Committee on Military Affairs "to accompany H.R.
11916," as stated on the title page of the document. This report,
which the committee had "ordered to be printed" on February 11,
1929, is another remarkable document in the long and ever evolving history of Congressional Cemetery.[39]

The first paragraph of the report presents the decision made
by the Committee on Military Affairs regarding H.R. 11916. "Having considered the same," the committee recommended "that it do
pass," that, in other words, the Secretary of War be "authorized and
directed to care for and preserve the land and monuments owned
by the United States in the Washington Parish Burial Ground (Congressional Cemetery)." The language of this recommendation indicates that the committee believed there were in essence two cemeteries: the larger cemetery—the Washington Parish Burial Ground,
which was owned by Christ Church, and a smaller, separate cemetery within the larger burial ground—Congressional Cemetery,
which was the property of the federal government.

The next two paragraphs expand upon the reference in H.R.
11916 to "the land and monuments owned by the United States" in
the burial ground. The narrative recalls in part the confused commentary made during the hearing regarding ownership of and responsibility for the cemetery:

This particular part of the Washington Parish Burial Ground
was deeded to the Government as a burial place for Government officials and is within a mile of the Capital down on
the Anacostia River. It is an isolated part of the cemetery,
and for 50 years has been allowed to go to decay. The Washington Parish Burial Ground itself is under the direction and
care of an Episcopal parish, but this section of the cemetery
has been left uncared for all these years.[40]

As indicated by this statement, as well as comments made during the hearing on H.R. 11916, the House Committee on Military Affairs proceeded in its deliberations about the burial ground in total isolation from Christ Church, identified merely as "an Episcopal parish," and without having visited the cemetery prior to conducting its hearing and issuing its report. There was, of course, no "particular part of the Washington Parish Burial Ground" that had been "deeded to the Government" and that was "an isolated part" down by the river. The reference in the above statement to "50 years" of neglect is particularly interesting in that Congress had not provided funds for cemetery maintenance during the preceding fifty-five years, not since the legislators had appropriated $2,000 on March 3, 1873, "for repairs and improvement" of the burial ground.[41]

The report concluded with the recommendations of U.S. Quartermaster General B.F. Cheatham, which were presented in a memorandum of November 30, 1928, given to the Assistant Secretary of War. Cheatham based his comments on information provided in cemetery records, which the vestry had made available to him, and on his own observations about cemetery infrastructure. While recognizing the historic legacy of Congressional Cemetery, he did not support H.R. 11916. In his introductory remarks, Cheatham dismissed any notion that there was a separate federal cemetery within the larger burial ground, stating that "the cemetery is owned by the Vestry of Christ Church, Washington Parish." He subsequently recommended that the cenotaphs, which he considered unsightly, be removed and then replaced by "suitable granite or marble monuments."[42]

Cheatham then addressed the "cost of maintenance" for the federal burial sites, which was a topic of increasing concern to the Christ Church vestry, the Daughters of the American Revolution as well as other organizations, and journalists keeping watch over the proceedings. His first comment had particular resonance—"The Government does not contribute toward the maintenance of these lots." He believed, however, that "arrangements" should be made for government care of government sites. His estimate was "that they could be maintained in good condition by one laborer at $1,200 per year and approximately $100 per year for supplies."[43] This was as far as the Quartermaster General would go in suggested support for the cemetery. He concluded by advising against passage of H.R. 11916 and then recommending the following—"that the attention of the Navy Department be called to the fact that there are 99 sailors and marines buried in this cemetery and that if their bodies are transferred to the Arlington National Cemetery their graves will receive perpetual care along with those of their comrades."

On December 6, 1928, the Assistant Secretary of War approved Cheatham's report, which he then sent to the Secretary of War, Dwight F. Davis. On December 19, Davis forwarded this decision, which he endorsed, to Representative Abernethy. He thereby stated that the Department of War did not want to assume responsibility for preservation of "the land and monuments owned by the United States" at Congressional Cemetery.[44] This was not, however, the end of the matter, which resurfaced in the 1930s with new initiatives focused on the responsibilities of the War Department for maintenance of the federal burial sites, as will be discussed below. As for Christ Church, it apparently issued no public comments regarding the testimony over H.R. 11916, which had been well intended even though it had mistakenly claimed that the federal graves had "been allowed to go to decay" "for 50 years."

Meanwhile, other parties both within and external to the federal government joined in ongoing deliberations over the most appropriate organization and/or individuals to assume responsibility for the federal graves at Congressional Cemetery. They included Helen Mar Pierce Gallagher, biographer of Robert Mills; the Washington Metropolitan Chapter of the American Institute of Architects; journalist Helen Essary; and members of the U.S. Congress, specifically Representative Edith Rogers of Massachusetts and Senators Theodore Green and Peter Gerry, both of Rhode Island. Henry Gibbins, Quartermaster General of the United States, summarized the substance of their understandings about the burial ground and then added something new in the 1939 *Quartermaster General's Report* he presented to Congress.

Helen Gallagher and the Washington Metropolitan Chapter of the American Institute of Architects worked to secure a monument for the gravesite at Congressional of Robert Mills (1781-1855), which had remained unmarked for some eighty years following his death. The unmarked grave of this distinguished architect, who had designed a number of landmark buildings in Washington, D.C., made all kinds of statements about changing national priorities, missed opportunities, and the inevitable, poignant loss of collective memory.

The accomplishments of Robert Mills as Architect of Public Buildings during 1836-1851 included not only the design of the Washington Monument, considered the primary achievement of his career, but also three prominent buildings in the federal capital: the Treasury, Patent Office, and Post Office. In addition to these efforts, he had long been interested in the development of a national memorial in Washington, D.C., to commemorate U.S. presidents and members of Congress who died in office, as discussed in Chapter 1 of this study. It is particularly ironic that Mills, propelled as he was by visions of great memorials and lasting buildings, would himself lie for so long in an unmarked grave.

The Mills family did not provide a gravestone, probably because they expected action by the federal government, given Mills' distinguished service to the nation. The U.S. government was, however, slow to act, preoccupied as it was by the increasing sectional discord preceding the Civil War, then by the war itself and the challenges of reconstruction. Congress did not begin to reawaken to its responsibility regarding this particular unmarked grave in its backyard until the 1920s and then only with initial, unsuccessful efforts to pass legislation providing for a marker.

Helen Gallagher and the Washington Metropolitan Chapter of the American Institute of Architects deserve primary credit for refocusing public attention on the contributions of Robert Mills. In her article published in the April 1929 issue of *The Architectural Record*, Gallagher stated that Mills was important as the creator of "an American school of architecture" but that he nonetheless had been forgotten by the broader public. She expanded on this statement in *Robert Mills, Architect of the Washington Monument, 1781-1855*, a full-length biography published in 1935.[45]

In one particularly interesting chapter of this study, entitled "Grave No. III," Gallagher asserted in italics that *"Surely this country carries an unpaid debt to the genius of Robert Mills."* By way of explanation/exclamation, she recalled her pilgrimage to Mills burial site:

The visit I made to his grave, in a cemetery full of old-time beauty, took place in springtime. My sensations were not happy as I stood by that pathetic mound of earth, one which should be revered by Americans. The air was full of the scent of roses; birds sang, while my guide in this especial God's acre counted the graves (incredible as it may seem) between designated trees in order to locate the one searched for. The grave of this distinguished man was known simply as No. III.

Gallagher commented in this same chapter on the particular irony associated with the bicentennial observation of the birth of George Washington. The elaborate year-long celebrations, which included countless pilgrimages to the Washington Monument, did not result in public recognition and remembrance of Robert Mills as the author of this national memorial. "It is a shame," she declared, "that the passing of 1932, the year of the bicentennial of George Washington's birth, has left behind it no record of the name and the face of Robert Mills, linked to his own masterpiece, the monument to George Washington."[46]

The Washington Metropolitan Chapter of the American Institute of Architects (Washington AIA) subsequently took action to secure a gravesite memorial for Robert Mills, as recounted in the history of the chapter written by architect Edwin Bateman Morris. The organization was, however, surprisingly slow to act. Founded in 1887, twenty-two years after the death of Mills, it took the members nearly fifty years to mark his grave. Meanwhile, the chapter "had been accustomed on successive Memorial Days" to visit the graves of the great architects buried in the city, specifically Peter Charles L'Enfant at Arlington; James Hoban at Mt. Olivet; and William Thornton, George Hadfield, and Robert Mills at Congressional. Morris stated that the chapter had "for years" sought congressional funding for a Mills monument. When that was not forthcoming, the Washington AIA secured donations from architects across the country, staged a national competition for design of the monument, which was won by architects Philip Golden and Harry Cunningham, and oversaw the "fabrication" and placement of the memorial at the cemetery.[47]

The Washington AIA also planned the dedicatory ceremony. As part of this effort, Morris invited President Franklin Roosevelt to the ceremony, scheduled to begin at 10:00 a.m. on May 30. In the letter, dated May 21, 1936, he recalled the major accomplishments of Mills' career, citing "the classic Treasury building . . . the old Patent Office, the old Land Office, and the Washington Monument." He then concluded on a mixed note: "No member of his profession doubts Mills' secure place in history. He was so great a man that one day the Congress will recognize it and erect a worthy National Memorial here in his honor. At least, we hope so."[48]

In his response, dated the next day, May 22, Roosevelt sent his regrets about not being able to attend the ceremony and then acknowledged Mills' major achievements, noting the structures Morris had itemized in his letter of invitation. In his commentary about the Washington Monument, Roosevelt went significantly beyond the prompt provided by Morris:

Of all the monuments in our National Capital the one outstanding in silent, solemn grandeur is that which Mills designed and which the Nation erected in memory of Washington. None but a very great genius could have evolved in his mind such a lofty conception of the greatness of a man and of a great Nation's love for that man. I am truly glad that belated tribute is to be paid to Mills' memory.[49]

This statement is in itself an historic marker. In commenting on the "silent, solemn grandeur" of the Washington Monument, President Roosevelt emphasized the link so often missing in the public record, identifying Robert Mills as the designer of the memorial.

During the ceremony, which was summarized the following day in *The Evening Star*, a great-granddaughter of Robert Mills unveiled the monument, which is neoclassical in design, measuring nine feet in height and four in width, and fashioned out of quality stone contributed by the Tennessee Marble Company and the Grey Knox Marble Company. The inscription identifies Mills as the "First Federal Architect, Whose Influence Moulded Our Architecture And Whose Genius Gave Us The Washington Monument, The Treasury Building, The Old Patent Office, And The Old Post Office." His grave is located appropriately within the historic center of the cemetery, near both the burial site of William Thornton, who designed the U.S. Capitol, and the cenotaphs of Benjamin Latrobe, once the mentor of Robert Mills. The monument over this site remains the sole memorial in Washington, D.C. for Robert Mills.

Following the 1936 ceremony in memory of Robert Mills, a new generation of congressional representatives discovered Congressional Cemetery. They were led by Representative Edith Rogers of Massachusetts and journalist Helen Essary, who comprised an effective team in securing funding for the burial ground. Rogers had been elected to Congress to fill the vacancy resulting from the death in 1925 of her husband, John Jacob Rogers, who had represented the Fifth District of Massachusetts. She continued to serve in this capacity for the next thirty-five years, until her death in 1960. During her long tenure as a congressional representative, Rogers was chairperson of the Committee on Veterans' Affairs and introduced various pieces of legislation that established, for example, the Women's Army Corps and that promoted enactment of the G.I. Bill of Rights. In addition, she became a champion of Congressional Cemetery, perhaps in part because of the many veterans interred at the site. In acting on this interest, she worked in tandem with Helen Essary, who wrote a daily column for *The Washington Times* and also published articles in other local newspapers. Rogers gave speeches and introduced legislation in the House of Representatives to provide federal funding for the cemetery, and Essary summarized and promoted Rogers' activities in her articles.

In "Congressional Oversight," published in *The Washington Daily News* on February 19, 1937, Essary said that Rogers had recently made these observations "in the gloom of a dying day of Congress"—that Christ Church did not have the resources to restore and preserve the cemetery, that Congress had an historic responsibility for the burial ground ("If we do not honor our own, no one else will"), that Congress had provided generously for ongoing care of the graves at Arlington, and that the legislators should approve as well the sums needed to renovate and preserve "the congressional plot" at Congressional Cemetery. Events moved swiftly thereafter. Essary's article, which Edith Rogers read to members of the House, was reprinted in the *Congressional Record*. Meanwhile, Senator Theodore Green, a Democrat from Rhode Island, introduced legislation that provided funding for the care of federal burial sites at Congressional and that was attached as a rider to the War Department Civil Appropriations Act for 1938. The language pertinent to Congressional Cemetery appeared in a section focused on "maintaining and improving national cemeteries," specifically "Arlington National Cemetery, and that portion of Congressional Cemetery to which the United States has title and the graves of those buried therein, including the burial site of Pushmataha, a Choctaw Indian Chief . . . ."⁵⁰ This was the first of subsequent appropriations made by the federal government for care of "that portion" of the burial ground considered by legislators to be property of the United States government.

Edith Rogers and Helen Essary congratulated each other on work well done. As narrated in "Old Cemetery Restoration Is Pushed," published in *The Washington Daily News* on July 17, 1937, Essary had contacted newspaper staff to request that they recognize Rogers "for her good work in persuading Congress to look after its own" and Rogers had asked that the publication acknowledge Essary "for stirring up the subject and presenting it in pictorial language which helped make it possible for her to persuade her fellow legislators to do something about it." The article ended with the wry statement that "both seemed to think that Senator Green, being a man, could look after himself, and see that he gets a bit of credit too."

While initiatives had been put in place for the preservation of Congressional Cemetery, considerable challenges remained, as delineated in the 1939 Quartermaster General's Report issued under the signature of Major General Henry Gibbins, who served as Quartermaster General of the U.S. Army during 1936-1940. Gibbins summarized the case for Congressional Cemetery as the first national burial ground in the sixteen-page "Memorandum" provided at the beginning of his report. He led with the observation that "in reality, the Congressional Cemetery was the first National Cemetery created by the Government. . . ." He continued by stating that "it was generally recognized as the official burying ground of Congress" by the end of 1832, when approximately forty government officials had been interred in the cemetery "by order of the

Government." He then documented all subsequent appropriations to the year 1939 made by the federal government for development and maintenance of the burial ground.[51]

In addition to citing federal appropriations, Gibbins underscored what he saw as inexcusable neglect and irregular behavior on the part of the U.S. government. It had not, for example, provided memorials for some major federal officials, including Thomas T. Tucker (1745-1828), who had been a veteran of the Revolutionary War, a Representative from South Carolina in the first Congress of the United States, and Treasurer of the United States during 1801-1828. With considerable restraint, Gibbins observed that "there is no marker at his grave, and it would seem fitting that Congress authorize a suitable monument." He also provided examples of other unmarked graves, such as that of Simon Knox, a 2nd Assistant Engineer of the U.S. Navy who had been buried at the cemetery on September 19, 1855, and that of Robert Quinlan, a corporal in the U.S. Marine Corps who had been interred on June 17, 1860. In addition, Gibbins observed that a number of burials had been made in "scattered sites" across the cemetery of military men who had died during the Civil War while in service to the nation. According "to the laws of war," these interments should have been made at "government expense." In many cases, however, the expenses were charged "to the estate of the deceased," as indicated in cemetery records. Gibbins went on to say that he had stepped into the breach:

> I have taken steps to supply headstones for the unmarked graves on the government owned plots and, in addition, those plots without [stet] the government area wherein veterans are buried and the graves are unmarked. I realize this action on my part is somewhat without [stet] the scope of existing law; however, I believe that the Congress will concur with me that my action is proper.[52]

It is significant that Gibbins understood that the entire cemetery, not merely the burial sites and monuments associated with prominent individuals, was an historic legacy. His understanding of the cemetery, as elaborated in his 1939 Quartermaster General's report, meshes with the definition of historic sites given six years earlier by the National Park Service. In commentary developed under the leadership of Verne Chatelain, the first chief historian of the NPS, the agency stated that these places had "certain matchless or unique qualities" and that they were locations where the "student of the history of the United States can sketch the larger patterns of the American story." As characterized by historian Charles Hosmer, these sites were "strongly associated with the lives of famous Americans" and with "especially dramatic incidents in American history."[53] The definition developed by the National Park Service, according to Hosmer, became the basis of the 1935 Historic Sites Act. While Quartermaster General Gibbins did not directly mention either the National Park Service or the 1935 law, his understanding that Congressional Cemetery was in itself an historic site provided a foundation for subsequent definition of the burial ground as an historic landmark and thus fully qualified for federal support under the Historic Sites Act.

The Burial Ground at Mid-Century

William M. Heinline, superintendent of Congressional Cemetery for seventeen years (1934-1951), and Joseph Mayhew, foreman for a remarkable half century (1890-1940), presided over the burial ground during a time of relative and memorable calm regarding the site. These years were followed by a period of new challenges that emerged during the 1950s in connection with the start of a sizable demographic shift within the surrounding neighborhood and the effects of this change on Christ Church in its operation of the burial ground.

In their long years of service to Congressional Cemetery, Heinline and Mayhew fit broadly within the tradition of many other dedicated supporters of the burial ground, including Henry and John Ingle in the first half of the nineteenth century. The survival of the cemetery over the long years has depended on these individuals, who clearly felt they were keeping the faith—with the members of their families interred at Congressional, the legacy of the burial ground as the first national cemetery, and the understanding that some things are truly unforgettable, lasting beyond personal commitment and recollection.

The cemetery and parish records at Christ Church do not in-

clude detailed biographical profiles of William Heinline or his predecessors in the position of cemetery superintendent. For Heinline,
as with some of the others, a biographical sketch can, however, be
fashioned from scattered information given in vestry minutes and
the local press. The sense of the man that emerges from these documents is compelling. Heinline clearly had deep and abiding commitments to his church, to the cemetery, particularly the long history associated with the burial ground, and to his family, both the
living and the dead.

As cemetery superintendent, Heinline demonstrated that he
was "an antiquarian at heart," as noted by Jessie Fant Evans in a
profile given in *The Evening Star* on May 26, 1940. He understood
the historic significance of the cemetery records, observing with
considerable enthusiasm that "Congressional Cemetery . . . is now
one of the greatest treasure houses of genealogical record in the
United States." Noting that the documents "are continuous from
as early as 1812 to 1813, many of them within their old jackets," he
expressed his appreciation of the contributions made in particular
by the War Department and the Daughters of the American Revolution. He stated as well that he hoped Congress would provide
the funds needed to photostat the documents so that they could
be made accessible to the public. A photograph published in *The
Washington, D.C., Star* on October 30, 1949, appropriately showed
the bespectacled, grey-haired superintendent examining "some of
the massive books in which early records were kept."[54]

Heinline maintained the confidence and trust of the vestry when
the cemetery was in general financially solvent, as it was during the
second half of the 1930s, when there were only occasional monthly
deficits, and during World War II, when the monthly shortfalls rose
in number and amount but never produced annual deficits. At the
beginning of the post-war period, the deficits increased but were
still manageable. In 1946, for example, they totaled $2402 for Janu-
ary, July, August, and September. The combined profit from the
other eight months was, however, $4114, thereby providing a posi-
tive balance for that year of $1712.

A seismic shift in cemetery finances emerged shortly thereafter.
The minutes of the vestry meeting on December 14, 1948, stated,
for example, that "the Cemetery was running in the red. . . ." In

a meeting conducted on January 11, 1949, the vestry accordingly approved a $1500 loan from Christ Church to pay for the repair of deteriorating fencing at the cemetery. The critical year was 1950. As of December 31, Christ Church had a healthy balance of $5,201, while the cemetery had a deficit totaling $2,082.[55] These figures underscored a substantial reversal of church/cemetery finances when compared to the numbers available for earlier periods, such as the late nineteenth century, when the cemetery regularly made profits and the church realized chronic deficits.

Given the accumulating deficits in cemetery accounts, Superintendent Heinline experienced increasing difficulties during the late 1940s in his efforts to maintain the burial ground. The vestry, meanwhile, expended increasing amounts of time discussing deteriorating conditions at the cemetery and the many needed repairs. As this happened, the parish rector, Reverend Carter S. Gillis, became progressively more involved in the cemetery. During a meeting on July 13, 1948, as in subsequent meetings, he urged each member of the vestry to visit the burial ground and to compile a list of needed repairs. The information provided in part from these lists was then incorporated into a separate cemetery report appended to the meeting minutes. In a special session on September 4, 1951, the vestry decided "that some way be arranged for the conduct of cemetery business other than at regular vestry meetings when time does not permit sufficient consideration to this side of parish affairs," or to the needs of the church itself. One week later, on September 11, 1951, the vestry agreed to separate the discussion of "church business and cemetery business" and to consider all matters pertinent to the burial ground during special meetings scheduled for the fourth Tuesday of each month.[56]

The first of the cemetery meetings was conducted on October 25, 1951, without the presence of Superintendent Heinline. During that session, one J. Russell Lowe moved and the vestry unanimously approved a motion specifying that the superintendent "submit his resignation effective the close of business December 31, 1951."[57] Following the departure as requested of Heinline, Al Rhea Johnson became cemetery superintendent. His appointment did not, however, alter the general decline at Congressional Cemetery, which was caused not by deficiencies on the part of William Heinline but by issues attendant upon the demographic shift beginning within the surrounding neighborhood (see Chapter 6). As for Superintendent Heinline, he returned to the burial ground some five years later, following his death in April 1956. Thereupon, he became part of the historical record he had long treasured as superintendent at Congressional Cemetery.

William Heinline was preceded in death by his old colleague, cemetery foreman Joseph A. Mayhew. As he had closed the gates at Congressional Cemetery for fifty years (1890-1940), so does Mayhew bring this chapter to an end. He does not speak to the reader directly, through any written words of his own, but through recollections summarized by an unidentified writer in "Grave Keeper Is Completing Fiftieth Year," an article published in *The Washington Post* on May 9, 1940. The author repeated the word "unforgettable" to describe the memories of Mayhew.

The cemetery foreman had been interviewed at the burial ground, standing "in the shade of an oak overlooking the Anacostia River." As he contemplated the graveyard, he "was seeing again the flow of 50 years" and the powerful scenes he had witnessed. He remembered, of course, the pomp and ceremony, especially the "powerful, splendid" funeral for hometown hero John Philip Sousa. In particular, he recollected the sounds of Sousa's great "Semper Fidelis," played in dirge tempo by the United States Marine Corps Band. He also remembered the impressive ceremony at the funerals of other local heroes, such as former Washington, D.C., police superintendents, whose names he recited "like a roll of honor." Mayhew seemed especially moved, however, by the burials that did not have much ceremony but that brought with them considerable grief. They included the many victims of the flu epidemic he had buried during World War I, as well as the veterans who survived "a dozen fronts" in Europe only to die at home of their wounds. He found the children to be particularly poignant: "'I never could get hard hearted,' he explained. 'You can't escape some of that—it worries you—although they may be complete strangers. Once I buried a woman, the mother of three small children. For two months after I couldn't sleep for hearing those children crying.'"

Mayhew said that nevertheless, despite such troubling memories, he felt an overriding sense of peace upon his fiftieth anniversary as foreman. In no mind to leave his post, he remained in this position, prominent at the cemetery gate, for another seven years. Following his death in February 1948, he was buried at the cemetery, as had been other family members. In addition to his mother Catherine, who had died in 1927, they included his father Basil, who expired in 1918, having spent his last thirty years as foreman at Congressional Cemetery. Together, Basil and Joseph Mayhew provided an impressive eighty-seven years of service at the burial ground. They accordingly compiled a record of longevity that seems a legacy of another time.

A photograph of Joseph Mayhew accompanies the 1940 profile published in *The Washington Post*. In this image, the foreman is standing at the main cemetery entrance, ready to close the gate for another day. Dressed in his official uniform, which is reminiscent of military wear, he conveys a sense of confidence, indicating that the gates of the cemetery can be closed in the evening and that all will be well until another day, another opening into this place of life and death. He seems, in sum, to represent in this pose the confidence of other keepers of the legacy, including Christ Church, members of Congress, Quartermaster General Henry Gibbins, the Daughters of the American Revolution, and journalist John Clagett Proctor. For all their hopes, these individuals and organizations were positioned at the end of one era and at the beginning of another, during which time it became possible that the gates might close for good on historic Congressional Cemetery.

6

A GATHERING CRISIS AT
THE OLD BURIAL GROUND

During a speech delivered in Congress on May 17, 1972, Representative Tom Railsback of Illinois declared that "Mr. Speaker, the Congressional Cemetery is in dire need of our help." He proceeded to state that the burial ground "has been seriously neglected": "Family vaults have been stripped of their doors. Trees and other foliage are overgrown. There are piles of beer cans and whiskey bottles. The small gray chapel built at the turn of the century has not been used since 1970." He then observed that "there is something that we in the Congress can do about these problems." The "something" he identified was that the cemetery "be acquired, protected, and administered by the Secretary of Interior with adequate sums" appropriated by Congress for its "proper development and operation."[1] In specifying the Department of the Interior as the most appropriate keeper of the burial ground, Railsback was supporting legislation that had been introduced on April 12, 1972, by Representative John P. Saylor of Pennsylvania and that would be advanced subsequently by Senator Vance Hartke of Indiana and Representative Joel Broyhill of Virginia.

This chapter focuses on the gathering crisis at Congressional Cemetery beginning in the 1950s. Christ Church, Congress, and federal agencies, particularly the Department of Defense and the Department of Interior, were the major participants in the unfolding narrative. Christ Church experienced challenges associated with a precipitous decline in its membership and revenues, as well as mounting expenses associated with cemetery maintenance. Congressional representatives, meanwhile, had difficulties in securing a federal agency willing to assume major responsibility for the repair and continuing operation of the site. Meanwhile, the cemetery continued to deteriorate, and long-time supporters of the burial ground confronted the real possibility of its temporary, if not permanent closure.

"Turbulence and Change on Capitol Hill"

In her history of Christ Church, published in 1994 upon the bicentennial anniversary of its establishment, Nan Robertson stated that "the 1950's ushered in a period of turbulence and change on Capitol Hill."[2] Christ Church was profoundly affected by these developments, which were driven by a significant demographic shift in the surrounding community. During the 1960s and 1970s, the congregation experienced a steady loss of members and revenue. As this occurred, a succession of rectors and vestry members confronted issues relevant to both the identity and survival of the parish, including its capacity to fulfill its historic responsibility for Congressional Cemetery.

The demographic change on Capitol Hill was part of a larger shift in the population of Washington, D.C., during 1940-1970, when the African-American population increased from approximately twenty-eight to seventy-one percent of the total. Three primary factors contributed to this change. The first was the historic migration of southern blacks to large urban areas in the north, including Washington, D.C. The second was implementation of the Redevelopment Act of 1946, which provided for the rebuilding of southwest Washington, D.C., and which resulted in the relocation of a significant part of the displaced population to "the black crescent reaching from the Navy Yard to Rock Creek in an arc about the central business district," as noted by historian Constance Green. Finally, the Supreme Court decision in Shelley versus Kramer on May 3, 1948, made racially restrictive housing covenants illegal. Anticipating the subsequent desegregation of their neighborhoods, many white residents in the Capitol Hill community moved to the Virginia and Maryland suburbs. As white relocation expanded, new housing opportunities became available in the area for black homeowners.[3]

Meanwhile, Christ Church experienced a significant erosion within its membership. Edward Gabler, who served as rector during 1928-1946, had presided over a stable, "thriving parish" that was large enough "to support three services on Sunday" and that had a membership of approximately five hundred by 1946, as documented by Nan Robertson. In contrast, his successors oversaw a steep decline in the size of the congregation as parishioners moved increasingly to the suburbs and were not replaced by new members. By 1956, the number of parishioners totaled fewer than one hundred. The congregation remained at approximately this size into the 1970s, as indicated by the annual report of the church for 1974, which listed ninety-eight "voting members."[4] This was a small group indeed to provide the financial and personnel support required to maintain both Christ Church and Congressional Cemetery, the latter of which was particularly in need at that time of a large infusion of monetary and other resources.

Six rectors presided over Christ Church during this period of transition: John H. Stipe (1951-1953), Ivan E. Merrick (1953-1956), James J. Greene (1956-1964), Donald Seaton (1964-1968), David Dunning (1968-1972), and Lynn McCullum (1973-1977). They all commented in vestry meetings and other forums on the demographic changes in the surrounding community and the effects of those changes on Christ Church. In 1955, Rev. Merrick stated that "we live in a neighborhood which displays more complex change than perhaps any other neighborhood in America" and that "we either move ahead or we slip behind." Rev. Greene expanded on this theme in his "Rector's Report" of April 15, 1963, observing that the ongoing "changes come too rapidly for many, who retreat back to 'the good old days', wishing they could reestablish the friendly atmosphere that once characterized our neighborhoods." He noted in addition that "our Day Nursery has been running this year at about half its capacity."[5]

In their efforts to address mounting problems associated with the ownership and operation of Congressional Cemetery, Christ Church rectors and members of the vestry raised profound, unanswered questions basic to their responsibilities for the burial ground. John Stipe, the first of the six pastors identified above, concluded during his initial year at Christ Church that the cemetery

was more a distraction from than an integral part of the parish min-
istry. In a letter dated June 8, 1952, he accordingly asked the vestry
to vote on a recommendation requesting that the bishop establish
a committee "to evaluate and clarify not only the financial and administrative relationships between Washington Parish and Congressional Cemetery, but also the extent to which funds deposited
in the name of one may be, or may not be, expended for the other."
He added that if it were determined that the church could never
use cemetery funds, he would "recommend the consideration" of a
legal separation between the two institutions: "The great amount of
energy and time expended by the vestry" on "the cemetery continues to be a disturbing problem, in that the church's program does
not receive all the attention it requires. . . ."[6]

Nothing came of Rev. Stipe's June 8 letter, although the vestry
"unanimously adopted" his recommendation on June 10, 1952, and
forwarded it on June 16 to Rev. Angus Dun, Episcopalian Bishop
of Washington. The bishop responded by letter on June 24, 1952,
saying that he had talked with "several gentlemen" willing to serve
on the specified committee and that the vestry should arrange "a
conference" with them. Expressing his hope that these individuals "may prove helpful to you,"[7] the bishop then removed himself
from the increasingly knotty issues relevant to the legal, "financial
and administrative relationships" between Christ Church and Congressional Cemetery. The vestry minutes do not provide a narrative
of subsequent events relative to the bishop's letter. It is clear, however, that the vestry did not secure assistance from this particular
initiative.

During the following two decades, Christ Church continued
to deliberate over questions about its responsibilities for the burial
ground. As indicated in the minutes of a meeting conducted on
September 11, 1969, for example, the vestry had determined that
the cemetery offered "diminishing returns in that there is only a
certain amount of land left for burials." Once the remaining sites
were used, the cemetery would constitute a chronic and increasing
"expense item." Given this situation, the vestry asked: "What are
our obligations to the cemetery?" In an effort to provide an answer,
the Cemetery Committee announced the "beginning of a monumental task"—that of determining "the basic financial structure of
the cemetery."[8]

In a report dated March 1970, the Cemetery Committee identified "manifold and sundry" conditions that required a "massive
restoration program." They included damage to the historic brick
wall, tombstones that had been "pushed over," underground crypts
that needed to be repaired or removed, "plus a 'thousand others'."
As indicated by this document, Christ Church had found one certain answer to its many questions about Congressional Cemetery—
it could no longer maintain the old burial ground. Ethel Robertson,
who was a member of the vestry, offered this observation in her
"Financial History" of the site: "During 1973-1974 it became apparent the cemetery was no longer deriving enough income from its
operation. The vestry hoped to have the government or some institution concerned with historic preservation take over its operation
and restoration."[9] Clearly, it had been a challenge for Christ Church
to realize and then acknowledge that it was at this crossroads. It
became even more problematic, however, to find another keeper
for the burial ground.

"Scrambled Ownership" and Federal Responsibilities

Regarding Congressional Cemetery, the relationship between Christ
Church and the federal government unraveled during the 1950s
and 1960s. The two primary areas of concern were the number and
locations of the federal burial sites and the respective responsibilities of the church and the U.S. government for their maintenance.
Questions about these matters surfaced during the 1950s as federal
officials explored the possibility of transferring ownership of the
sites to Christ Church. This initiative had most likely been driven
by federal agreement in 1937 to cut the grass around the graves and
by federal confusion since that time regarding their placement. In
characterizing the situation, legal counsel, legislators, and the press
referred over and again to "scrambled ownership" of the burial
sites. Viewed a half century later, the phrasing appears singularly
cavalier, underscoring as it does a lack of historical curiosity and
understanding about the federal and military personnel memorialized at these sites, as well as the role of Christ Church in maintaining their graves.

The Corps of Engineers, U.S. Army, initiated the deliberations
by proposing in a letter of June 20, 1950, to sell four-hundred burial

sites owned by the U.S. government to Christ Church for $10,800. The letter of response, dated December 21, 1950, came from Edward C. Cox, who was then treasurer of Christ Church. Speaking on behalf of the vestry, he stated that the proposed price was inappropriate:

> The major portion of the . . . sites have been cared for by the cemetery for almost 100 years at no additional cost to the Government; whereas, other lot owners are charged a nominal annual fee for special care, except sites which are perpetually endowed. It is apparent, therefore, that even at a nominal cost of $1 per site per year for the upkeep of these lots the Government has received a benefit which would represent 10 times the original cost per site for those sites acquired by act of Congress, August 18, 1856.

Cox concluded by asking that the federal government either make "an outright donation" of the sites to the church or request a "consideration" of no more than $100.[10]

Lacking specifics about the four-hundred burial sites, the federal government sought legal advice from Roger Kent, General Counsel in the Office of the Secretary of Defense. While he could not clarify the locations of all the sites, he carried the day by interjecting "scrambled ownership" into the discourse via a letter of March 31, 1953, to Senator Leverett Saltonstall of Massachusetts, chairman of the Senate Committee on Armed Services:

> At numerous times, prior to 1871, the Government acquired many burial lots and released others. Apparently meticulous records were not kept and preserved. Government burials were made in lots not acquired and private burials were made in lots sold by the vestry but previously having been acquired by the Government. Several unsuccessful attempts have been made to clarify this scrambled ownership.

As examples of the problem, Kent noted that the vestry had "inadvertently used" 188 of the 400 government sites for "private burials" and the government had unintentionally used eight private sites for federal "burials, cenotaphs, or monuments." In addition, "48 burial lots are occupied or obstructed by an unused receiving vault without authority of the vestry." Neither Kent nor his audience understood that the "unused receiving vault" was and remains an important memorial site, having served as a temporary place of interment for three U.S. Presidents—William Henry Harrison, John Quincy Adams, and Zachary Taylor—as well as for many members of Congress and other notable individuals. Kent proceeded to recommend that the government "convey the excess receiving vault and about 392 excess burial lots to the vestry, at a consideration of $100" and that Christ Church relinquish its "claim for reimbursement of moneys expended by the vestry for upkeep and special care of Government lots . . . ."[11] This recommendation led to the passage of federal legislation on June 6, 1953, that was designed "to clarify the scrambled ownership of a number of burial lots located in the Washington Parish Burial Ground."

Local journalists, who had a field day with the proceedings, generally sided with Christ Church, stating in one way or another that the federal government had not fulfilled its responsibilities regarding Congressional Cemetery. In "U.S. Acts to Return Old Cemetery Lots," carried in the April 28, 1953, issue of *The Washington Post*, an unidentified author stated, for example, that "once again, the Government and Washington Parish Christ Church are dickering over burial lots," that "the current transaction . . . may close the deal once and for all," and that Christ Church would be the loser—"the vestry will keep right on maintaining the Government cenotaphs and monuments just the same, as it has for 169 years."

The issue of federal responsibility for the federal burial sites came into sharp focus during 1960 with an important meeting at the burial ground on February 15, a subsequent exchange of quotable memoranda and letters, and speeches in Congress. Organized by the Quartermaster General, Military District of Washington, D.C., the February 15 meeting was conducted "to gain some knowledge and insight as to the feelings of responsible persons relative to their contracted maintenance of the 806 gravesites for which the government is responsible," as stated in a summation provided by Samuel H. Davis, Superintendent of Alexandria National Cemetery. The two sides to these deliberations were characterized as "representing Christ Church" and "representing the government's interests." The former consisted of Rev. James Greene, cemetery superintendent Al Johnson, and four members of the Christ Church vestry. The latter comprised leading figures responsible for the national military cemeteries in the Washington, D.C., area—Col. Ambrose T. McGuckian, Quartermaster General, Military District of Washington, D.C.; Jesse Myers, Acting Chief of the Cemetery Branch, Memorial Division of the Office of Quartermaster General, Military District of Washington, D.C.; John C. Metzler, Superintendent of Arlington National Cemetery; and, as noted above, Samuel H. Davis, Jr.[12]

The meeting focused primarily on the fee Christ Church "would charge" per annum to maintain the 806 government lots at the cemetery by conducting tasks that included the following and that would be "subject to unannounced inspections . . . at any time": "mowing the grass to a height of two inches" in areas where federal graves were located; neatly "trimming the grass adjacent to and around all government monuments, headstones and cenotaphs on the lots each time the grass is mowed"; "cleaning government headstones, using the standard cleaning formula and procedure"; raising and straightening "government headstones on a unit cost as directed"; and filling, reseeding, and/or sodding "sunken graves on a unit cost . . . ." Superintendent Al Johnson provided the answer, stating that $2,015, or $2.50 per grave, would be required to conduct the specified tasks. Rev. Greene spoke on behalf of the representatives from Christ Church, saying that "they would be governed by Mr. Johnson's judgement in such matters." While the discussion about this figure and related matters was apparently "genial," the spokespersons for the national military cemeteries drew differing conclusions, as noted by Samuel Davis in his summation: "The resultant figures appeared to be far in excess of costs experienced in national cemeteries."[13]

On February 16, 1960, one day after the meeting at Congressional Cemetery, Superintendent Al Johnson responded in a letter to comments provided by Superintendent Samuel Davis of Arlington National Cemetery. He was clearly angry over statements made during the preceding day by the officials associated with the national military cemeteries, as indicated by the statement given in his final paragraph:

If the Government wants to take the Care and Maintenance of the 806 graves over again we will not feel badly about it. Feel free to do as you desire. We hanv't [sic] made any money on the contract, as it is now written. It has been quite a Headache [sic] to us. Of course, you figure this work at cost, when you say we should be able to keep the areas owned by the Government for $1,000.00 per annum. We don't figure the same way; we must figure cost, Plus. If we are doing this work at cost we should turn it back to you, when the contract expires next June 30th. If we can't make some money on the contract it should be the responsibility of the Government, and we should not renew the contract again.

This statement, clearly spoken from the heart, represented not only the views of Superintendent Johnson but also those of Christ Church. The following words appear at the end of the letter: "By Direction of Rector And Vestry of Christ Church, Washington Parish."[14]

Meanwhile, the debate was joined by Representative George Mahon of Texas, who was chairman of the Armed Services Subcommittee of the House Appropriations Committee. He had "been particularly interested in the upkeep of the Government-owned lots in the Congressional Cemetery for more than two years," as noted in a Memorandum for the Record dated September 16, 1960.[15] As part of his advocacy on behalf of the burial ground, he gave persuasive testimony in support of increased federal funding on at least two occasions before the House of Representatives. The first was on May 24, 1960, when the House was deliberating over appropriations under H.R. 12326 "for civil functions administered" in part by the Department of the Army for the fiscal year ending June 30, 1961. During that session, Mahon commended his colleagues for their recommendation that $2,100 be allocated for the maintenance of federal graves at Congressional Cemetery as part of their larger appropriation for federal "cemeterial expenses." He noted that the $750 appropriated for the previous fiscal year was insufficient in that the federal graves were not conveniently grouped in one area but were instead "scattered throughout nine burial locations in the cemetery." In his most memorable statement on this occasion, Ma-

In the Shadow of the Unites States Capitol

hon characterized Congressional as the first national burial ground, noting that "from the beginning it was intended that this cemetery would be used in part as a burial ground for Members of Congress and other officials of the U.S. Government. . . ."[16]

Mahon sharpened these comments in a speech before the House of Representatives on July 2, 1960. Throughout his presentation, he focused on Congressional as the forerunner of Arlington. He noted, for example, that "until the establishment of the Arlington National Cemetery, additional sites in Congressional Cemetery were, from time to time, reserved for Government use and, in return, the Government appropriated moneys, labor, and material toward the upkeep and improvement of the cemetery property." He then provided an important identification of Congressional as the first national cemetery based on its inclusivity, its availability to all Americans regardless of military status:

It is not surprising that this cemetery has been known almost from its establishment as Congressional Cemetery and is usually so designated in acts of Congress and by the public generally. It is often referred to as our first national cemetery and is perhaps our one true national cemetery due to the fact that Arlington and all other so-called national cemeteries are dedicated primarily for interment of the remains of those who have served in our Armed Forces, whereas Congressional Cemetery is primarily civilian.[17]

Without indicating or perhaps knowing, Representative Mahon recalled in this statement observations provided in 1937 by Quartermaster General Henry Gibbins, who had characterized Congressional as "in reality, the first national cemetery."

Representative Mahon did not prevail in his efforts to secure additional funding for maintenance of the 806 federal burial sites at Congressional Cemetery. He acknowledged his frustration in a letter he wrote on July 7, 1960, to Wilber M. Brucker, Secretary of the Army. After noting that he and the Secretary had spoken "some time ago" regarding "the maintenance of the Congressional Cemetery," he recalled a conversation with a combat veteran of World War II and the Korean War who had definite ideas about the meaning of "national cemetery" and did not think Congressional Cemetery fit the definition. While Mahon did not summarize their conversation, he was irritated by the exchange, as suggested by the final two paragraphs in his letter to Secretary Brucker:

> I have been rather kind to the Army, as you know, and it disturbs me a bit that I have had indications that perhaps the Army, rather than make a reasonably fair contract with Christ Church, was going to go through a much more elaborate and expensive process and undertake to keep up the graves by having people go into the Cemetery from other areas.
>
> If this is right and fair, it is all right with me, but I hope the Army will do the right thing about this matter and act in accordance with the implied mandate of Congress.[18]

The end of this episode in the saga of Congressional Cemetery was that Congress did not at that time appropriate $2,100 or any other sum to Christ Church for maintenance of the federal burial sites. The members apparently agreed with the conclusion reached by Jesse Myers of the Memorial Division of the Office of Quartermaster General, Military District of Washington. In a Memorandum for the Record, he had stated "that the government can maintain these lots at a higher standard and at less cost than they would be maintained by Congressional Cemetery even if additional money were provided for that purpose."[19]

In his letter of February 16, 1960, written at the direction of the Christ Church rector and vestry, Al Johnson had stated that maintenance of the federal lots "has been quite a Headache to us" and that "we will not feel badly about it" if the federal government wanted to assume this responsibility. The determination that government personnel could maintain the burial sites better and at a lesser cost than could the cemetery staff must, nonetheless, have been discouraging, even insulting, to Al Johnson and the Christ Church vestry, who generally believed that they had not been sufficiently compensated by the federal government for their services provided at Congressional Cemetery.

Questions Regarding Congressional as a National Cemetery

The decision by Congress that it would not provide funds to Christ Church for maintenance of the federal burial sites at Congressional concluded one episode in the long history of Congressional Cemetery. It did not, however, end debate about the historical significance of the burial ground, particularly its status as a national cemetery. The discussion focused on these key questions: What is a national cemetery? Is Congressional a national cemetery? The respective parties in these informal deliberations provided opposing understandings of the burial ground in their answers to these queries. The differing views had, of course, been part of the ongoing discussion about Congressional Cemetery since the establishment of the national military cemetery system during the Civil War. The divergent understandings of the burial ground were exacerbated during the 1960s, however, as the infrastructure of the cemetery continued to deteriorate and as Christ Church experienced increasing difficulties in maintaining the site.

Two incidents, one at the beginning and the other at the end of the 1960s, exemplified the ongoing deliberations. The first centered on the March 8, 1961, issue of *The Pentagram News*, which was produced by Domenick J. Arone, a newspaper publisher based in Arlington, Virginia, who identified himself in the periodical as "a private individual, in no way connected with the Department of the Army." The issue included "Here Lies Push-Ma-Ta-Ha," an article that focused not on the Choctaw chief who had fought alongside Andrew Jackson (see Chapter 4) but on Congressional Cemetery as the first national burial ground. The opening paragraphs made this claim in comparing Congressional to Arlington National Cemetery:

> While Arlington National Cemetery is one of the best known burial grounds in the world, its predecessor in Washington lies almost unnoticed amid the headstones of statesmen, soldiers and even Indians.
>
> Although Arlington bustles daily with services and ceremonies, 80,000 men and women lie in the comparative stillness of the old Congressional Cemetery on the banks of the Anacostia River near the D.C. General Hospital.

The 30-acre burial ground was the United States' first national cemetery long before Arlington was begun during the Civil War as a last resting place for battle victims.[20]

Objections to these statements appear in brief, typewritten comments provided on the copy of this article maintained at the National Archives, Washington, D.C. These comments summarize the views of John C. Metzler, Superintendent of Arlington National Cemetery; Jesse Myers of the Memorial Division, Quartermaster General, Washington Military District; and Colonel Harry D. Temple, Army veteran. They read as follows:

Mr. Myers and Colonel Temple objected to the implication that the Congressional Cemetery was the "First National Cemetery."

Mr. Myers talked to Mr. Metzler who arranged with his Headquarters that such stories would in the future be cleared.

Metzler, Myers, and Temple did not, however, have the last word in this particular matter. The final typewritten comment states that a "Mrs. McDonald," who was a civilian staff member in the Memorial Division of the Quartermaster General, Washington Military District, "pointed out" that Congressional Cemetery was identified as the first national cemetery in official records maintained by the Memorial Division.

The three officials did prevail, nonetheless, in connection with the subsequent issue of *The Pentagram News*, dated March 22, 1961. This publication carried a short, pithy article with this combative title: "Congressional Cemetery Not 'National'." The first three paragraphs of this five-paragraph narrative read as follows:

Washington's Congressional Cemetery may have been the first cemetery for burial of national leaders, but it wasn't the first national cemetery.

Officials of Arlington National Cemetery point out that the National Cemetery System wasn't established until 1861-62.

278   *In the Shadow of the Unites States Capitol*

Congressional Cemetery, which has graves dating to 1803 [sic], never was a part of the system; so, contrary to information received earlier by the Pentagram News, it was not a National Cemetery.[21]

In 1969, the National Park Service (NPS) joined the ongoing debate over the national significance of Congressional Cemetery. Shortly thereafter, it emerged as the major federal participant in deliberations that continued into the 1970s and became increasingly complex, involving extended negotiations over the agency's responsibilities for the burial ground. This narrative was initiated on May 25, 1969, when William J. Murtagh, Keeper of *The National Register of Historic Places*, and Ernest Allen Connally, Chief of the NPS Office of Archeology and Historic Preservation, certified the inclusion of Christ Church in this list, which had been authorized by the National Historic Preservation Act of 1966. Administered by the NPS, *The National Register* remains part of a national effort to identify and preserve historic resources, defined as "districts, sites, buildings, structures, and objects that are significant in American history, architecture, archeology, engineering, and culture . . . ."[22]

On June 23, 1969, Murtagh and Connally approved the inclusion of Congressional Cemetery in *The National Register of Historic Places*. Both the church and cemetery were accordingly cited in the inaugural issue of this publication, issued during 1969. Landmarks historian Nancy C. Taylor, National Capitol Planning Commission, had prepared the nomination for Congressional Cemetery, which was submitted on April 3, 1969. In her statement, she focused on the singularity of the burial ground, recalling comments made previously by Quartermaster Henry Gibbins and Representative George Mahon:

Although privately owned by Christ Church, Congressional Cemetery was the first true National Cemetery in the U.S. and is perhaps still the only truly National Cemetery due to the fact that Arlington and other national cemeteries are principally reserved for military dead. . . . There are perhaps more early historical figures buried within this 'American Westminster Abbey' than in any other cemetery in the country.[23]

Taylor underscored the unique status of Congressional Cemetery in the remaining sections of the nomination form, specifying that the site was "National" as opposed to "State" or "Local." The inaugural issue of *The National Register of Historic Places* did not include these comments. It did, however, note that the burial ground "continued to be called the Congressional Cemetery" for these reasons: "its close association with the national legislature," the interments of congressmen in "100 burial sites" that had been reserved "for the use of the Federal Government," and the appropriations made by Congress "between 1824 and 1834" "for the construction of a keeper's house, a receiving vault, and a wall around the grounds." The 1976 edition of *The National Register* and all subsequent issues to date have identified Congressional as "the first national cemetery."

Two statements in particular provide definitions relevant to the inclusion of Congressional in *The National Register of Historic Places*. The first appeared in *With Heritage So Rich* (1966), a report issued in May by a committee that included representatives from the legislative and executive branches of the U.S. government, as well as the National Trust for Historic Preservation. According to William Murtagh, this volume "provided guidelines for the philosophy of preservation planning deemed necessary at the time." They stated in sum that "if the preservation movement is to be successful, it must go beyond saving bricks and mortar. It must go beyond saving occasional historic houses and opening museums. It must be more than a cult of antiquarians. It must do more than revere a few precious national shrines. It must attempt to give a sense of orientation to our society, using structures and objects of the past to establish values of time and place."[24]

The publication of *With Heritage So Rich* led to passage on October 15, 1966, of the National Historic Preservation Act, which was designed to preserve "historic properties significant to the Nation's heritage," specifically to its "historical and cultural foundations." The legislation recognized, at least in theory, the need for federal support of such institutions:

Although the major burdens of historic preservation have been borne and major efforts initiated by private agencies and individuals, and both should continue to play a vital role, it is nevertheless necessary and appropriate for the Federal Government to accelerate its historic preservation programs and activities, to give maximum encouragement to agencies and individuals undertaking preservation by private means, and to assist State and local governments and the National Trust for Historic Preservation in the United States to expand and accelerate their historic preservation programs and activities.[25]

In terms of this study, the above statement with its reference to federal support for "private agencies and individuals" could certainly be interpreted to include Christ Church in its efforts to maintain Congressional Cemetery. There was seemingly, then, no legislative obstacle in working to secure government assistance in preserving the burial ground as a site expressive of the "historical and cultural foundations" of the nation, specifically of the national capital in its formative years. There were, however, other obstacles, including ongoing controversy over identification of the burial ground as a national cemetery.

John C. Metzler, Superintendent of Arlington National Cemetery, Jesse Myers of the Quartermaster General's Memorial Division, and many others maintained that only a military cemetery could qualify as a national cemetery. Because Congressional Cemetery was not specifically and exclusively a military burial ground, it could not be supported as a national cemetery. In her nomination of Congressional for *The National Register of Historic Places*, Nancy Taylor offered a more inclusive interpretation of national cemetery, stating that Congressional "is perhaps still the only truly National Cemetery due to the fact that Arlington and other national cemeteries are principally reserved for the military dead." The problem for those sharing this view was that no legislation had been passed espousing this more inclusive understanding of national cemetery. For this reason, no federal agency had been expressly tasked with the preservation of a burial ground that did not fit the definition of "national military cemetery," no matter its other claims and distinctions.

In addition, neither established precedent nor federal legislation had ever tasked any particular federal agency with supporting Congressional Cemetery as a national historic site. In the early 1970s, then, no one agency emerged as the champion of the burial ground, although a number of federal organizations, particularly the National Park Service, considered various proposals for providing support to the cemetery. Their enthusiasm waned, however, as the projected costs increased and as other initiatives competed for limited federal appropriations.

Representative John Saylor and His Vision of the Burial Ground

From 1812 into the early 1970s, the federal government and Christ Church had collaborated periodically in efforts focused on the development and maintenance of Congressional Cemetery. During those many years, however, neither party had urged or pursued clarification of their relationship in these activities. Their occasional partnership had accordingly never been defined or codified. Finally, during 1972-1973, efforts were undertaken to end this extended period of ambiguity and to define at long last federal responsibilities for the preservation of Congressional Cemetery. Representative John P. Saylor of Pennsylvania was the dominant legislative figure in these deliberations. The key participating agencies were the Department of the Army, the Veterans Administration, and the National Park Service. Christ Church, curiously, was not directly involved in the discussions but did, nonetheless, make clear its support of Saylor's initiatives.

The developments relative to Congressional Cemetery during this period do not constitute a neat and tidy story. They include instead the circulation of controversial proposals recommending that various federal agencies assume ownership of and responsibility for the burial ground; increased anxiety on the part of Christ Church, which concluded that it could not by itself rescue the cemetery; and deepening public concern over its ongoing deterioration. While the narrative does not have a clear ending, it constitutes the most deliberative, extensive effort by the federal government to that time in identifying a federal keeper for the burial ground.

Representative Saylor stood steady at the center of the ongoing deliberations, confident in his understanding that Congressional Cemetery was a national legacy and that substantive federal sup-

port was critical to its preservation. As a public official, he was remarkable for the character and length of his service to the nation, for
his appreciation of history and the historical legacy of Congressional Cemetery, and for his efforts as a conservationist and environ-
mentalist. Elected to Congress in 1949, Saylor served in the twelve
succeeding Congresses until his death at the age of sixty five on
October 28, 1973. Among other legislative responsibilities, he had
served for twenty-four years on the House Committee on Veterans
Affairs, and he was the ranking minority member of the House Interior and Insular Affairs Committee at the time of his death. Both
of these committees had responsibilities for cemeteries under the
control of the federal government, with the former overseeing the
Civil War burial grounds and the latter the network of cemeteries
for U.S. veterans. Through his participation in these committees,
Saylor refined his definition of U.S. national cemeteries, which he
came to understand included Congressional Cemetery.

Saylor's work as a legislator was impelled in part by his interests in history and conservation. As an expression of these interests, he expended considerable time and energy in ongoing efforts
focused on the preservation of Congressional Cemetery, which he
considered a national legacy. He received no awards for these initiatives. Instead, he was repeatedly frustrated over what he saw
as unreasonably narrow definitions of national cemeteries and the
rite of burial in such cemeteries. He did, however, gain the support
of the Christ Church vestry, which hoped that he could ultimately
find a solution to the increasingly weighty challenges posed by the
deteriorating burial ground. In addition, he brought issues relevant
to the preservation of Congressional Cemetery into sharp focus on
the national stage, initiating action that forced federal agencies,
particularly the National Park Service, to define their responsibilities or lack thereof for the burial ground.

Both the legislative skills of John Saylor and his commitment to
the preservation of Congressional Cemetery were on full display
in a lively hearing before the House Committee on Veterans' Affairs over proposed legislation that eventually became the National
Cemetery Act of 1973. The hearing, staged during March 28 and
29, 1972, focused on H.R. 12674, entitled "National Cemeteries and
Burial Benefits for Veterans." The key elements of this proposed

legislation were to establish a national cemetery system within the Veterans' Administration and to transfer responsibility for the national cemeteries, with the exception of Arlington National Cemetery and the U.S. Soldiers' Home in Washington, D.C., from the Department of the Army to the Veterans' Administration.

The centerpiece of the hearing was a presentation by Charles R. Ford, who was Chief of Civil Functions in the Office of the Under Secretary of the Army, Department of the Army. He stated that the Department of the Army was united in its support of H.R. 12674: "We are confident that the Veterans' Administration will do an excellent job of operating the proposed new national cemetery system and will provide for the needs of the families of those who die on active duty and are buried in these cemeteries." He was equally confident that the Army was the appropriate authority for continued operation of Arlington National Cemetery. By way of example, he delineated the progress made on implementation of the Arlington National Cemetery master plan, which Congress had approved in 1966 with the appropriation of $8,760,000: "Ten major programs have been completed including land development for burial purposes, an irrigation system, a service complex and a visitor's center and parking area." Ford was then asked about eligibility requirements for burial at Arlington. The "overriding criterion," he explained, was "honorable active service in the Armed Forces of the United States." Qualifications were, however, attached to this standard in that "only certain categories of men and women" were entitled to burial at Arlington, including active duty personnel and individuals who had retired after twenty years of service, as well as "the spouses, minor children, and certain dependent adult children of the foregoing . . . ."[26]

John Saylor, who had been sitting quietly during this recitation, could finally take it no longer. He was likely pushed beyond silence by Ford's reference to the large federal appropriation for Arlington and the caveats regarding burial at the cemetery. Recognized by Chairman Olin E. Teague of Texas, Saylor said this: "I hate to tell you that it [Ford's statement] is a broken record. The needle scratches. I have heard this same story for 20-plus years, except that you now admit that everybody can't be buried in Arlington Cemetery." During all the talk in this hearing about national military cemeteries, budgets, and responsible federal authorities, Saylor had been thinking about Congressional Cemetery. He went on to say that the ongoing deterioration of this burial ground ought to make Ford and his supporters think twice about the supposed federal record of accomplishment in the preservation of national burial grounds:

> Now, you say you are proud of your record of 110 years. Let me give you a couple of examples of which you should not be proud. Don't ever go out to Congressional Cemetery, because if you do you will hang your head in shame. Don't have anybody come out there and have the military taking a look at the graves they are supposed to be responsible for because they are in horrible condition. That is one right here under your very nose in Washington that the Army should not be proud of.[27]

By the force of his personality, particularly his inimitable use of language, Saylor dominated the hearing conducted over H.R. 12674, as recorded in the published transcript. He did not change the expected course of events resulting from the hearing in that President Nixon signed H.R. 12674 into law on August 13, 1973. Saylor did, however, succeed in reminding his fellow legislators that there was another cemetery of national significance in the capital city and that the federal burial sites at this cemetery needed attention. By his comments and subsequent actions, he was instrumental in preparing the basis for a congressional hearing on June 22, 1973, designed "to provide that the historic property known as the Congressional Cemetery may be acquired, protected, and administered by the Secretary of the Interior as part of the park system of the National Capital, and for other purposes."

A complex series of events preceded the June 22, 1973, hearing that engaged the familiar players in such deliberations: Christ Church, the federal government, and the general public. During the early 1970s, Christ Church came to the certain understanding that it could no longer continue in its historic role as owner and operator of the burial ground. At the same time, Congress and various federal agencies expressed their general understanding that the cemetery was indeed an historic site but ultimately concluded that some other organization should assume responsibility for its continuation. Meanwhile, concerned citizens, particularly lot owners, wrote letters to their congressional representatives urging federal action to arrest the deterioration of Congressional Cemetery. The narrative of these events emerges from a rich trove of unpublished material—including correspondence and memoranda in the archives of the Department of the Interior, Department of the Army, and Christ Church—as well as official government publications, particularly the *Congressional Record* and *The National Register of Historic Places*. These documents underscore two key points: one, the national prominence of Congressional Cemetery as an historic site and two, its uniqueness, given the difficulty government organizations had in placing it within a particular category of historic sites.

As before, Representative Saylor initiated the federal debate. On April 12, 1972, just a couple of weeks following the congressional hearing on H.R. 12674, he introduced H.R. 14339, identified in general as "A Bill to provide that the historic property known as the Congressional Cemetery may be acquired, protected, and administered by the Secretary of the Interior as part of the park system of the National Capital, and for other purposes." With the introduction of this legislation, he established a framework for the subsequent debate, positioning the Department of the Interior, specifically the National Park Service, at the center of the discussion.

The proposed legislation gained force as three other congressmen advanced the same bill but with different identification numbers. On May 4, 1972, Senator Vance Hartke, a Democrat from Indiana, stated in Congress that Congressional Cemetery was "a national disgrace," given its ongoing deterioration, and then introduced S. 3580, which was identical to Saylor's bill. About two weeks later, on May 17, 1972, Representative Tom Railsback, a Republican from Illinois, advanced H.R. 15039, also identical but for the identification numbers to Saylor's bill. Approximately one year later, on June 21, 1973, Representative Joel Broyhill, a Republican from Virginia, reintroduced Saylor's bill as H.R. 8883. Meanwhile, on January 11, 1973, Representative Saylor had reintroduced his bill as H.R. 1891.[28] The repeated, insistent introduction of the same bill by a bipartisan group of legislators kept the spotlight on the National Park Service, prompting uncertainty, controversy, and ultimately a unified approach within the agency as it deliberated over proposals regarding its responsibilities for Congressional Cemetery.

This initiative also brought new life and hope to the Christ Church vestry, which had been apprised of Saylor's intentions prior to his introduction of H.R. 14339. During their meeting on April 10, 1972, for example, the members were optimistic, even joyous, over the possibility that the federal government would assume responsibility for the burial ground. Woodruff Price, Senior Warden of Christ Church, had a lead role in the deliberations, which he initiated by exclaiming that "We're about to be expropriated!" He then proposed this resolution, which the vestry approved unanimously:

> RESOLVED, that the Vestry of Christ Church feels that it is in the best interest of Christ Church and Congressional Cemetery that custodianship of the Cemetery be placed in the hands of an appropriate agency of the Federal Government; PROVIDED that assurances are received that the rights of existing plot holders will be respected and that upkeep of the Cemetery will be continued consistent with its historic and memorial character.[29]

The phrasing of this resolution, particularly the statement about placing "custodianship of the Cemetery" with "an appropriate agency of the Federal Government," suggests that the vestry was not certain at that time about its intentions regarding the burial ground. While the members clearly wanted to relinquish responsibility for the cemetery, they were not so sure about transferring ownership, as conveyed by their use of the word "custodianship." As indicated by the minutes of the April 10 meeting, the vestry did not deliberate at that time over the possible legal or practical meanings of this term. The members did, however, reconsider the phrasing during the following week.

On April 17, 1972, the vestry drafted a one-page statement on the "Proposed Acquisition of Congressional Cemetery by the Secretary of the Interior." The last sentence in this document stated that the Saylor bill would have the best chance of passage "if, at an early date, Christ Church expressed its willingness to donate the Cemetery if the bill should become law."[30] The shift in phrasing had major significance, indicating that Christ Church was willing to relinquish ownership of the burial ground it had controlled for 165 years. Given the sense of responsibility the members collectively felt for the cemetery, they could never have agreed to this shift of phrasing, with all the attendant implications, unless they had not only recognized but also accepted the understanding that they could no longer do what John Ingle and so many other heroic members of earlier vestries had done—operate and maintain the historic burial ground.

The vestry formalized its decision in a resolution of May 8, 1972, which read in part as follows:

> Resolved: The Vestry of Christ Church – Washington Parish endorses HR-14339 and S3580 legislation [Saylor's and Hartke's bills] which would authorize the Secretary of the Interior to acquire and maintain Congressional Cemetery, which is presently owned by Christ Church; the Vestry urges the prompt enactment of this legislation by the Congress; and the Vestry expresses its intention to donate without restriction the real property known as Congressional Cemetery to the United States as soon as practicable after enactment of legislation authorizing its acquisition and maintenance by the Secretary of the Interior.

The vestry directed that copies of this resolution be sent to Representative John Saylor; Senator Vance Hartke; Rogers Morton, Secretary of the Interior; Henry M. Jackson, senator from the state of Washington and chairman of the Senate Interior and Insular Affairs Committee; and Wayne N. Aspinall, chairman of the House Interior and Insular Affairs Committee.[31]

Meanwhile, interested, indignant, even angry members of the public entered the debate over Congressional Cemetery, stating in letters to the editors of various newspapers and to their congressional representatives that the federal government needed to do something at long last to save the burial ground. They were inspired to action by media coverage of the funeral events staged for J. Edgar Hoover, Director of the Federal Bureau of Investigation. He died in Washington, D.C., on May 2, 1972, and was buried at Congressional

Cemetery on May 4, following a funeral conducted that day at the National Presbyterian Church in the District of Columbia. Long before his death, Hoover had directed that he be interred at Congressional next to the graves of his parents. As noted by Brian C. Kates in "Forsaken Heritage," published in *American Cemetery: The Magazine of Cemetery Management*, government officials had accordingly been "faced with fulfilling his wish to be buried at Congressional — a desire he put in writing long before it had become an eyesore."[32]

While the funeral was televised, the proceedings at the cemetery were not. Newspapers across the country, however, published accounts of preparations for the burial and descriptions of the cemetery at the time of interment. An article by Donald P. Baker in *The Washington Post* of May 7, 1972, exemplifies the coverage. Entitled "City's Oldest Cemetery: History Oft Interred with Bones," the article made two major points: that Congressional had long been the cemetery of choice by "official Washington" but that official Washington had not fulfilled its responsibilities to the historic burial ground. The article began with this memorable quotation, which was also cited in other journalistic accounts: "'When we heard Mr. Hoover was coming here, we got out there ourselves and cut the grass,' said Alverta Price, who lives in the caretaker's house at Congressional Cemetery." As indicated in the second paragraph, Alverta Price was the grandmother of a cemetery employee. Discerning legislators and members of the public saw a disturbing disconnect between the pomp and ceremony of the funeral and the seemingly haphazard preparation of the grounds for Hoover's burial. Baker provided illustrative quotations, noting that Senator Vance Hartke had described Congressional Cemetery as "a national disgrace" on the day of Hoover's burial and had introduced legislation at that time.

In the days following the interment of Hoover, a number of concerned citizens who had watched televised coverage of the funeral and/or read reprints of articles about the cemetery wrote to their congressional representatives and to President Nixon urging them to take action. Many of these letters, a number of which have been preserved in archives of the National Park Service, included clippings of articles reprinted in publications identified as the *Milwaukee Journal* and the *Oregonian*, among other periodicals.

One of the most memorable letters came from Mrs. Helen P. Anthony of Water Valley, Mississippi, who had watched the televised coverage of Hoover's funeral at the National Presbyterian Church. On the same day, May 4, 1972, she wrote directly to "Mr. President," voicing her concerns about ongoing deterioration at the cemetery. She said that she had visited the graves of her mother and grandmother at Congressional during the preceding September and had been "shocked and heartbroken at the disgraceful condition of the cemetery. Grass was knee high, some tombstones overturned and it looked like a forgotten place." She then cited the statement she remembered in particular from Nixon's remarks about Hoover during the funeral: "I heard you say 'Let us cherish his memory.' I hope we will do just that." She concluded with this statement, focused on her vision of Congressional as a burial ground for all Americans:

> What better way could we do that [cherish Hoover's memory] than preserve Congressional Cemetery. Not only for a tribute to J. Edgar Hoover, but for other great Americans, like John Philip Sousa, many of our early Senators and Congressmen, many D.C. firemen & police and the average citizen whose resting place is Congressional. . . . Any effort you may be able to give this matter, Mr. President, will be wholeheartedly appreciated by me.[33]

The congressmen and federal officials who received messages from concerned citizens appear to have read them with care. The letter to "Mr. President" from Helen Anthony, for example, was extensively underscored, beginning with this sentence in the brief introductory paragraph: "Now with the passing of Mr. Hoover and his burial in Congressional Cemetery the concern [about this burial ground] has been re-kindled." The letters were forwarded to responsible federal officials, most frequently within the Department of Interior/NPS but also on occasion to the Office of the President. In their responses, the federal officials sometimes provided strong endorsements of the attached statements, as did Congressman William A. Steiger of Wisconsin in his letter to R.A. Whitlock, Congressional Services Officer, National Park Service:

A resident of my District has written a forceful letter concerning . . . the Congressional Cemetery in Washington, a copy of which is enclosed.

I too am concerned that the cemetery be assured of being kept in good condition. Your consideration of Mrs. King's request, and of my concern, would be most appreciated.[34]

The correspondence indicates that the National Park Service had come to center stage in federal deliberations over Congressional Cemetery. The letter from Helen Anthony to President Nixon provides a case in point. A Deputy Special Assistant to the President sent her a response during May 1972, saying that "this is a matter outside the jurisdiction of the Federal Government." He then, however, directed the letter to the attention of the Department of Interior, as well as to the mayor's office in Washington, D.C. In correspondence dated June 20, 1972, Russell E. Dickenson, Director of National Capital Parks, thanked Mrs. Anthony for her letter to President Nixon and informed her of John Saylor's bill, providing "that Congressional Cemetery be operated as a part of the National Capital Parks System."[35] The rest of this particular saga in the history of Congressional Cemetery focuses on actions taken by the National Park Service in response to the emerging consensus that it acquire and manage Congressional Cemetery.

The National Park Service as Possible Owner of the Site

The NPS initially supported efforts focused on its acquisition and management of the burial ground. Perhaps the most compelling evidence of this support was agency participation in the development of H.R. 14339, "A Bill to provide that the historic property known as the Congressional Cemetery may be acquired, protected, and administered by the Secretary of the Interior as part of the park system of the National Capital, and for other purposes." The NPS prepared the accompanying documentation at the request of Representative Saylor. In a memorandum dated April 27, 1972, Richard L. Stanton, Assistant Director of Cooperative Activities for the National Capital Parks, informed Robert M. Utley, Director of the NPS Office of Archeology and Historic Preservation, that "we have been requested to prepare Legislative Support Data" for the Saylor bill and asked Utley to evaluate the historical significance of Congressional Cemetery.[36]

In a memorandum that reached Stanton's office on May 4, Utley reported that the cemetery was "a property of outstanding significance in the history of the National Capital" and thus "would be a wholly appropriate addition to its system of parklands."[37] This assessment provided the basis for a document entitled "Justification: Congressional Cemetery," which was completed in June 1972 and incorporated into the requested Legislative Support Data. The "Justification," which constituted the most detailed appraisal of the burial ground provided to that date by a federal agency, indicated that top officials within the National Park Service seriously contemplated its acquisition. The document was prepared by a team comprising a maintenance specialist, landscape architect, park planner, legislative assistant, and two engineers, one of whom had expertise in archeology. They all were familiar with issues relevant to possible incorporation of the burial ground into the National Capital Parks System.[38]

The "Justification" comprised eleven sections focused on central areas of interest. The "Introduction" stated that Congressional "may be considered the first 'national cemetery' of the United States" because federal funding was provided for its maintenance during the antebellum period and "many high-ranking U.S. officials and early American historical figures were buried there." The following section, entitled "Acquisition by NPS," credited both the historical evaluation provided by Utley and the citation of the cemetery in the inaugural issue of *The National Register of Historic Places* (1969):

Acquisition of Congressional Cemetery by the National Park Service, as proposed by Congressional Bills H.R. 14339 (Saylor) and S. 3580 (Hartke), can be supported by the historical evaluation of our Office of Archeology and Preservation as an addition to the park system of the Nation's Capital. This acquisition is further supported by its inclusion in the National Register of Historic Places as approved by the President's Advisory Council on Historic Preservation.

The remaining sections of the "Justification" delineated significant challenges attendant upon NPS acquisition of Congressional Cemetery and then advanced a visionary concept of the burial ground as an historic site within the National Capital Park System. As part of this narrative, the agency identified characteristics of the burial ground that have always attracted individuals and groups interested in its preservation, as well as the problems that frequently drove them away. The section entitled "Development by National Park Service" noted, for example, that the NPS would restore "the cemetery to that period of time established by historic studies as being most significant in the history of the cemetery," which would have been the first half of the nineteenth century. This effort would not be easy because the burial ground was in "such a state of disrepair that the expenditure of considerable funds over a period of years would be necessary" to repair and stabilize the infrastructure and "to bring the entire property to a level of maintenance and development of which our entire Nation can be proud."[39]

On September 7, 1972, Manus Fish, Acting Director of National Capital Parks, submitted the "Justification" to Ronald Walker, Director of the NPS. He included the other Legislative Support Data, consisting of boundary, land ownership, and general development maps; a development schedule; an environmental impact statement; the resolution by Christ Church to donate the cemetery to the United States; and a photograph album, the contents of which were not specified. At the end of the accompanying memorandum, Fish articulated the vision of the team that had developed the document: "We feel that Congressional Cemetery will have to be operated and maintained in the same Class A standards as Arlington National Cemetery." The "we" in this statement did not include other agency officials who thought that the NPS did not have the resources to both restore and maintain Congressional and who did not want to establish precedent requiring the agency to become "cemetery keepers across the nation wherever noble remains are interred."[40]

The NPS testified at the congressional hearing of June 22, 1973, on H.R. 1891, providing that the burial ground "may be acquired, protected, and administered by the Secretary of the Interior as part of the park system of the National Capital, and for other purposes."

A large part of the narrative relevant to this hearing occurred in the months preceding the event. Representative Saylor introduced H.R. 1891 on January 11, 1973, at the beginning of the first session of the 93rd Congress. He signaled thereby that he remained convinced that the National Park Service should assume control of Congressional Cemetery. NPS administrators, however, reconsidered their initial support of the legislation. They ultimately concluded that they could not support the bill, as indicated by a June 14, 1973, memorandum from Russell Dickenson, Director of National Parks, to Ronald Walker, Director of the NPS:

The support data points out the extraordinary costs to be provided for if this cemetery is to be stabilized and brought to [an] acceptable standard. We seriously question, in view of the present atmosphere of fiscal restraint, the propriety of supporting this proposal at this particular time although the project is a worthy one. For this reason we would recommend against supporting such a bill at this time.[41]

While the surviving documentation does not detail Walker's subsequent actions, it is likely that he accepted Dickenson's recommendation and then forwarded this decision to the Secretary of the Interior, Rogers Morton. John H. Kyle, Assistant Secretary of the Interior, articulated the NPS position regarding the proposed legislation in a letter that was dated June 21, 1973, and sent to James A. Haley, chairman of the House Committee on Interior and Insular Affairs. As chairman, Haley had oversight of the Subcommittee on National Parks and Recreation, which conducted the hearing on H.R. 1891 during the following day.

Kyle summarized the NPS position regarding the proposed legislation at the beginning of his letter, stating that "the objectives of H.R. 1891 can be better accomplished by means other than National Park Service administration." The agency, he said, recommended "deferral" of congressional action on the bill "until there has been a full opportunity to explore" other options. Kyle noted that the greater part of the cemetery was not a national burial ground and that the NPS, if it assumed control, would have to maintain the graves of not only prominent federal officials but also of thousands "of citizens not involved in public life." The primary obstacle to NPS acquisition was, however, cost:

> The grounds and structures of Congressional Cemetery are in an advanced state of deterioration. We have studied the cost of bringing the property up to a standard appropriate for interpretation as part of the National Capital Park system . . . . We estimate that development costs, including the cost of stabilization of structures and headstones, landscape planting and installation of a new water system, reconstruction of roadways, installation of a storm drainage system, and restoration of walk ways and steps would cost over $3 million. Estimated annual operating and maintenance costs would be over $450,000 a year by the fifth year after authorization.

In short, the NPS had concluded that it would not "be a wise use of financial resources for the Congress to delegate to the National Park Service the responsibility for carrying out this task."

Kyle stated that the agency was ready, however, to assume a much more limited role. Toward the end of his letter to James Haley, he said that "we would be delighted to cooperate with the Committee in exploring alternatives that would provide the cemetery with the improved management that this historical site deserves."[42] So introduced, the search for suitable "alternatives" became central to the federal debate about Congressional Cemetery, including the hearing conducted on June 22, 1973, before the Subcommittee on National Parks and Recreation.

This hearing was an extraordinary event, replete with ironies involving both the schedule and participants. The discussion about H.R. 1891 and the future of the historic cemetery was planned for just one hour—10:00-11:00 a.m.—during which time the subcommittee was also to discuss another bill. The date of the hearing, June 22, was but one day after John Kyle had informed James Haley that the NPS did not support H.R. 1891. Haley, in turn, transmitted this decision to the chairman of the subcommittee, Representative Roy A. Taylor, who informed the other five members. This information was not, however, provided to the representatives of Christ

Church who were scheduled to provide statements. The result was a disconnect between their hope, even expectation, that the NPS would acquire Congressional Cemetery and the understanding of the legislators that the agency had no intention of assuming this responsibility.

The surviving record of the hearing is the unpublished "Report of Proceedings," comprising thirty-four pages.[43] This report documents the participation, or lack thereof, of the key players, the first of whom was to be the author and sponsor of the proposed legislation, John Saylor. He did not, however, attend the hearing, most likely because he had concluded that NPS acquisition of the cemetery was unlikely. Of his absence, Chairman Taylor simply said that "he could not be here today." While the "Report of Proceedings" indicated he had provided a statement, it did not include such a document.

Three representatives of the National Park Service did attend the hearing: Stanley W. Hulett, Associate Director of the NPS; Robert M. Utley, Director of the NPS Office of Archeology and Historic Preservation; and Richard L. Stanton, Assistant Director of Cooperative Activities, National Capitol Parks. They all previously had gone on record in support of Saylor's bill.[44] Stanley Hulett, who was the first witness, provided testimony, however, in opposition to the proposed legislation. Utley and Stanton did the same with occasional comments made during the discussion following Hulett's statement.

In his commentary, Hulett spoke first about the "advanced state of deterioration" of both "grounds and structures" at the burial ground. He concentrated next on costs, noting that "preliminary... estimates, which we developed just prior to today's hearing, are very high—more than $3.2 million for initial development and almost half a million dollars per year for maintenance and operation...." Given the "tight budgetary and personnel constraints" then experienced by the NPS, he stated that "other alternatives for preserving the cemetery must be explored." He noted, for example, that Congress could "contract directly with a private concern for maintenance of the cemetery" or perhaps the Architect of the Capitol could assume responsibility. Hulett then came to this conclusion: "Mr. Chairman, we therefore recommend that action on H.R. 1891 be deferred. We would be pleased to cooperate with your committee in exploring alternatives that would provide the cemetery with the improved management that this historical site deserves." He requested, and the NPS was granted, a ninety-day period during which the agency would "explore the various alternatives."

The discussion that followed was notable in particular for Hulett's statement that the burial ground was historic and "it should be properly maintained." He then voiced the central issue: "Our only question at this point is who should maintain it. . . ."[45] This question, repeated twice by a subcommittee member, was, of course, the central concern. It was easy to say that the historic burial ground should be preserved. The true stumbling block was in identifying the responsible party. Christ Church had a clear understanding that it could no longer serve in this capacity, as stated by Charles Turbyville, who identified himself as "Junior Warden of the Vestry of Christ Church," and Hazel Detwiler, a parishioner who had long been active in her support of Congressional Cemetery. Turbyville reminded the legislators that Christ Church endorsed H.R. 1891. The reasons were that the cemetery would "be a valuable addition to the National Capitol park system" given its national significance and that Christ Church no longer had the resources to maintain the burial ground.

Some of the legislators had heard previous commentary about the historic significance of the cemetery, as given by congressmen including Representative John Saylor. Many of them likely did not know, however, that the cemetery was owned by a local parish and that this parish could no longer maintain the site. Charles Turbyville explained that "we," the vestry and members of Christ Church, "believe the cemetery should have better care than we can afford to give it." The "operating income" was derived primarily from burials and was insufficient to allow even basic maintenance: "It is a constant struggle to keep the grass cut, trash picked up, gravestones upright and to do other such minor chores." The church could not even consider larger tasks, including "restoration" of the cenotaphs and other historic monuments, repair of the walkways, and installation of a new water system, all of which were pressing needs. The central statement Turbyville provided in his testimony was that the "current difficulties" were not "temporary" and that the church was rapidly approaching a crossroads at which it would have to make "some agonizing choices between maintaining the cemetery and [the] needs of our church and its members that are of equal importance."[46]

Hazel Detwiler provided the last word, literally. She spoke from the heart, appealing to the legislators as a citizen who valued Congressional Cemetery as "the first national cemetery until Arlington was established." She focused her remarks on the burial ground as a national legacy, observing in part the symbolism of the gravestone emplaced in memory of one Thomas America, then visible at the Seventeenth Street gate. In her concluding remarks, she stated that the burial ground was "a national heritage" and that "it means a great deal to anyone who is interested in American history." As the hearing drew toward an end, Representative Roy Taylor, chairman of the Subcommittee on National Parks and Recreation, thanked Hazel Detwiler for her "testimony." He noted that, "in a few words," she had underscored the "definite historic significance" of the burial ground, observing that "it was in its day what Arlington is today." Hazel Detwiler responde by saying "Exactly."[47]

The final word of Detwiler's testimony conveyed a conviction about the burial ground that was not shared by the other participants, save for Charles Turbyville. The only decision made during the hearing was that the National Park Service would be given the requested ninety days to develop "alternatives" for the preservation of Congressional Cemetery and that these alternatives would then be presented during a resumption in January 1974 of the hearing conducted by the Subcommittee on National Parks and Recreation. The subsequent search for "alternatives" became an effort on the part of the NPS to find another agency to assume control of the old burial ground.

Alternatives for Preservation of the Burial Ground

Richard Stanton, Assistant Director of Cooperative Activities at the National Park Service, led a study at the agency that resulted in a twenty-page report entitled, "Congressional Cemetery Alternatives." While this document was not dated, it was probably completed in October 1973 according to the given schedule.[48] The report is unique in that it records the results of the only formal attempt by a federal agency to identify the historic relationships between various government organizations and the cemetery and to assess federal responsibilities for the burial ground based on those connections. As noted, the cemetery clearly had a claim on the federal government for some type of support. This claim was, however, shared among several agencies, each of which had a partial interest in the burial ground. Herein lay both the special legacy and the challenge posed by the cemetery. It was widely recognized as an historic site, even as the first national burial ground. It did not, however, fit neatly into any particular category of historic sites.

The NPS study delineated six possibilities for the preservation of Congressional Cemetery:

- *Alternative One:* "The Department of the Interior, National Park Service, would acquire Congressional Cemetery, restore, maintain, protect, and interpret."
- *Alternative Two:* "Full or partial responsibility to continue with Christ Church."
- *Alternative Three:* "Christ Church to be subsidized partially or in full."
- *Alternative Four:* "Department of the Interior, National Park Service, acquires selected historic and interpretive areas only."
- *Alternative Five:* "Acquisition, restoration, maintenance, protection, and interpretation by the Veterans Administration or the Department of the Army."
- *Alternative Six:* "Architect of the Capitol accepts title; restores, maintains, and protects. The National Park Service interprets."

The order of these alternatives is important, in that the NPS led with the three it immediately rejected, advanced another two (Alternatives Four and Five) that had some merit, and then provided its recommendation, Alternative Six. The agency wanted to make it clear from the start that it did not consider itself the likely keeper of the legacy and thus stated in connection with Alternative One that "the National Park Service is under tight budgetary and personnel constraints" and thus, "in view of the high cost of this project," had concluded that the "other alternatives for preserving the cemetery should be explored." In support of this statement, the NPS provided five pages enumerating expected costs, which totaled $3,274,000 for restoration of the burial ground, $376,000 for annual maintenance and protection, and $81,800 for interpretation per year.[49]

The NPS summarily dismissed Alternatives Two and Three, having concluded that neither of them was "realistic." The agency focused on budgetary problems in connection with Alternative Two, providing by way of example a letter of May 17, 1972, from Woodruff N. Price, Senior Warden of Christ Church, to Representative John Saylor. In this two-page document, Price explained that the vestry was concerned about "the long term future of this historic cemetery" in that the church had funds "for normal upkeep, but not for needed capital investment" critical to restoration of the burial ground. Regarding Alternative Three—"Christ Church to be subsidized partially or in full"—the agency had concluded from "extended discussions with the church officials" that there was "no hope of outside subsidies of sufficient amount to make any inroads into the critical areas of restoration, maintenance, and protection."

The agency lingered over Alternative Four, giving it "a great deal of thought" before concluding that "we do not recommend this" approach. Alternative Four focused on NPS acquisition of "selected historic and interpretive areas only," which the agency determined was "not appropriate." The problem was that "the historic enclaves are scattered throughout the cemetery and there is no continuity," as demonstrated with an attached map, identified as "Congressional Cemetery: General Development Plan." This document clearly showed that the so-called "historic enclaves," including the cenotaphs, the Public Vault, and the graves of J. Edgar Hoover and John Philip Sousa, were not grouped in any one area but were instead located across six of the nine cemetery squares. The NPS was correct in asserting that it would be more costly to maintain the historic graves because they were not grouped together. The agency did recognize, however, that the scattering of the historic graves among those of the general public underscored the unique status of Congressional as a national public burial ground and thus as a site that would fit more readily under the aegis of the

NPS than of the Veterans Administration or the Department of the Army, both of which were cited in Alternative Five.

The NPS considered the Veterans Administration and the Department of the Army as possible keepers of the cemetery because they were both "involved in the maintenance and operation of Federal cemeteries in the United States and overseas." Agency officials anticipated, however, that the VA might not want to assume this responsibility because of "the preponderance of civilians interred" at the site. They proceeded, nonetheless, to contact the agency. The VA declined the offer, but for another reason, delineated in a letter from John W. Mahan, Acting Director of the Veterans Administration, to Manus Fish, Acting Director of National Capital Parks. Mahan acknowledged that the Veterans Administration had assumed responsibility under the National Cemeteries Act of 1973 for the maintenance at Congressional of 806 burial sites containing the remains of 467 "prior interments." For this reason, "we now have a vested interest in the cemetery and its future status."

Mahan went on to explain that the VA had, nonetheless, to be "guided in our thinking by the basic mission of providing for veterans" and that the acquisition of "Congressional Cemetery would do little towards" meeting that responsibility. By way of explanation, he noted that "only 3,000 unsold plots or gravesites" remained at the cemetery. If these sites were "made available to those eligible for interment in . . . national cemeteries," they "would be completely used in a period of 150 days excluding Saturdays, Sundays and Holidays." Moreover, "there is no room for further expansion of the cemetery." Mahan ended his letter by asserting that the NPS, not the VA, seemed the more likely organization to assume responsibility for the burial ground:

> We are persuaded to think that in the final analysis, the National Park Service is more appropriately the proper element of the federal government to assume the responsibility for this historic cemetery which dates back to 1807 when it was established.

In its consideration of Alternative Five, the NPS also contacted the Department of the Army, proceeding "through the office of the

Superintendent of Arlington Cemetery." The Army did not want to engage in conversation about its possible acquisition of the burial ground and did not provide the NPS with a "formal response." The NPS accordingly understood "that the Department of the Army would prefer not to consider this proposal as their responsibilities deal primarily with interments of veterans and care of veterans' cemeteries."

This left Alternative Six, recommended by the National Park Service "as priority no. 1." Agency officials had concluded that it would be appropriate for the Architect of the Capitol (AOC) to assume both the title to and responsibility for the cemetery. They noted that the AOC was responsible for operation of the United States Capitol Complex and that Congressional Cemetery appeared to be part of that complex in that its "history is linked to the Congress and should be an integral part of the interpretation of the Capitol Building and the history of Capitol Hill." The NPS officials understood, moreover, that the partnership delineated between the Architect of the Capitol and the agency would be "unique between entities of the Federal establishment" but "would seem to be a proper mixing of roles." In addition, this arrangement would be advantageous to the NPS because it would cost the agency no more than $81,800 per year "for interpretation and visitor services." Most important of all, it "would . . . preclude any semblance of a precedent for the National Park Service to acquire, restore, maintain, and protect other cemeteries on the National Register of Historic Places, a role not fully suited to the National Park Service mission."[50]

While the NPS supported Alternative Six, this approach was problematic in part because Congress did not appropriate funds for the operation and maintenance of Congressional Cemetery by the Architect of the Capitol or by any other federal office or agency. In a memorandum dated January 18, 1974, Richard Stanton, then Assistant Director of Cooperative Activities at the NPS, stated that the legislative counsel for the Speaker of the House "is personally opposed to the Architect of the Capitol undertaking such an acquisition and it is my feeling that the Architect is not now enthusiastic over the proposal." Stanton proceeded to recommend that the National Park Service should make it clear that the NPS did not have the resources to assume responsibility for the cemetery, although it was ready to provide the interpretive services identified in Alternative Six.[51]

During these deliberations, it had become clear that no federal agency wanted to acquire Congressional Cemetery and that the search for a federal keeper of the burial ground was at an end. Rogers Morton, Secretary of the Interior, spoke for the NPS in a letter that was dated August 23, 1974, and directed to James Haley, Chairman of the House Committee on Interior and Insular Affairs. He summarized the NPS position in his concluding comments, which read as follows:

> As you know, the National Park Service development budget is concentrating on priority objectives such as the Bicentennial, facilities to provide for public health and safety, and pollution control. The reconstruction of Congressional Cemetery would not, in our opinion, command a very high priority when development needs for the National Park System throughout the country are considered.

As funds were available, the agency would, however, "assist in the interpretation of Congressional Cemetery if requested to do so by the owner or whatever agency the Congress determines ought to have responsibility for its administration."[52]

The Morton letter marked the end of the effort initiated by Representative John Saylor to identify a federal agency as owner and operator of Congressional Cemetery. Two primary factors figured into the conclusion of this important chapter in the saga of the burial ground. The first was the death of Saylor on October 28, 1973. A forceful, outspoken advocate on behalf of this historic site, he was one of a kind, impossible to replace. The second factor was accumulating documentation indicating that Congressional itself was one of a kind, unique among national cemeteries in that it did not fit easily under the mandate of any one federal agency.

Memorial services were conducted for Representative Saylor in the House and the Senate on October 29 and 30, respectively. The ceremonies were particularly memorable in the House, where Saylor had served as the ranking minority member of both the Interior and Insular Affairs Committee and the Veterans' Affairs Committee. A total of 150 members provided statements that day about the large presence of Saylor as both an individual and a legislator. Thomas E. Morgan, a representative from Saylor's home state of Pennsylvania, recalled, for example, that Saylor had "played important roles" in the federal capital in "setting up a corporation for the redevelopment of Pennsylvania Avenue," creating "the C. & O. Canal National Park" and, among other projects, "in keeping up the Congressional Cemetery." Among the eleven legislators who spoke during the memorial service conducted in the Senate, Vance Hartke recalled the "common interest" he shared with Saylor "in the restoration and preservation" of the burial ground and then commended the congressman for his "legislative efforts in [sic] behalf of the restoration of Congressional Cemetery just blocks away from where I now stand."[53] While other members of Congress shared these views, it is clear that the introduction of yet additional legislation would not have been sufficient to save the burial ground. With the death of John Saylor, the momentum for this approach had come to an end.

Representative Saylor had been astute in identifying the National Park Service as the most likely federal keeper of Congressional Cemetery. Among other factors, the agency had an administrative structure in its National Capital Region that seemingly could have accommodated the burial ground. This unit, the largest of eight such authorities within the agency, operated forty-six diverse historic sites, including Civil War battlefields (Antietam and Manassas), national parks (the Chesapeake and Ohio Canal and Harper's Ferry), national historic sites (the Custis-Lee Mansion within Arlington Cemetery, Pennsylvania Avenue, the Clara Barton House, and the Frederick Douglass House), and performing arts centers (Wolf Trap and Ford's Theatre). The National Capital Region was also responsible during the 1970s for more than 150 memorials, including the monuments for George Washington, Thomas Jefferson, and Abraham Lincoln, as well as 8500 acres of park land within the District of Columbia.

Congressional Cemetery is connected geographically to Anacostia Park, which comprises 1200 acres of land along the Anacostia River. Established in 1911 and incorporated into the National Capitol Region of the NPS in 1933, the park gradually expanded in size so that by 1936 its southwestern border juxtaposed the south-eastern boundary of the burial ground. In their "Justification: Congressional Cemetery," developed in connection with possible NPS acquisition of the burial ground, the agency team led by Ben Howland had developed a "General Development Plan" that included maintenance offices, a storage facility, and a staff parking lot along the southwestern boundary of the park. Planned for access by a road through the Anacostia Park, these facilities had been projected for use in the restoration of Congressional Cemetery.

Various senior administrators within the NPS recognized possible advantages associated with the incorporation of Congressional Cemetery into the National Capital Parks system. They ultimately determined, however, that the NPS "would not at this time accept the property" for "administration as a unit of the National Park Service," as stated by Rogers Morton in his August 23, 1974, letter to James Haley. He explained that the agency did not want to acquire Congressional Cemetery for two primary reasons: one, acquisition of the burial ground was not "a high priority when development needs for the National Park System throughout the country are considered" and two, it could establish a "precedent for the National Park Service to acquire, restore, maintain, and protect other cemeteries," as stated in the "Congressional Cemetery Alternatives" developed by the NPS.[54] The deliberations were important nonetheless because they advanced a formula specifying that the "Architect of the Capitol accepts title; restores, maintains, and protects" the burial ground. The Architect of the Capitol emerged as an integral part of the formula subsequently developed for the preservation of Congressional Cemetery (see Chapter 7).

Meanwhile, the Christ Church vestry was devastated by the NPS decision regarding the burial ground. Gerald Connolly, Chairman of the Cemetery Committee, expressed the collective angst in his 1974 annual report. He led with this statement: "What started out as a year in which we hoped to get some firm financial footing at the Cemetery . . . has turned into a disaster. The Congressional Cemetery is in worse health, both financially and physically, than it was at this same time last year." Moreover, "the Cemetery has become a great drain on the physical and financial health of Christ Church," and fellow parishioners seemed no longer willing to help address the gathering crisis. He wondered why the church even tried to continue as owner and manager of the burial ground: "We have a small, loyal crew of workers at the Cemetery, but we can barely pay them a living wage. When a man has worked for you for 35 years and he is only making $8,000 a year with no health benefits, no pension, and a $35 Christmas bonus, it makes you wonder if you should be in that business."

In his conclusion, Connolly said in no uncertain terms that Christ Church had run out of the ingredients—personnel, funds, ideas, and optimism—vital to continued ownership and management of the burial ground: "Nobody on the current Vestry or the Cemetery Committee knows what to do about this problem as far as any long term solutions are concerned. Something must be done in the next few months to begin finding the solution or next year's report will be even bleaker."[55] Thus in the mid-1970s, some 160 years after Christ Church had acquired Congressional Cemetery, the vestry and the congregation in general understood that it could no longer maintain the facility. The problem was that no other organization, federal or otherwise, seemed willing to assume responsibility for the first national burial ground.

7

A RACE AGAINST TIME

On June 16, 1997, the National Trust for Historic Preservation included Congressional Cemetery in its list of America's 11 Most Endangered Historic Places. This list, which was established in 1988 and is updated annually, draws attention to and thereby assists in the preservation of historic buildings, places, and landscapes. The three primary criteria used in making the selections, as specified by the Trust, are the "significance" of the site within its "cultural context," the "urgency" in relation to "the need for immediate action to stop or reverse serious threats," and "potential solutions" to eliminate or alleviate these threats "in the short- and/or long-term." Congressional Cemetery fully met the requirements focused on significance and urgency. The burial ground also met the requirement for "potential solutions" in the milestones realized to that date by the Association for the Preservation of Historic Congressional Cemetery (APHCC), a volunteer, nonprofit organization established in 1976.

The history of the APHCC comprises a compelling narrative, given its substantial achievements in what has been described as a "race against time" to preserve cemetery infrastructure and historic documentation reaching back to the early nineteenth century. This narrative has not, however, circulated widely. A significant contributing factor is that "traditional historians" have largely "overlooked the magnitude and diversity of volunteer efforts," as noted by Susan J. Ellis and Katherine H. Noyes in *By the People: A History of Americans as Volunteers*. This chapter attempts to address this omission in connection with the APHCC by delineating its formation, its efforts in connection with federal supporters to articulate a private/public alliance focused on preservation of the burial ground, and then the challenges and achievements of the Association and its supporters in the public sector.[1]

New Management for the Old Cemetery

The years 1974 to 1979 constituted a critical juncture in the history of Congressional Cemetery. During this period, Christ Church realized that it could no longer manage the burial ground. The vestry accordingly transferred its responsibilities for the site to the APHCC. Select documents in parish archives, particularly memoranda to the vestry, statements by the rector, and annual congregational reports, provide compelling insight into the final years of Christ Church as operator of the burial ground. In sum, they record the ending of what was surely one of the most extended volunteer efforts of national significance in the United States— management of America's first national cemetery for a period of 164 years, extending from 1812 to 1976.

The first of these documents is a memorandum of October 21, 1974, from Willis D. (Don) Brown to his fellow members of the vestry. This document specifies the need for a permanent endowment, the interest from which would be used to maintain the cemetery. Brown stated that the size of the endowment, which he identified as a fund to be provided by the "Friends of Congressional Cemetery," should be approximately two million dollars.[2] The creation of such a fund would have been a reach for the vestry, which did not include professional fund raisers among its members.

Lynn McCallum, then rector of Christ Church, substantially advanced the conversation by recommending that the vestry adopt an eleven-point proposal during its meeting on June 2, 1975. Three comments given within this proposal are particularly noteworthy, signaling that Christ Church had indeed proceeded into new terrain in its management of the burial ground. Rev. McCallum's first statement was perhaps the most significant in that he recommended "that we stop the performance of all burials at Congressional Cemetery except" for the interments of "plot owners," relatives of individuals already buried at the site, and "members of

Christ Church." While not specifying any schedule, he seemingly intended a temporary reduction in the interments so that the vestry could assess current operations and future directions. The recommendation is noteworthy in that the vestry had never before—not from 1812 to the June 2, 1975, meeting—considered a decrease in the burials for any reason.

Rev. McCallum proceeded to recommend the formation of a three-person committee "to oversee the short term operation of the cemetery" and of another committee to develop "a long range resolution of the Cemetery problem." After minimal adjustments to the phrasing, the vestry adopted his proposal in full recognition that the burial ground was an historic legacy but also an increasingly weighty "problem." The members then appointed a long-range planning committee comprising four members, one of whom was Don Brown, who had captured the attention of the vestry by his prior recommendation of a "Friends of Congressional Cemetery" endowment.[3]

The long-range planning committee made swift and significant progress on "the Cemetery problem," as noted in a July 23, 1975, memorandum to the vestry by fellow parishioner and lawyer William A. Stringfellow. He reported that the members had "agreed to recommend" the creation "of a separate entity to take ownership, direction, and management of the cemetery once it is established." He then enumerated the many benefits—particularly the enormous relief—resulting from such action:

> It would relieve the church and the vestry of the responsibility of running the cemetery. It would relieve them henceforth of further financial responsibility as to any deficit. It would mean that the cemetery would not be an operational item on future vestry agendas.

Stringfellow sharpened his phrasing in subsequent statements, asserting that "the basic idea of in effect getting the church out of the cemetery business is fundamental to the recommendation." As was understood by the vestry, Christ Church could no longer continue as caretaker. For this reason, "a new entity would take over the operation of the cemetery with our blessings." Stringfellow observed that this organization would "seem to have a good chance of ensuring the proper and successful perpetuation of the cemetery on a sound basis, because it would offer the opportunity for others to participate in all ways, and thereby broaden the base of our support." This "separate entity" would accordingly "relieve the church and the vestry of the responsibility of running the cemetery." At long last, "the cemetery would not be an operational item on future vestry agendas."[4]

In commentary he provided for the 1975 "Annual Report of Christ Church," Don Brown summarized as follows the progress made by the long-range planning committee:

This Fall [sic], the task force proposed to the Vestry that a non-profit cemetery association be formed with a board of directors of 9 to 12 members, three of whom must be members of Christ Church. The association would lease the cemetery from the church for a symbolic amount, and would not be able to alter its purpose or dispose of any part of it. The association and the board would be composed of people who are interested in the welfare of the cemetery and be willing to devote their energy toward the solution of its problems. The proposal was passed, incorporation papers have been signed, and selection of the board members is in process.

Brown concluded by stating that the planning committee could envision "a brighter future," even though "the condition of the cemetery is possibly at its worst": "Our hope is to someday see the Congressional Cemetery restored, and with an endowment sufficient to provide for its future." With this statement, Brown advanced the vision that propelled not only his task force but also the APHCC, the organization established to oversee the restoration and preservation of the old burial ground.[5]

Events moved swiftly thereafter. On March 24, 1976, the "Articles of Incorporation of the Association for the Preservation of Historic Congressional Cemetery" were notarized and filed. These Articles are significant in part because they specified the following efforts, among others, that remain central to continuing operations of the APHCC: "to conduct or sponsor research into the history of said Cemetery and its ties to the Nation's Capital," "to make the public aware of the significance and importance of Congressional Cemetery to the City and the Nation," and "to create and maintain endowment funds for the purpose of carrying out its objects and purposes. . . ." The document underscored the importance of the endowment funds, stating that the APHCC was "specifically authorized" to establish these accounts, which have proved a major factor in securing a future for the burial ground. The concluding section of the Articles of Incorporation identified the three members of the original APHCC Board of Directors as Gerald Connolly, Don Brown, and Peter Jones, all of whom were active members of Christ Church and understood both the historic legacy of and the significant challenges associated with the burial ground.[6]

On March 30, 1976, leaders in Capitol Hill restoration activities met at the Smithsonian Castle in Washington, D.C., to discuss the preservation of Congressional Cemetery. Francis Kraemer, elected as the first chairman of the APHCC during this meeting, provided information about this session in the first issue of the organizational newsletter, dated April 1977:

> Exactly one year ago today a few individuals who realized the importance of historic Congressional Cemetery assembled at the Smithsonian Institution to officially form this organization. There has been much progress in the intervening 12 months, but the real job has only just begun. The Association has one purpose — to ensure the restoration and preservation of this important historic site.

In the same newsletter, Kraemer noted that the APHCC had conducted its annual election of officers on March 30, 1977, the first anniversary of the initial organizational meeting. After acknowledging that he had been "honored by being re-elected Chairman of the Board," Kraemer identified the other officers for the coming year: Donald Brown, Vice-Chairman; George Didden, Treasurer; William A. Stringfellow, Secretary; and Ethel Robertson, who was a faithful, generous supporter of both Christ Church and Congressional Cemetery, as Executive Director.[7]

George Didden, who served as chairman of the Board of Directors during 1978-1980, recalled that the first task for the Association was to secure a long-term lease of the cemetery from Christ Church. This was not easy: "While Christ Church was eager for us to assume the task of running Congressional, they remained protective of the congregation's historic interests in the cemetery." After much "time and energy" and "negotiation," some of which was "a bit heated at times," the APHCC Board of Directors acquired a lease, not initially for the forty years they had wanted but for a provisional, three-year period, extending from August 1, 1976, to July 31, 1979. They secured the forty-year lease they had originally sought upon expiration of the provisional lease.[8]

By the end of the provisional lease, the APHCC had made significant progress in expanding both the size and revenues of the organization, as indicated by presentations made by members of the Board of Directors at the third annual meeting of the organization, convened on February 16, 1980, at Christ Church. Joel Truitt, co-chairman of the membership committee, and Ethel Robertson, who was then treasurer of the Association, reported increases in significant organizational indicators. As noted by Truitt, the Association had at that time a membership of "about 680," which constituted a gain of approximately 150 members over the previous year. Robertson reported an annual gain in Association revenues of approximately sixty percent, noting that "the calendar year 1979 fund balances increased by $15,488.52, from a total of $23,111.37 to $38, 599.89."[9]

Chairman George Didden summarized these and other statements in his declaration that "1979 was a banner year for us." As he recalled later, "we did not solve all the cemetery's problems but we laid the basis, I think, for the later improvements that have continued to come." The time seemed right for him to step down from his position as chairman of the board. In announcing his resignation, he offered a succinct summation of the ongoing challenge for the Association: "I leave this post with a great sense of respect for the vibrant group of people who comprise the Board for their unfailing support and integrity in the face of great odds."[10] It is the final words in this statement—"great odds"—that linger when viewed in retrospect.

Participation by the Architect of the Capitol

As in previous decades, various organizations within the federal government, particularly Congress, continued to deliberate over their responsibilities for Congressional Cemetery during 1976-1982, a period that coincided with the formative years of the Association for the Preservation of Historic Congressional Cemetery. The debate centered on two events: the discussion in Congress over Public Law 94-495, which constituted the sole piece of legislation passed by both houses to that time focused on preservation of the burial ground; and an extraordinary meeting conducted on February 22, 1979, by the Veterans Administration to examine options the administrators believed they had to determine the future course for the cemetery. The attendant negotiations engaged, in addition to the U.S. Congress and the Veterans Administration, all the familiar players, particularly the Department of Interior, the Architect of the Capitol, and Christ Church. They did not, however, involve in a substantive way the new participant in the unfolding drama: the APHCC. This was most likely because Congress and the federal agencies were as yet unaware of the Association.

Public Law 94-495, which was approved by President Gerald Ford on October 14, 1976, focused on two efforts to be conducted by the Architect of the Capitol: (1) "to perform such work as may be necessary to prevent further deterioration of, and to maintain, those sections of the cemetery . . . which are of historical significance, including those sections in which former Members of the Senate and House of Representatives are buried," and (2) to "conduct a study for the purpose of determining the continuing maintenance and preservation needs for those historical sections of the Congressional Cemetery . . . including the costs which he estimates would be associated with various maintenance actions which he may recommend for the cemetery." The rule specified the appropriation of $175,000 for the fiscal year ending on September 30, 1978, and $75,000 for the fiscal year ending on September 30, 1979, for maintenance efforts. It authorized the provision of an additional $50,000 for the fiscal year ending on September 30, 1978, for the identified study. While no mention was made of the APHCC, the bill did state that the Architect of the Capitol "shall obtain the consent and approval of the person or persons who have legal responsibility for the care and maintenance of the cemetery" before embarking on the initiatives identified in the bill.[11]

The formulation of Public Law 94-495 involved bicameral and bipartisan participation at the top levels of the U.S. Congress. On May 13, 1976, Thomas "Tip" O'Neil, who was Majority Leader of the House of Representatives and a Democrat from Massachusetts, introduced H.R. 13789 in the House with the support of John J. Rhodes, who was House Minority Leader and a Republican from Arizona. On May 17, Hugh Scott, the Senate Minority Leader, introduced S. 3441 in the Senate with the support of Mike Mansfield, Senate Majority Leader. Scott was a Republican from Pennsylvania and Mansfield a Democrat from Montana. Representative Lindy (Corinne Claiborne) Boggs, a Democrat from Louisiana and chairperson of the Joint Committee on Arrangements for the Commemoration of the Bicentennial, had a major role in subsequent actions relevant to the proposed legislation.[12]

Two significant letters to members of the Senate and House accompanied the proposed legislation. The first, dated May 17, 1976, and signed by Senators Scott and Mansfield, underscored the connection between Congressional as the first national cemetery and Arlington as its successor in this role:

> In this Bicentennial Year, we ask you to project yourself ahead a century to the tricentennial. What would be your reaction to a newspaper story in 2076 A.D. about Arlington National Cemetery that told of vandals tipping over gravestones, grave robbers rifling through coffins, weeds growing waist high, and real estate speculators drawing up plans to turn the site into a high-rise condominium complex?
>
> We know you would find such a story outrageous and implausible. One would think that our honored dead deserve a less inglorious fate. Yet, that is precisely the fate that has befallen the Americans who are buried in our first National Cemetery. This cemetery, now called the Congressional Cemetery . . . served as the national cemetery until Arlington National Cemetery was established after the Civil War.[13]

In the second letter, dated May 24, 1976, Representative Lindy Boggs stated that Congressional was not only the first national cemetery but also the only national burial ground in the United States in that it was available for use by everyone: "It has often been called the nation's first national Cemetery [sic] and is certainly the only one that is not reserved exclusively for the burial of those who have served in the armed forces." Boggs' understanding of the cemetery was shared by a select group of federal leaders who reached back into the nineteenth century and included Quartermaster General Montgomery Meigs. Boggs understood very well the special relationship between Congress and the cemetery, as evidenced by the congressional burials at this site, the "many" congressional appropriations, and the "sandstone 'cenotaphs' designed by Benjamin Latrobe" in remembrance of individual members of Congress.[14] The commentary by Boggs about the cenotaphs has particular resonance in that her husband, Representative Hale Boggs, had died in a plane crash in Alaska four years earlier and his body had never been found. She would place a cenotaph in his memory at Congressional Cemetery in 1981.

Boggs was notable among her congressional colleagues in her appreciation of the challenge confronting the APHCC, which had been established shortly before she wrote her letter. She understood that "their task is a large one" and that "the Joint Committee after surveying the situation has concluded that it will be extremely difficult for the association to save the cemetery without some assistance from Congress." Lindy Boggs thought that the time was right for Congress to fulfill a "neglected obligation to their predecessors" at rest in the burial ground and to support the proposed legislation.[15]

The U.S. Senate and House Subcommittees on National Parks and Recreation conducted their respective hearings on S. 3441 and H.R. 13789 on July 27 and August 6, 1976. The surviving documentation of these deliberations makes a compelling read in part because of the testimony provided by Senator Hugh Scott and by the Department of the Interior.

Senator Scott spoke before both subcommittees in support of the proposed legislation. In a press release issued on July 28, the day following the Senate hearing, he expressed urgency about the proposed legislation, referring twice to the "obligation" and then to "the duty" of Congress "to honor our patriots whose final resting place has been so severely neglected." When addressing the House Subcommittee, he declared that "it is important, indeed it is im-perative, that Congress take charge of this situation and pass H.R. 13789 in order that the Congressional Cemetery be restored to the dignified status it deserves." He then recalled legislation advanced during 1972-1973 by the late Representative John P. Saylor, also from Pennsylvania: "The time is now—we cannot afford to let this bill fall by the wayside, as we did H.R. 1891 and H.R. 8883 in the 93ʳᵈ Congress." In his conclusion, Scott characterized the old burial ground as an important place of national memory: "A country that forgets its past can have no future. I urge that we honor our great American heritage by supporting this important legislation that would restore the historic sections of Congressional Cemetery."[16]

The spokesperson for the Department of the Interior, who is not identified in the extant documentation, did not offer any new ideas. Instead, he reiterated the five alternatives advanced by Rogers Morton, Secretary of the Interior, in his letter of August 23, 1974, to James Haley—that (1) no action be taken at that time, (2) a federal subsidy be provided to Christ Church for "development, restoration, maintenance, protection, and interpretation" of the burial ground, (3) the District of Columbia government assume control, (4) the Veterans' Administration or the Department of the Army take responsibility, or (5) the Architect of the Capitol acquire, restore, maintain, and interpret the cemetery.[17]

As in 1974, the Department of Interior was concerned about budgetary limitations and the accompanying need to prioritize initiatives. When viewed against other agency imperatives, "the reconstruction of Congressional Cemetery would not in our opinion command a high priority."[18] S. 3441 and H.R. 13789 did not, of course, specify that the agency assume full responsibility for the burial ground. The Department of Interior was concerned, nonetheless, that the study identified in the two bills might lead eventually to this end. And thus as demonstrated by the testimony provided during the August 6, 1976, hearing before the House Subcommittee on National Parks and Recreation, the Department of Interior remained firm in its position that it did not want to assume any caretaker role for the burial ground.

The subsequent history of Public Law 94-495, as recorded in congressional correspondence and reports, as well as a couple of choice journalistic accounts, constitutes another telling narrative of federal ambivalence over its responsibilities for Congressional Cemetery. Passage of the legislation, while significant, did not assure the provision of $250,000 for restoration and maintenance of the historical sections of the burial ground and $50,000 to conduct a study focused on requirements for preserving those areas. In a letter to Senator Walter D. Huddleston, Chairman of the Subcommittee on Legislative Matters of the Senate Appropriations Committee, Senator Hugh Scott expressed his concerns:

It would be a pity if Congress failed to appropriate the small amount of funds authorized to restore the historic sections of the cemetery to a modicum of respectability. I fear that the warm bicentennial feelings that prompted us to act last year have waned to such a degree that the decades of neglect will continue uninterrupted.[19]

A hearing conducted on June 7, 1977, by the House Subcommittee on Cemeteries and Burial Benefits, Committee on Veterans Affairs, surfaced the views that had made Scott uneasy. This hearing is of major significance in that it focused a spotlight on the Department of Veterans Affairs as an emerging, albeit unwilling candidate for keeper of the cemetery. In terms of this study, the two major speakers at this forum were Marian P. Connolly, who was then senior warden at Christ Church and who articulated the views of the parish, and George M. White, who was Architect of the Capitol and thus had special interest in legislation that identified his office as the responsible party for preserving "the historical sections" of the burial ground and for conducting a study focused on restoration and maintenance of those areas. The comments provided by Connolly and White are extraordinary in part because neither acknowledged the responsibilities of the other for the burial ground, thereby demonstrating the critical lack of dialogue among key participants in the continuing conversation about Congressional Cemetery.

Marian Connolly expressed the concern of Christ Church over congressional inaction in funding PL 94-495. As she noted, "the actual appropriation of the funds is now in jeopardy" because the House Subcommittee on Legislative Appropriations had "fixed upon the Congressional Cemetery appropriation as an expendable item" in their attempt to control the budget. She concluded her testimony as she had begun by asserting that Congressional Cemetery had been established and had always been sustained as "a joint venture" involving both "private and Federal contributions." To secure its future, "this partnership must be resumed."[20]

In his testimony, George White focused on the inadequacies he saw in PL 94-495, which he said specified the restoration and maintenance of only twenty percent of the cemetery in its exclusive focus on the historic sections. He noted in addition that the legislation did not include funds to increase security, which he considered essential to any restoration effort. White reserved his primary concern for his conclusion, saying "I believe that entering upon this project bears with it the consequences of having to maintain the property into the foreseeable future."[21] The Office of the Architect of the Capitol, as well as all other candidate organizations, clearly did not want to assume major, long-term responsibility for the burial ground.

Shortly thereafter, the saga of PL 94-495 came to a swift and inconclusive end. During June 1977, the Senate Appropriations Committee agreed to appropriate the funds specified in the bill, while the House Appropriations Committee did not. "And the House prevailed," Lindy Boggs recalled during yet another Congressional hearing about the burial ground, conducted in March 1978. She went on to say, in her memorable phrasing, that "in the conference, there was a smarting in the participating subcommittees on appropriations at that time over the 'billion-dollar Congress' label, and they were unwilling to spend the money."[22]

As recorded in the *Congressional Record*, the legislators were "not unsympathetic to the plight of the Congressional Cemetery." They had concluded, however, that under the provisions of the National Cemeteries Act of 1973, the Veterans Administration was the appropriate agency to assume responsibility for the burial ground:

> The Conferees believe the Veterans Administration could and should become more active in fulfilling its responsi-

bilities regarding the maintenance of the Cemetery. Last year the Veterans Administration expended only $2,000 for maintenance of the Congressional Cemetery out of a total $26 million budget for National Cemeteries. The Conferees strongly believe that the Veterans Administration should greatly improve its maintenance activities at the Cemetery.[23]

In subsequent deliberations, legislators sharpened their focus on the Veterans Administration as heir apparent. Lindy Boggs propelled this turn of events by additional commentary she provided during the March 1978 congressional hearing. After observing that "there was a smarting . . . over the 'billion-dollar Congress' label," she went on to say that the VA, specifically one "Mr. McGee," mowed the grass around veteran graves at Congressional "once every 8 days during the summer, and once a month, approximately, from October to May." She then fixed her attention on Max Cleland, who was Administrator of the Veterans Administration and in attendance at this hearing: "I would like to know if according to the Senate's desire expressed in the 1973 act, the Administrator could give close and favorable attention to acquiring, as part of the National Cemetery System, the whole of Congressional Cemetery." Cleland, who seemed surprised by this query, said this in response: "Thank you very much for your interest. We shall indeed give it our close attention."[24]

In the following months, VA administrators gave their "close attention" to making sure that the agency did not acquire "the whole of Congressional Cemetery." As part of this effort, top officials staged a remarkable meeting at agency facilities on February 22, 1979, to address the future role of the Veterans Administration in relation to the burial ground. The participants represented the federal organizations that had long been considered the prime candidates to assume responsibility for the site. Totaling thirteen in number, they comprised two representatives from the National Park Service; one from the Office of the Architect of the Capitol; nine from the Veterans Administration, among whom were Robert Beller and Robert Hannon, who were the VA Director and Deputy Director of Cemetery Services; and the Superintendent of Arlington National Cemetery, Ray Costanzo.[25] The attendees did not include representatives from either Christ Church or the APHCC, who likely knew nothing of this meeting and would have been alarmed over the proceedings.

As summarized by Robert Beller, who chaired the session, the attendees appeared "in agreement" on two major actions: (1) "to disinter" the remains from government-owned lots at Congressional and reinter those remains at Arlington National Cemetery and (2) to emplace a restored cenotaph from Congressional Cemetery at "a park close to the Capitol." A "bronze plaque" would be affixed to this cenotaph that would identify the history of these monuments at the burial ground. The minutes of this meeting do not indicate whether the attendees reached consensus on action regarding the remaining cenotaphs, although "Relocate cenotaphs," in the plural, was identified as one of the options. At the conclusion of this session, Beller said to the attendees that the VA Department of Memorial Affairs would prepare a document summarizing the decisions reached during this session, as well as "make a formal presentation to the Veterans' Affairs Committee in March, and advise them that we have general acceptance of the Architect of the Capitol, National Park Service, and Arlington National Cemetery, and suggest that they initiate specific legislation."[26]

Approximately ten weeks later, on May 1, 1979, the Comptroller General of the United States ruled that the Veterans Administration could use agency funds to maintain only the "government-owned portions" of Congressional Cemetery, not for the "repair and maintenance of the private areas." This decision essentially froze in place for that time the status quo regarding VA responsibilities for the burial ground. The agency was authorized to mow the grass around the federal gravesites, as before. The Comptroller General said nothing about decisions reached during the February 22, 1979, meeting about transferring to Arlington the remains from government-owned lots at Congressional and about emplacing a restored cenotaph from Congressional at a site near the U.S. Capitol.[27]

Representative Lindy Boggs gained control thereafter in the deliberations by Congress and federal agencies over Congressional Cemetery. She did so by two definitive actions: (1) dedicating a cenotaph at the burial ground in memory of her husband, Representative Thomas Hale Boggs, Sr., (1914-1972), and (2) co-sponsoring legislation that provided a workable definition of federal responsibility for Congressional Cemetery and that remains in place to this day. She accordingly emerged as the most successful congressional advocate to that date for federal support of the burial ground. Her success was attributable to her vision of the cemetery and her tenacity in securing federal support, as well as to the efforts of her predecessors in Congress who had recognized the historic legacy of the burial ground.

Representative Hale Boggs, as he was known to friends and family, had served in Congress as a Democrat during 1941-1943 and 1947-1972 and was majority leader at the time of his death. On October 16, 1972, he was on a flight that disappeared somewhere between Anchorage and Juneau, Alaska. His body was not recovered, and he was later presumed dead. The dedicatory service at Congressional Cemetery, conducted on May 19, 1981, was a powerful, dramatic event, evocative of the ceremonies attendant upon congressional burials at the graveyard during the nineteenth ceremony. The attendees, totaling some two hundred, represented "the full swath of Capitol life—the leaders, the lobbyists, the doorkeepers," as characterized by journalist Francis Cline in *The New York Times* on the following day. The family was represented by Lindy Boggs; her two daughters, Cokie Boggs Roberts and Barbara Boggs Sigmund; and her son, Thomas Hale Boggs, Jr.; among others. As had been customary during the preceding century, the ceremony included the participation of both Congress and the U.S. military. Thomas "Tip" O'Neil, Speaker of the House, gave a tribute to his friend and colleague, while Reverend James Ford, House Chaplain, offered the dismissal. The United States Army Brass Quintet provided both the prelude and recessional music. The latter included "The Battle Hymn of the Republic," which the Army Brass Quintet began "in dirge time" and then shifted "into a Dixieland version for the New Orleans lawmaker that had people smiling as they left the cemetery."

While the ceremonies were reminiscent of nineteenth-century memorial services at the graveyard, they also underscored the significant changes in place. As indicated in the bulletin provided to attendees, the "Welcome" was offered not by a member of Congress but by Ethel Robertson, identified as "President, Congressional Cemetery Associates." The last page of the bulletin, entitled "Congressional Cenotaphs," summarized the history and significance of the memorial stones, noting that the cenotaph for Representative Hale Boggs was the first emplaced at Congressional in 105 years.[28]

The press coverage of the ceremony focused on the cenotaph as a testament in stone to the contributions of Hale Boggs. In his article for *The New York Times*, Francis Cline contrasted the permanence of the marker against the impermanence of this mortal condition: "His body was never recovered, and in the gray dampness of this morning his widow, successor in Congress and lifetime campaign and office manager, Representative Lindy Boggs, beamed when the stone monument, commemorating one whose body lies elsewhere, was dedicated as a permanent mark of Hale Boggs' presence in the life and politics of Congress." Jayne O'Donnell, in the May 21, 1981, issue of *Roll Call*, reported that Thomas Hale Boggs, Jr., "said he considers the memorial to be 'a place of permanence' where the Congressman's family can go to pay their respects." In a coauthored article published in *The City Paper* on October 5, 2001, Cokie and Steve Roberts focused on the significance they found in the cenotaph: "For Cokie's family to have that marker in a place of quiet and solitude turned out to be incredibly comforting. It means there's a place to go on the anniversaries of her father's death and on Memorial Day and All Souls' Day. It means there's a place to put flowers, to say prayers, to shed tears."[29]

The cenotaph for Hale Boggs had additional significance, important to the preservation of Congressional Cemetery as a site of national memory. By emplacing the memorial stone for her husband, Representative Lindy Boggs asserted that the historic markers had ongoing meaning, for the nation as well as for individual families. They provided "a place to go" to recall the contributions of individual members of Congress, as well as the linkage between current and past Congresses. In making this emphatic statement, she effectively blocked the Veterans Administration, or any other organization, from proceeding with plans to remove the historic cenotaphs from the cemetery or in any other way diminish their special import at the burial ground.

Lindy Boggs reinforced and extended this statement on April 1,

1982, when she introduced H.R. 6033, identified as "a bill relating to the preservation of the historic Congressional Cemetery in the District of Columbia for the inspiration and benefit of the people of the United States." This legislation succeeded as no other had in the long history of the burial ground in that it identified the basic formula regarding federal support that remains in place to this day. It specified that a particular agency, originally identified as the Department of Interior, "enter into a cooperative agreement or agreements with the Association for the Preservation of Historic Congressional Cemetery . . . pursuant to which the Secretary [of that agency] may assist in the protection, restoration, and maintenance of the Congressional Cemetery for the benefit of the public." The bill authorized $300,000 "to carry out the provision of this Act."

In proposing H.R. 6033, Boggs delivered a statement carefully designed to secure congressional approval. She observed at the start that she was supported in her action by "the general public" and "by a number of our colleagues in the House and Senate," particularly by Senator Thomas Eagleton, a Democrat from Missouri.[30] She noted, in addition, that "we break no new ground" in the recommendation of a cooperative agreement. Authorized by the 1935 Historic Sites and Building Act, such agreements had been instrumental to the preservation of institutions including the Corcoran Gallery of Art and Folger Shakespearean Library in Washington, D.C. Surely, Boggs was suggesting, it would be appropriate, in keeping with legislative precedent, for Congress to authorize a cooperative agreement for the rescue of Congressional Cemetery. She concluded by sharing her understanding of Congressional as one of a kind—a "truly national cemetery" and a locus of special national memory:

This is our first national cemetery and, as some would have it, our only truly national cemetery since the others are dedicated primarily for the interment of deceased veterans of our Armed Forces. Not only would the restoration of this cemetery, with its close historical relationship with Congress, serve to bring to public attention important pages from the history of the U.S. Congress, but it would also reaffirm a commitment to the memories of the individuals through history who have helped to make this country great.[31]

While Lindy Boggs advanced a special, inclusive understanding of "national cemetery," the Department of the Interior, placed yet again in the spotlight regarding Congressional Cemetery, adhered to its previous position. As indicated by internal agency documentation, top officials were in agreement that H.R. 6033 not be enacted. Russell Dickinson, then Director of the National Park Service, expressed the prevailing view in a memorandum to legislative counsel dated May 17, 1982. He recalled that PL 94-495, which had been approved by Congress on October 14, 1976, had directed the Architect of the Capitol to maintain the historic sections of the cemetery and had authorized $250,000 for this effort over a two-year period. Congress had not, however, appropriated funds for this initiative. This precedent, as well as other unfunded mandates, was not encouraging in that it raised the possibility that the agency might have to use its own funds to accomplish the specified task: "Funding priorities of the National Park Service are concentrated on maintaining and improving the resources currently under our jurisdiction. Funds for the restoration and maintenance of Congressional Cemetery would not be a high priority. Our position in this regard has not changed since 1974."[32]

On August 26, 1982, Congress approved an amended PL 97-245, which specified the participation of the Architect of the Capitol, not the Department of the Interior:

> In order to assist in the restoration and preservation of the historic values of the Congressional Cemetery, the Architect of the Capitol is authorized and directed to make grants to the Association for the Preservation of Historic Congressional Cemetery . . . to be carried out under terms and conditions to be prescribed by the Architect of the Capitol. The Association shall maintain adequate records and accounts of all financial transactions and operations carried out under such program, and such records shall be available at all times for audit and investigation by the Architect or the Comptroller General of the United States. . . . There is au-

thorized to be appropriated $300,000 for grants to be made under section 2 of this Act, such sums to remain available until expended.[33]

This was a fitting conclusion to the extended deliberations focused on identifying a federal partner in the effort to maintain Congressional Cemetery. To begin, the historic linkage between the Office of the Architect of the Capitol and Congressional Cemetery reaches back to the formative years of Washington, D.C., as the nation's capital. Dr. William Thornton (1759-1828), the original designer of the U.S. Capitol Building, is interred at Congressional, as is George Hadfield (1764-1826), who served as superintendent of construction for the U.S. Capitol during 1795-1798. Benjamin Latrobe (1764-1820), Architect of the Capitol during 1815-1817, designed the cenotaphs, the signature funeral monuments at Congressional Cemetery. In addition, the Architect of the Capitol is responsible for maintenance of the United States Capitol Complex, including the U.S. Capitol Building and grounds, the Supreme Court, and congressional office buildings, as well as the U.S. Botanic Garden. It takes not a stretch of the imagination to think that Congressional Cemetery, situated in close proximity to these structures, could be understood to fit in some capacity within these responsibilities. Most important of all, PL 97-245, as amended, preserved the spirit of the public/private initiative responsible for the establishment of the cemetery at the beginning of the nineteenth-century and its subsequent development as the first national burial ground. In sum, this statute identified what appears in retrospect to be the most appropriate federal authority for the envisioned task.

The Formative Years of the Cemetery Association

The Association for the Preservation of Historic Congressional Cemetery, as viewed in its entirety, constitutes a unique case study in efforts by a volunteer organization to rescue and maintain a site of national significance. Its elongated name, unwieldy though it may seem at times, conveys the group's singularity. It is, to begin, an "Association" of private citizens, not an organization based on statutory law or assured of governmental funding. It is focused solely on a preservation effort, hence the positioning of this term at the center of its name. More specifically, the organization is intent upon the conservation of a unique historic institution, the only burial ground in the United States identified as "Congressional Cemetery." In short, the name of the organization identifies an Association that is in itself worthy of study.

An examination of the challenges confronting and the gains made by the APHCC is facilitated by the minutes of organizational meetings, issues of the Association newsletter, and recollections of both founding and long-term members of the society. These resources document the evolution and maturation of the organization from its establishment in 1976 to the present. This development occurred in two stages. During the first of these periods, extending from 1980 to 1996, the members celebrated the historic legacy of the burial ground, even as they confronted increasingly challenging urban realities. In the years extending from 1996 to the present, the APHCC has established a solid foundation for continuing, long-term preservation of the cemetery. The commentary given in this section focuses on developments during 1980-1996.

In the first half of the 1980s, APHCC spokespersons emphasized the historic legacy of the cemetery in the Victorian period, particularly during the 1860s through the 1880s. They did not focus on the overall layout of the grounds, which incorporated the linear design basic to Peter Charles L'Enfant's plan for the federal city.[34] They concentrated instead on select monuments at the cemetery, and they staged events at the burial ground that they associated with the Victorian period. Through these efforts, the APHCC secured the participation in their Board of Directors of leaders within the Daughters of the American Revolution (DAR).

Michael Richman of the National Trust for Historic Preservation provided commentary on the sculpture in a presentation he made during the 1985 annual meeting of the APHCC, conducted on March 30 at Christ Church. The summer 1985 issue of the Association newsletter provided this summation of his remarks, which concentrated on the mid-Victorian period, extending from 1848 to 1870:

> Mr. Richman considered the mid-Victorian monuments of Congressional Cemetery, which he encourages the Board

to catalogue, to be of a quality comparable to any in the high artisan-craftsman tradition that preceded the late-nineteenth century evolution of cemetery monuments into a distinctive, sculptural public art. He tantalized the room with a brief survey of handsome monuments, signed and unsigned, and with hints of the kind of research that could be undertaken into this unexplored corner of Victorian symbolism and industry.

In addition to presenting Richman's assessment of the "mid-Victorian monuments" at the burial ground, the newsletter noted that he was by that time a member of the APHCC Board of Directors.[35] Serving in this capacity, he provided linkage that would become increasingly important between the APHCC and the National Trust for Historic Preservation.

In staging events at the cemetery during the 1980s, the Association proceeded with the understanding that the cemetery would function at times as a park, in keeping with Victorian ideas about burial grounds. The members accordingly organized occasional, elaborate celebrations at Congressional that included dinners and concerts. They were joined during select events by members of the DAR, who participated in preservation activities at the burial ground.[36] The summer 1983 issue of the APHCC newsletter described one such gathering in a front-page article entitled, "DAR Hosts Victorian May Day Garden Fete." The first paragraph set the scene:

Blessed with beautiful spring weather, Congressional Cemetery on May 1 was transformed into a stately, elegant Victorian park graced by lovely ladies in hoop skirts, shawls, and lace parasols; gents in waistcoats, bowlers, and watch-fobs, with a proper smattering of kilts. At 3 p.m., the guests assembled to stroll about the grounds accompanied by the City of Alexandria Pipe and Drum Corps. Munching popcorn and sipping lemonade, they enjoyed our unparalleled collection of funerary sculpture and lovely vistas.

The following paragraphs focused on the formal dinner provided for 114 participants who were seated outdoors in front of the chapel and on the success of this celebration: "Not only was it a most enjoyable and unique afternoon, it also brought us $1500.00 closer to completion of our chapel."

Chris Hermann, who ably wrote and edited the Association newsletter during 1980-1989, constructed the front page of the summer 1983 issue so that it underscored a confrontation at Congressional between Victorian values and contemporary urban realities. The summary of the "Victorian May Day Garden Fete" was on the left side of the page. The right side presented a brief but powerful piece entitled "Interstate Highway Threatens Cemetery." As evidenced by the contrasting realities delineated in these two narratives, the burial ground could not be enjoyed simply as a lovely garden, emblematic of times past.

During the 1980s, the APHCC confronted two primary challenges to the burial ground: (1) an expansion of the District of Columbia prison complex at the eastern boundary of the cemetery that would house seven-to-eight hundred inmates and (2) construction of the Barney Circle interchange along its southern perimeter, adjacent to the Anacostia River Park. The first of these initiatives had an immediate, negative impact upon the burial ground. Deliberations over the proposed Barney Circle interchange fueled debate within the Capitol Hill community, including the APHCC, that extended well into the 1990s.

On March 21, 1986, Marion Barry, then mayor of Washington, D.C., delineated a plan to add an eight-story unit to the D.C. prison for inmates with drug and mental problems and to locate this facility on land adjacent to Congressional Cemetery. He explained later that he had been surprised by the opposition to this initiative because the land next to the proposed site was either a park or "just a graveyard." Those who opposed this development stated in varying ways that the plan, including Barry's injudicious phrasing, dishonored the legacy of the first national burial ground. Chris Herman voiced his objections in the fall 1986 newsletter, noting that the mayor's proposal took the surrounding community by surprise in that it came "out of the blue": "The proposed site had been on no list previously under discussion between responsible local and

Federal officials. Much less had the affected community any prior indication of the Mayor's plan . . . ." "The affected community," particularly the APHCC and the larger Capitol Hill neighborhood, thereafter joined forces. Among other efforts, they issued a statement opposing expansion of the prison because the multi-level facility would constitute a "visual intrusion" upon the neighborhood and would encourage additional developments in the neighborhood.[37]

On March 21, 1987, exactly one year from the day Marion Barry had advanced his proposal regarding the prison, the Capitol Hill Neighborhood Prison Task Force convened to develop a strategy opposing the plan. Margaret Hobbs, then chairperson of the APHCC Board of Directors, spoke for the Association, positioning herself thereby within the historic lineage of individuals who understood the larger meaning of the cemetery. She saw it both literally — as "the historic burying place of many Congressmen and many others notable in our country's history" — and figuratively — "it is, in a real sense, a memorial and a symbol of the United States Congress, of this Nation's history, and of the National Capital." Given this understanding, she viewed expansion of the prison as an act that would both "dishonor" the community at rest and "endanger" and "degrade" the surrounding neighborhood. Hobbs understood accordingly that the APHCC had a large responsibility "to the past, to the present and to the future": "We must speak for those whom we honor because of their service to our country. We must speak for those who help us protect this part of our national heritage. We must speak for those to whom we will pass on that national heritage."[38]

As construction began on the eight-story unit, an event occurred that confirmed the worst fears of those opposing expansion of the prison. On August 22, 1988, an inmate who had escaped from the facility sought refuge among the dead at Congressional Cemetery. As a correctional officer fired bullets into the burial ground, Lee Jenney, who was then cemetery administrator, John Hanley, the grounds superintendent, and two other "workers took cover behind tombstones," as reported in "Cemetery Officials Protest D.C. Jail Guards' Gunfire," published in *The Washington Post* on August 25, 1988. While the prisoner was captured shortly thereafter, the

Association was not mollified. The *Post* article gave the final word to Lee Jenney: "We are outraged. That guard could have killed any of us who work here or any visitors to the cemetery. Not only do we have to worry about the threat of escaping prisoners, we now have to worry about being shot by an employee of the jail."[39]

The September 12, 1983, issue of *Capitol Streets*, identified on the masthead as "The Hill Rag," addressed the Barney Circle proposal with two articles, entitled "DOT Wants To Bury Congressional Cemetery" and "Why DOT Wants To Bury Congressional Cemetery." As noted, the National Park Service had "preliminarily agreed" to transfer thirty-five acres of the Anacostia National Park to the District of Columbia in exchange for prime acreage along the Georgetown riverfront. Following this exchange, the D.C. Department of Transportation planned to construct a highway along the Anacostia River that would proceed through Capitol Hill and then across the Potomac River to the Virginia shore via an interstate bridge that would be forty feet high and would cost an estimated $95 million. The negatives intrinsic to this plan were as follows: "In the words of the environmental impact statement, the bridge would become the 'dominant' feature of the view from the Cemetery. And the incessant noise of cars and trucks on the bridge and four-lane highway immediately adjacent to the Cemetery would end nearly two-hundred years of rare, pastoral quiet."

In his editorial for the winter 1985-1986 issue of the Association newsletter, Chris Herman recalled the observations of Jane W. Gemmill, a Philadelphian who had visited Congressional Cemetery one-hundred years earlier. In her *Notes on Washington* (1884), she described two arresting perspectives afforded by the burial ground, one of which was literal and the other figurative. The former was the view across the gravestones, beyond the Anacostia River, to the beautiful "high hills on the Maryland side." The latter came from within the cemetery itself, which offered "a beautiful calm retreat where the living may spend a quiet hour, away from the noise, bustle and weariness of the city," where the visitor might find the calm to contemplate "that long, long sleep which awaits each mortal."[40] The contemplation of these perspectives was "reason enough to protect the first national cemetery," Herman observed. While the commentary he and others provided was meaningful to the APHCC, it did not cut short the long life of the Barney Circle proposal, as will be addressed later in this chapter.

The APHCC realized substantial accomplishments in organizational development and in the repair of cemetery infrastructure during the 1980s, even as the leadership addressed challenges associated with the prison and Barney Circle. The gains were attributable in part to the efforts of successive chairpersons of the Board of Directors: Ethel Robertson (1980-1982, 1989-1990), Florian Thayn (1982-1986), and Margaret Hobbs (1986-1989). They all had important connections. Ethel Robertson was a long-time, active member of Christ Church, proprietor of the burial ground. Florian Thayn was Director of the Art and Reference Division, Office of the Architect of the Capitol, which had been authorized by PL 97-245 to provide grants to the APHCC for maintenance of the graveyard. As for Margaret Hobbs, she was a long-time resident of Capitol Hill who understood very well the potential impacts of the prison and the proposed Barney Circle interchange on both the cemetery and the surrounding neighborhood.

The individuals on the APHCC Advisory Board also had important connections, as exemplified by the membership in place during 1988. At that time, the Board comprised fourteen persons who were affiliated with Congress, the U.S. military, and the National Trust for Historic Preservation, among other organizations. The individuals with connections to Congress were Representative Lindy Boggs; Dr. Edward L. Elson, Chaplain of the Senate; and Dr. James Ford, Chaplain of the House of Representatives. The military was represented by Rear Admiral John D.H. Kane, who had been Chief Historian of the U.S. Navy, and by Colonel John Ray Bourgeois, Director of the Marine Corps Band. The National Trust for Historic Preservation had a spokesperson in Michael L. Ainslie, who had been president and chief executive officer of the organization during 1980-1984. Each issue of the APHCC newsletter identified members of the Advisory Board. Given the stature of these individuals, the recitation of their names provided an important endorsement of the ongoing effort to preserve the first national burial ground.

During 1980-1989, the newsletter provided effective outreach to the surrounding community. Written and edited by Chris Herman, it was distributed two times a year in 1980, 1981, 1983, 1984, 1985/86, 1988, and 1989 and then three times per annum during 1982 and 1987. Commenting in retrospect on his work with the publication, Herman remarked that "I enjoyed it all."[41] His pleasure in the task was evident in part by the editorials, including the titles, which are a substantial cut above such narratives in standard organizational periodicals. Among the representative examples are "Tempus Fugit . . . Et Manet," cited above, "Vignettes from a Summer Palette" (fall 1985), "Checking the Exchequer" (spring 1987), and "Fall-De-Rol: Turtles, Water Music, the Town Crier, and More" (winter 1987). While special events at the cemetery came and went, the newsletter remained, providing memorable summations of APHCC activities and interests. The publication accordingly provides the most detailed information about the organization during 1980-1989, including the gains it realized in repairing historic cemetery infrastructure.

The most significant of these achievements were restoration of the chapel, built in 1903, and replacement of the original water works system. The former included repair of the chapel roof, doors, and foundation, as well as installation of a small organ and also electricity, heat, and water. The precise cost of this stage of chapel restoration is not identified in the surviving documentation. The winter 1989 issue of the newsletter noted, however, that financial support came from contributions made to a "$90,000 restoration fund drive" by organizations including Christ Church, recognized for its "princely contribution," the Dolley Madison Chapter of the D.A.R., and the Walter A. Bloedorn Foundation, based in Washington, D.C.

The funding for replacement of the water works system, which totaled $78,000, came from the $250,000 authorized by PL 94-495 for "restoration and preservation" of the burial ground. An article in the winter 1987 newsletter announced that "a brand-new system of pipes and standpipes is now in place" and that this system, unlike the old infrastructure, had the capacity to carry water "to all corners of the Cemetery." In addition, the narrative provided information about the "baptism" of the new water works during Halloween festivities at the cemetery, which were open to the public. The ceremony included "an al fresco fanfare from Handel's Water

Music and some words of thanks to Congress from Chairman Margaret Hobbs."[42] Clearly, the Association, beleaguered though it was by ongoing discussion of the Barney Circle interchange, still knew how to celebrate.

The APHCC experience from 1990 to 1996 has not been remembered for celebratory "al fresco fanfares" from the music of Handel or anyone else. These years constituted instead "a difficult period," as characterized by Jim Oliver, who served on the Board of Directors from 1989 to 2001, was vice-chairman during 1990-1991, and then served as chairman during 1992-1994 and 1997-2001. Oliver explained that his "remembrance of that time," particularly 1989 and the early 1990s, was that the Board of Directors did not have "the energy and enthusiasm" of the "first generation of visionaries."[43] The leadership was focused instead on two major issues that respectively posed external and internal challenges to the organization. The former involved continuing deliberations over the Barney Circle proposal and its anticipated effects on the integrity of the cemetery as a geographic and historic entity. The internal matter centered on the cemetery superintendent in his management of APHCC financial resources and constituted the most serious concern of this type ever experienced by the organization.

Chris Herman resigned as editor of the Association newsletter on August 1, 1989, to focus on opposition to the Barney Circle proposal. His resignation had a profound effect on the periodical as the main vehicle of outreach to the wider membership. Under his leadership, the publication provided an engaging, informative read, signaling that the APHCC was alive and well and was making progress in maintaining the cemetery. The message enunciated by the newsletter was altogether different during 1990-1994. In those five years, only two newsletters were distributed, one during fall 1992, which was inexplicably identified as "Volume 1, No. 1," and the other in spring 1994, presented as "Volume II, No. 1." The two issues represented a radical departure from the newsletters of the 1980s in both format and content.

The fall 1992 publication, comprising but one page, led with a half-page article by John Hanley, who was superintendent of the cemetery during 1989-1997. He noted that only twenty-six percent of the APHCC membership had responded to a request during the

summer for financial contributions. Previous such appeals had resulted in donations from some "eighty to eighty five percent of the
membership." Hanley concluded by asking members to "remem-
ber that you have someone here who cares." If one asked, "Who
cares???" he would respond with, "I care!!!" To long-time readers
of the newsletter, this article signaled that the APHCC was undergoing a sea change and that all was not well with the organization
or, by extension, with efforts to preserve the burial ground.

The spring 1994 issue suggested a larger story in two abbreviated statements, one on each page of this two-page number. The first,
given under the heading "Thank You," indicated that the APHCC
had significant financial problems but did not explain why: "1993
was a difficult year for the Association. We kept our expenses a bit
below those of last year but our income fell by a crushing 40%. We
ended the year with an operating deficit that adds a particular burden to this year's budget and threatens our small trust fund." The
second statement said that a way had been found to address this
"particular burden" through negotiation of "a mitigation agreement" with the Federal Highway Administration and the D.C.
Department of Public Works over the Barney Circle project. According to the terms of this arrangement, which were not specified, the cemetery would gain "a new water drainage system, new
roadways, a new wall to replace the chain link fences and extensive
plantings of trees and shrubbery." Careful readers of the newsletter
must have been left wondering about the larger narrative residing
between the statements about financial problems and the "mitigation agreement."

References in the newsletter to this agreement ceased with the
decision by the Washington, D.C., City Council in December 1996
to reject the initial $15 million construction contract, thereby bring-
ing a close, at least for that time, to any further negotiations about
Barney Circle. The APHCC leadership did not make an official
public statement about Barney Circle, focused as it was on substantial problems within the organization. A summation of these difficulties was given in a "Notice to Association Members," which
was published in the spring 2000 Association newsletter, after the
problems had been resolved. As stated, the Board had concluded
that "the cemetery was in capable and caring hands" in that John

Hanley had managed the burial ground "virtually alone and made a great deal of progress" during "more than half a decade."

This judgment had proved wrong, as the subsequent paragraphs explained with references to "complaints," "commitments that were not kept," "bills that were not paid," and financial problems that brought the APHCC to "the verge of insolvency" by 1996. The Board had proceeded "to resolve all outstanding claims in order to recover our good name." As part of this effort, the members "sought the assistance" of the U.S. Attorney's Office for the District of Columbia, which had worked with the FBI in reviewing cemetery records and interviewing both past and current members of the Board. The leadership explained that it had published this "Notice to Association Members" because the investigation was nearing an end and the Board "wanted our members and friends to be aware of this in the event it is reported by the news media," as it was in the April 1, 2001, issue of *The Washington Post*. The article noted that Hanley had been indicted by a grand jury and accused of having embezzled some $175,000 from cemetery funds over a ten-year period. Following court proceedings, he was required to serve a prison sentence of eighteen months and to repay the $175,000 to the Association.

The Hanley incident constituted a difficult challenge for the APHCC, particularly for the leadership of the organization. It is most appropriately viewed, however, as an aberration within the larger volunteer effort that has been responsible for management of the cemetery since 1807. The years extending from 1980 to 1996 were significant in the history of the Association in that they comprised the period during which the leadership realized gains in organizational development that were critical to the operation and preservation of the first national burial ground.

A New Partnership with the Federal Government

During 1997, Congressional Cemetery was identified as one of America's 11 Most Endangered Historic Places, as noted in the beginning of this chapter. In 2007, the Association for the Preservation of Historic Congressional Cemetery celebrated the bicentennial anniversary of the burial ground. During the years extending between these milestones, three organizations—the Association for the Preservation of Historic Congressional Cemetery, the U.S. Congress, and the National Trust for Historic Preservation—provided critical leadership in activities focused on long-term preservation of the burial ground. They accordingly reformulated the private/public partnership basic to the operation and maintenance of the cemetery from its establishment in 1807.

Richard Moe, president of the National Trust for Historic Preservation, presided over a ceremony conducted at Congressional Cemetery on June 16, 1997, upon its identification as one of America's 11 Most Endangered Historic Places. In his comments, summarized in the summer 1997 issue of the Association newsletter, he described the burial ground as "an undiscovered treasure" that had been selected for citation to underscore the cultural significance and the critical needs of historic cemeteries across the nation. The results of this designation were "overwhelming": "For a moment, the story of Congressional Cemetery was heard in almost every corner of the world." Among the purveyors of this narrative were *The Washington Post*, C-SPAN, the Associated Press, National Public Radio, the British Broadcast Corporation, and Japanese Public Television. This coverage, in turn, was instrumental in generating contributions totaling some $75,000 and in mobilizing volunteer support for the burial ground. As noted in information provided by the National Trust, approximately 1,600 volunteers launched a one-day "rescue mission" at the cemetery. Most of these volunteers were members of the armed forces, which collectively had an historic connection with the site.[44]

Among the gains resulting from designation of the burial ground as an Endangered Place, the most significant was the establishment of a $1 million congressional matching fund for its "care and maintenance." This fund had inauspicious beginnings, originating as it did from a cleanup effort at the burial ground during October 1997. Jim Oliver, who was at that time chairperson of the APHCC Board of Directors, had secured the participation of Representative James Walsh, a Republican from New York who was then chairman of the Legislative Branch Appropriations Subcommittee. During this event, Walsh said that he would approach the Architect of the Capitol about giving the APHCC access to equipment used in maintaining the U.S. Capitol grounds. The conversation that followed led to a substantive dialogue about the burial ground between Representative Walsh and Alan M. Hantman, who had been appointed in 1997 to a ten-year term as Architect of the Capitol.

As part of this dialogue, Hantman wrote a letter to Walsh on October 29, 1997, that constitutes a landmark document in the history of Congressional Cemetery. In five pages typed single space, Hantman summarized the historic challenge posed by the burial ground, which was neither a public nor a private cemetery but a blend of the two: "This mixture of government-owned and privately-owned lots has been a troublesome factor in structuring federal support for the cemetery as a whole." Given his understanding about the singularity of the site, Hantman realized that a unique solution was required for its preservation. In articulating alternatives, he identified one approach that substantively advanced the conversation about Congressional Cemetery. He said, in short, that "funds sufficient to create a viable trust fund" could be provided on "a one-time-basis" to a federal organization, specifically to the Department of Veterans Affairs, the National Park Service, the Architect of the Capitol, "or the National Trust for conveyance to an appropriate fiduciary."[45]

Representative Walsh, in consultation with the Architect of the Capitol, concluded that the National Trust would be the most appropriate manager of a trust fund designed for the support of Congressional Cemetery. On June 23, 1998, he accordingly introduced language into the legislative appropriations bill for the fiscal year ending on September 30, 1999, that specified the creation of a $1 million matching grant for "the perpetual care and maintenance" of Congressional Cemetery. The resulting legislation, approved by President Bill Clinton on October 21, 1998, as Public Law 105-275, directed the Architect of the Capitol to provide the specified sum to the National Trust for Historic Preservation. The National Trust, in turn, was to "administer, invest, and manage such grant funds in the same manner as other National Trust endowment funds" and to distribute funding to the APHCC only as matched by identical sums raised by the Association.[46]

During a festive ceremony conducted at Congressional Cemetery on May 12, 1999, James Walsh and Alan Hantman presented a $1 million check to Richard Moe, President of the National Trust for Historic Preservation. This event was of particular note because it was a celebration of the private/public partnership established to preserve the burial ground. Moe, who was once again master of ceremonies at the cemetery, established the theme, observing that "what has happened here is the same thing that has helped save thousands of America's irreplaceable treasures: an effective partnership among private individuals, government agencies and nonprofit organizations." He proceeded to introduce Representative Walsh, who spoke about this collaboration as "an example of public and private cooperation to maintain a national historic site in our nation's capital." Alan Hantman, the final speaker, recalled that his organization had been instrumental in its focus on National Trust participation: "I am pleased that Chairman Walsh and the Congress adopted our suggestion that the National Trust play an important role to assure the improved maintenance of Congressional Cemetery."[47]

Public Law 105-275 was worthy of celebration in that it marked the end of congressional deliberations over funding mechanisms for Congressional Cemetery that reached back to 1928. On April 24 of that year, Representative Charles L. Abnernethy of North Carolina introduced H.R. 11916, which "directed" the Secretary of War to maintain "the land and monuments owned by the United States" at the burial ground. During the following seventy years, Congress deliberated over a succession of bills that identified various federal agencies as likely caretakers of the cemetery. The sponsors of these bills comprised a long list of articulate and determined legislators, including Representatives Lindy Boggs of Louisiana, Vance Hartke of Michigan, George Mahon of Texas, and John Saylor of Pennsylvania, along with Senators Joel Broyhill of Virginia, Theodore Green and Peter Gerry of Rhode Island, Tom Railsback of Illinois, and Hugh Scott of Pennsylvania. Public Law 105-275 was, however, the only one of the bills that focused directly on the private/public partnership central to the establishment and operation of Congressional Cemetery. For this reason, it was the only one that offered a viable formula for its preservation.

On May 19, 1999, one week after the ceremony staged at Congressional in celebration of the $1 million matching grant, First Lady Hillary Clinton announced a series of matching grants under the Save America's Treasures program. Established by Executive Order in February 1998 as a public-private partnership involving the White House, the National Park Service, and the National Trust for Historic Preservation, this initiative focuses on the preservation and celebration of historic sites and monuments, as well as documents and artifacts, expressive of the United States as a nation. The grant given to the APHCC under this program totaled $52,800. The sum when matched comprised $105,600 and was used during summer 2002 in the restoration of approximately eighty tombstones, table top markers, and box tombs at Congressional.[48]

Shortly thereafter, individual members of Congress, beginning with Senator Byron Dorgan of North Dakota, advanced legislation that provided funding for the burial ground. As was the case with other congressional representatives, Dorgan had become an advocate for the cemetery as the result of an initial visit to the site. In comments delivered subsequently in Congress, he recalled that in early 2001 he had paid his respects at the grave of Scarlet Crow, a member of the Wahpeton-Sisseton Sioux Tribe who had come to Washington, D.C., in 1867 "with some other American Indians from my part of the country" to negotiate a treaty with the U.S. government. His body was found shortly thereafter under the Occoquan Bridge, and the investigation that followed determined that he had been murdered.

While at Congressional, Dorgan had noted in particular a disconnect between the historic legacy of the cemetery, as exemplified by the congressional cenotaphs, and the deterioration of the infrastructure, including the roads. He accordingly urged Congress to provide additional funding for the burial ground in the appropriations bill for fiscal year 2003. In making this statement, he articulated his vision of the cemetery as a place of national memory:

I think all recognize that this is something to which we should pay some attention. I know there are many other very big issues we deal with here in the Senate. But this is something that I think is important to the memory of who we are, who served our country, how we treat them in death, and how we respect their memories. We can and should do better to bring a sense of repair and majesty to Congressional Cemetery.[49]

During spring 2002, following his initial visit to Congressional Cemetery, Dorgan sponsored legislation that established a second $1 million matching grant for the cemetery that was also to be managed by the National Trust for Historic Preservation and used for repair and maintenance of the grounds. Preparatory to these efforts, the grant required an in-depth assessment of the cemetery landscape and infrastructure, including the monuments and buildings. The stated purpose of this effort was to collect the types of information needed in developing a master plan to guide long-term development and preservation of the burial ground.[50]

As required by the 2003 congressional appropriation, representatives of the Architect of the Capitol, National Trust for Historic Preservation, and APHCC selected the firm to oversee the evaluation. They included Linda Harper, who was chairperson of the APHCC Board of Directors as well as Interim Director of the Southern Field Office of the National Trust. Their choice was Turk, Tracey & Larry Architects, LLC, based in Portland, Maine. To conduct parts of the larger effort, the company retained subcontractors that provided engineering assessments of the buildings and other physical structures (Robert Silman Associates), evaluated some 1400 gravestones (Integrated Conservation Resources, Inc.), examined the trees and shrubs (Bartlett Tree Experts), and provided an historical overview of the burial ground (Cathleen Breitkreutz).

The resulting "Historic Landscape and Structures Report for Historic Congressional Cemetery" was approximately one foot in width, comprising five volumes that, according to the APHCC newsletter, assessed "virtually every aspect of the cemetery" and prioritized recommendations for its restoration. The estimated cost was $53 million, to be expended largely as follows:

- $26 million for overall restoration and development of the grounds, including the reconstruction of both roads and walking paths, installation of a new water system, as well as stabilization and enhancement of the cemetery grounds by planting some 1,250 shrubs and 450 trees, among other activities
- $20 million for the repair of individual gravestones, as well as an additional $1.1 million for the repair of family mausoleums and burial vaults

- $5.4 million for repair of the existing brick and iron fencing around the cemetery and for construction of new fencing as needed
- $1.7 million for substantial repairs of structures including the chapel, gatehouse, and tool shed.[51]

While the above recommendations were critical to planning for restoration activities, the projected total sum of approximately $53 million for these initiatives was considerable indeed for a volunteer organization that was working at that time to meet the requirements of two $1 million matching grants.

The APHCC leadership conducted three "visioning" sessions during 2002-2003 on planning for the next century. During the first session, the Board of Directors discussed current conditions and possible future uses of the cemetery grounds. They concentrated in the next session on facilities, including a possible new maintenance building that would include space for conservation workshops. In the final visioning session, the Board addressed programming initiatives, particularly in connection with restoration of the burial ground; plans for developing an educational initiative; and ideas for expanding fundraising initiatives. While the members understood that "third century planning is likely to continue for some time," they emphasized the ongoing importance of volunteer contributions, which were instrumental in the establishment of the cemetery in 1807 and have been essential to its operation since that time.

A critical part of the volunteer effort has focused on preserving and facilitating the use of historic records maintained at Congressional Cemetery. As part of this initiative, Jim Oliver, who served on the Board of Directors from 1989 to 2001, developed a computerized list of burials from 1807 to 2007. This task took seven years to complete in large part because the index cards were handwritten and sometimes difficult to decipher and because records were missing for the period 1807-1820, thereby necessitating research in original cemetery documentation. Oliver also took digital photographs of the 3,000-page Daily Log Book for the years 1898-1982 and of some 14,000 gravestones.[52]

In addition to these records, the documentation includes obituaries of individuals interred at Congressional over the past 200 years. Sandra Schmidt, cemetery historian, has provided the lead since 1999 in the development of an extensive obituary database. This resource has unique value, in large part because of the philosophy basic to its compilation. In walks through the cemetery during the early 1990s, Schmidt would pause before the inscriptions on particular gravestones, wondering about the individuals interred at these sites. She then proceeded to the Library of Congress to read their obituaries as given in *The National Intelligencer* and *The Evening Star* during the nineteenth century and subsequently in *The Evening Star* and *The Washington Post*. During 1999, she began to transcribe the narratives, proceeding chronologically through the lists of everyone interred at the site on a permanent or a temporary basis, including U.S. presidents, members of Congress, top military leaders, Native American negotiators, and explorers of the American frontier, as well as housewives, day laborers, individuals living outside conventional social norms, and children. Given this approach, the collected obituaries not only offer many fascinating, unforgettable narratives about the individuals buried at Congressional but they also comprise an invaluable resource for reading the larger culture.[53]

Since its establishment in 1970, the APHCC has been supported in meaningful ways by a broad and diverse group of organizations. They have included, among many others, the following: Boys & Girls Clubs of Greater Washington; Capitol Hill Garden Club; Congressional Pages; Georgetown University Freshmen Volunteers; Job Corps; National Defense University; National Urban League; Professional Lawn Care Association; Department of Forensic Anthropology, Smithsonian Museum of Natural History; and the Washington, D.C., Chapter of Wittenberg University. They have also included federal agencies formerly considered as possible keepers of the burial ground. The spring 2007 Association newsletter delineated, for example, the partnership between the National Park Service's Historic Preservation Training Center and the Veteran Administration's National Cemetery Administration in preserving 166 congressional cenotaphs.

As the Association proceeded with plans for the bicentennial celebration of the burial ground in 2007, C. Dudley Brown provid-

ed commentary in an interview about the challenges and achievements of the organization. He had a long view in that he had served
on the Board of Directors since 1979 and had thus witnessed nearly
the entire history of the Association. In thinking about the early
years, he remembered the substantial contributions of Francis
Kraemer, along with George Didden, Barbara Held Reich, Ethel
Robertson, Florian Thayne, Joel Truitt, and others in establishing
the organization. When asked how he would characterize the difficulties they experienced during the formative period of the Association, extending from 1976 through the 1980s, he declared that "the
challenges seemed at times to be overwhelming." The members of
the Board confronted a cemetery that was "overgrown with grass
and weeds, cluttered with debris, and marked by large numbers of
overturned tombstones." "They were able to rescue the cemetery at
a critical period," he added, because "they understood its historic
legacy and they had the energy and commitment that allowed them
to act according to this understanding." In his reflections about the
burial ground during the preceding decade, Brown observed that
"the cemetery has been in a renaissance," although "significant
challenges remain." He accordingly underscored the need for continuing volunteer participation: "The operation and preservation
of Congressional Cemetery has always depended on the contributions of individual and organizational volunteers."[54]

Patrick Crowley provided an appraisal of APHCC initiatives in
"Looking Beyond Two Hundred Years," a "Letter from the Board"
that was published in the spring 2007 *Heritage Gazette*. He began by
stating that the organization had "met most of the strategic goals set
in 2000," including resetting 500 gravestones, restoring 20 percent
of the historic brick vaults, and planting 300 trees, as well as developing a master plan for continuing efforts. He noted in addition
that considerable work remained: "We have hundreds of stones to
right, and as many stories to research and tell. We have gardens
to tend, trees to plant, fences to mend, and structures to restore."
The operative word in this narrative is the "beyond" given in the
title. While there is "much still left to do," Crowley as well as other
members of the Board and the larger organization demonstrated
the energy, confidence, and astute planning that will be required
for ongoing preservation of the historic burial ground. Given its

composition, the Board was well situated to proceed with this effort. As identified in the spring 2007 newsletter, it comprised representatives from the key constituencies: three from Christ Church; three lot owners; six members of the APHCC; and two ex-officio members, one representing the Architect of the Capitol and the other the National Trust for Historic Preservation.

In an address delivered in 1991 upon the twenty-fifth anniversary of the National Historic Preservation Act, William J. Murtagh, first Keeper of *The National Register of Historic Places*, discussed both the challenges and the benefits of historic preservation. The controlling idea of his presentation, entitled "Janus Never Sleeps," was that "in a changing society, preservation is a stabilizing force, a continuum that provides us visual and psychological evidence of where we have been." At the same time, it serves "as a guide to where we might go." Poised strategically between the past and the future, the larger historic preservation movement has "achieved much in a relatively short period of time. This, however, should be seen only as prologue."[55]

These statements provide a framework for viewing the APHCC as it celebrated the bicentennial anniversary of Congressional Cemetery. The Association was collectively committed to preservation of the rich historic legacy of the burial ground. At the same time, the organization was articulating visions for various uses of the cemetery in the next century. It takes confidence, energy, and good ideas to engage in visioning statements. The individuals providing leadership within the APHCC clearly had these requisites. They were fully engaged in a "race against time" and were making notable progress in the ongoing challenges associated with preservation of the first national burial ground.

CONCLUSION

CONGRESSIONAL CEMETERY AND NATIONAL MEMORY

"The world around a monument is never fixed. The movement of life causes monuments to be created, but then it changes how they are seen and understood. The history of monuments themselves is no more closed than the history they commemorate."[1] This statement by Kirk Savage is relevant to Congressional Cemetery as a place of national memory. Widely recognized as the national burial ground during the antebellum period, it was then progressively forgotten by the general public until the 1970s and the establishment of a volunteer organization focused on restoration and preservation of the burial ground. This concluding section focuses on the creation, the loss, and then the recovery of national memory regarding Congressional Cemetery as the first national burial ground and as a place of ongoing historic significance.

Memories Caught in Stone and Text

The complex legacy of the cemetery is recorded in two diverse but complementary forms: the unique memorials at the site, particularly the congressional cenotaphs and the historic Public Vault, and the written documentation maintained in archives located across Washington, D.C. The monuments in their eloquent silence and the records with all their words convey similar statements about the national significance of Congressional Cemetery. In so doing, they provide commentary on the manifold issues relevant to the making of public memory.

The monuments at all cemeteries make statements about memory, usually about the lives of individuals as remembered by their descendants. Thousands of markers at Congressional convey such statements. The cenotaphs and the Public Vault, the latter of which was used in part for the temporary interment of several U.S. presidents, provide another message relevant to this burial ground, specifically its singular status as a national cemetery. The narrative is complicated, beginning with the physical presence of these memorials at the cemetery and continuing with the puzzling saga of their deterioration over more than a century.

The cenotaphs are notable for their distinguished authorship, by architect Benjamin Latrobe, and because of their special status as the only collective memorials ever erected at a burial ground or anywhere else in memory of individual members of the U.S. Congress and, by extension, of Congress itself. They have extraordinary placement, virtually in the backyard of the U.S. Capitol Building, thereby establishing a type of connection, as well as contrast, between the silence of the gravestones and the frequently vociferous debates in Congress. The cenotaphs accordingly bring a certain richness and resonance to the ongoing congressional presence in federal Washington, D.C. Given their unique legacy, it is remarkable that the quotation most frequently recalled about the monuments is George Hoar's observation in 1876 that they bring "new terrors to death" by their very appearance, which the representative from Massachusetts considered singularly unattractive.[2] It is significant as well that in the years following Hoar's statement, the cenotaphs were left to decay in close proximity to the U.S Capitol, the house of the U.S. Congress.

Over its long history, the Public Vault has posed statements similar to those offered by the cenotaphs. It has been used for the temporary interment of approximately "4,600 people—presidents, generals, and common folk," as noted in *The Heritage Gazette*, newsletter of the Association for the Preservation of Historic Congressional Cemetery (APHCC). No other burial ground in the United States has such a structure, designed as a pause along the way for individuals within all sectors of the broader community. Given its availability to everyone, the Public Vault comprises a unique historic site in itself. Nonetheless, the structure was "empty and decaying" as late as 2003, as was also reported by the APHCC: "Our venerable old Public Vault is in sad shape, its doors hanging on by a thinning strip of a wrought iron hinge. Once a grand way station with brick pillars and wrought iron fencing suitable for hosting the remains of three presidents, the Public Vault is now just a shadow of its former grandeur."[3] While the Public Vault has since been restored with the use of funds provided by the federal government, both this structure and the cenotaphs made large statements during their long decline about vulnerabilities on the surface level, in the stone used for these monuments, and on a much deeper level, about collective memory.

The Public Vault, the cenotaphs, and numerous individual gravestones at Congressional Cemetery were fashioned from Aquia Creek sandstone, as were the Executive Mansion, the U.S. Capitol, the original Treasury Building and Patent Office, and also the first aqueduct bridges along the Chesapeake and Ohio Canal. This sandstone afforded many advantages as well as disadvantages, as was soon discovered. Among the persuasive advantages were its immediate availability at sites along the Potomac River, the ease with which it could be carved, and its warm tones. It is possible that because of these qualities, its primary disadvantage—a critical lack of durability—was overlooked. As repairs were later made to the federal structures, so have they been made at Congressional Cemetery.

The memories about the burial ground captured on paper complement and extend the commentary provided by the Public Vault and the cenotaphs. Diverse in their origins as well as archival locations within both the private and public sectors, these documents delineate the singularity and the importance of the site. At the same time, they underscore the challenges associated with achieving broad consensus within the surrounding community regarding its historic legacy.

Perhaps the most striking fact about this documentation is that the foundational records, those essential to understanding the establishment and long-term operation of the first national burial ground, were created and continue to be maintained by Christ Church on Capitol Hill, established in 1794. They comprise a rich trove of primary resources, including the minutes of vestry meetings extending from 1812 to 1976, when the APHCC assumed responsibility for the site; rules and regulations governing its operation during the nineteenth and twentieth centuries; reports by cemetery superintendents summarizing both progress realized and chronic problems at the old burial ground; as well as correspondence and other documentation delineating communication between spokespersons for the vestry and federal officials on matters relevant to the site.

One of the primary documents providing insight into the understanding of the congregation regarding its responsibilities for operation and maintenance of the cemetery is *Washington Parish Burial Ground (Congressional Cemetery), 1807-1913*, which was published by the vestry in 1913. Issued approximately one-hundred years after Christ Church had assumed ownership of the burial ground, this document declared that the congregation shared a "sacred trust and duty" in its "management" role. In addition, the publication underscored the understanding of parishioners that this cemetery, the operation of which posed substantial and increasing challenges for the congregation, was an "historic" site.[4]

Among other documents maintained by Christ Church, the minutes of vestry meetings are essential in addressing the historic legacy of the burial ground. These narratives, which were drafted by hand through the 1940s, delineate the vision of the original founders of the cemetery, their impressive dedication to its maintenance, and the many challenges they confronted. Particularly notable are the fifty years of summations provided by the father and son team of Henry and John Ingle, who served as registrars during 1812-1822 and 1822-1863, respectively. Their neat script records in considerable detail the types and the extent of the volunteer service required not only to establish but also to maintain a burial ground that included the federal government among its constituents.

While the records archived at Christ Church focus on the establishment and operation of the site, documents maintained by the federal government underscore its status as the first national burial ground. They are diverse in origin, having been developed within both the legislative and executive branches of the U.S. government, and in location, scattered as they are in collections maintained by the Library of Congress, National Archives, National Park Service,

Washington Navy Yard, and Office of the Architect of the U.S. Capitol. They are also diverse in presentation, including memoranda
and letters, reports, historical summations, and the transcripts
of hearings on proposed legislation that read like small dramas,
featuring cameo performances by memorably articulate congressional leaders. Viewed together, these documents underscore the
significance of Congressional as an historic site and the challenges
experienced by both the legislative and the executive branches of
the federal government in understanding and then meeting their
respective responsibilities for the cemetery.

National Memory Lost and Recovered

The complexity of Congressional Cemetery as an historic site
emerged in the century following the Civil War. During this period, the first national burial ground and the rich memories associated with the site faded from public memory. This happened in
part because the cemetery was not reducible to a specific category
of historic sites. Other contributing factors were the establishment
of the military cemetery system and the location of Congressional
Cemetery east of the National Mall and thus away from the energy
and the activity moving in the opposite direction.

The challenge from the beginning was that Congressional was
not a traditional burial ground. While the founders established
the site as a municipal cemetery, they deeded it in 1812 to Christ
Church on Capitol Hill. Christ Church proceeded to identify the
cemetery as the Washington Parish Burial Ground. In 1816, however, the vestry offered Congress 100 lots for the interment of members who died in Washington, D.C., while the legislature was in session. Owned by a church, used for the burials for District residents,
including indigents, and available as needed by the federal government, the new cemetery blurred the line between private and
public. The Department of Interior accordingly ruled in 1857 that
the cemetery was not "public grounds," regardless of the federal
burials and monuments at the site. This decision led to the eventual
withdrawal of federal support for the burial ground and contributed to its decline as a place of national memory.

There was a seismic shift in federal recognition of and support for the cemetery during the Civil War. This conflict gave rise

to a new kind of burial ground in the American experience—national military cemeteries. These sites, particularly Arlington National Cemetery given its proximity to federal Washington, D.C., made powerful statements regarding the enormous price paid to preserve the Union. In the aftermath of the war, the symbolism attendant upon Arlington overshadowed memories focused on the historic legacy of Congressional, founded during the antebellum period. National cemetery came to mean national military cemetery, although the qualifying word "military" was not used in official parlance. Because there was no clear and certain place in the lexicon for national public burial ground, Congressional faded into the background while Arlington emerged as the premier national cemetery. As this happened, Congress shifted its focus and its funding to Arlington, largely forgetting about its responsibilities for the crumbling cenotaphs, the old Public Vault, and Congressional as the first national burial ground.

The last great funeral procession to Congressional Cemetery was staged in 1850 prior to the temporary interment there of President Zachary Taylor. Subsequent presidential interments were conducted within a refashioned monumental center in the federal city. This occurred in connection with development of the National Mall, which had been envisioned by Peter Charles L'Enfant in his 1791 plan for Washington, D.C. The Smithsonian Institution opened as a museum in 1855 and the Arts and Industries Building, which housed the 1876 centennial exhibits, in 1881. The Washington Monument was completed in 1884. During the next two decades, Congress authorized funds for restoration of the National Mall. In 1902, the Park Commission recommended expansion of the area west of the Washington Monument to include a site for a Lincoln Memorial and a bridge across the Potomac River to Arlington National Cemetery. The emerging federal landscape of buildings, museums, monuments, and wide avenues became the setting that Americans increasingly embraced as the nucleus of monumental Washington, D.C.

Depending on the individual, the landscape incorporated certain ironies. When looking at the Washington Monument, for example, many would not have known that Robert Mills, who designed the memorial, was buried at Congressional Cemetery following his death in Washington, D.C., during 1855. In addition, a sizable number of those who focused on Arlington Cemetery across the Potomac would not have recognized that the first national burial ground was Congressional Cemetery and that it was situated approximately 1.5 miles east of the U.S. Capitol.

Meanwhile, little had changed within the community surrounding Congressional Cemetery. The neighborhoods developed during the antebellum period remained largely in place, as were military institutions that included the Navy Yard, Marine Barracks, and Fort McNair. Established within this setting, Congressional Cemetery was, however, increasingly forgotten by the broader public. Historian John Bodnar provided applicable commentary, stating that public memory often emerges from "a political discussion that involves . . . fundamental issues about the entire existence of a society: its organization, structure of power, and the very meaning of its past and present." In addition, he observed that public memory can emerge out of "an argument about the interpretation of reality," which can function "as a cognitive device to mediate competing interpretations and privilege some explanations over others."[5] In the decades following the Civil War, and particularly by the early twentieth century, Congressional Cemetery was largely left out of the "political discussion" focused on the "meaning" of the nation both "past and present." Once the preeminent national burial ground, a site associated with both federal and military leaders, as well as everyone else, the cemetery still made eloquent statements. According to many, however, they came from a bygone era.

Two events subsequently helped shift the prevailing "interpretation of reality" toward a context that would contribute substantially to the rediscovery and renewal of historic sites, including Congressional Cemetery. In 1966, amidst growing public concern over the potential loss of significant parts of the national historic legacy, Congress passed the National Historic Preservation Act. The legislation stated in part that "the preservation of this irreplaceable heritage is in the public interest so that its vital legacy of cultural, educational, aesthetic, inspirational, economic, and energy benefits will be maintained and enriched for future generations of Americans." To advance these goals, the law established the National Register of Historic Places and authorized the creation of state historic preservation offices. Three years later, Congress instituted the

Bicentennial Commission to organize the 200th anniversary celebration of the Declaration of Independence. For the next seven years, the Commission proceeded to remind Americans of the historical events that led to creation of the nation.

The National Historic Preservation Act and the Bicentennial Commission were instrumental in establishing a context that encouraged Christ Church and Congress to persevere in challenging efforts focused on the preservation of Congressional Cemetery and its historic legacy. In 1973, Representative John Saylor and other legislators urged the National Park Service to assume responsibility for the site. Upon the failure of this effort and with funds in short supply, Christ Church briefly halted burials two years later. In 1976, the year of the bicentennial, the congregation established the Association for the Preservation of Historic Congressional Cemetery. Since that time, the organization has worked with federal supporters and private citizens to restore the site and to reaffirm its legacy as the first national burial ground. While major goals have been realized, efforts focused on long-term preservation of the cemetery will continue into the foreseeable future. Although the challenge is considerable, the goal is worthy. The burial ground is, after all, positioned in the shadow of the U.S. Capitol. So situated, Congressional Cemetery has a significant hold on the memory of the nation.

Notes

Introduction: The First National Burial Ground

1   George Watterston, *A New Guide to Washington* (Washington, D.C.: Robert Farnham, 1842), 71-80. The cemetery was originally recognized as "the burying ground at the east end of the city of Washington." After assuming control of the site in 1812, Christ Church identified the cemetery as the "Washington Parish Burial Ground." In 1849, the vestry changed the name to "Washington Cemetery." By the early 1840s, however, the graveyard had become generally recognized within the broader community as "Congressional Burial Ground" or "Congressional Cemetery" because of the substantial number of federal interments, as noted by Watterston. "Congressional Cemetery" continues as the accepted denominator for the burial ground to this day.

2   Montgomery Meigs, *Annual Report of the Office of the Quartermaster-General to the Secretary of War for the Fiscal Year Ending June 30, 1881* (Washington, D.C.: Government Printing Office, 1881), 23. Meigs had provided essentially the same statement in his Annual Reports for the fiscal years ending on June 30, 1879, and June 30, 1880.

3   Office of the Quartermaster General, U.S. Army, Untitled Report to Congress on Congressional Cemetery, submitted by Major General Henry Gibbins to the House Appropriations Committee, 76th Congress, 1st Session, in connection with the War Department Civil Functions Appropriations Bill for Fiscal Year 1939, 1. A photocopy of this document is maintained at the Congressional Cemetery archives.

4   Among many others, the legislators who urged federal support for the restoration and maintenance of Congressional Cemetery included the following: Representatives Charles L. Abernethy (1872-1955) of North Carolina, James P. Glynn (1867-1930) of Connecticut, George H. Mahon (1900-1985) of Texas, Edith Nourse Rogers (1881-1960) of Massachusetts, John P. Saylor (1908-1973) of Pennsylvania, and James T. Walsh (1947 -) of New York; as well as Senators Byron L. Dorgan (1942 -) of North Dakota, Theodore F. Green (1867-1966) of Rhode Island, and Peter G. Gerry (1879-1957), also of Rhode Island.

5   Congress, House of Representatives, Senator George H. Mahon speaking about "The Congressional Cemetery of Washington, D.C.," 86th Congress, 2nd sess., *Congressional Record – Appendix* (July 5, 1960): A5846-A5818.

6   Congress, Senate, Senator Dorgan of North Dakota speaking about Congressional Cemetery, 108th Cong., 1st sess., *Congressional Record* (June 27, 2003): S8826-27.

7   In discussing the cemetery grounds and monuments, this study incorporates information from the following documents: "Historic Landscape and Structures Report for Historic Congressional Cemetery," authorized by Congress in 2002; and "Congressional Cemetery (Washington Parish Burial Ground)," a study completed in 2005 by the Historic American Landscape Survey, a program of the National Park Service.

Chapter 1: A New Cemetery for the New Federal City

1   Samuel C. Busey, *Pictures of the City of Washington in the Past* (Washington, D.C.: Wm. Ballantyne & Sons, 1898), 235, quoting William Janson, unidentified source; Henry Adams, *John Randolph* (New York: Houghton Mifflin Company, 1898), 217.

2   Regarding L'Enfant's first name, Kenneth R. Bowling states that (1) after he immigrated to the United States, L'Enfant always identified his first name as Peter and that (2) he was accordingly recognized as Peter L'Enfant until the beginning of the twentieth century, when the French minister to the United States referred to him as Pierre while citing his accomplishments. See Bowling's book entitled *Peter Charles L'Enfant: Vision, Honor, and Male Friendship in the Early American Republic* (Washington, D.C.: Friends of the George Washington University Libraries, 2002).

3   Iris Miller, *Washington in Maps, 1606-2000* (New York: Rizzoli International Publications, Inc., 2002), 39.

4   Wesley Pippenger, "District of Columbia Ancestors: A Guide to Records of the District of Columbia," 1997, 36, Library of the Historical Society of Washington, D.C.

5   Paul E. Sluby, Sr., and Stanton L. Wormley, *Rock Creek Cemetery, Washington, D.C., 1822-1893*, vol. 1, *Old Interment Records, 1822-1906* (Washington, D.C.: Columbian Harmony Society, 1992), v-vii.

6   Christian Hines, *Early Recollections of Washington City* (Washington, D.C.: Chronicle Book and Job Print, 1866; reprint, Washington, D.C.: Junior League of Washington, 1981), 38-41. Hines had a high sense of purpose in drafting his *Recollections*, stating in the beginning of the volume that his "principal object . . . will be to reserve, or preserve, from oblivion accounts of incidents, events and facts which may be very useful as well as interesting, to the future historian of Washington, and which, otherwise, would be lost to posterity, as the generation to which he belongs has nearly passed away, and the few who remain will, in a few years, be with us no more."

7   Ibid., 38.

8   Ibid.

9   U.S. Senate, *History of the Congressional Cemetery* (Washington, D.C.: Government Printing Office, 1906), 4-5.

10   Paul E. Sluby, Sr., and Stanton L. Wormley, *Holmead's Cemetery (Western Burial Ground), Washington, D.C.* (Washington, D.C.: Columbian Harmony Society, 1985), 4-5.

11   Harvey W. Crew, *Centennial History of the City of Washington, D.C.: With Full Outline of the Natural Advantages, Accounts of the Indian Tribes, Selection of the Site, Founding of the City, Pioneer Life, Municipal, Military, Mercantile, Manufacturing, and Transportation Interests, the Press, Schools, Churches, Societies, Public Buildings, etc., to the Present Times* (Dayton, OH: United Brethren Publishing House, 1892), 696. In 1879, the District of Columbia was given title to the land occupied by the Western Burial Ground, which was known by the local citizenry as Holmead's because of its long association with the Holmead family.

12   Thomas Munroe, Superintendent of the City of Washington, to Henry Ingle, Agent for the Purchase of Square 1115, March 23, 1808, in *History of the Congressional Cemetery*, 6.

13   *History of the Congressional Cemetery*, 5; George Watterston, *A New Guide to Washington* (Washington, D.C.: Robert Farnham, 1842), 72, 79. Purchased for incorporation into a cemetery, Square 1115 was returned to one of its earlier uses. A married couple known as William and Ruth Young once had substantial land holdings in what later became the southeastern section of the city of Washington. This real estate included the property subsequently designated as Square 1115. Located on this site were the Youngs' sizable home—twenty-four by thirty-six feet with an attached kitchen eighteen feet square—and the family graveyard, twenty feet square. When the new cemetery was established on Square 1115, the only remains of the home were the foundation and of the graveyard just "a little dust," as noted in "Site of the Navy Yard," published in *The Evening Star* on November 17, 1900.

14   *History of the Congressional Cemetery*, 5. Information is not available in this *History* or other extant documentation regarding efforts to survey or lay out the burial ground.

15   Ibid.

16   Virginia Campbell Moore, "Reminiscences of Washington as Recalled by a Descendant of the Ingle Family," *Records of the Columbia Historical Society* 3 (1900): 97. Moore observed that Capitol Hill at the turn of the nineteenth century "was all of Washington, between which and Georgetown was a 'great gulf fixed,' almost impassable by reason of the mud and clay in winter and the dust and sun in summer."

17   Ibid., 99; Robert Brooks Ennis, "Christ Church, Washington Parish," *Records of the Columbia Historical Society*, 47 (1969-70): 129-130.

18   Kemnitzer, Reid & Haffler, Architects, "Historical Notes on Christ Church, Washington Parish," in Proposal Number P8620, p. 2; File Box: "Vestry Minutes & Annual Meetings, 1970-1974," Christ Church Archives.

19   Ennis, 133, note 11; John C. Van Horne, ed., *The Correspondence and Miscellaneous Papers of Benjamin Henry Latrobe, 1805-1810*, vol. 2 (New Haven: Yale University Press, 1986), 869.

20   Madison Davis, "The Navy Yard Section During the Life of the Rev. William Ryland," *Records of the Columbia Historical Society*, 4 (1901): 211-212.

21   Washington Topham, "Dr. Frederick May," *Records of the Columbia Historical Society*, 32 (1930): 307-308.

22   Ibid., 307-310; Bob Arnebeck, *Through a Fiery Trial: Building Washington, 1790-1800* (Lanham, MD: Madison Books, 1991), 499.

23   Arnebeck, 431.

24   Davis, "The Navy Yard Section During the Life of Rev. Wm. Ryland," 210; Allen C. Clark, "Samuel Nicholls Smallwood, Merchant and Mayor," *Records of the Columbia Historical Society*, 28 (1926): 23-61.

25   Constance McLaughlin Green, *Washington: A History of the Capitol, 1800-1950*, vol. 1 (Princeton: Princeton University Press, 1962; First Princeton Paperbook Printing, 1976), 21; Taylor Peck, *Round-Shot to Rockets: A History of the Washington Navy Yard and the U.S. Naval Gun Factory* (Annapolis, MD: United States Naval Institute, 1949), 11.

26   Office of the Quartermaster General, U.S. Army, Untitled Report to Congress on Congressional Cemetery, submitted by Major General Henry Gibbins to the House Appropriations Committee, 76th Congress, 1st Session, in connection with the War Department Civil Functions Appropriations Bill for Fiscal Year 1940, 47, note 140, Photocopy, Congressional Cemetery Archives, cited subsequently in this chapter as the Gibbins Report; Peck, 12; Arnebeck, 557; and Ennis, 130, note 9.

27   Ennis, 130. See Anthony S. Pitch, *The Burning of Washington: The British Invasion of 1814* (Annapolis: Naval Institute Press, 1998), 44.

28   Ennis, 126-127; Reverend Ethan Allen, "Washington Parish, Washington City" (unpublished manuscript, circa 1857), entry for 1796, Manuscripts Division, Library of Congress. Reverend Allen, rector of Christ Church from 1823 to 1830, was for many years the official historiographer of the Diocese of Maryland.

29   Allen, entry for 1794; John Claggett Proctor, "Churches Attended by the Presidents," in *Proctor's Washington and Environs*, articles written for *The Washington Sunday Star* (1928-1949) (Washington, D.C.: by the author, 1950), 260.

30   Nan Robertson, *Christ Church, Washington Parish: A Brief History* (Washington, D.C.: Christ Church, 1994), 4.

31   John Claggett Proctor, "Marine Plant Shared in City's Rise," *The Sunday Star*, Washington, D.C., November 13, 1934; John Claggett Proctor, "Anacostia and John Howard Payne," *The Sunday Star*, Washington, D.C., November 25, 1934.

32   Ennis, 133.

33   Ibid., 148, 133; Minutes of the Christ Church vestry meeting on August 4, 1806, Vol. 1, May 1795 – April 1862, Archives, Christ Church, Washington, D.C.

34   Allen C. Clark, *Greenleaf and Law in the Federal City* (Washington, D.C.: Press of W.F. Roberts, 1901), 62.

35   Kemnitzer, Reid, & Haffler, 1; Ethan Allen, entry for 1794 in unpublished manuscript, Manuscripts Division, Library of Congress.

36   Kemnitzer, Reid & Haffler, 2; Robertson, *Christ Church, Washington Parish*, 1.

37   *History of the Congressional Cemetery*, 7, 9.

38   The eleven regulations are identified in pages 7-9 of *History of the Congressional Cemetery*.

39   Edward C. Carter II, John C. Van Horne, and Lee W. Formwalt, eds., *The Journals of Benjamin Henry Latrobe, 1799-1820, From Philadelphia to New Orleans*, vol. 3 (New Haven: Yale University Press, 1980), 70.

40   Green, 42.

41   *History of the Congressional Cemetery*, 7.

42   *Washington Diocese* 48 (November 1979): 3; Robertson, *Christ Church, Washington Parish*, 4; Audrey Jones, One-Page Typed Summation of the All Saints Service at Congressional Cemetery on November 4, 1979, Archives, Office at Congressional Cemetery, Washington, D.C. Of the regulations not addressed in this section, the third focused on the duties of the sexton, the fifth on specifications for "the interment of strangers and others who take less than three sites," and the eighth on the required depth of all graves, which had to be "at least 5 feet 6 inches from the natural surface of the earth to the bottom of" the excavation.

43   *History of the Congressional Cemetery*, 15, 11, 14.

44   Ibid., 10-15; Samuel H. Williamson, "Seven Ways to Compute the Relative Value of a U.S. Dollar Amount, 1774 to Present," Economic History Services, http://www.measuringworth.com/calculators/uscompare/result.php. Accessed on May 20, 2012. The dollar value of $274,900 was determined according to the Historic Opportunity Cost, meaning the relative cost of a dollar using the index of all input into the economy.

45   *History of the Congressional Cemetery*, 10-15.

46   Ibid., 10-12. These pages identify the actions taken by the Christ Church vestry during 1816-1824 to secure the $2,000 appropriation provided by the U.S. Congress on May 4, 1824, to erect a brick wall around Congressional Cemetery.

47   Pages 13 and 14 of the *History of the Congressional Cemetery* summarize the actions taken by the Christ Church vestry to encourage the six congressional appropriations provided during 1832-1835.

48   *History of the Congressional Cemetery*, 14. The interior of the Public Vault, which is partly submerged, measures 12 feet and 1 inch in width, 22 feet and 2 inches in depth, and 8 feet and 9 inches in height, as noted on page 11 of the "Report to Congress, Restoration Summer – 2003," which was prepared by the Association for the Preservation of Historic Congressional Cemetery. Other nineteenth-century cemeteries had receiving vaults used for the temporary deposition of remains while arrangements were made for a permanent place of burial. The first receiving tomb at Mount Auburn Cemetery in Boston, for example, was constructed in the early 1830s, during the period when the receiving vault was emplaced at Congressional. See Blanche M.G. Linden, *Silent City on a Hill: Picturesque Landscapes of Memory and Boston's Mount Auburn Cemetery* (Amherst and Boston: University of Massachusetts Press in Association with the Library of American Landscape History in Amherst, 2007), 230-231.

49   *History of the Congressional Cemetery*, 14.

50   Ibid., 15.

51   Gibbins Report, 45, 163 note 30.

52   *History of the Congressional Cemetery*, 3.

53   Ibid., 16.

54   Ibid., 17.

55   Minutes of the Christ Church vestry meeting on April 19, 1854, Vol. 1, May 1795 – April 1862, Archives, Christ Church.

56   In their efforts on behalf of Congressional Cemetery, the Ingle family contributed a substantial legacy. Henry Ingle provided key leadership as one of the three trustees given primary responsibility in establishing the cemetery. His son John was arguably the central figure in developing infrastructure for the cemetery, in partnership with Congress, and then in enlarging the size of the burial ground to its current boundaries.

57   Cathleen Breitkreutz, "Developmental History: Landscape and Architectural Assessment," vol. 1, "Historic Landscape and Structures Report for Historic Congressional Cemetery" (Washington, D.C.: Architect of the Capitol, September 26, 2003), 7, Turk Tracey & Larry Architects, LLC, AOC 020057 Project No. 020026. The "Historic Landscape and Structures Report" was funded by the 2002 Omnibus Appropriation Bill of the U.S. Congress. The legislation provided $1,250,000 for cemetery restoration and preservation, of which $250,000 was designated for preparation of the "Historic Landscape and Structures Report." The Architect of the Capitol, who administered the appropriation, selected the firm of Turk, Tracey & Larry, based in Portland, Maine, to develop the document. Com-

pany representatives evaluated site infrastructure, recommended appropriate restoration procedures and treatments, and provided cost estimates relevant to accomplishing the recommended actions.

58   Cathleeen Breitkreutz noted on page 20 of her "Developmental History: Landscape and Architectural Assessment" that beginning with the establishment of Mount Auburn in Cambridge, Massachusetts, during 1831, "the landscape of the new American cemetery was based on English picturesque landscape with curved roads, varied topography, small bodies of water, and ornamental trees and plants." For commentary on the rural cemetery movement, see Blanche Linden's *Silent City on a Hill* and David Charles Sloane's *The Last Great Necessity: Cemeteries in American History* (Baltimore: Johns Hopkins University Press, 1991), 44-64.

59   Benjamin Latrobe, *The Journals of Benjamin Henry Latrobe, 1799-1820; From Philadelphia to New Orleans*, vol. 3, ed. Edward C. Carter, III, John C. Van Horne, and Lee W. Formwalt (New Haven: Yale University Press, 1980), 259, note 18. In her "Developmental History" of Congressional Cemetery, Cathleen Breitkreutz stated that the cenotaphs emplaced at the burial ground were "designed by" Latrobe but that "it has long been uncertain exactly when" he "designed the cenotaph form and when the first was installed at the burying ground" (p. 14).

60   Ibid., 259. Pamela Scott and Antoinette J. Lee described the cenotaphs as being "starkly abstract in their geometry" and noted that they figure among "the few examples in this country of late eighteenth-century visionary architecture." See their coauthored book: *Buildings of the District of Columbia* (New York: Oxford University Press, 1993), 266.

61   Peggy McDowell and Richard E. Meyer, *The Revival Styles in American Memorial Art* (Bowling Green: Bowling Green State University Press, 1994), 62

62   House of Representatives, "Contingency Expenses of the House Dec 4, 1822 to Dec 1829" [date of Congresses and document unidentified], H.R. 17 11 CA.4, Photocopy, Congressional Cemetery Files, Washington, D.C.; Clerk, House of Representatives, Contingency Accounts, 1843, National Archive—Legislative Reference, Photocopy, Congressional Cemetery Files, Washington, D.C.; *History of Congressional Cemetery*, 39. In addition to providing information about the cost of the cenotaphs, the *History of Congressional Cemetery* identified stonecutters who prepared the monuments. They included Hugh Lochrey, who had provided almost all the cenotaphs emplaced at Congressional from 1846 to 1860.

63   George Watterston, *A New Guide to Washington* (Washington: Robert Farnham, 1842), 72-74. While Watterston was critical of the cenotaphs, he praised Congressional Cemetery. In "Grave Yards of Washington," published in the May 10, 1839, issue of *The National Intelligencer*, he

declared that Congressional was "the most frequented and best known [burial ground] in Washington." He considered the site "beautiful," "surrounded" as it was "by a substantial brick wall, with three handsome gateways leading into the cemetery, through which run several fine avenues and smaller walks, ornamented with trees and shrubs, that are now beginning to give it the appearance of a garden."

64   Report of the Commissioner of Public Buildings, October 13, 1859, Photocopy, Congressional Cemetery Files, Washington, D.C.

65   Allen C. Clark, "Robert Mills, Architect and Engineer," *Records of the Columbia Historical Society* 40-41 (1940): 2-3.

66   Kirk Savage, "The Self-Made Monument: George Washington and the Fight to Erect a National Memorial," in *Critical Issues in Public Art,* ed. Harriet F. Senie and Sally Webster (New York: Harper Collins, 1992), 10-12.

67   John Quincy Adams, *Memoirs of John Quincy Adams,* vol. 5, ed. Charles Francis Adams (Philadelphia: J.B. Lippincott, 1875), 221.

68   H.M. Pierce Gallagher, *Robert Mills: Architect of the Washington Monument, 1781-1855* (New York: Columbia University Press, 1935), 176; Rhodri Windsor Liscombe, *Altogether American: Robert Mills, Architect and Engineer, 1781-1855* (New York: Oxford University Press, 1994), 160; Pamela Scott, "American Monuments," in *Robert Mills, America's First Architect,* ed. John M. Bryan (Washington, D.C.: American Institute of Architects Press, 1989), 162. Architectural historian Pamela Scott notes in the cited document that "Mills had submitted to Congress a design for a national cemetery in Washington located in a picturesquely landscaped square originally designated on L'Enfant's plan of the city as the site of the national pantheon." In 1836, after Congress did not act on his proposal for a national mausoleum, Mills designed the U.S. Patent Office building for the same site. Today, the original Mills structure houses the National Portrait Gallery on the corner of 9th and H Streets, N.W.

69   Gallagher, 176, note 1.

70   Ibid.

71   Jonathan Elliot, *Historical Sketches of the Ten Miles Square Forming the District of Columbia: With a Picture of Washington, Describing Objects of General Interest or Curiosity at the Metropolis of the Union* (Washington: J. Elliot, Jr., 1830), 307-310.

Chapter 2: The Grand Procession To The National Burial Ground

1   William E. Ames, *A History of the National Intelligencer* (Chapel Hill: University of North Carolina Press, 1972), 113. On December 31, 1864, William Seaton sold *The National Intelligencer* to Snow, Coyle and Company, a Washington, D.C. publishing firm. The publishing company of Gales and Seaton was dissolved on that date.

2   John Quincy Adams, *Memoirs of John Quincy Adams, Comprising Portions of His Diary from 1795 to 1848*, vol. 10, ed. Charles Francis Adams (Philadelphia: J.B. Lippincott & Company, 1876), 460.
3   Samuel C. Busey, *Pictures of the City of Washington in the Past* (Washington, D.C.: Wm Ballantyne & Sons, 1898), 268.
4   Samuel Sewall, *Diary of Samuel Sewall, 1674-1729*, vol. 3 (New York: Arno Press, 1972), 326. This publication includes all three volumes of Sewall's *Diary*. He began his diary at the age of twenty-one and continued providing entries for fifty-seven years (1673-1730).
5   Sewall, *Diary*, vol. 1, 454; Gordon E. Geddes, *Welcome Joy: Death in Puritan New England* (Ann Arbor: UMI Research Press, c. 1981), 135; Sewall, *Diary*, vol. 3, 387.
6   Sewall, *Diary*, vol. 3, 326.
7   Ibid., 390; *The New England Weekly Journal*, February 16, 1728, quoted in Geddes, 137-138.
8   *Virginia Gazette*, October 18, 1770, quoted in Isaac Rhys, *The Transformation of Virginia, 1740-1790* (Chapel Hill: University of North Carolina Press, 1999), 326-327.
9   Steven C. Bullock, *Revolutionary Brotherhood: Freemasonry and the Transformation of the American Social Order, 1730-1840* (Chapel Hill: University of North Carolina Press, 1996), 53-56; William Preston, *Illustrations of Masonry*, 2d ed. (London: J. Wilkie, 1775; reprint, Bloomington, Illinois: The Masonic Book Club, 1973), 135-137, 145 (page citations are to the reprint edition).
10   Preston, 137.
11   Washington Irving, *Life of George Washington*, edited and abridged by Jess Stein (New York: Putnam, 1855-59; reprint, Tarrytown, New York: Sleepy Hollow Restorations, 1975), 684 (page citation is to the reprint edition).
12   Francis Trollope, *Domestic Manners of the Americans*, ed. Donald Smalley (London: Whittaker, Treacher and Company, 1832; reprint, New York: Alfred A. Knopf, 1949), 235 (page citation is to the reprint edition).
13   The U.S. government conducted funerals and burials for the following members of the House of Representatives before the U.S. Congress relocated from New York/Philadelphia to Washington, D.C.: Theodorick Bland of Virginia (who died on June 1, 1790), interred in New York City; Nathan Bryan of North Carolina (June 4, 1798), buried in Philadelphia; and John Swanwick (August 1, 1798), also buried in Philadelphia. With these interments, the federal government initiated procedures that were subsequently incorporated into funeral ceremonies conducted in Washington, D.C. They included establishing a committee responsible for the arrangements, suspending on a temporary basis all legislative business,

establishing a one-month period of mourning, and conducting a funeral that was attended by both houses of Congress and that concluded with a formal procession to the designated burial ground.

14   Mary Ryan, "The American Parade: Representations of the Nine-teenth-Century Social Order," in *The New Cultural History*, ed. Lynn Hunt (Berkeley: University of California Press, 1989), 133. Susan G. Davis inter-preted parades as "political actions, rhetorical means by which performers attempted to accomplish practical and symbolic goals." This commentary is provided in her *Parades and Power: Street Theatre in Nineteenth-Century Philadelphia* (Philadelphia: Temple University Press, 1986), 5.

15   The sources used in compiling this table are as follows: *Biographi-cal Directory of the American Congress, 1774-1996*, ed. Joel D. Treese (Alex-andria, VA: C.Q. Staff Directories, 1997); and Jim Oliver, "Congressional Cemetery, Washington, D.C., Index of Interments, 1807 to Present."

16   "Dr. Mitchell's Letters from Washington: 1801-1813," April 1879, *Harper's New Monthly Magazine*, vol. 58, December 1878 to May 1879 (New York: Harper & Brothers, 1879), 754.

17   The two pallbearers were Representative Richard Bland Lee (1761-1827) and Thomas Tudor Tucker (1745-1828). Representative Lee, elected from Virginia to the First, Second, and Third Congresses, had been buried at Congressional on March 14, 1827, seventeen months before the re-interment there of his old friend, Theodorick Bland. Much later, in 1976, Lee was reinterred at Sully Plantation, Virginia. Thomas Tudor Tucker of South Carolina was interred at Congressional on May 4, 1828, about four months before Bland's re-interment there. Tucker had capped a distinguished legislative career with twenty-seven years of service as U.S. treasurer, having been appointed to this position by President Thomas Jefferson in 1801.

18   David R. Goldfield and Blaine A. Brownell, *Urban America: From Downtown to No Town* (Boston: Houghton Mifflin Company, 1973), 115-118.

19   Robert W. Habenstein and William M. Lamers, *The History of American Funeral Directing* (Milwaukee: Bulfin Printers, 1955), 263-264.

20   Ibid., 264. Advertisements for other innovative coffins surfaced at approximately the same time. On October 21, 1853, for example, the *Washington Star News* carried an advertisement placed by J.W. Plant, an undertaker in Washington, D.C., who wanted "to call the attention of the public to his PATENT CORPSE PRESERVER [sic], which has been already been tested in the families of several in this city, to whom he can refer as to its efficacy in preserving the body from decomposition for any length of period."

21   Irving H. Bartlett, *John C. Calhoun: A Biography* (New York: W.W.

Norton & Company, 1993), 374; Charles M. Wiltse, *John C. Calhoun: Sectionalist, 1840-1850* (New York: Bobbs-Merrill, 1951), 475.

22   *Obituary Addresses Delivered on the Occasion of the Death of the Hon. John C. Calhoun, A Senator of South Carolina, in the Senate of the United States, April 1, 1850. With the Funeral Sermon of the Rev. C.M. Butler, D.D., Chaplain of the Senate, Preached in the Senate, April 2, 1850* (Washington: Jno. T. Towers, 1850), 22.

23   Ibid., 23, 26.

24   Ibid., 33, 39.

25   Margaret L. Coit, *John C. Calhoun: American Portrait* (Boston: Houghton Mifflin, 1950), 513; Wiltsie, 478.

26   Robert V. Remini, *Henry Clay: Statesman for the Union* (New York: WW. Norton & Company, 1991), 783-785.

27   George Ticknor Curtis, *Life of Daniel Webster* (New York: D. Appleton and Company, 1872), 703.

28   Robert V. Remini, *Daniel Webster: The Man and His Time* (New York: W.W. Norton & Company, 1997), 762; Curtis, 703-705.

29   The *Washington Star News* of January 4, 1864, said this about the demise and burial of Lemuel Bowden: "Senator Bowden died of black small pox, and consequently, fear of contagion prevented many from attending his funeral who would otherwise have done so. As it was, however, there was a goodly number of persons in attendance, among whom were many Senators and Representatives. The remains were interred in the Congressional Cemetery, the procession moving through Pennsylvania Avenue."

30   Busey, 286, 272-273.

31   Adams, 458-459.

32   Ibid., 460.

33   The design of Harrison's coffin facilitated his relatively lengthy stay in the Public Vault. As noted by James A. Green, Harrison's "body had been placed in a leaden coffin which was enclosed in one of mahogany. The latter had been hermetically sealed with zinc sheets and then these—the lead, mahogany and zinc—were put in a coffin of walnut which was covered by a black silver velvet pall trimmed with gold fringe and ornate gold tassels"—*William Henry Harrison: His Life and Times* (Richmond, VA: Garrett and Massie, 1941), 405.

34   The reason for the delay in the burial of Alexander McCormick remains a mystery. As noted in Chapter 1 of this study, the cemetery regulations adopted by the Christ Church vestry on March 30, 1812, had reserved five sites at the cemetery free of charge for "the exclusive privilege of the burial of Rev. Alexander T. McCormick and his family."

35   *The National Intelligencer* of June 28, 1841, observed that the re-

mains of President Harrison were "removed from the Government burial grounds . . . at the hour and under the ceremonies prescribed by the order of Congress." James A. Green delineated the passage home in *William Henry Harrison*, 405-406.

36   Lynn Hudson Parsons, "'The Splendid Pageant': Observations on the Death of John Quincy Adams," *New England Quarterly* 53 (December 1980): 471. Among the Whigs he appointed to the Committee of Arrangements, Speaker Robert Winthrop included young Abraham Lincoln, who had joined Adams in opposing the Mexican War as an extension of proslavery interests.

37   *Token of a Nation's Sorrow: Addresses in the Congress of the United States and Funeral Solemnities on the Death of John Quincy Adams* (Washington, D.C.: J. and G.S. Gideon, 1848), 28.

38   William H. Seward, *Life and Services of John Quincy Adams* (Auburn, NY: Derby, Miller, and Company, 1849; reprint, Port Washington, New York: University Press of America, 1971), 359-360 (page citations are to the reprint edition).

39   In reproducing this list, the authors of this study have provided first names when not given by *The National Intelligencer*.

40   Thomas Hart Benton, *Thirty Years' View*, vol. 2 (New York: D. Appleton & Company, 1879), 707-708.

41   *Token of a Nation's Sorrow*, 39-40; Oliver, "Index of Interments, 1807 to Present."

42   Parsons, 466; Bemis, 541. For a fuller discussion of the events following the demise of John Quincy Adams, see Abby Arthur Johnson and Ronald M. Johnson, "Funereal Pageantry and National Unity: The Death and Burial of John Quincy Adams," in *Ceremonies and Spectacles: Performing American Culture*, ed. Teresa Alves, Teresa Cid, and Heinz Ickstadt (Amsterdam: Vu University Press, 2000), 144-151.

43   *The National Intelligencer* of July 12, 1850, delineated the format for the funeral parade to Congressional Cemetery for the temporary interment of President Zachary Taylor.

44   *The National Intelligencer*, July 15, 1850; Oliver, "Index of Interments, 1807 to Present"; Karl Jack Bauer, *Zachary Taylor: Soldier, Planter, Statesman of the Old Southwest* (Baton Rouge: Louisiana State University Press, 1985), 318-319.

45   The organization of the procession staged in Washington, D.C., in memory of President Abraham Lincoln is delineated in "[Handbill] [April 19, 1865] Order of the Funeral Procession [of] President Abraham Lincoln," in *I Remain: A Digital Archive of Letters, Manuscripts, and Ephemera* [database on-line] (Bethlehem, PA: Lehigh University Digital Library, accessed on May 7, 2006). The format for this parade is presented as given in

the original documentation except for the first line—"FUNERAL ESCORT IN COLUMN OF MARCH"—which was not provided in bold type.

46   The following texts provide detailed coverage of the funeral procession that transferred the remains of President Lincoln from the Executive Mansion to the U.S. Capitol Building: Dorothy and Philip Kunhardt's *Twenty Days* (North Hollywood, California: New Castle Publishing Company, 1965), Victor Searcher's *The Farewell to Lincoln* (New York: Abingdon Press, 1965), Merrill D. Peterson's *Lincoln in American Memory* (New York: Oxford University Press, 1994), Harry Garlick's *The Final Curtain: State Funerals and the Theatre of Power* (Amsterdam: Rodopi B.V., 1999), and Barry Schwarz's *Abraham Lincoln and the Forge of National Memory* (Chicago: University of Chicago Press, 2000). In his account of plans for the Lincoln funeral, Victor Searcher noted that Congressional Cemetery had been one of three alternative sites proposed to Mary Todd Lincoln for the burial of her husband. He added that she rejected all three sites in favor of burial in Springfield, Illinois. The following statement appeared in "The Succession," an article published in *The New York Times* on April 16, 1865: "It is expected, though nothing has been determined upon, that the funeral of the late President Lincoln will take place on or about Thursday next. It is supposed that his remains will be temporarily deposited in the Congressional Cemetery."

47   Harry Garlick, 188.

48   While the remains of President Lincoln were not interred on a temporary basis at Congressional, thirty-five people with diverse roles relevant to his death and interment were buried at the cemetery. They include David Herold (1842-1865), a member of Christ Church who functioned in part as a guide for John Wilkes Booth as he proceeded into southern Maryland following the assassination of the president and who was hanged with other conspirators at the federal arsenal in Washington, D.C., on July 7, 1865; Joseph G. Shelton (1829-1907), who was one of Lincoln's body guards and who had helped carry the wounded president to the house across the street from Ford's Theater; Dr. Charles M. Ford and Dr. James Crowhill Hall, who were among the sixteen physicians that attended Lincoln during his final hours; Dr. Joseph Bell Alexander (1824-1871), co-owner of the undertaking firm of Brown and Alexander, which prepared Lincoln's body for transport to Springfield, Illinois, and burial there; Henry Pratt Cattell (1838-1915), who was an employee of the firm Brown & Alexander and who embalmed the body of Lincoln; Benjamin Brown French (1800-1870), who designed and oversaw the construction of two catafalques used in ceremonies conducted respectively at the Executive Mansion and U.S. Capitol; and Representative Henry Gaither Worthington (1828-1909) of Nevada, who served as a pallbearer at Lincoln's funeral.

Chapter 3: Civil War Memories at Congressional and Arlington Cemeteries

1   Karl Decker and Angus McSween, *Historic Arlington* (Washington, D.C.: Decker and McSween Publishing Company, 1892), 3-4. The Decker and McSween Publishing Company was listed in the "Business Directory" of *Boyd's City Directory* in the year 1893. From 1892 to 1898, the two authors were included in the "Journalists" section of this publication.

2   Decker and McSween, 63.

3   Ibid., 63, 65-66. In *The Story of Arlington*, published in 1899 as the second history of the cemetery, author John Ball Osborne stated his belief "that in a few isolated instances soldiers were buried at Arlington prior to May 13, 1864," referencing a comment by a member of the Seventh Wisconsin Infantry who claimed to be part of a firing squad that had participated during 1863 in the burial of a comrade at a site near the Custis graves. *The Story of Arlington* (Washington, D.C.: Press of John F. Sheiry, 1899), 30. David Miller noted that the narrative about Abraham Lincoln and Montgomery Meigs at Arlington emerged originally from recollections shared from "within the Meigs family." This comment is provided in his *Second Only to Grant: Quartermaster General Montgomery C. Meigs* (Shippenburg, Pennsylvania: White Marc Books, 2001), 259.

4   William C. Dickinson, Dean A. Herrin, and Donald R. Kennon, eds., *Montgomery C. Meigs and the Building of the Nation's Capital* (Athens: Ohio University Press, 2002), x.

5   MacCloskey, *Hallowed Ground: Our National Cemeteries* (New York: Richards Rosen Press, 1968), 138, 21-23. The United States government claimed title to the Arlington estate through legislation of February 6, 1863, that required the payment of taxes in person. Because Mary and Robert Lee could not venture into what was then enemy territory to pay the assessed sum of $92.07, the U.S. government purchased the estate for the assessed value of $26,810. See Miller, 258.

6   MacCloskey, 24.

7   Ibid., 39-40.

8   Ibid., 37.

9   James M. Good, *The Outdoor Sculpture of Washington, D.C.: A Comprehensive Historical Guide* (Washington, D.C.: Smithsonian Institution Press, 1974), 202. Louisa Meigs made the final entries in her son's pocket diary, writing on October 3 that "Lt. J.R. Meigs was killed by guerrillas on the 3[d] of October about 7 oclock in the eveng [sic], returng [sic] to camp at Genl [sic] Sheridans H[d]. Quarters. He was Chief Engineer of the Army of the Valley of the Shanandoah [sic] & aid to Genl Sheridan." Her emotions surfaced in the final entry, on October 7 — "Was brought home this day, the loving remains of my noble precious son." Russell F. Weigley, *Quar-*

termaster General of the Union Army: A Biography of M.C. Meigs (New York: Columbia University Press, 1959), 309.

10   *Annual Report of the Office of the Quartermaster-General to the Secretary of War for the Fiscal Year Ending June 30, 1879* (Washington, D.C.: Government Printing Office, 1879), 20-21.

11   *Annual Report of the Office of the Quartermaster-General to the Secretary of War for the Fiscal Year Ending June 30, 1880* (Washington, D.C.: Government Printing Office, 1880), 22; *Annual Report of the Office of the Quartermaster-General to the Secretary of War for the Fiscal Year Ending June 30, 1881* (Washington, D.C.: Government Printing Office, 1881), 23.

12   Constructed during 1833-1843 by the Alexandria Canal Company, the Aqueduct Bridge connected the C&O Canal on the Georgetown waterfront to the Alexandria Canal at what was then the hamlet of Rosslyn. The bridge was an elevated waterway used for the transport of boats and barges across the Potomac River to Virginia. In 1861, at the beginning of the Civil War, the federal government assumed control of the bridge, drained the water, and used the canal trough primarily for the transport of troops and military equipment. In 1868, the Alexandria Canal Company resumed control of the structure, reopening the waterway and placing a roadway above the canal trough for the passage of pedestrians and vehicular traffic. During 1886, the federal government purchased the Aqueduct Bridge for $125,000 and then rebuilt it as an iron-truss structure in 1888, just in time for the funeral procession for General Philip Sheridan, discussed later in this chapter.

13   *Annual Report for the Fiscal Year Ending June 30, 1879*, 21; *Annual Report for the Fiscal Year Ending June 30, 1880*, 22; *Annual Report for the Fiscal Year Ending June 30, 1881*, 22.

14   Decker and McSween, 69; *Annual Report of the Office of the Quartermaster-General to the Secretary of War for the Fiscal Year Ending June 30, 1868* (Washington, D.C.: Government Printing Office, 1868), 109; *Annual Report of the Office of the Quartermaster-General to the Secretary of War for the Fiscal Year Ending June 30, 1870* (Washington, D.C.: Government Printing Office, 1870), 80.

15   In *Historic Arlington*, pages 72-74, Karl Decker and Angus McSween delineated efforts by the Quartermaster General's department to recover the remains of Union dead from battlefields around Washington, D.C. James Edward Peters provided details about the construction of the Tomb of the Unknown Dead of the Civil War in *Arlington National Cemetery: Shrine to America's Heroes* (Kensington, Maryland: Woodbine House, 1986), 26-27.

16   *Annual Report of the Quartermaster General for the Year 1870*, 80.

17   Ibid., 91.

18   The Association for the Preservation of Historic Congressional Cemetery is an organization of volunteers established in 1976. Chapter 7 of this monograph provides information about the APHCC. *The Evening Star*, later known as *The Washington Star-News* and *The Washington* Star, was published in Washington, D.C., during 1852-1981. Sandy Schmidt, cemetery historian, has transcribed obituaries published in this periodical that summarize in memorable detail the lives of numerous individuals interred at Congressional. Information about the scope of this effort is given in Chapter 7 of this study. Janice Hume has addressed the historical importance of obituaries, stating that an examination of these narratives "can help in understanding an important aspect of American culture, the public memory of its citizens." See Janice Hume, *Obituaries in American Culture* (Jackson: University Press of Mississippi, 2000), 12.

19   Henry Pratt Cattell, who was an embalmer for the firm of Messrs. Harvey & Marr, prepared the body of John Rawlins for burial, as noted in *The Evening Star* of September 7, 1869. Previously, he had embalmed the bodies of both President Abraham Lincoln and his son Willie. See Stephen M. Forman, *A Guide to Civil War Washington* (Washington, D.C.: Elliott & Clark Publishing, 1995), 149. Following his death on December 8, 1915, Henry Cattell was buried at Congressional Cemetery.

20   Julia A. Sienkewicz, a landscape historian, provided two views of Congressional Cemetery within the context of the funeral ceremonies for General Rawlins. She observed that as the end stop for the procession, "the cemetery plays its role perfectly. It offers age, dignity, nature, stability and memory to the ritual of mourning." In terms of its "appearance," however, it "may not have played quite such a seamlessly perfect role," as noted in "The Congressional Cemetery," published in the September 10, 1869, issue of *The New York Times*. This article, which she cited, stated that "there is a general neglect about everything," including the "painfully gloomy" brick walls and the "unpretending entrance," the latter of which had "nothing of the magnificent solemnity of Green-Wood," a rural cemetery in New York. See Julia A. Sienkewicz, "Historic American Landscapes Survey: Congressional Cemetery (Washington Parish Burial Ground)," No. DC-1 (Washington, D.C.: Historic American Landscapes Survey, National Park Service, 2005), 52.

21   Juliet Opie Hopkins was widely respected within the Confederacy for her contributions during the Civil War, which included the establishment of three hospitals in Richmond, Virginia, for the care of wounded Alabama soldiers. Her portrait appeared on the twenty-five-cent coin and the fifty-dollar bill issued by Alabama during the war.

22   Alexander Dallas Bache (1806-1867), a great-grandson of Benjamin Franklin, is also interred at Congressional. A prominent man in his

time, he was professor of natural philosophy and chemistry at the University of Pennsylvania during 1828-1836, superintendent of the U.S. Coast Survey from 1843 to his death, a regent of the Smithsonian Institution, and the first president of the National Academy of Sciences. Louis Agricola Bauer, "Alexander Dallas Bache," *Dictionary of American Biography*, ed. Allen Johnson, vol. 1 (New York: Charles Scribner's Sons, 1957), 461-462.

23   Ethel Stephen Arnett, *Mrs. James Madison: The Incomparable Dolley* (Greensboro, NC: Piedmont Press, 1972), 238.

24   Stewart Sifakis provided a biographical sketch of Charles F. Henningsen in his *Who Was Who in the Civil War* (New York: Facts on File, 1998), 303.

25   Harry Wright Newman, *The Smoots of Maryland and Virginia* (Washington, D.C.: n.p., 1936), 43.

26   Roy Morris, Jr., *Sheridan: The Life and Wars of General Phil Sheridan* (New York: Crown Publishers, 1992), 390-391.

27   *The Evening Star*, August 10 and 11, 1888; Morris, Jr., 392.

28   The "lower road" was the Georgetown and Alexandria Turnpike, built in 1809. Constructed along the eastern boundary of Arlington, this thoroughfare provided direct access to the cemetery through its three main gates.

29   Osborne, 40. As indicated in *The Evening Star* of August 11, 1888, Sheridan had purchased Guy four years earlier because he had a white star on his forehead and looked like Rienzi, whom he later renamed Winchester in memory of his valor at the great battle waged there. Guy was saddled for the procession in military style, ready for mount but for the general's boots, affixed within the stirrups in reverse order. See also Morris, Jr., 392.

30   David W. Blight, *Race and Reunion: The Civil War in American Memory* (Cambridge, MA: The Belknap Press of Harvard University Press, 2001), 65, 68-70. The title Blight provided for Chapter 3 of *Race and Reunion* was "Decoration Days." In discussing the ceremonies both in Chapter 3 and elsewhere in his book, he referenced both Decoration Day and Memorial Day, using the terms interchangeably.

31   Ibid., 71.

32   During 1869-1875, *The Evening Star* identified the annual day of remembrance as Decoration Day in 1869, 1870, 1872, and 1874 and as Memorial Day in 1871, 1873, and 1875. Following 1875, the periodical referred to the occasion as Memorial Day.

33   On May 30, 2003, the Sons of Union Veterans of the Civil War reenacted the Order of Exercises for the sixth Memorial Day ceremony at Arlington, conducted on May 30, 1873. As stated in the "Preface" provided in the program distributed on May 30, 2003, "the ceremony (exercises)

on these hallowed grounds will follow with exacting detail the music, speeches, poems, and prayers recited that day with only slight modifications where documentation is not possible" (David R. Curfman, M.D., Chairman, Historic Decoration/Memorial Day Ceremonies, Sons of Union Veterans of the Civil War).

34   A sizable number of the visitors who attended the ceremonies of remembrance at Arlington crossed the Potomac River by ferry, characterized by *The Evening* Star of May 30, 1870, as a vessel "of pic-nic notoriety," given the festivities associated with the transport that year of some "five thousand persons at the lowest estimate" to the Virginia shore.

35   Frederick Douglass, *Life and Times of Frederick Douglass* (London: Collier Books, 1962; reprint, Boston: DeWolf, Fiske, and Company, 1892, revised edition), 413-415 (page citations are to the reprint edition). *The Evening Star* of May 30, 1871, summarized the address given by Douglass in its coverage of the 1871 Memorial Day celebrations at Arlington.

36   Stuart McConnell, *Glorious Contentment: The Grand Army of the Republic, 1865-1900* (Chapel Hill: The University of North Carolina Press, 1992), 183-184. Organized in 1866, the Grand Army of the Republic consisted of Union veterans who had served in the Civil War.

37   The McClellan cap, which had a flat top and a squared visor, was named after George B. McClellan, who organized the Army of the Potomac and was general-in-chief of the Union Army during November 1861-March 1862.

38   The Women's Relief Corps was founded in 1883 as an auxiliary to the Grand Army of the Republic. From that time through the 1890s, the organization sought to keep alive the memory of contributions made by those who had fought in the Civil War. They did this primarily by helping stage annual Memorial Day observances. In addition, the various chapters worked on cemetery maintenance and the creation of war memorials. See Blight, 71-72. The summation of Memorial Day activities at Congressional Cemetery in 1886, 1889, 1898, and 1899 is based on information given in *The Evening Star* published on May 30 of those years.

Chapter 4: A Truly National Assembly

1   John Quincy Adams, *Memoirs of John Quincy Adams*, vol. 5, ed. Charles Francis Adams (Philadelphia: J.B. Lippincott, 1875), 220-221.

2   George Watterston, *A New Guide to Washington* (Washington, D.C.: Robert Farnham, 1842), 75-76. Watterston quoted from Thomas Gray's "Elegy in a Country Churchyard" in his recollection of these words: "and all that beauty, all that worth e'er gave."

3   David Charles Sloane, *The Last Great Necessity* (Baltimore: The Johns Hopkins University Press, 1991), 30, 7.

4   "Congressional Cemetery's American Heritage: The Public Vault," *The Heritage Gazette* (Spring 2003), 4; Brian C. Kates, "Forsaken Heritage: The Neglect and Ravishment of Congressional Cemetery in Washington, D.C.," *American Cemetery* 51 (June 1978): 25. *The Heritage Gazette* is the newsletter of the Association for the Preservation of Historic Congressional Cemetery. Commentary on construction of the Public Vault is given in Chapter 1 of this history, "A New Cemetery for the New Federal City."

5   Built in 1835, the Causten Vault is a red brick structure with white marble entablature bearing this inscription: "Inexorable Death's Doing." Situated on the eastern side of the cemetery, the Causten Vault is located in close proximity to the historic Public Vault.

6   On March 3, 1823, Congress passed legislation that authorized the placement of a substantial marker over the Elbridge Gerry grave and provided an appropriation to cover the costs. James M. Goode characterized the resulting memorial, fashioned by American sculptor John Frazee (1790-1852), as a "handsome neoclassical" monument: "The 12-foot-high shaft, a truncated pyramid of marble, is surmounted by an urn and flame." See Goode's *The Outdoor Sculpture of Washington, D.C.: A Comprehensive Historical Guide* (Washington, D.C.: Smithsonian Institution Press, 1974), 91.

7   Lorenzo D. Johnson, *Chaplains of the General Government with Objections to Their Employment Considered. A List of All the Chaplains to Congress, in the Army and in the Navy, from the Formation of the Government to This Time* (New York: Sheldon, Blakeman & Co., 1856), 60.

8   The Secretary of the Navy was a member of presidential cabinets from 1798 to 1947, when Congress reorganized the American military, placing the Department of Navy under the Department of Defense. As a result of this reorganization, the Secretary of Defense remained part of the cabinet, while the Secretary of the Navy no longer served in this capacity.

9   Ihna T. Frary, *They Built the Capitol* (Richmond, VA: Garret & Massie, 1940), 44-45. Among the other builders of the U.S. Capitol interred at Congressional are Peter Lenox (1771-1832) and William Swinton (1759-1807). Lenox served as chief carpenter at the Capitol from 1817 to 1829, when the building was considered complete. Swinton, widely considered the finest stonecutter in Philadelphia, had been recruited by Benjamin Latrobe (1764-1820) in August 1806 to work on the Capitol Building. On April 11, 1807, he died in Washington, D.C., and became the first person interred at the Washington Parish Burial Ground.

10   The Congressional Cemetery website, accessible at http://www.congressionalcemetery.org, provides information as available on veterans interred at the burial ground. Sandra Schmidt, cemetery historian, has compiled this information.

11   In addition to those who were celebrated for illustrious service during the Revolutionary War, the veterans interred at Congressional Cemetery include many others long forgotten by the surrounding community. Among those is Abraham Broom, who died on February 21, 1835. He is recalled in a Revolutionary War record as having signed a receipt on August 8, 1781, confirming simply that he had exchanged horses with General Kazimierz Pulaski, a Polish exile who was a celebrated cavalry officer in the Revolutionary War, and that he had received $100 for this exchange. If remembered at all, most of the other veterans of the Revolutionary War are identifiable in public records only by their military unit.

12   Ray Brighton, *The Checkered Career of Tobias Lear* (Portsmouth, New Hampshire: Portsmouth Marine Society, 1985), 330.

13   Ibid.

14   John D. Morris, *Sword of the Border: Major General Jacob Jennings Brown, 1775-1828* (Kent, Ohio: Kent State University Press, 2000), 273.

15   The Jacob Brown monument elicited these comments from George Watterston, first Librarian of Congress: "What thrilling events does not this mute memorial of the dead recall! But even they, too, are fast passing away from the memory of his countrymen, and the succeeding generation will know them only from the page of history." Watterston, *A New Guide to Washington*, 73. According to Cathleen Breitkreutz, a landscape and architectural historian, Jacob Brown's memorial is "one of the early important monuments" and Alexander Macomb's "one of the most ornate monuments in the original" section of the cemetery. The "crowning glory" of the Macomb memorial, which is "overflowing with Greek, Roman, and Egyptian details and symbolism . . . is a Greek helm with a small bird supporting the plume." Cathleen Breitkreutz, "Developmental History: Landscape and Architectural Assessment," vol. 1, "Historic Landscape and Structures Report for Historic Congressional Cemetery" (Washington, D.C.: Architect of the Capitol, September 26, 2003), 68, Turk Tracey & Larry Architects, LLC, AOC 020057 Project No. 020026.

16   Robert V. Remini, *The Life of Andrew Jackson* (New York: Penguin Books, 1990), 99.

17   K. Jack Bauer, *The Mexican War, 1846-48* (New York: Macmillan Publishing Company, Inc., 1974), 397; Richard Bruce Winders, *Mr. Polk's Army: The American Military Experience in the Mexican War* (College Station, Texas: Texas A&M University Press, 1997), 164-166.

18   Owen Thomas Edgar (June 17, 1831 – September 3, 1929) was the last U.S. veteran of the Mexican-American War interred at Congressional Cemetery. An enlisted man, he served during the war aboard the frigates *Potomac, Allegheny, Pennsylvania*, and *Experience*. He lived in Washington, D.C., for more than fifty years.

19   Tamara K. Hareven, "Preface," in *Anonymous Americans: Explorations in Nineteenth-Century Social History*, ed. Tamara K. Hareven (Englewood Cliffs, N.J.: Prentice-Hall, Inc., 1971), vii.

20   Sandra Schmidt and Jim Oliver have made major contributions in ongoing efforts to preserve Congressional Cemetery, as noted in Chapter 7 of this study, entitled "A Race Against Time."

21   Janice Hume observed that "the importance of wealth and power in America is evidenced by omissions of the poor and powerless from obituary pages in all eras." She noted that the standard exception to this practice involves the occasional "nontraditional obituaries" for individuals who had exceptional lives, perhaps because of unusual longevity, or who experienced deaths that were beyond the norm, as in accidents or by murder. See Hume's *Obituaries in American Culture* (Jackson: University Press of Mississippi, 2000), 135.

22   *The National Intelligencer* noted on June 30, 1826, that Tobias Martin had been "an excellent artisan" and that "at the time of his death, and for some months past, his mechanical ingenuity and skill had been employed in the construction of a power press, for the use of the proprietors of this paper—which was so far advanced and previously tested by a small model, as to leave little doubt of its entire success and efficiency had he lived to complete it." The press, according to the article, "was an original invention, neither he [Martin] nor any one concerned in it ever having seen one on that principle, the pressure being produced, as it is in the English presses, by a revolving cylinder."

23   James M. Goode, *The Outdoor Sculpture of Washington, D.C.: A Comprehensive Historical Guide* (Washington, D.C.: Smithsonian Institution Press, 1974), 96. Congressional Cemetery is also a memorial site for victims of the *Wawaset* tragedy, which was the largest civil disaster in Washington, D.C., during Reconstruction. On August 8, 1873, this passenger and freight vessel was destroyed by fire on the Potomac River some forty miles downstream from Washington, D.C. Among the more than fifty victims were the following members of the family of Joseph Reed, who was a police officer in the federal city: his pregnant wife, who was twenty-eight years old; three children from a previous marriage, all of whom were under nine years of age; as well as an aunt, a cousin, and a seventeen-year-old niece. The monument emplaced over the Reed graves, located immediately inside the main entrance to the cemetery, bore an inscription that summarized the disaster but has since been washed away by time except for the first three words: "Potomac River, Wawaset." John Clagett Proctor, "Congressional Cemetery; The Reed Family and the Steamer *Wawaset*," in Proctor's *Washington and Environs, Articles Written for the Washington Sunday Star* (1928-1949) (Washington, D.C.: Privately Printed, 1950), 440-442.

24   Leonard Matlovich's death, funeral, and important details about his burial memorial can be found in the Chicago Tribune July 3, 1988. Many journalists have visited the site and written eloquently about Matlovich's life as a gay activist. See, for example, Neely Tucker, "Gay Veterans Gather to Honor Their Own," Washington Post, 11/12/08. A compelling biography is Mike Hippler, Matlovich: The Good Soldier (1989, New York City). Other LGBT burials near the monument include Cliff Anchor (1936-2000), Peter Doyle (1843-1907), Frank Kameny (1925-2011), and Frank O'Reilly (1921-2001). See Congressional Cemetery's informative 'Walking Tour" of the LGBT Community for additional information.

25   Jim Oliver, "Historical Congressional Cemetery" (Data Base, Archives, Congressional Cemetery Files, June 18, 1994), 5-7.

26   Ibid.

27   Vestry minutes of Christ Church, June 16, 1888, Journal of Minutes, 1883-1911.

28   U.S. Senate, History of the Congressional Cemetery, 6; Constance McLaughlin Green, Washington: A History of the Capital, 1800-1950 (Princeton: Princeton University Press, 1962), 41-42.

29   Kenneth T. Jackson and Camilo Jose Vergara, Silent Cities: The Evolution of the American Cemetery (New York: Princeton Architectural Press, 1989), 37.

30   The extant documentation delineates ceremonies at Congressional conducted in memory of Native Americans that reach back to at least 1874, when Peter Pitchlynn (1807-1881), who represented the Choctaw Nation in Washington, D.C., decorated their burial sites. See Herman J. Viola, Diplomats in Buckskins: A History of the Indian Delegations in Washington City (Washington, D.C.: Smithsonian Press, 1981), 187. The June 7, 1879, issue of the Van Buren Press, published in Van Buren, Arkansas, commented on another such ceremony, noting that a delegation of Cherokees, Choctaws (including Pitchlynn), and Creeks visited the graves of Native Americans at Congressional on Memorial Day of that year "while our own race were paying the tender tributes due to the memory of our illustrious and gallant dead."

31   Herman Viola noted that the United States negotiated "some 370 treaties . . . with Indian tribes [that] were formally ratified, perfected, or proclaimed as part of the law of the land." Of those treaties, a total of sixty-five were formulated in Washington, D.C. He added that "because of unproductive negotiations in the field, government officials would summon tribal leaders to Washington where, under pressure, even the most sophisticated Indians would eventually come to terms." Diplomats in Buckskin, 29.

32   Ibid., 79; Calvin Colton, Tour of the American Lakes, and Among the

Indians of the North-West Territory, in 1830: Disclosing the Character and Prospects of the Indian Race (London: Frederick Westley and A.H. Davis, 1833), 2:171-172; quoted in Viola, 79.

33   John Ehle, *Trail of Tears: The Rise and Fall of the Cherokee Nation* (New York: Anchor Books/Doubleday, 1988), 351.

34   The "Act of Union Between the Eastern and Western Cherokees" was accessed on April 17, 2012, at http://www.yvwiiusdinvnohii.net/Cherokee/LegalDocuments/ActOf UnionOf1839.htm.

35   Cherokee Nation, *Memorial of the Delegates of the Cherokee Nation to the President of the United States and the Senate and House of Representatives in Congress* (Washington, D.C.: Washington Chronicle Print, 1866), 7; Grace Steele Woodward, *The Cherokees* (Norman: University of Oklahoma Press, 1963), 299-300.

36   John Clagett Proctor, "Pushmataha, Famous Indian Buried in District," in Proctor's *Washington and Environs*, a collection of articles written by Proctor for the *Washington Sunday Star* from 1928 to 1949 (self-published, 1950), 91.

37   Angie Debo, *The Rise and Fall of the Choctaw Republic* (Norman: University of Oklahoma Press, 1961), 49.

38   Ibid., 188, 193-195. On July 13, 1921, the Pushmataha Memorial Society conducted a ceremony of remembrance at his gravesite. The participants, including an unspecified number of congressional representatives, understood that Pushmataha was a substantial historical figure. In general, however, they did not recognize the totality of his legacy, focusing instead on the statement given on his tombstone that said he had been "on all occasions, and under all circumstances, the white man's friend." The keynote speaker, Representative Benjamin G. Humphreys (1863-1923) of Mississippi, observed, for example, that "Pushmataha was a firm believer in the white man's civilization" and that he had been "convinced that the only hope which the future held for his people lay in their adoption of this higher social order." As indicated by this statement, the gravesite of Pushmataha has surfaced complex memories focused on the possible meanings of being "the white man's friend."

39   Charles Dickens, *American Notes* (New York: St. Martin's Press, 1985), 150-152.

40   Ibid.

41   W. David Baird, *Peter Pitchlynn: Chief of the Choctaws* (Norman: University of Oklahoma Press, 1972), 209-210.

42   Viola, 164; Gibbins Report, 142, note 1.

43   *Magnificent Voyagers: The U.S. Exploring Expedition, 1838-1842,* Herman J. Viola and Carolyn Margolis, eds. (Washington, D.C.: Smithsonian Institution Press, 1985).

44   James Allen's manuscript was published by the U.S. Congress in 1832 as *Journal of an "Expedition into Indian Country" to the Sources of the Mississippi*.

45   Martha Coleman Bray, *Joseph Nicollet and His Map* (Philadelphia: The American Philosophical Society, 1980), 91.

46   A memorial was dedicated at the unmarked grave of Joseph Nicollet on May 7, 1997, 154 years after his burial at Congressional Cemetery. The summer 1997 issue of the *Congressional Cemetery Association Newsletter* provided this information relevant to the occasion: "The South Dakota red granite marker was donated by Rausch Brothers Monument Company of Ortonville, Minnesota, and placed at the urging of Harold L. Torness," a banker based in Sisseton, South Dakota, and "an admirer of Nicollet." The dedicatory ceremony was attended by Edmund C. Bray and Martha Coleman Bray, who translated from French and edited *Joseph N. Nicollet on the Plains and Prairies: The Expeditions of 1838-39, with Journals, Letters, and Notes on the Dakota Indians* (Minnesota Historical Society Press, 1976). The inscription on the memorial is a statement by Nicollet: "He will triumph who understands how to concentrate and combine with the greatest skill the benefits of the past and the demands of the future."

47   Charles Preuss, *Exploring with Fremont: The Private Diaries of Charles Preuss, Cartographer for John C. Fremont on His First, Second, and Fourth Expeditions to the Far West*, trans. and ed. Erwin G. and Elisabeth K. Gudde (Norman: University of Oklahoma Press, 1958), xix.

48   John C. Fremont, *Report of the Exploring Expedition to the Rocky Mountains in the Year 1842, and to Oregon and North California in the Years 1843-44* (Washington: Gales and Seaton, 1845), 123.

49   William H. Goetzmann, *Army Exploration in the American West, 1803-1863* (New Haven: Yale University Press, 1959), 106.

50   Charles Preuss, *Exploring with Fremont*, xx.

51   Ibid. While Preuss had a successful life, he came to an untimely end. As noted in *The Evening Star* of September 2, 1854, he hung himself on August 31, 1854, in the barn of a farm near Bladensburg, Maryland. Erwin and Elisabeth Gudde provided this comment about his death: "He put an end to his life, said Jessie Fremont [wife of John Fremont], because he realized that his glad, free days in the open were over" (Ibid., xxix).

52   Robert M. Utley, *A Life Wild and Perilous: The Mountain Men and the Paths to the Pacific* (New York: Henry Holt and Company, 1997), xiv; LeRoy R. Hafen and W.J. Ghent, *Broken Hand: The Life Story of Thomas Fitzpatrick, Chief of the Mountain Men* (Denver: The Old West Publishing Company, 1931), v.

53   In *A Life Wild and Perilous*, Robert Utley noted that Fitzpatrick acquired two sobriquets—White Hair and Broken Hand—as a result of

his "wild and perilous" life. The former came from his "nearly fatal escape from the Gros Ventres in 1832, which was said to have turned his hair white overnight," and the latter was associated with "a rifle accident that shattered his left wrist" (159).

54   Ibid., 253, 252, 254.

55   Goetzman, 142.

56   Georgia Willis Read and Ruth Gaines, eds., *Gold Rush: The Journals, Drawings and Other Papers of J. Goldsborough Bruff, Captain, Washington City and California Mining Association, April 2, 1849—July 20, 1851* (New York: Columbia University Press, 1949), xviii. As a draftsman, Bruff drew designs for decorative elements within the United States Treasury Building, including elaborate railings and chandeliers. See Pamela Scott, *Fortress of Finance: The United States Treasury Building* (Washington, D.C.: Treasury Historical Association, 2010), 142-145.

57   J.S. Holliday, *The World Rushed In: The California Gold Rush Experience* (New York: Simon and Schuster, 1981), 229, 99.

58   William James Morgan, David B. Tyler, Joye L. Leonhart, and Mary F. Loughlin, eds., *Autobiography of Rear Admiral Charles Wilkes, U.S. Navy, 1798-1877*, intro. Rear Admiral John D.H. Kane, Jr., USN (Ret.) (Washington, D.C.: Naval History Division, Department of the Navy, 1978), v, 927, and 543. Wilkes also praised William Speiden (1798-1861), who served as paymaster in the U.S. Exploring Expedition of 1838-1842, as well as in Commodore Perry's Expedition to Japan (1852-1854), and was buried at Congressional Cemetery on December 18, 1861. On page 383 of his *Autobiography*, Wilkes observed that Speiden "was true to himself and would be at all times true to the Expedition and do what he could, though he felt it was little, to carry it out successfully."

59   In addition to the individuals profiled in this section, Congressional is the burial site of others who had notable roles in continental explorations, including Andrew Atkinson Humphreys (1810-1883). In his capacity as chief of the Office of Western Exploration and Surveys during 1854-1861, Humphreys oversaw surveys authorized by the U.S. Congress to identify the most efficient and economical railway route from the Mississippi River to the Pacific Ocean. His co-written *Report Upon the Physics and Hydraulics of the Mississippi River*, which was published by Congress in 1855, identified five routes that proved "practical and economical" and have remained largely intact to this day for use by transcontinental railroads. Goetzman, 11.

60   William E. Ames, *A History of the National Intelligencer* (Chapel Hill: University of North Carolina Press, 1972), 113.

61   Alan Trachtenberg, *Reading American Photographs: Images as History, Mathew Brady to Walker Evans* (New York: Hill and Wang, 1989), 33.

378   Notes

62   Mary Panzer, *Mathew Brady and the Image of History* (Washington, D.C.: Smithsonian Institution Press, 1997), 106, xx, 108-109.

63   "Women's Legal History Biography Project," 11-12, Robert Crown Law Library, Stanford Law School, accessed on December 19, 2005, at http://www.stanford.edu/group/WLHP/papers/lockwood.htm.; Julie Davis, "A Feisty Schoolmarm Made the Lawyers Sit Up and Take Notice," *Smithsonian Magazine*, 11 (March 1981): 142, 146-147.

64   "Women's Legal History Biography Project," 15.

65   John Clagett Proctor, "Belva Ann Lockwood: Only Woman Candidate for President of the United States," in *Records of the Columbia Historical Society*, vols. 35-36, ed. Maud Burr Morris (Washington, D.C.: Columbia Historical Society, 1935), 203-204.

66   Adelaide Johnson chose the busts of Susan Anthony and Elizabeth Cady Stanton to serve as bridesmaids in her 1896 marriage to Alexander Frederick Jenkins, an English businessman. A female minister presided over the ceremony, which was conducted at Johnson's studio in Washington, D.C. Edith Mayo, "Adelaide Johnson," in *Notable American Women: The Modern Period* (Cambridge: Belknap Press of Harvard University Press, 1980), 380.

67   The Adelaide Johnson papers, which are archived at the Library of Congress, comprise 55.6 linear feet and some 40,000 items, including documentation about her work on the *Portrait Monument*, correspondence with individuals including Susan B. Anthony, Emmeline Pankhurst, Alice Paul, and May Wright Sewall, as well as diaries and speeches.

68   In addition to John Philip Sousa, the following directors of the Marine Corps Band are interred at Congressional Cemetery: Venerando Pulizzi (1816, 1824-1827), John B. Cuvillier (1827-1829), Joseph Cuvillier (1829-1835), Raphael R. Triary (1836-1843, 1848-1855), Antonio Pons (1843-1844, 1846-1848), and Francis Maria Scala (1855-1871).

69   "A Salute to John Philip Sousa," a pamphlet developed and made available by the Association for the Preservation of Historic Congressional Cemetery.

70   Neil Harris, "John Philip Sousa and the Culture of Reassurance," in *Perspectives on John Philip Sousa*, ed. Jon Newsom (Washington, D.C.: Library of Congress, 1983), 11-12.

71   Paul E. Bierley, *John Philip Sousa: American Phenomenon* (Englewood Cliffs, New Jersey: Prentice-Hall, 1973), 92-97.

72   Congressional Cemetery constitutes in part a memorial site for the extended Sousa family. John Philip Sousa's wife Jane and their three children were interred in his burial plot. His parents, John Antonio and Marie Sousa, as well as five of their ten children, were buried in three adjoining sites. Still other members of the Sousa family are interred elsewhere at the cemetery. Ibid., 236, note 3.

73   Norman P. Scala, who was the son of Francis Maria Scala and who was himself buried at Congressional on January 20, 1953, donated his father's papers to the Library of Congress in 1952. This collection comprises 608 titles, including the march Francis Scala drafted for the inaugural ball of President Ulysses Grant, which he considered "the most important achievement of my musical career." "Francis M. Scala," an article drafted by Captain Frank Byrne, USMC (Ret), in November 1989 and accessed on January 7, 2006, at http://www.marineband.usmc.mil.

74   Bierley, 176. John Philip Sousa organized the Sousa Band in 1892, the year he resigned from the Marine Corps Band. Under Sousa's leadership, the band toured from 1892 to 1931.

75   Office of the Quartermaster General, U.S. Army, Untitled Report to Congress on Congressional Cemetery, submitted by Major General Henry Gibbins to the House Appropriations Committee, 76th Congress, 1st Session, in connection with the War Department Civil Functions Appropriations Bill for Fiscal Year 1940, page 1. The Congressional Cemetery archives include a copy of this report.

Chapter 5: Keepers of the Legacy

1   Among other activities, John Clagett Proctor served as chief editor of *Washington, Past and Present* (1930), a five-volume series of books, two of which focused on the history of the federal capital and the remaining three on prominent residents. Proctor's correspondence and manuscripts are maintained by The Historical Society of Washington, D.C., under this heading: John Clagett Proctor and Maud Proctor Callis Papers.

2   *History of the Congressional Cemetery*, "presented" to Congress by Senator Elmer Jacob Burkett, chairman of the drafting committee (Washington, D.C.: Government Printing Office, 1906), 20-21. This publication does not identify the committee or committee members who researched and wrote this document. The *History* is useful in identifying key dates in the development of the burial ground. It does not, however, provide interpretive commentary.

3   Specifics relevant to the iron fence are given in pages 21-26 of the *History of the Congressional Cemetery*.

4   The quotations about the cenotaphs appear on pages 42 and 35 of the *History of the Congressional Cemetery*.

5   Ibid, 35.

6   In "A Bill That Has Excited Considerable Opposition To Its Passage," *The Evening Star* of January 22, 1895, summarized the protest of lot owners over proposed federal legislation that would allow Congressional Cemetery to use sections of city streets that had been incorporated within the burial ground.

7   *History of the Congressional Cemetery*, 56-57. Clifford Howard, Acting Secretary, prepared the minutes, providing summaries, not verbatim quotations, of the statements made.

8   In a letter sent on March 17, 1898, to Hon. John W. Ross, President of the District of Columbia Board of Commissioners, O.B. Hallam provided documentation buttressing the claims he had made about lot ownership the preceding day: "As to lot owners I herewith inclose [the] form of certificate [regarding the sale of lots] from which it appears that the title does not pass to the purchaser or so-called lot owner, but merely the right to use the burial sites, subject to all rules then or thereafter to be made. . . ." Ibid.

9   House Committee on the District of Columbia, *Burial Sites in Congressional Cemetery*, report submitted by Samuel W. Smith, 59th Cong., 1st sess., March 12, 1906. As indicated in the minutes of a special meeting conducted on March 18, 1907, the Christ Church vestry unanimously resolved to pay a law firm identified as "Wolf & Rosenburg" a total of $8500 for their services "in securing the passage" of the legislation that became Public Law 207. As noted in the minutes of another special meeting, conducted on March 25, 1907, the vestry had contracted with this firm on December 5, 1904, for services not delineated in the minutes. The minutes of the meetings on March 18 and 25, 1907, are filed in Journal of Minutes, 1883-1911, Archives, Christ Church, Washington, D.C.

10   *Burial Sites in Congressional Cemetery*, 5.

11   In her study of the southeast section of Washington, D.C., Ruth Ann Overbeck briefly noted demographic shifts in the decades following the Civil War. The Navy Yard, she wrote, "helped a new immigrant group establish an American foot" in the blocks nearby while many middle-class families followed the developers "north and east of the older sections." See Ruth Ann Overbeck, "Capitol Hill: The Capitol Is Just Up the Street," in *Washington at Home*, ed. Kathryn S. Smith (Washington, D.C.: Windsor Press, 1988), 39-40. David L. Lewis noted similar changes during the same period, observing that "Southeast sank below the consciousness of establishment Washington. . . . Lighting, sewage, paving, and streetcar lines flowed downhill and away from Southeast Washington." See David L. Lewis, *District of Columbia: A Bicentennial History* (New York: W.W. Norton & Company, 1976), 131.

12   Minutes of the Christ Church vestry meeting on February 14, 1888, Journal of Minutes, 1883-1911, Archives, Christ Church.

13   During a vestry meeting held on June 13, 1876, a committee established to clarify the financial relationship between the church and the cemetery recommended an annual transfer of no more than $1400 from the cemetery to the church funds. While this recommendation was not ad-

opted during that meeting, the vestry apparently proceeded accordingly. The minutes of the meeting on June 13, 1876, are filed in Journal, 1862-1883, Archives, Christ Church.

14   The October 13, 1873, minutes of the Christ Church vestry meeting summarize the history of this first trust fund. These minutes are filed in Journal, 1862-1883, Archives, Christ Church.

15   Ibid. See Robert H. Weibe, *The Search for Order, 1877-1920* (New York: Hill & Wang, 1967), 1-7, for commentary on the banking crisis of 1873.

16   Minutes of the Christ Church vestry meetings on March 8, 1887, October 12, 1893, and March 12, 1906, Journal of Minutes, 1883-1911, Archives, Christ Church.

17   Minutes of the Christ Church vestry meeting on January 8, 1889, Journal of Minutes, 1883-1911, Archives, Christ Church; *Rules and Regulations*, 1897, 27; Vestry of Washington Parish, *Rules and Regulations of the Washington Parish Burial Ground (Congressional Cemetery)* (Washington, D.C.: The Sudwarth Company, November 1913), 4.

18   *Rules and Regulations*, 1897, 26.

19   "Congressional Cemetery Endowments," files maintained at Congressional Cemetery.

20   The Christ Church vestry agreed during a meeting on September 11, 1905, to contribute fifty dollars to the Association of American Cemetery Superintendents (AACS). There is no evidence indicating, however, that either vestry members or the cemetery superintendent attended the Association's 1905 annual meeting, which was convened in Washington, D.C., or any of its other gatherings.

21   *Proceedings of the Twelfth Annual Meeting of the Association of American Cemetery Superintendents Held in Omaha, Nebraska, during 13-15 September 1898* (Place of Publication Not Specified: Association of Cemetery Superintendents, 1898), 60-61. James J. Farrell noted that "after 1891, the AACS conventions always discussed and promoted perpetual care." See Farrell's *Inventing the American Way of Death, 1830-1920* (Philadelphia: Temple University Press, 1980), 137.

22   *Proceedings of the Thirteenth Annual Meeting of the Association of American Cemetery Superintendents Held in New Haven, Connecticut, during 5-7 September 1899 and in Hartford, Connecticut, on 8 September 1899* (Place of Publication Not Specified: Association of Cemetery Superintendents, 1899), 14-15.

23   Cathleen Breitkreutz, "Developmental History: Landscape and Architectural Assessment," vol. 1, "Historic Landscape and Structures Report for Historic Congressional Cemetery" (Washington, D.C.: Architect of the Capitol, September 26, 2003), 30, Turk Tracey & Larry Architects, LLC, AOC 020057 Project No. 020026.

24   Ibid., 33-34, 49-50. The gatehouse, as renovated in 1874, was used until 1923, when a new structure was built on the site of the original 1832 building.

25   Some of the other roads in the cemetery were identified as follows: Prout Avenue, after William Prout, who was a member of the Christ Church vestry for 16 years (1806-1822), and his son Jonathan Prout, who served as a vestryman for 38 years (1821-1859); and Tingey Avenue, after Thomas Tingey, who was a vestryman at Christ Church for twenty-two years (1806-1828): Ibid., 35.

26   *History of the Congressional Cemetery,* 4, 3.

27   The potter's field was located in close proximity to the northeastern boundary of Congressional Cemetery, overlooking the Anacostia River. Extant documentation provides scant information about this burial ground, which was identified in "Busy Night Doctors," published in *The Washington Post* of January 22, 1896, as a "graveyard of the poor, the forgotten, and the unknown," as "a makeshift of a cemetery," and as a source of cadavers used "for dissection" in medical schools.

28   In addition to highlighting the "Old Washington" series, the obituary for James Croggan that was published in *The Evening Star* on August 22, 1916, emphasized his coverage of the assassination of President James Garfield, saying that the articles were "one of the most important pieces of work" he did for the newspaper.

29   The Vestry, Washington Parish, *Washington Parish Burial Ground (Congressional Cemetery), 1807-1913* (Washington, D.C.: The Sudwarth Company, 1913), 5.

30   Ibid., 6.

31   John Bodnar, *Remaking America: Public Memory, Commemoration, and Patriotism in the Twentieth Century* (Princeton: Princeton University Press, 1992), 173-174.

32   Ibid., 176-179.

33   Margaret Gibbs, *The DAR* (New York: Holt, Rinehart and Winston, 1969), 12, 73.

34   Nelson McDowell Shepard, "Cenotaphs and Epitaphs in Congressional Cemetery," *Daughters of the American Revolution Magazine* 55 (April 1921): 192.

35   *Hearing Before Subcommittee No. 9, Committee on Military Affairs, House of Representatives, Seventieth Congress, First Session, on H.R. 11916,* Statements by Mrs. Edwin C. Gregory [Margaret Gregory] and Hon. Charles L. Abernethy (Washington, D.C.: Government Printing Office, 1928), 1.

36   In the conclusion to her letter, Grace Brosseau urged approval of H.R. 11916, observing that "the preservation of" the cenotaphs at Con-

gressional "is strictly in line with the objects of our society [the DAR]: 'To perpetuate the memory and spirit of the men and women who achieved American independence by the acquisition and protection of historic spots and the erection of monuments.'" Ibid., 3, 2, 1.

37   Ibid., 4.

38   Ibid., 5, 4, 7.

39   Ibid., 7, 8; U.S. Congress, House Committee on Military Affairs, *Care and Preservation of Certain Land and Monuments in the Washington Parish Burial Ground (Congressional Cemetery)*, Report #2463 (Washington, D.C.: Government Printing Office, 1929).

40   *Care and Preservation of Certain Land and Monuments in the Washington Parish Burial Ground (Congressional Cemetery)*, 1.

41   *History of the Congressional Cemetery*, 32.

42   *Care and Preservation of Certain Land and Monuments in the Washington Parish Burial Ground (Congressional Cemetery)*, 2-3.

43   Ibid., 3-4.

44   Ibid., 4.

45   Introduction by Fiske Kimball to H.M. Pierce Gallagher, "Robert Mills, 1781-1855, America's First Native Architect," *The Architectural Record* 65 (April 1929): 387; H.M. Pierce Gallagher, *Robert Mills, Architect of the Washington Monument, 1781-1855* (New York: Columbia University Press, 1935), 176.

46   Gallagher, *Robert Mills*, 388.

47   Edwin Bateman Morris, "A Monument to Robert Mills," *Journal of the AIA* (June 9, 1948): 258. The guidelines issued by the Washington AIA specified that "this competition is limited to architects and architectural draftsmen resident in Washington who are not, during the period of the competition, otherwise employed in architectural work," that "the character of the design should be expressive of the man and his works," and that the cost of the proposed monument was "not to exceed $1,500.00." "Allied Architects' Sketch Competition for a Memorial to Robert Mills in Congressional Cemetery, Washington, D.C.," May 23, 1932. The American Institute of Architects Archives, Washington, D.C.

48   Press release issued on May 30, 1936, by The Association of Federal Architects, Circular File, Congressional Cemetery, Washingtoniana Collection, Martin Luther King Library, Washington, D.C.

49   Ibid.

50   *War Department Civil Appropriation Act, 1938, Statutes at Large* 50, part 1, 515 (1937). Senator Theodore Green supported federal funding for Congressional Cemetery as a result of a visit to the burial ground. As narrated in an article by Charter Heslep in *The Washington Daily News* of May 15, 1939, he and Senator Peter Gerry of Rhode Island had come to the

cemetery one Sunday morning to visit the graves of their great grandfa-
thers, who were Senator James Burrill of Rhode Island and Vice President
Elbridge Gerry, respectively. While it took Gerry "hours" to find the grave
of Vice President Gerry, Green never did find the grave of his great grandfather. Both were surprised over the "sad state" of the burial ground,
which was reportedly covered by "rank weed growth." In addition, many
of the "cenotaphs and headstones . . . were crumbling and falling."

51   Office of the Quartermaster General, U.S. Army, Untitled Report
to Congress on Congressional Cemetery 1939, submitted by Major General
Henry Gibbins to the House Appropriations Committee, 76th Congress, 1st
Session, in connection with the War Department Civil Functions Appropriations Bill for Fiscal Year 1940, 1-3. Comprising 177 pages, this report
is based on a rich trove of historical resources. As identified in the preface
to the document, they include papers maintained at the burial ground; records of the Veterans Administration, such as pension files of veterans of
the Revolutionary War, War of 1812, Mexican War, and Civil War; Francis
B. Heitman's *Historical Register of Officers of the Continental Army During
the War of the Revolution, April 1775 to December 1783* (1914); documents
accessible at libraries of the Bureau of Indian Affairs, Daughters of the
American Revolution, and National Archives; and the "old files" of *The
National Intelligencer, The Washington Post,* and *The Evening Star.*

52   Office of the Quartermaster General, Untitled Report to Congress
on Congressional Cemetery, 3-4, 16.

53   Charles B. Hosmer, Jr., *Preservation Comes of Age: From Williamsburg to the National Trust, 1926-1947,* vol. 1 (Charlottesville: University
Press of Virginia, 1981), 565. Published for the Preservation Press, National Trust for Historic Preservation in the United States.

54   Cemetery records of the late nineteenth and early twentieth centuries include the names of many Heinlines, a number of whom were part
of the extended family of William M. Heinline. As cemetery superintendent, Heinline was well positioned to watch over their graves, a factor that
likely contributed to his twenty-year tenure at the burial ground.

55   The minutes of the vestry meetings on December 14, 1948, and
January 11, 1949, are filed in the Journal of Minutes, February 1944 to December 1949, Archives, Christ Church. The financial information relevant
to Christ Church and to Congressional Cemetery as of December 31, 1950,
is provided in File Box, Vestry Minutes and Annual Meetings – 1950s, Archives, Christ Church.

56   The minutes of the vestry meetings on September 4 and 11, 1951,
are maintained in File Box, Vestry Minutes and Annual Meetings – 1950,
Archives, Christ Church.

57   Minutes of the Christ Church vestry meeting on October 25, 1951,

File Box, Vestry Minutes and Annual Meetings – 1950s, Archives, Christ Church.

Chapter 6: A Gathering Crisis at the Old Burial Ground

1   Tom Railsback, Congress, House, 92nd Congress, 2nd sess., *Congressional Record*, 118, pt. 14 (May 17, 1972): 17854. Congressional Cemetery has forty family vaults, of which twenty-three are brick and seventeen stone.

2   Nan Robertson, *Christ Church, Washington Parish: A Brief History* (Washington, D.C.: privately printed, 1994), 16.

3   The population figures are cited from these sources: Constance M. Green, *The Secret City: A History of Race Relations in the Nation's Capital* (Princeton, NJ: Princeton University Press, 1967), 200, 283-284; David R. Goldfield and Blaine A. Brownell, *Urban America: From Downtown to No Town* (Boston: Houghton Mifflin Company, 1979), 260.

4   Robertson, 16; Mary D. Hewes, "Christ Church, Washington Parish: Historical Perspectives on the Role the Church Played from 1887 to 1987," 12, unpublished manuscript; List of Voting Members, "Annual Report: Christ Church, Washington Parish," 1974, File Box, Vestry Minutes and Annual Meetings – 1970-74, Archives, Christ Church, Washington, D.C.

5   Hewes, 31-32; Rev. Ivan Merrick, "Rector's Report," 1955 [month and date not specified], File Box, Vestry Minutes and Annual Meetings – 1950s, Archives, Christ Church; Rev. James Greene, "Rector's Report," April 15, 1963, File Box, Vestry Minutes and Annual Meetings – 1960s, Archives, Christ Church.

6   Reverend John Stipe, Letter to Vestry, Trinity Sunday, June 8, 1952, File Box, Vestry Minutes and Annual Meetings – 1950s, Archives, Christ Church.

7   Minutes of Christ Church vestry meeting on June 10, 1952, File Box, Vestry Minutes and Annual Meetings – 1950s, Archives, Christ Church; Donald J. Detwiler, Christ Church Register, to Rt. Rev. Angus Dun, June 16, 1952, and Rev. Dun to Donald Detwiler, June 24, 1952, File Box, Vestry Minutes and Annual Meetings – 1950s, Archives, Christ Church.

8   Minutes of Christ Church vestry meeting on September 11, 1969, File Box, Vestry Minutes and Annual Meetings – 1960s, Archives, Christ Church.

9   "Congressional Cemetery Report," March 1970, File Box, Vestry Minutes and Annual Meetings – 1970-1974, Archives, Christ Church; Ethel Robertson, "Congressional Cemetery Financial History, 1960-1974" (January 30, 1979), 2, File Box, Vestry Minutes and Annual Meetings, 1970-1974, Archives, Christ Church.

10   Senate Committee on Armed Services, *Authorizing the Secretary of the Army to Convey Certain Government-Owned Burial Lots and Other Property in the Washington Parish Burial Ground, Washington, D.C., and to Exchange Other Burial Lots*, 83d Cong., 1st sess., 1953, 3-4. This report includes the December 21, 1950, letter from Edward Cox.

11   Ibid., 3.

12   Samuel H. Davis, Jr., Superintendent of Alexandria National Cemetery, "Report of Meeting with Officials of Washington Parrish [sic] of Christ Church," summation of meeting at Congressional Cemetery, February 15, 1960, Box 36, Congressional Cemetery, File 2, Entry 24, located in Veterans Administration, Record Group 15, National Archives, Washington, D.C.

13   Ibid.

14   A.H. Johnson to Lieutenant Charles E. Nolte, III, Assistant Adjutant General, February 16, 1960, File Box, Vestry Meetings and Annual Meetings – 1950s, Archives, Christ Church.

15   Mrs. McDonald, Memorandum for the Record, September 16, 1960, Box 36, Congressional Cemetery, File 2, Entry 24, located in Veterans Administration, Record Group 15, National Archives.

16   Congress, House, Senator George H. Mahon of Texas speaking about "The Congressional Cemetery," 86th Congress, 2nd sess., *Congressional Record – Appendix* 106, pt. 6 (May 24, 1960): 1582.

17   Congress, House, Senator George H. Mahon of Texas speaking about "The Congressional Cemetery of Washington, D.C.," 86th Congress, 2nd sess., *Congressional Record – Appendix* 106, pt. 6 (July 2, 1960): 5846-5818.

18   George Mahon to Wilber M. Brucker, July 7, 1960, Box 40, File 5, Entry 25, Veterans Administration, Record Group 15, National Archives.

19   Jesse Myers, Memorandum for the Record, February 24, 1960, Box 36, Congressional Cemetery, File 1, Entry 24, Veterans Administration, Record Group 15, National Archives.

20   "Here Lies Push-Ma-Ta-Ha; He Wanted 'Big Guns' Fired," *The Pentagram News*, March 8, 1961, Box 36, Congressional Cemetery, File 2, Entry 24, Veterans Administration, Record Group 15, National Archives. Arone Publications, the company established by Dominick Arone (1920-2005), issued approximately thirty publications, as noted in the obituary for Arone published in *The Washington Post* on February 10, 2005.

21   "Congressional Cemetery Not 'National'," *The Pentagram News*, March 22, 1961, Box 36, Congressional Cemetery, File 2, Entry 24; Veterans Administration, Record Group 15, National Archives.

22   James A. Glass, *The Beginnings of a New National Historic Preservation Program, 1957 to 1969* (Nashville: American Association for State and Local History, 1990), 57.

23   Nan Robertson, 18-19; Nancy C. Taylor, "National Register of Historic Places Inventory – Nomination Form," April 3, 1969. This document is maintained by the National Register of Historic Places, National Park Service, Department of the Interior, Washington, D.C.

24   William Murtagh, *Keeping Time: The History and Theory of Preservation in America*, revised ed. (New York: John Wiley & Sons, Inc., 1997), 64-65.

25   Ibid., 64.

26   Congress, House, Committee on Veterans' Affairs, *National Cemeteries and Burial Benefits for Veterans*, 92nd Cong., 1st sess., March 28 and 29, 1972, 2182-2183.

27   Ibid., 2184.

28   John S. Saylor, Congress, House, "Acquisition and Protection of Congressional Cemetery," April 12, 1972, speech in support of H.R. 14339, *A Bill to provide that the historic property known as the Congressional Cemetery may be acquired, protected, and administered by the Secretary of the Interior as part of the park system of the National Capital, and for other purposes*, 92d Congress, 2nd sess., *Congressional Record* 118, pt. 14: H3020-3021; Vance Hartke, Congress, Senate, May 4, 1972, speech in support of S.3580, *Congressional Record* 118, pt. 14: S7233-7234; Tom Railsback, Congress, House, May 17, 1972, speech in support of H.R. 15039, *Congressional Record* 118, pt. 14: H17854; Joel Broyhill, Congress, House, June 21, 1973, speech in support of H.R. 8883, *Congressional Record* 119, pt. 16: H20778; John Saylor, Congress, House, January 11, 1973, speech in support of H. 1891, *Congressional Record* 119, pt. 1: H865.

29   Minutes of Vestry Meeting, April 10, 1972, File Box, Vestry Minutes and Annual Meetings – 1970-1974, Archives, Christ Church.

30   "Proposed Acquisition of Congressional Cemetery by the Secretary of the Interior," April 17, 1972, Ibid.

31   Resolution by the Christ Church vestry endorsing H.R. 14339 and S. 3580, May 8, 1972, Ibid.

32   Brian Kates, "Forsaken Heritage: The Neglect and Ravishment of Congressional Cemetery in Washington D.C.," *American Cemetery* 51 (June 1978): 27.

33   File: "Congressional Cemetery," National Capital Region, National Park Service, Washington, D.C.

34   Ibid.

35   Ibid.

36   Richard L. Stanton to Robert M. Utley, April 27, 1972, File: "Congressional Cemetery," National Capital Region, National Park Service.

37   Robert M. Utley to Richard L. Stanton, May 4, 1972, Ibid.

38   Gary Everhardt to Hon. Charles McC. Mathias, Jr., Senate,

July 18, 1975, Ibid. Mary Marcer, legislative assistant, was captain of the team that developed the "Justification." The other members were Alva Conner as maintenance specialist, John Longworth as engineer, Darwina Neal as landscape architect, Joseph Prentice as archeological engineer, and Robert Romanowski as park planner.

39   "Justification: Congressional Cemetery," File: "Congressional Cemetery," National Capital Region, National Park Service.

40   Manus J. Fish, Jr., to Ronald Walker, September 7, 1972, Ibid.

41   Russell Dickerson to Ronald Walker, June 14, 1973, Ibid.

42   John H. Kyle to James A. Haley, June 21, 1973, Ibid.

43   Congress, House, Subcommittee on National Parks and Recreation, Committee on Interior and Insular Affairs, Hearing on H.R. 1891, "To Provide That the Historic Property Known as the Congressional Cemetery May Be Acquired, Protected, and Administered by the Secretary of the Interior as Part of the Park System of the National Capital, and for Other Purposes," 93rd Cong., 1st sess., June 22, 1973. Record Group 233, Box 48; File of Committee on Interior and Insular Affairs, Room 1324, Longworth Building, House of Representatives, Washington, D.C.

44   The statement Stanley Hulett developed in support of H.R. 1891 was accompanied by a map entitled, "Congressional Cemetery: General Development Plan." This map identified an Interpretive and Administrative Center, which was located near the main entrance on E Street, Southeast, and was to include "Visitor Information – Orientation – Comfort Facilities," as well as an "Historical Research Library." The map also identified meditative and rest areas across the cemetery, a "Maintenance & Service Area" at the southeastern part of the cemetery, and plantings along the borders of the major sections within the burial ground. "Congressional Cemetery," National Capital Region, National Park Service.

45   Congress, House, Subcommittee on National Parks and Recreation, Committee on Interior and Insular Affairs, Hearing on H.R. 1891, "To Provide That the Historic Property Known as the Congressional Cemetery May Be Acquired, Protected, and Administered by the Secretary of the Interior as Part of the Park System of the National Capital, and for Other Purposes."

46   Charles Turbyville, "Statement of Christ Church, Washington Parish, to The Subcommittee on Parks and Recreation, United States House of Representatives," June 22, 1973, 20-24, Ibid.

47   Hazel S. Detwiler, Testimony provided to the Subcommittee on Parks and Recreation, June 22, 1973, 30-32, Ibid.

48   "Congressional Cemetery Alternatives." File: "Congressional Cemetery," National Capital Region, National Capital Park Service.

49   In connection with Alternative One, the National Park Service

stated that if Congress determined that the NPS was "the most appropriate custodian" of Congressional Cemetery, "legislation should provide that the Department of the Interior be precluded from accepting title to the cemetery until funds are made available in a sufficient amount to provide for this project as this office is not presently funded to undertake this responsibility." Ibid.

50   Ibid.

51   Richard L. Stanton to Manus Fish, "Subject: Congressional Cemetery – H.R. 1891," January 18, 1974, Ibid.

52   Rogers Morton to James Haley, August 23, 1974, Ibid.

53   *Memorial Services Held in the House of Representatives and Senate of the United States, Together with Tributes Presented in Eulogy of John P. Saylor, Late a Representative from Pennsylvania* (Washington, D.C.: Government Printing Office, 1974), 12, 11, 5, 158-159.

54   Rogers Morton to James Haley, August 23, 1974. File: "Congressional Cemetery," National Capital Region, National Capital Park Servicer. In his letter to James Haley, Rogers Morton noted that he had been asked "to explore alternatives for the administration of Congressional Cemetery during a hearing conducted on June 22, 1973, before the Subcommittee on National Parks and Recreation. He noted that the following alternatives had been identified: "1. No action at this time," "2. Special Federal grant" provided "to Christ Church for development, restoration, maintenance, protection, and interpretation," 3. "District of Columbia government" as manager of the site because the "administration of cemeteries is traditionally a local responsibility," 4. "Acquisition, restoration… and interpretation" of the burial ground by "the Veterans Administration or the Department of the Army," both of which are "concerned with the provision and maintenance of cemeteries for veterans," 5. "Management" and "interpretation" by the Architect of the Capitol because of the communications between this office and Congress.

55   Gerald Connolly, "Congressional Cemetery," 1974 Annual Report of Christ Church. File, "Vestry Minutes and Annual Reports, 1970-1974," Christ Church Archives.

Chapter 7: A Race Against Time

1   "A Race Against Time: 2004 Vault Restoration Plans," *The Heritage Gazette*, Winter 2004, 1, 3; Susan J. Ellis and Katherine H. Noyes, *By the People: A History of Americans as Volunteers* (San Francisco: Jossey-Bass, 1990), xi. Prior to spring 2003, when the Association newsletter was designated as *The Heritage Gazette*, the publication was issued under these labels: *The Association for the Preservation of Historic Congressional Cemetery* (first number, not dated); *News from the Association for the Preservation of Historic*

Congressional Cemetery (second issue, April 1977); *Congressional Cemetery Association Newsletter* (Spring 1978 [third issue] through Fall 2000); *Spring 2002 Newsletter; Summer 2002 Newsletter;* and *Fall 2002 Newsletter.*

2   Willis D. Brown, "Memo to the Vestry," October 21, 1974, File Box, Vestry Minutes and Annual Meetings—1970-1974, Archives, Christ Church, Washington, D.C.

3   Minutes of Vestry Meeting, June 2, 1975, File Box, Vestry Minutes and By-Laws and Annual Meetings—1975-1979, Archives, Christ Church.

4   William A. Stringfellow, "Memorandum for Vestry," July 23, 1975, Ibid.

5   Don Brown, "Congressional Cemetery," in "Annual Report of Christ Church, Washington Parish," 1975, p. 2, Ibid.

6   In establishing the Association for the Preservation of Historic Congressional Cemetery, Christ Church worked within a broader context of volunteerism at that time on Capitol Hill. As noted by Ruth Ann Over-beck, the local community gained a reputation during the 1970s for "civic activism" focused on preservation of their historic neighborhood, which had been established largely during the mid-Victorian period. Their achievements included the creation of the Capitol Hill Restoration Society in 1955 and the inclusion of the Capitol Hill Historic District in the 1976 *National Registry of Historic Places.* While Christ Church was within the Capitol Hill Historic District, Congressional Cemetery was approximately four blocks east of the boundary. Ruth Ann Overbeck, "Capitol Hill: The Capitol Is Just Up the Street," in *Washington at Home,* ed. Kathryn S. Smith (Washington, D.C.: Windsor Publications, Inc., 1988), 41.

7   Frank W. Kraemer, Jr., Letter to "Dear Friends of Congressional Cemetery," *News from the Association for the Preservation of Historic Congressional Cemetery,* April 1977, 1-2.

8   George Didden III, interview by Ronald M. Johnson, April 19, 2004, Washington, D.C., summary of interview; "Lease," July 31, 1979, File Box, Vestry Minutes and By-Laws and Annual Meetings, 1975-1979, Archives, Christ Church; *Congressional Cemetery Association Newsletter,* October 1, 1979, 3.

9   "Third Annual Report for 1979," *Congressional Cemetery Association Newsletter,* May 1980, 2-3; "Membership Drive To Be Launched," *Congressional Cemetery Association Newsletter,* February 1979, 2.

10   "Third Annual Report for 1979," 2. George Didden III, interview by Ronald M. Johnson, Washington, D.C., summary of interview.

11   *Public Law 94-495, U.S. Code,* 90 stat., 2373 (October 14, 1976). Public Law 94-495 emerged from proposed legislation considered respectively by the Senate and the House of Representatives as S. 3441 and H.R. 13789, which had authorized "a study by the Secretary of the Interior to

formulate proposals for renovation and permanent maintenance" of the "historical sections" of Congressional Cemetery.

12   Congress, House and Senate, *A bill to authorize the Architect of the Capitol to perform certain work on and maintain the historical sections of the Congressional Cemetery for a two-year period, and to authorize a study by the Secretary of the Interior to formulate proposals for renovation and permanent maintenance of such sections by the United States*, 94th Cong., 2d sess., H.R. 13789, *Congressional Record*, 122, prt. 25, daily ed. (September 27, 1976): H32643-H32695; S. 3441, *Congressional Record*, 122, prt. 12, daily ed. (May 17, 1976): S14124.

13   Senators Hugh Scott and Mike Mansfield to "Dear Colleague," May 17, 1976, Congressional Cemetery File, Archives of the U.S. Architect of the Capitol, U.S. Capitol Building, Washington, D.C.

14   Representative Lindy Boggs to "Dear Colleague," May 24, 1976, Congressional Cemetery File, Archives of the U.S. Architect of the Capitol.

15   Ibid.

16   Office of Senator Hugh Scott, Press Release, July 28, 1976, Congressional Cemetery File, Archives of the U.S. Architect of the Capitol; "Statement by Senator Hugh Scott" before the Subcommittee on National Parks and Recreation, House Committee on Interior and Insular Affairs, August 6, 1976, Congressional Cemetery File, Archives of the U.S. Architect of the Capitol.

17   "Statement of Witness for the Department of the Interior Before the Subcommittee on National Parks and Recreation, House Committee on Interior and Insular Affairs, Concerning H.R. 13789," Congressional Cemetery File, Archives of the U.S. Architect of the Capitol; Rogers Morton to James Haley, August 23, 1974, File: "Congressional Cemetery," National Capital Region, National Park Service, Washington, D.C.

18   "Statement of Witness for the Department of Interior Before the Subcommittee on National Parks and Recreation, House Committee on Interior and Insular Affairs, Concerning H.R. 13789," Congressional Cemetery File, Archives of the U.S. Architect of the Capitol.

19   Hugh Scott to Walter D. Huddleston, 1977 (the year is handwritten on the letter), Congressional Cemetery File, Archives of the U.S. Architect of the Capitol.

20   "Statement of Marian P. Connolly, Senior Warden of Christ Church, Washington Parish, before the House Subcommittee on Cemeteries and Burial Benefits; Committee on Veterans Affairs, House of Representatives, on Congressional Cemetery, on Tuesday, June 7, 1977," Record Group 15, Entry 24, Box 36, Folder 2, "Congressional Cemetery," National Archives, Washington, D.C.

21   "Statement of George M. White, Architect of the Capitol, before

the Committee on Veterans' Affairs, Subcommittee on Cemeteries and Burial Benefits," Record Group 15, Entry 25, Box 40, Folder 5, "Congressional Cemetery, DC," National Archives.

22   Excerpt from House Appropriations Committee Hearings, p. 118, Record Group 15, Entry 25, Box 41, Folder 2, "Congressional Cemetery DC," National Archives.

23   Congress, House, *Legislative Branch Appropriation Act, 1978*, 95ᵗʰ Cong., 1ˢᵗ sess., *Congressional Record*, 123, prt. 17, daily ed. (June 29, 1977): 21372.

24   Excerpt from House 1979 Appropriations Committee Hearings, p. 119, Record Group 15, Entry 25, Box 41, Folder 2, "Congressional Cemetery, DC," National Archives.

25   "Meeting – Congressional Cemetery – February 22, 1979," p. 1, Record Group 15, Entry 25, Box 41, Folder 2, "Congressional Cemetery, DC," National Archives.

26   Ibid., pp. 5, 2, 5.

27   Representative Edward Patrick Boland of the Committee on Appropriations submitted a report that included this statement about the meeting on February 22, 1979: "The Committee is disturbed to learn that an option was discussed within the Veterans Administration regarding the feasibility of disinterment from Congressional Cemetery of the remains of individuals buried in plots which are the responsibility of the Federal government. Such action would be contrary to the stated Federal policy to encourage historic preservation and would represent a serious breach by the Nation of its obligation to deceased service personnel. In addition, the Committee expects the Veterans Administration to work as closely as possible with the Historic Congressional Cemetery Association in its efforts to beautify and renovate this cemetery where many thousands of America's military personnel, public servants and other notables are interred." House Committee on Appropriations, *Report Together with Additional Views* [To Accompany H.R. 4394, *Department of Housing and Urban Development—Independent Agencies Appropriation Bill, 1980*], 96ᵗʰ Cong., 1ˢᵗ sess., Report No. 96-249, June 7, 1979. Representative Boland, a Democrat from Massachusetts, served in eighteen Congresses, extending from January 1953 to January 1989.

28   The words on the front cover of the bulletin distributed at the memorial service for Representative Hale Boggs read as follows: "The United States Congress and the Congressional Cemetery Association Honor Hale Boggs, Louisiana, May 19, 1981." A copy of this bulletin is maintained in the Congressional Cemetery File, Archives of the U.S. Architect of the Capitol.

29   On December 12, 1980, the U.S. Congress approved $7,000 for

preparation of a cenotaph in memory of Hale Boggs. In a February 1981 letter to George M. White, Architect of the Capitol, sculptor Harold C. Vogel specified that he would "cut" a cenotaph "from Aquia sandstone" that would be "identical" to the nineteenth-century cenotaphs at Congressional. "Department of the Treasury Appropriation Warrant," No. 399-01-1-12, December 12, 1980, Congressional Cemetery File, Archives of the U.S. Architect of the Capitol; Harold C. Vogel to George M. White, February 1981, Congressional Cemetery File, Archives of the U.S. Architect of the Capitol.

30   Following the wanton destruction of some 120 monuments at Congressional during September 1981, Senator Thomas Eagleton had announced "his support for a long-talked about plan to turn the responsibility for the maintenance of the cemetery's facilities over to the federal government." He noted, in addition, "that he would like the Capitol Police to assume responsibility for guarding the cemetery." Congress, House, Representative Lindy Boggs speaking about "Preserving Historic Congressional Cemetery," 97th Cong., 2nd sess., *Congressional Record* 128 (April 1, 1982): 1398-1399.

31   Ibid., 1399.

32   Russell Dickinson to Legislative Counsel, May 17, 1982, Congressional Cemetery File, National Capital Region, National Park Service, Washington, D.C.

33   *Public Law 97-245*, Statute 96, 313 (August 26, 1982).

34   The extant documentation provides scant information regarding the participation of professional landscape designers at Congressional Cemetery during the nineteenth and twentieth centuries. The vestry minutes for a meeting conducted during July 1917 do indicate, however, that Christ Church retained George Burnap, landscape architect for the Office of Public Buildings and Grounds, Washington, D.C., for unspecified "services rendered in making drawings for improvements at Congressional Cemetery" (Records of Washington Parish, June 1911 to September 1926, Archives, Christ Church).

35   "Association Members Hear Richman," *Congressional Cemetery Association Newsletter*, Summer 1985, 3.

36   The Daughters of the American Revolution also had a voice on the APHCC Advisory Board, which remained in place during 1980-1989. As indicated by the Association newsletter, Annette Nevin Shelby, President General of the D.A.R. and wife of Alabama Senator Richard D. Shelby, served on the Advisory Board from 1982 to 1987.

37   Chris Herman, "Threatened Prison Construction Adds Insult to Highway Injury," *Congressional Cemetery Association Newsletter*, Fall 1986, 3.

38   Margaret Hobbs, "Statement on Behalf of the Congressional Cem-

etery Association," Files of the Association for the Preservation of Historic Congressional Cemetery (APHCC), APHCC Office, Congressional Cemetery.

39   The APHCC Advisory Board initiated a campaign in 2007 to plant three-hundred trees at Congressional Cemetery. The landscape plan specified that a number of these trees, specifically evergreens, would be positioned to "help screen the Jail, integrating with other [unspecified] materials working along the boundary" ("Canopy Restoration," accessed on July 3, 2008, at www.congressionalcemetery.org).

40   Chris Herman, "TEMPUS FUGIT . . . ET MANET," *Congressional Cemetery Association Newsletter*, Winter 1985/1986, 1; Jane W. Gemmill, *Notes on Washington* (Philadelphia: E. Claxton and Company, 1884), 229-230.

41   Chris Herman, interview by Ronald M. Johnson, August 22, 2005, Washington, D.C., summary of interview.

42   "Water Works-In-Progress," *Congressional Cemetery Association Newsletter*, Fall 1987, 2; "Fall-De-Rol: Turtles, Water Music, the Town Crier, And More," *Congressional Cemetery Association Newsletter*, Winter 1987, 1.

43   Jim Oliver, interview by Ronald M. Johnson, March 1, 2005, Washington, DC., summary of interview.

44   "Eleven Years of the Eleven Most," accessed on June 24, 2004, from the web site of the National Trust for Historic Preservation: http://www.nationaltrust.org/11most/eleven_years.html.

45   Alan M. Hantman to Representative James Walsh, October 28, 1997, Congressional Cemetery File, Archives of the U.S. Architect of the Capitol. One other alternative identified by Alan Hantman was "declaring by statute that the Cemetery is a National Cemetery and allocating funds from the general cemeterial budget of the Department of Veterans Affairs on a one-time basis to create a viable trust fund either within the National Cemetery Gift Fund or through another fiduciary."

46   Congress, House, *Making Appropriations for the Legislative Branch for the Fiscal Year Ending September 30, 1999, and for Other Purposes*, 105th Cong., 2nd sess., H.R. 4112, *Congressional Record*, 144, part 18, daily ed. (October 16, 1998): 25400-25401; *National Trust Endowment for Care and Maintenance of Congressional Cemetery, Statutes at Large*, 112 Stat., 2448, Public Law 105-275, sec. 209 (October 21, 1998).

47   Press Release: "Congressional Cemetery Receives $1 Million from Congress: Check Presented at Special National Preservation Week Event," May 12, 1999, Congressional Cemetery File, Folder 1, Archives of the U.S. Architect of the Capitol.

48   "An Update," *Congressional Cemetery Association Newsletter*, Summer 1999, 2; "SAT Grant To Begin in April," *Congressional Cemetery As-*

sociation Newsletter, Spring 2002, 2. Upon matching the Save America's Treasures grant, the APHCC selected the Dean Ruedrich Company of North Carolina to conduct restoration work on selected memorials. As noted in "SAT Work Completed," published in the fall 2002 issue of the APHCC newsletter, the grant also funded "a complete restoration" of the mid-nineteenth century Labbe Vault. The price of this effort was a sobering "indicator of future costs": "Although it is one of the smaller vaults, the restoration cost almost $20,000."

49   Congress, Senate, Senator Byron Dorgan of North Dakota urging his colleagues to provide additional federal funding for Congressional Cemetery, 108th Cong., 1st sess., *Congressional Record* 149, pt. 2 (June 26, 2003): 8826-8827.

50   "Scarlet Crow & Senator Dorgan Come to Aide of Congressional," APHCC *Spring 2002 Newsletter,* 1-2. By his advocacy of congressional support for the burial ground, Dorgan encouraged two additional $100,000 appropriations, included in the 2003 and 2004 Omnibus Appropriation Bills and sponsored respectively by Representatives Sam Farr, a Democrat from California, and Rodney Frelinghuysen, a Republican from New Jersey. As summarized in the APHCC newsletters of spring 2003 and spring 2004, the first grant was to be used for "emergency repairs" of the cemetery's physical plant, including the brick wall and the Public Vault, "both of which were originally constructed through Congressional Appropriations way back in the 1830s." The second grant was to be expended in removing dead trees, preparing a master landscape plan, and proceeding with ongoing efforts focused on vault restoration. The article in the spring 2004 newsletter concluded with this statement of appreciation for much-needed congressional support: "The Association is deeply grateful to our friends in Congress for keeping this historic place on their agenda."

51   "Resources Study Completed: Long-Term Restoration Plan," *The Heritage Gazette,* Winter 2004, 1, 6. During spring 2003, the APHCC renamed the Association newsletter as "The Heritage Gazette." "The Historic Landscape and Structures Report" draws in part on "A Strategic Plan for Congressional Cemetery" for the years 2001 through 2007. Developed during summer 2000, this twenty-page document focuses on efforts that include stabilizing the gravestones and burial vaults, restoring the chapel and the gatekeeper's house, and facilitating public outreach. Linda Harper, who was then Interim Director of the Southern Field Office, National Trust for Historic Preservation, participated in this effort as a consultant.

52   Jim Oliver, interview by Ronald M. Johnson, March 1, 2005, Washington, D.C., summary of interview; "Jim Oliver Photography Feat," *Spring 2002 Newsletter,* 4. While the Daily Log Books were initiated in 1820, they incorporated more information from death certificates beginning in

1898. Jim Oliver served on the APHCC Board of Directors from 1989 to 2001, during which time he was vice chairperson (1990-1991) and then chairperson (1992-1994 and 1997-2001).

53   Sandy Schmidt, interview by Abby A. Johnson and Ronald M. Johnson, August 6, 2005, Washington, D.C., summary of interview.

54   C. Dudley Brown, interview by Ronald M. Johnson, June 1, 2005, Washington, D.C., summary of interview.

55   "Janus Never Sleeps," in *Past Meets Future: Saving America's Historic Environments*, ed. Antoinette J. Lee (Washington, DC: The Preservation Press, 1992), 57.

Conclusion: Congressional Cemetery and National Memory

1 Kirk Savage, "The Past in the Present: The Life of Memorials," *Harvard Design Magazine*, no. 9 (Fall 1999): 3.

2 United States Senate, *History of the Congressional Cemetery* (Washington, D.C.: Government Printing Office, 1906), 35.

3 "Congressional Cemetery's American Heritage: The Public Vault" and "$100,000 for Repair Work! Appropriations for the Public Vault," *The Heritage Gazette* (Spring 2003), 4, 1.

4 The Vestry, Washington Parish, *Washington Parish Burial Ground (Congressional Cemetery) 1807-1913* (Washington, D.C.: The Sudwarth Company, 1913), 5.

5 John Bodnar, *Remaking America: Public Memory, Commemoration and Patriotism in the Twentieth Century* (Princeton: Princeton University Press, 1992), 14.

SELECTED BIBLIOGRAPHY

Archival Collections

Christ Church Archives, Christ Church, Washington. D.C.: Minutes of vestry meetings and annual reports of the congregation maintained in files or boxes according to the following labels: Vol. I, May 1795-April 1862; Journal,1862-1883; Journal of Minutes, 1883-1911; Records of Washington Parish, June 1911 to September 1926; Journal of Minutes, October 1926 to January 1944; Journal of Minutes, February 1944 to December 1949; File Box, Vestry Minutes and Annual Meetings 1950s; File Box, Vestry Minutes and Annual Meetings 1960s; File Box, Vestry Minutes and Annual Meetings 1970-1974; and File Box, Vestry Minutes and By-Laws and Annual Meetings, 1975-1979.

Congressional Cemetery Archives, Congressional Cemetery, Washington, D.C.: Burial Records; Office Files; Minutes of the Board of Directors, Association for the Preservation of Historic Congressional Cemetery (APHCC); APHCC Newsletter File; Newspaper Clippings File.

Georgetown University Archives and Special Collections, Washington, D.C.: David Rankin Barbee Papers.

Historical Society of Washington, D.C., Library and Archives, Washington, D.C.: John Claggett Proctor Papers.

Indiana University of Pennsylvania Archives, Indiana, Pennsylvania: John P. Saylor Congressional Collection.

Library of Congress, Washington, D.C.: Manuscript Division: Ethan Allen Papers, Montgomery C. Meigs Papers, George Watterston Papers; and Special Collections and Rare Books: Toner Collection.

Martin Luther King Public Library, Washington, D.C.: Washingtoniana Collection.

National Archives, Washington, D.C.: Records of the Veterans Administration, Record Group 15.

National Park Service, National Capital Region, Washington, D.C.: Congressional Cemetery File.

Office of the Architect Archives, United States Capitol Building, Washington, D.C.: Congressional Cemetery Files.

Government Publications

Congressional Hearings: U.S. Congress:

House. Committee on Veterans Affairs. *National Cemeteries and Burial Ben-*

efits for Veterans. 92nd Cong., 1st sess., March 28-29, 1972.
House. Committee on Military Affairs, Subcommittee No. 9. *Washington Parish Burial Ground (Congressional Cemetery)*. 70th Cong., 1st sess., April 24, 1928.
Congressional Reports: U.S. Congress:
House. Committee on the District of Columbia. Report No. 2223, Accompanying H.R. 5972. "Burial Sites in Congressional Cemetery." Report submitted by Representative Samuel W. Smith. 59th Cong., 1st sess., March 12, 1906. Committee Print.
House. Committee on Military Affairs. Report No. 2463, Accompanying H.R. 11916. "Care and Preservation of Certain Land and Monuments in the Washington Parish Burial Ground (Congressional Cemetery)." Report submitted by Representative James Glynn. 70th Cong., 2nd sess., February 11, 1929. Committee Print.
Senate. Committee on the District of Columbia. Report No. 72, Accompanying H.R. 5972. "History of the Congressional Cemetery." Report submitted by Senator Elmer Burkett. 59th Cong., 2nd sess., December 6,1906. Committee Print.
Senate. Committee on the Armed Services. Report No. 161, Accompanying S.1545. "Authorizing the Secretary of the Army to Convey Certain Government-Owned Burial Lots and Other Property in the Washington Parish Burial Ground, Washington, D.C., and to Exchange Other Burial Lots." Report submitted by Senator Leverett Saltonstall. 83rd Cong., 1st sess., April 23, 1953. Committee Print.
Executive Branch Reports:
Department of Interior. National Park Service. *The National Register of Historic Places 1969*. Report prepared by Ernest A. Connally and William J. Murtagh. Washington, D.C. Government Printing Office, 1969.
Department of Interior. National Park Service. *The National Register of Historic Places 1976*. Report prepared by William J. Murtagh. Washington, D.C.: Government Printing Office, 1976.
Department of War. *Annual Report of the Quartermaster General Made to the Secretary of War*. Washington, D.C.: Government Printing Office, 1868, 1870, 1879, 1880, and 1881.

Other Published Government Documents

Memorial Services Held in the House of Representatives and Senate of the United States, together with tributes presented in eulogy of John P. Saylor, Late a Representative from Pennsylvania, Ninety-third Congress, First Session. Compiled under the direction of the Joint Committee on Printing. Washington, D.C.: Government Printing Office, 1974.
Token of a Nation's Sorrow: Addresses in the Congress of the United States and

Funeral Solemnities on the Death of John Quincy Adams: Who Died in the Capitol at Washington, on Wednesday Evening, February 23, 1848. 30th Congress, 1st Session. Printed by J. and G.S. Gideon, 1848.

Unpublished Government Documents

U.S. Congress. House of Representatives. Committee on Appropriations. Hearing Held for Appropriation Request of the U.S. Army Department of Civil Functions, "Memorandum on Congressional Cemetery." Submitted by Henry Gibbins, Quartermaster General, U.S. Army, 1939. A copy of the memorandum was accessed in the Congressional Cemetery Archives.

U.S. Congress. House of Representatives. Committee on Resources. Hearing Held Before the Subcommittee on National Parks and Recreation of the Committee on Interior and Insular Affairs on H.R. 1891, "To provide that the historic property known as the Congressional Cemetery may be acquired, protected, and administered by the Secretary of the Interior as part of the park system of the National Capital, and for other purposes." A copy of the transcript of this hearing, which was held on June 23, 1973, was accessed in Record Group 233, Box 48; File of Committee on Interior and Insular Affairs, Room 1324, Longworth Building, House of Representatives, Washington, D.C.

Newspapers

The National Intelligencer (1810-1866) and *The Washington Evening Star* (1852-1981) provided detailed, memorable commentary about the funeral processions to Congressional Cemetery as well as individuals interred at the site.

Books

Adams, Charles Francis, ed. *Memoirs of John Quincy Adams*. Vol. 5. Philadelphia: J. B. Lippincott & Company, 1875.

Adams, Henry. *John Randolph*. New York: Houghton, Mifflin and Company, 1882.

Ames, William. *A History of the National Intelligencer*. Chapel Hill: University of North Carolina Press, 1972.

Arnebeck, Bob. *Through a Fiery Trial: Building Washington, 1790-1800*. Lanham, Maryland: Madison Books, 1991.

Baird, W. David. *Peter Pitchlynn: Chief of the Choctaws*. Norman, Oklahoma: University of Oklahoma Press, 19.

Bartlett, Irving H. *John C. Calhoun: A Biography*. New York: W.W. Norton & Company, 1993.

Bauer, Karl Jack. *The Mexican War, 1846-48*. New York: Macmillan Publishing Company, Inc., 1974.

_____. *Zachary Taylor*. Baton Rouge, Louisiana: Louisiana State University Press, 1985.

Benton, Thomas Hart. *Thirty Years View*. New York: D. Appleton & Company, 1879.

Bierley, Paul E. *John Philip Sousa: American Phenomenon*. Englewood Cliffs, New Jersey: Prentice-Hall, Inc., 1973.

Blight, David W. *Race and Reunion: The Civil War in Memory*. Cambridge, Massachusetts: The Belknap Press of Harvard University, 2001.

Bodnar, John. *Remaking America: Public Memory, Commemoration, and Patriotism in the Twentieth Century*. Princeton, New Jersey: Princeton University Press, 1992.

Boggs, Lindy, with Katherine Hatch. *Washington Through a Purple Veil: Memoirs of a Southern Woman*. New York: Harcourt Brace & Company, 1994.

Bray, Martha Coleman. *Joseph Nicollet and His Map*. Philadelphia: American Philosophical Society, 1980.

Bremer, Richard G. *Indian Agent and Wilderness Scholar: The Life of Henry Rowe Schoolcraft*. Mount Pleasant, Michigan: Clarke Historical Library/ Central Michigan University, 1987.

Brighton, Ray. *The Checkered Career of Tobias Lear*. Portsmouth, New Hampshire: Portsmouth Marine Society, 1985.

Bruff, Goldsborough. *Gold Rush: The Journals, Drawings, and Other Papers of J. Goldsborough Bruff, Captain, Washington City and California Mining Association, April 2, 1849-July 20, 1851*. 2 Volumes. Edited by Georgia Willis Read and Ruth Gaines. New York: Columbia University Press, 1949.

Bryan, John M., ed. *Robert Mills, Architect*. Washington, D.C.: American Institute of Architects Press, 1989.

Bullock, Steven C. *Revolutionary Brotherhood: Freemasonry and the Transformation of the American Social Order, 1730-1840*. Chapel Hill, North Carolina: University of North Carolina Press, 1996.

Busey, Samuel C. *Pictures of the City of Washington in the Past*. Washington, D.C.: Wm. Ballantyne & Sons, 1898.

Clark, Allen C. *Greenleaf and Law in the Federal City*. Washington, D.C.: Press of W. F. Roberts, 1901.

Coit, Margaret L. *John C. Calhoun: American Portrait*. Boston: Houghton Mifflin Company, 1950.

Cole, Donald B., and John J. McDonough, eds. *Benjamin Brown French: Witness to the Young Republic, A Yankee's Journal, 1828-1870*. Hanover: New University Press of New England, 1989.

Crew, Harvey W. *Centennial History of the City of Washington, D.C.* Dayton, Ohio: United Brethren Publishing House, 1892.

Curl, James Stevens. *The Victorian Celebration of Death.* London: David & Charles Publishers, 1972.

Curtis, George Ticknor. *Life of Daniel Webster.* New York: D. Appleton and Company, 1872.

Davis, Susan G. *Parades and Power: Street Theatre in Nineteenth-Century Philadelphia.* Philadelphia: Temple University Press, 1986.

Dearing, Mary R. *Veterans in Politics.* Baton Rouge, Louisiana: Louisiana State University Press, 1952.

Debo, Angie. *The Rise and Fall of the Choctaw Republic.* Norman, Oklahoma: University of Oklahoma Press, 1961.

Decker, Karl, and Angus McSween. *Historic Arlington: A History of the National Cemetery from its Establishment to the Present Time.* Washington, D.C.: Decker and McSween Publishing Company, 1892.

Delano, Judah. *The Washington Directory: Showing the Name, Occupation, and Residence of Each Head of a Family and Person in Business, the Names of Members of Congress, and Where They Board, Together with Other Useful Information.* Washington, D.C.: R.L. Polk & Company, 1822.

De Toledano, Ralph. *J. Edgar Hoover.* New Rochelle, New York: Arlington House, 1973.

Dickens, Charles. *American Notes.* New York: St. Martin's Press, 1985. A reproduction of the 1868 edition.

Dickinson, William C., Dean A. Herrin, and Donald R. Kennon, eds. *Montgomery C. Meigs and the Building of the Nation's Capital.* Athens, Ohio: Ohio University Press, 2002.

Douglass, Frederick. *Life and Times of Frederick Douglass.* London: Collier Books, 1962; reprint, Boston: DeWolf, Fiske, and Company, 1892, revised edition.

Ehle, John. *Trail of Tears: The Rise and Fall of the Cherokee Nation.* New York: Doubleday, 1988.

Elliot, Jonathan. *Historical Sketches of the Ten Miles Square Forming the District of Columbia; with a Picture of Washington, Describing Objects of General Interest or Curiosity at the Metropolis of the Union.* Washington, D.C.: by the author, 1830.

Ellis, John B. *The Sights and Secrets of the National Capital: A Work Descriptive of Washington City in All Its Various Phases.* Chicago: Jones, Junkin & Company, 1869.

Farrell, James J. *Inventing the American Way of Death, 1830-1920.* Philadelphia: Temple University Press, 1980.

Frary, Ihna Thayer. *They Built the Capitol.* Richmond, Virginia: Garrett and Massie, 1940.

Gallagher, H. M. Pierce. *Robert Mills: Architect of the Washington Monument, 1781-1855.* New York: Columbia University Press, 1935.

Garlick, Harry. *The Final Curtain: State Funerals and the Theatre of Power.* Amsterdam: Rodopi B.V., 1999.

Geddes, Gordon E. *Welcome Joy: Death in Puritan New England.* Ann Arbor, Michigan: UMI Research Press, 1981.

Glass, James A. *The Beginnings of a New Historic Preservation Program, 1957 to 1969.* Nashville, Tennessee: American Association for State and Local History, 1990.

Goetzmann, William H. *Army Exploration in the American West, 1803-1863.* New Haven: Yale University Press, 1959.

Goode, James M. *The Outdoor Sculpture of Washington, D.C.: A Comprehensive Historical Guide.* Washington, D.C.: Smithsonian Institution Press, 1974.

Green, Constance McLaughlin. *Secret City: A History of Race Relations in the Nation's Capital.* Princeton, New Jersey: Princeton University Press, 1967.

_____. *Washington: A History of the Capital, 1800-1950.* 2 vols. Princeton, New Jersey: Princeton University Press, 1962.

Green, James A. *William Henry Harrison: His Life and Times.* Richmond, Virginia: Garrett and Massie, Inc., 1941.

Habenstein, Robert W., and William M. Lamers. *The History of American Funeral Directing.* Milwaukee, Wisconsin: Bulfin Printers, Inc., 1955.

Henry Ingle (1763-1822): His Ancestry and Descendants (1690-1914). Privately Printed, n.d.

Hines, Christian. *Early Recollections of Washington City.* Washington, D.C.: Chronicle Book and Job Print, 1866; reprint, Washington, D.C., Junior League of Washington, 1981.

Holmead's Cemetery (Western Burial Ground) Washington, D.C. Compiled by Paul E. Sluby, Sr. Edited by Stanton L.Wormley. Washington, D.C.: Columbia Harmony Society Publication, 1985.

Holt, Dean W. *American Military Cemeteries.* Jefferson, North Carolina: McFarland & Company, 1992.

Hosmer, Charles B., Jr. *Preservation Comes of Age: From Williamsburg to the National Trust, 1926-1949.* 2 vols. Charlottesville: University Press of Virginia for the Preservation Press, 1981.

Hume, Janice. *Obituaries in American Culture.* Jackson, Mississippi: University Press of Mississippi, 2000.

Irving, Washington. *Life of George Washington.* Edited by Jess Stein. New York: Putnam, 1855-1859; reprint, Tarrytown, New York: Alfred A. Knopf, 1949.

Isaac, Rhys. *The Transformation of Virginia.* Chapel Hill: University of North Carolina Press, 1999.

Jackson, Kenneth, and Camilo Jose Vergara. *Silent Cities: The Evolution of the American Cemetery.* New York: Princeton Architectural Press, 1989.

Johnson, Lorenzo D. *Chaplains of the Central Government, with Objections to Their Employment Considered. A List of all the Chaplains to Congress, in the Army and in the Navy, From the Formation of the Government to This Time.* New York: Sheldon, Blakeman, and Company, 1856.

Kammen, Michael. *Mystic Chords of Memory: The Transformation of Tradition in American Culture.* New York: Alfred A. Knopf, 1991.

Latrobe, Benjamin. *The Correspondence and Miscellaneous Papers of Benjamin Henry Latrobe.* Edited by John C. Van Horne. New Haven: Yale University Press, 1986.

_____. *The Journals of Benjamin Henry Latrobe; 1799-1820, From Philadelphia to New Orleans.* Edited by Edward C. Carter, III, John C. Van Horne, and Lee W. Formwalt. 3 Volumes. New Haven: Yale University Press, 1980.

Lee, Antoinette J., ed. *Past Meets Future: Saving America's Historic Environments.* Washington, D.C.: The Preservation Press, 1992.

Levinson, Sanford. *Written in Stone: Public Monuments in Changing Societies.* Durham, North Carolina: Duke University Press, 1998.

Levy, Leonard W. *The Establishment Clause: Religion and the First Amendment.* New York: Macmillan Company, 1986.

Lewis, David L. *District of Columbia: A Bicentennial History.* New York: W.W. Norton & Company, Inc., 1976.

Linden, Blanche M.G. *Silent City on a Hill: Picturesque Landscapes of Memory and Boston's Mount Auburn Cemetery.* Amherst and Boston: University of Massachusetts Press in Association with the Library of American Landscape History, 2007.

Linenthal, Edward. *Sacred Ground: Americans and Their Battlefields.* Urbana, Illinois: University of Illinois Press, 1991.

Liscombe, Rhodri Windsor. *Altogether American: Robert Mills, Architect and Engineer, 1781-1855.* New York: Oxford University Press, 1994.

Loudon, J.C. *On the Laying Out, Planting, and Managing of Cemeteries; and on the Improvement of Churchyards.* London: Privately Printed, 1843.

MacCloskey, Monro. *Hallowed Ground: Our National Cemeteries.* New York: R. Rosen Press, 1968.

McConnell, Stuart. *Glorious Contentment: The Grand Army of the Republic, 1865-1900.* Chapel Hill, North Carolina: University of North Carolina Press, 1992.

McDowell, Peggy, and Richard E. Meyer. *The Revival Styles in American Memorial Art.* Bowling Green, Ohio: Bowling Green State University Press, 1994.

Meserve, Dorothy, and Philip B. Kunhardt, Jr. *Twenty Days: A Narrative in*

Text and Pictures of the Assassination of Abraham Lincoln and the Twenty Days and Nights that Followed – The Nation in Mourning, the Long Trip Home to Springfield. North Hollywood, California: Newcastle Publishing Co., Inc., 1985.

Meyer, Richard E., ed. *Cemeteries and Gravemarkers: Voices of American Culture.* Logan, Utah: Utah State University Press, 1992.

Miller, David W. *Second Only to Grant: Quartermaster General Montgomery C. Meigs; A Biography.* Shippensburg, Pennsylvania: White Mane Books, 2000.

Mills, Robert. *Guide to the Capitol and National Executive Offices of the United States.* Washington, D.C.: W.M.Greet, 1847-1848.

Morris, Edwin Bateman. *A History of the Washington Metropolitan Chapters of the American Institute of Architects.* Washington, D.C.: Privately Printed, 1951.

Morris, John D. *Sword of the Border: Major General Jacob Jennings Brown, 1775-1828.* Kent, Ohio: Kent State University Press, 2000.

Morris, Roy, Jr. *Sheridan: The Life and Wars of General Phil Sheridan.* New York: Crown Publishers, 1992.

Murtagh, William J. *Keeping Time: The History and Theory of Preservation in America.* New York: John Wiley & Sons, Inc., 1997.

Newsom, Jon, ed. *Perspectives on John Philip Sousa.*Washington, D.C.: Music Division Research Services, Library of Congress, 1983.

Norgren, Jill. *Belva Lockwood: The Woman Who Would be President.* New York: New York University Press, 2007.

Obituary Addresses Delivered on the Occasion of the Death of the Hon. John C. Calhoun, a Senator of South Carolina, in the Senate of the United States, April 1, 1850. Washington, D.C.: Printed by Jno. T. Towers, 1850.

Osborne, John Ball. *The Story of Arlington: A History and Description of the Estate and National Cemetery, Containing a Complete List of Officers of the Army and Navy Interred There, with Biographical Sketches of Heroes of the Civil and Spanish Wars, and Notable Memorial Addresses and Poems.* Washington, D.C.: Press of John F. Sheiry, 1899.

Panzer, Mary. *Mathew Brady and the Image of History.* Washington, D.C.: Smithsonian Institution Press, 1997.

Peck, Taylor. *Round-Shot to Rockets: A History of the Washington Navy Yard and U.S. Naval Gun Factory.* Annapolis, Maryland: United State Naval Institute, 1949.

Pitch, Anthony S. *The Burning of Washington: The British Invasion of 1814.* Annapolis: Naval Institute Press, 1998.

Polk, John K. *Polk: The Diary of a President, 1845-1849, Covering the Mexican War, the Acquisition of Oregon, and the Conquest of California and the Southwest.* Edited by Allan Nevins. New York: Longmans, Green and Company, 1929.

Porter, Sarah Harvey. *The Life and Times of Anne Royall.* Cedar Rapids, Iowa: Torch Press, 1908.

Proctor, John Clagett. *Proctor's Washington and Environs: Written for the Washington Sunday Star (1928-1949).* Washington, D.C.: Privately Printed, 1950.

Ragon, Michel. *The Space of Death: A Study of Funerary Architecture, Decoration, and Urbanism.* Translated by Alan Sheridan. Charlottesville: University Press of Virginia, 1983.

Remini, Robert V. *Daniel Webster: The Man and His Time.* New York: W.W. Norton & Company, 1997.

_____. *Henry Clay: Statesman for the Union.* New York: W.W. Norton & Company, 1991.

_____. *The Life of Andrew Jackson.* New York: Penguin Books, 1990.

Roberts, Rebecca Boggs, and Sandra K. Schmidt on Behalf of the Historic Congressional Cemetery. *Images of America: Historic Congressional Cemetery.* Charleston, South Carolina: Arcadia Press, 2012.

Robertson, Nan. *Christ Church Washington Parish: A Brief History.* Washington, D.C.: Privately Printed, 1994.

Rules and Regulations of the Washington (Congressional) Cemetery, Adopted by the Vestry of Christ Church (Protestant Episcopal), Washington, D.C. Washington, D.C.: Terry Bros., Printers, 1897.

Rules and Regulations, Washington Parish Burial Ground (Congressional Cemetery), Washington, D.C. Revised and Amended by the Vestry of Washington Parish. Washington, D.C.: Privately Printed, 1913.

Senie, Harriet F., and Sally Webster, eds. *Critical Issues in Public Art: Content, Context, and Controversy.* New York: HarperCollins Publishers, 1992.

Schoolcraft, Henry R. *Personal Memoirs of a Residence of Thirty Years with the Indian Tribes on the American Frontiers.* Philadelphia: Lippincott, Grambo and Company, 1851.

Scott, Pamela. *Fortress of Finance: The United States Treasury Building.* Washington, D.C., Treasury Historical Association, 2010.

Schwartz, Barry. *Abraham Lincoln and the Forge of National Memory.* Chicago: University of Chicago Press, 2000.

Searcher, Victor. *The Farewell to Lincoln.* New York: Abington Press, 1965.

Seward, William H. *Life and Services of John Quincy Adams.* Reprint of 1849 Edition. Port Washington, New York: University Press of America, 1971.

Sloane, David Charles. *The Last Great Necessity: Cemeteries in American History.* Baltimore: Johns Hopkins University Press, 1991.

Stannard, David E., ed. *Death in America.* Philadelphia: University of Pennsylvania Press, 1975.

Utley, Robert M. *A Life Wild and Perilous: Mountain Men and the Paths to the Pacific.* New York: Henry Hold and Company, 1997.

Trollope, Frances. *Domestic Manners of the Americans.* Edited by Donald Smalley. New York: Alfred A. Knopf, 1949.

Viola, Herman J. *Diplomats in Buckskins: A History of Indian Delegations in Washington City.* Washington, D.C.: Smithsonian Institution Press, 1981.

Washington Parish Burial Ground (Congressional Cemetery) 1807-1913. Published by the Vestry, Washington Parish. Washington, D.C.: Privately Printed, 1913.

Watterston, George. *A New Guide to Washington.* Washington, D.C.: Robert Farnham, 1842.

Wilson, James Harrison. *The Life of John A. Rawlins: Lawyer, Assistant Adjutant General, Chief of Staff, Major General of Volunteers, and Secretary of War.* New York: The Neale Publishing Company, 1916.

Wilson, Derek. *The Circumnavigators.* New York: M. Evans & Company, 1989.

Wiltse, Charles M. *John C. Calhoun: Sectionalist, 1840-1850.* New York: Bobbs-Merrill Co., Inc., 1950.

Winders, Richard Bruce. *Mr. Polk's Army: The American Military Experience in the Mexican War.* College Station, Texas: Texas A & M University Press, 1997.

Woodward, Grace Steele. *The Cherokees.* Norman, Oklahoma: University of Oklahoma Press, 1963.

Articles and Chapters in Books

Ames, Kenneth L. "Ideologies in Stone: Meanings in Victorian Gravestones." *Journal of Popular Culture* 14, no. 4 (1981): 641-656.

Barrett, Wayne. "A Heritage Preserved: America's First National Cemetery." *American Heritage* 33, no. 4 (June/July 1982): 65-69.

Baumann, Roland M. "John Swanwick: Spokesman for 'Merchant-Republicanism' in Philadelphia, 1790-1798." *The Pennsylvania Magazine of History and Biography* 42 (January 1973): 131-182.

Bender, Thomas. "The 'Rural' Cemetery Movement: Urban Travail and the Appeal of Nature." *New England Quarterly* 47 (June 1974): 196-211.

Ennis, Robert Brooks. "Christ Church, Washington Parish." *Records of the Columbia Historical Society* 47 (1969-1970), 126-175.

Francaviglia, Richard V. "The Cemetery as an Evolving Cultural Landscape." *Annals of the Association of American Geographers* 61, no. 3 (September 1971), 501-509.

French, Stanley. "The Cemetery as Cultural Institution: The Establishment of Mount Auburn and the 'Rural Cemetery' Movement." *Ameri-*

can Quarterly 26 (1974), 37-59.

Gallagher, H. M. Pierce. "Robert Mills, 1781-1855: America's First Native Architect [Introduction by Fiske Kimball]." *The Architectural Record* 65, no. 4 (April 1929), 387-393, and no. 5 (May 1929), 478-484.

Glassberg, David. "Public History and the Study of Memory." *The Public Historian* 18, no. 2 (Spring 1996), 7-23.

Hale, Madge. "Congressional Cemetery." *Daughters of the American Revolution Magazine* 98, no. 5 (May 1964), 564.

Haugh, Elizabeth Oglesby. "Crisis in Historic Congressional Cemetery." *Daughters of the American Revolution Magazine* 131, no. 8 (October 1997), 610-612.

Hobsbawm, Eric. "Introduction: Inventing Tradition." In *The Inventing of Tradition*, ed. Eric Hobsbawm and Terence Ranger, 1-15. Cambridge, U.K.: Cambridge University Press, 1983.

Johnson, Abby Arthur, and Ronald M. Johnson. "Funereal Pagentry and National Unity: The Death and Burial of John Quincy Adams." In *Ceremonies and Spectacles: Performing American Culture*, ed. Teresa Alves, Teresa Cid, and Heinz Ickstadt, 144-151. Amsterdam: VU University Press, 2000.

Johnson, Abby Arthur. "'The Memory of the Community': A Photographic Album of Congressional Cemetery." *Washington History* 4 (Spring/Summer 1992), 26-45.

Johnson, Abby Arthur, and Ronald M. Johnson. "A Legacy in Stone: The Latrobe Cenotaphs at Congressional Cemetery." *The Capitol Dome* 47 (Summer 2010): 21-32. *The Capitol Dome* is published quarterly by the U.S. Capitol Historical Society.

Kates, Brian C. "Forgotten Heritage." *American Cemetery* 51, no. 6 (June 1978), 24-29, 32.

Morris, Edwin Bateman. "A Monument to Robert Mills." *Journal of the American Institute of Architects* 9, no. 6 (June 1948), 257-261.

Overbeck, Ruth Ann. "Capitol Hill: The Capitol Is Just Up the Street." In *Washington At Home*, ed. Kathryn S. Smith, 31-41. Washington, D.C.: Windsor Publications, Inc., 1988.

Parsons, Lynn Hudson. "The 'Splendid Pageant': Observations on the Death of John Quincy Adams." *The New England Quarterly* 53 (December 1980), 464-482.

Ryan, Mary. "The American Parade: Representations of the Nineteenth-Century Social Order." In *The New Cultural History*, ed. Lynn Hunt, 131-153. Berkeley: University of California Press, 1989.

Shepard, Nelson McDowell. "Cenotaphs and Epitaphs in Congressional Cemetery." *Daughters of the American Revolution Magazine* 65, no. 4 (April 1 921), 192-202.

Index

412   Index

Croggan, James, articles published
in *The Evening Star* during
1912 about the history of
Congressional Cemetery and
the inclusive community at rest
in the burial ground: 242-245
Crowley, Patrick, Member of the
APHCC Board beginning in
2001: 343

Darby, Ezra, Representative from
New Jersey: 24
Daughters of the American
Revolution: advocacy
for federal support of
Congressional Cemetery: 245-
252, 261, 264; organization of
a "Victorian May Day Garden
Fete": 326-328
Dickens, Charles: 164-165
Dorgan, Byron, Senator from
North Dakota, initial visit to
Congressional Cemetery: 2-3,
339; sponsor of legislation
establishing a $1 million
matching grant: 340
Douglass, Frederick: 126-127

Essary, Helen, journalist who
advocated federal support for
Congressional Cemetery: 253,
257-258
expansion of the District of
Columbia prison complex
along the eastern boundary of
Congressional Cemetery: 328-
329; escaped inmate seeking
refuge in the burial ground:
329-330

Forsyth, John, Secretary of State
in the administrations of

Presidents Andrew Jackson and
Martin Van Buren: 103, 141-142

Gales, Joseph, an owner and editor
of *The National Intelligencer* from
1810 to 1860: 177
Gallagher, Helen Mar Pierce,
biographer of Robert Mills and
participant in the placement
of a gravesite monument in
his memory at Congressional
Cemetery: 253-255
Galliard, John, Senator from South
Carolina: 70-71
Gerry, Elbridge, Vice President of
the United States during 1812-
1814: 35, 104, 137, 140
Gerry, Peter, Senator from Rhode
Island: 253
Gibbins, Henry, Quartermaster
General of the U.S. Army
during 1936-1940: 2, 184, 212,
253, 258-260
Green, Theodore, Senator from
Rhode Island: 253, 258
Gregory, Margaret C., DAR
National Chairman of
Legislation during 1926-1929:
248-251

Hadfield, George, Superintendent
of Construction of U.S. Capital
during 1795-1798: 143-144, 325
Hanley, John, Superintendent of
Congressional Cemetery from
1989 to 1997: 329, 333-335
Hannon, Robert, VA Deputy
Director of Cemetery Services:
319
Harper, Linda, Chairperson of
APHCC Board of Directors
during 2001-2007: 340

administration of Congressional
Cemetery: 297-302
*The National Register of
Historic Places*: definition of
Congressional as "The First
National Cemetery": 278-281,
291
National Trust for Historic
Preservation: inclusion of
Congressional Cemetery in
its 1997 list of America's 11
Most Endangered Historic
Places: 307, 335-339; comments
provided at the ceremony by
Richard Moe, President of the
Trust: 336; decision to assist
Congress in establishing a
matching fund for preservation
of Congressional Cemetery:
336-338
Native American negotiators with
the U.S. Government interred
at Congressional Cemetery:
Apache: Chief Taza: 158;
Cherokee: Coodey, William:
159-160; Fields, Richard:
161-162; Looney, John: 160-
161; McDaniel, James: 161-
162: Pegg, Thomas: 161-162;
Rogers, John, Jr.: 159-161; Starr,
Ezekiel: 159-161; Chippewa:
A-Moose, Shawbo-Wis, and
St. Germain: 166; Choctaw:
Chief Pushmataha: 162-164;
Pitchlynn, Peter: 162, 164-165;
Kiowa: O-Com-O-Cost (Yellow
Wolf): 166-167; Pawnee: Tuck-
a-Lix-Ta (Owner of Many
Horses): 167; and Santee Sioux:
Chief Kan-Ya-Tu-Duta (Scarlet
Crow): 166, 339: numbers
of Native American burials

at Congressional Cemetery
according to nations: 158
Number of interments at
Congressional Cemetery for
veterans of the Revolutionary
War, Tripolitan and Algerian
Wars, War of 1812, and Mexican
War: 144

O'Brien, Richard Henry, U.S.
consul-general to Algeria, 1797-
1803: 145
Oliver, Jim, Chairperson of the
APHCC Board of Directors
during 1992-1994 and 1997-
2001: 333, 336; development of
a computerized list of burials
at Congressional from 1807 to
2007: 341; digital photographs
of the 3,000 page Daily Log
Book for the years 1888-1982
and of approximately 14,000
gravestones: 341
O'Neil, Thomas, Speaker of the
House of Representative during
1977-1987: 314, 321

Parks, Tilman Bacon,
Representative from Arkansas:
140-141
participants in continental and
oceanic explorations interred
at Congressional Cemetery:
Joseph Goldsborough Bruff:
173-174; William H. Cross:
174-175; William Helmsley
Emory: 170, 172-174; Thomas
Fitzpatrick: 170, 171-172; Joseph
Nicollet: 169-170, 176; Charles
Ludwig Preuss: 170-171, 176;
William Rich: 168; Henry
Rowe Schoolcraft: 168-170, 176;

Frederick D. Stuart, Sr.: 175-176; and William M. Walker: 168.
Pinkney, William, Attorney General of the United States during the presidency of James Madison: 142
processions to Congressional Cemetery in memory of federal leaders: the route to the burial ground: 53-59; Puritan, Anglican, and Masonic traditions incorporated into the parades: 59-65; parades honoring U.S. presidents William Henry Harrison, Zachary Taylor, and former President John Quincy Adams (temporary interments): 80-90; parades for individual members of Congress: Edward Dickinson Baker, Senator from Oregon: 78-79; Thomas Blount, Representative from North Carolina, 68; James Burrill, Senator from Rhode Island, 137; Levi Casey, Representative from South Carolina, 9; and John Galliard, Senator from South Carolina, 70-71
Proctor, John Clagett, articles published in *The Evening Star* about the historic legacy of Congressional Cemetery: 223, 264
Prout, William, donator of land to Christ Church in 1806 for a new church building: 26, 28
Public Law 94-495: approved by President Gerald Ford on October 14, 1976, the legislation specified the responsibilities of the Architect of the Capitol

relevant to preservation of Congressional Cemetery: 313-318, 324; Public Law 97-245: approved by Congress on August 26, 1982, the amended bill directed the Architect of the Capitol to provide grants to the APHCC for the preservation of Congressional Cemetery: 324-325; Public Law 105-275: approved by President William Clinton on October 21, 1998, the statute specified the creation of a fund to be administered by the National Trust for the Preservation of Historic Congressional Cemetery: 337-338; Public Law 207: approved by President Theodore Roosevelt on March 2, 1907, the legislation allowed Christ Church to incorporate specified sections of city streets into Congressional Cemetery: 229-230
Public Vault at Congressional Cemetery: 37-38, 75, 139, 271, 346-347

Railsback, Thomas, Representative from Illinois: 265, 285
Rawlins, John A., Secretary of War; Interment at Congressional Cemetery: 108-111, 125-126; reinterment at Arlington National Cemetery: 95-96, 106, 113
Revolutionary War Officers interred at Congressional Cemetery: General Peterson Goodwyn, 145; General Thomas Hartley, 145; General Daniel

George Holcombe at
Congressional Cemetery: 65
Turk, Tracey & Larry Architects:
"Historic Landscape and
Structures Report for Historical
Congressional Cemetery"
(2003): 340-341

U.S. Department of the Interior:
225-226, 265, 285, 313, 316, 324-
325
U.S. Marine Corps Band: 182-184
U. S. Presidents of the United
States referenced in documents
relevant to Congressional
Cemetery: John Quincy Adams:
49, 57-58, 70, 80-87, 93, 137,
139, 142; James Buchanan: 225;
Grover Cleveland: 121; Bill
Clinton: 337; Millard Fillmore:
76, 87, 179; Gerald Ford: 313;
Ulysses Grant: 95, 108-110;
William Henry Harrison: 56,
80-83, 93; Thomas Jefferson:
25-26, 56, 167, 177, 242; Andrew
Jackson,: 141-142, 147, 163;
Andrew Johnson: 161-162; John
F. Kennedy: 54, 93: Abraham
Lincoln: 54, 78-79, 90-94, 97,
153-154, 184, 228; William
McKinley: 95; James Madison:
56, 67, 139, 177; James Monroe:
56, 142, 148, 168, 177; Richard
Nixon: 284, 288-289; Franklin
Pierce: 225; James K. Polk:
39, 148-149, 172; Franklin D.
Roosevelt: 246, 256; Theodore
Roosevelt: 229; Zachary Taylor:
56, 76, 86-90, 93, 121, 179, 350;
Martin Van Buren:

142; John Tyler: 81-82; George
Washington: 64-65, 120, 143,
145, 242, 246

Veterans Administration: support
for VA maintenance of
Congressional Cemetery: 318-
320

Walsh, James, Representative from
New York: 336-338
War of 1812 Officers interred at
Congressional Cemetery: Major
General Jacob Jennings Brown,
120, 147-148; Major General
Alexander Macomb, 120, 147-
148, 169; Commodore Todd
Patterson, 147-148; Commodore
John Rodgers, 103, 145-148;
Commodore Thomas Tingey,
20-22, 26, 35
Washington Metropolitan Chapter
of the American Institute of
Architects: placement of a
monument at Congressional
Cemetery in memory of Robert
Mills: 255-257
Watterston, George, First Librarian
of Congress: 1, 14-15, 138, 150
Webster, Daniel, Senator from
Massachusetts: 75-77, 179
Wirt, William: Attorney General
in the administrations of
Presidents James Monroe and
John Quincy Adams, 113, 142;
candidate of the Anti-Masonic
Party for the U.S. Presidency in
1832: 142